In Darkness and Secrecy

IN DARKNESS AND SECRECY

The Anthropology of Assault Sorcery and
Witchcraft in Amazonia
Edited by Neil L. Whitehead and Robin Wright

Duke University Press   Durham & London 2004

© 2004 Duke University Press
All rights reserved
Typeset in Melior by Tseng Information Systems, Inc.
Library of Congress Cataloging-in-Publication Data
appear on the last printed page of this book.

Contents

1   Introduction: Dark Shamanism, *Neil L. Whitehead and Robin Wright*

21   The Order of Dark Shamans among the Warao, *Johannes Wilbert*

51   Dark Shamans and the Shamanic State: Sorcery and Witchcraft as Political Process in Guyana and the Venezuelan Amazon, *Silvia Vidal & Neil L. Whitehead*

82   The Wicked and the Wise Men: Witches and Prophets in the History of the Northwest Amazon, *Robin Wright*

109   Sorcery Beliefs, Transmission of Shamanic Knowledge, and Therapeutic Practice among the Desana of the Upper Río Negro Region, Brazil, *Dominique Buchillet*

132   The Glorious Tyranny of Silence and the Resonance of Shamanic Breath, *George Mentore*

157   A Blend of Blood and Tobacco: Shamans and Jaguars among the Parakanã of Eastern Amazonia, *Carlos Fausto*

179   The Wars Within: Xinguano Witchcraft and Balance of Power, *Michael Heckenberger*

202 Siblings and Sorcerers: The Paradox of Kinship among the Kulina, *Donald Pollock*

215 Being Alone amid Others: Sorcery and Morality among the Arara, Carib, Brazil, *Márnio Teixeira-Pinto*

244 Sorcery and Shamanism in Cashinahua Discourse and Praxis, Purus River, Brazil, *Elsje Lagrou*

272 The Enemy Within: Child Sorcery, Revolution, and the Evils of Modernization in Eastern Peru, *Fernando Santos-Granero*

306 Commentary, *E. Jean Langdon*

314 Afterword: Substances, Powers, Cosmos, and History, *Andrew Strathern & Pamela J. Stewart*

321 Contributors

324 Index

In Darkness and Secrecy

Introduction: Dark Shamanism

Neil L. Whitehead & Robin Wright

Shamanism is a burgeoning obsession for the urban middle classes around the globe. Its presentation in popular books, TV specials, and on the Internet is dominated by the presumed psychic and physical benefits that shamanic techniques can bring. This heightened interest has required a persistent purification of the ritual practices of those who inspire the feverish quest for personal meaning and fulfillment. Ironically, as Fausto points out in his essay in this volume, given the self-improvement motivations that have brought so many into a popular understanding of shamanism, two defining aspects of shamanism in Amazonia—blood (i.e., violence) and tobacco—have simply been erased from such representations (see also Lagrou, this volume). Such erasure is not only a vain self-deception but, more important, it is a recapitulation of colonial ways of knowing through both the denial of radical cultural difference and the refusal to think through its consequences. This volume is intended to counteract that temptation.

All of the authors whose works are presented herein are keenly aware of the way in which salacious and prurient imagery of native peoples has serviced the purposes of conquest and colonization over the past five hundred years. In missionary writings, for example, ideas about "native sorcery" and the collusion of shamans with "satanic" forces meant that such individuals were ferociously denounced and their ritual equipment and performances were banned from the settlement of the converts. In this context no distinction was made between the forms and purposes of ritual practice: curers as well as killers were equally persecuted. Thus, the rehabilitation of shamanism as a valid spiritual attitude and a culturally important institution that has taken place over the past twenty years through the enthusiastic, if ill-informed, interest of the urban middle classes might be seen in a more positive light—that is, as rescuing a form of cultural variety that would otherwise be lost in the cultural homogeneity of globalization. Nonetheless, such a rehabilitation through a positive, almost cheery, presentation of the native shaman as psychic healer distorts the actual ritual practice of Amazonians and other native peoples in a number of ways, as the materials collected here will show. Moreover, the notion that shamanism should be "rehabilitated" in this way misses the important point that it is the supposed illegitimacy of shamanic practice that should be questioned, rather than trying to justify cultural difference merely through the possible benefits it might have for ourselves. Taking seriously cultural difference in this context means that we have also to ask what other reasons there were for the colonial desire to repress this particular facet of native culture. As the essays in this volume indicate, a large part of the answer to that question must be the very centrality of shamanic ritual power to the constitution of native society and culture, as well as the role that "shamans" thus played in resisting, ameliorating, and influencing the course of indigenous and colonial contacts and subsequent histories. The consequence of this issue must also be to recognize that shamanic idioms are still very much present in the exercise of political power from the local to the national levels and that this recognition makes an understanding of all aspects of such ritual action a fundamental project for an anthropology of the modern world.

What then is "shamanism"? Anthropological debate in Amazonia has considered whether or not the term describes a unitary phenomenon, and has persistently questioned its institutional existence and its presence as a defined social role (Campbell 1989; Hugh-Jones 1996; Fausto, Heckenberger, Pinto, this volume). Nonetheless, there is a utility to the term that has underwritten its persistence in the literature and its continuing adoption in the present. This utility consists in the fact that the performance of ritual specialists throughout Amazonia shows a number of resemblances that, although they do not represent a clear and distinct category of ritual action, nonetheless reveal ethnographically a variety of symbolic analogies and indications of historical relatedness. Moreover, native terms such as *pajé* or *piaii* have passed easily from their original linguistic contexts into the mouths of many different speakers across Amazonia. Part of the reason for this may well be an apparent homogenization of ritual practice in the face of evangelism by Christian missionaries or other agents of colonial domination, but even if this were the only reason it would still be an important ethnographic fact about contemporary Amazonian cultures. Equally, anthropologists have tended to overlook or ignore the issue of violence. No doubt this is partly due to cultural prejudice against the exercise of violence, because it is held that its representation among others will only serve to lessen the authority and validity of their culture differences as something to be cherished and respected. Unfortunately, this has meant that we have not properly examined the "dark" side of shamanism, which is often integral to the efficacy of shamanism overall (Mentore, Santos-Granero, this volume).

The idea that shamanism thus expresses a recurrent moral ambiguity —for the same abilities that cure can also kill—recognizes a fundamental aspect of shamanic power through the presentation of shamanism as a personal or individual dilemma. However, shamanism's role in the reproduction of society and culture suggests that this view is incomplete and partial because it deals only with the appearance of shamanism in the routines of daily life. Indeed, in the case of the Parakanã (Fausto, this volume) the dark associations of shamanism, its past connections to warfare, and the uncertainty as to the status of those who might claim to have shamanic powers, have all but occluded its light or curing aspects. The deep mythohistorical presence of dark shamanism, contemporary with, if not actually preceding, the original emergence of persons and shamanic techniques, indicates that dark and light, killing and curing, are complementary opposites—not antagonistic possibilities. In the same way that shamanism itself has been historically shaped by forces conceived of as external to the originating shamanic cosmologies, so too the ritual practices of curers are intimately linked to the assaults of shamanic killers and cannot be understood apart from them (see Heckenberger, this volume). The loci of these cosmological contests become the bodies, both physical and political, that are created and destroyed through the ritual-political actions of chiefs, warriors, and shamans.

Dark Shamans

The concept of "dark shaman" comprises the notions of sorcery and witchcraft, terms that have their own particular and complex histories. A significant starting point for any anthropological consideration of witchcraft and sorcery must be the definition that Evans-Pritchard developed for these terms to describe the ritual and magical practices of *mangu* and *gbegbere ngua* among the Azande/Zande in Africa. For Evans-Pritchard, "the difference between a sorcerer and a witch is that the former uses the technique of magic and derives his power from medicines, while the latter acts without rites and spells and uses hereditary psycho-physical powers to attain his ends" (1937:387). This does not, however, apply to Amazonian cultures, for in all cases presented in this volume, sorcerers and witches act with an overt intentionality unlike those thought of as witches among the Azande (Evans-Pritchard 1937:42). The notion of a psycho-physical inheritance of a "witchcraft substance" (*misimo mangu*) is likewise absent, except perhaps in the case of the Xinguano and Kulina (see Heckenberger and Pollock, this volume). This does not mean that magical techniques do not pass from one generation to the next along kinship lines, but rather that such inheritance is not inevitable and that magical assaults are never "unconscious" to the same degree that Evans-Pritchard suggested for Zande witches.

We introduce the term dark shaman in this volume to reflect both the distinct features of Amazonian assault sorcery and of malicious witchcraft, as well as to capture the ambiguity inherent in shamanic practice, one that shades into the darkness of assault sorcery but also implies a broader knowledge and power than that of the witch or sorcerer who has often been pictured as a figure marginal to the central spiritual or religious notions of the society from which they come. Our usage of the term dark shamans is inspired principally by Johannes Wilbert's pioneering study of the shamanic order among the Warao (Wilbert 1972; 1993:92–125; and this volume). The work in this book, building on that detailed ethnography of Warao dark shamanism, argues for the centrality and importance of dark shamanism to the overall spiritual and cosmological ideas of Amazonian peoples in general. This reconceptualization of Amazonian shamanism also stems from the fact that both editors of the volume have recently completed extensive studies of the shamanism and cosmological practices of two Amazonian peoples—the Baniwa (Wright 1998) and the Patamuna (Whitehead 2002)—in which the significance of dark shamanism is very apparent.

Whitehead's (2002) study of the *kanaimà*, a major complex of dark shamanism among the peoples of the Guyana highlands, underscores the importance of these other works and links the practice of shamanism to wider sociopolitical goals, especially in the face of colonialism, epidemic disease, and modern development (see also Vidal and Whitehead, this volume). It is also evident that there are important ethnological similarities, as well as differences, in the social position and cultural practice of dark shamans, as indicated by a comparison of the *hoaratu* among the Warao, *manhene-iminali* among the Baniwa, and *kanaimà* among the Patamuna. The Warao themselves have a number of shamanic complexes, which include the *hoaratu*, dark shamans capable of inflicting pain and death; as with the *kanaimà*, the *hoaratu* are engaged in a cosmic quest, not merely assassination for political gain or personal and familial vengeance. This however, provides a point of contrast with the *manhene-iminali*, or "poison-owners," that is the very antithesis of shamanism (see Wright, this volume): the *manhene-iminali* incarnate the primordial spirits of destruction and chaos present in the universe from the beginning of time.

As with the most adept *piya* (shamans) of the Patamuna, among the Warao the *daunonarima*, "fathers of the wooden figurine," are also assault sorcerers. In Patamuna accounts of shamanic killing, reference is made to the "spirit masters" that are used to assail enemies, and these effigies seem highly reminiscent of the figurines used by the *daunonarima*. Usually this kind of assault sorcery, known as *iupithatem* among the Baniwa, is used to settle village conflicts or to assist in collective warfare, as with the Patamuna *piya* (see also Wright and Buchillet, this volume). However, this kind of shamanic assault does so in a generalized or relatively indiscriminate manner that, it has been argued in the case of the Patamuna (Whitehead 2002), made it inappropriate to the emergent era of gun warfare in the nineteenth century. This meant that the specificity involved in *kanaimà* assault sorcery made it a perfect adjunct to the emergence of smaller-scale political and military leadership. This historical change in intervillage and interethnic relations was therefore an important factor in the growing prevalence of *kanaimà* practice over the last hundred years or so (see Butt-Colson 2001; Whitehead 2001).

The historicity of shamanism and its abilities to adapt to the novel challenges of colonial and national intrusion are also evident among the Baniwa. The class of chants and evil spells comprised by *hiuiathi* (sorcery) is employed by Baniwa shamans to assail their enemies in a wide variety of social contexts (see Wright, this volume). However, such chants and spells are not themselves an exclusive part of shamanic techniques because they may be employed by anyone who knows them. In this sense such aggressive magic is also present among the Patamuna in the form of *talen*, which requires no special initiation to learn and use but is very much part of a family inheritance, being passed on largely within extended families. Although the knowledge of such spells and chants might be general for the Warao, Patamuna, or Baniwa, there is an extreme secrecy among the Baniwa as to who may commit acts of assault sorcery. In contrast, both the *hoaratu* and the *kanaimà* are often well-known individuals, and the *kanaimà* in particular may choose to openly brag of their deeds, or supposed deeds.

These brief comparisons allow a provisional discrimination among the various forms of dark shamanism, in particular between the existence and possession of certain magical techniques (*hiuiathi, talen*) that may be widely known; the counteraggression of shamans against the attacks by outsiders (*iupithatem, daunonarima, piya*); and the classes of dark shamans who are initiates to a distinct system of ritual practice (*hoaratu, kanaimà, manhene-iminali*).

Wilbert (1993:92–125) has previously discussed the *hoaratu* at great length. The cosmological origins of the *hoaratu* lie in the relations between humanity and the *hebo* (ancient ones) that still reside at the cardinal points of the earth. It has been the particular responsibility of the *hoaratu* to ensure that the scarlet macaw and his spirits do not become enraged and are appeased with a supply of human victims. So, as with *kanaimà* killing, to be killed by the *hoaratu* is to be utterly extinguished without hope of an immortality in the spirit world. The dismemberment of the Warao who dies at the hands of the *hoaratu*, like the anal and oral mutilations carried out by the *kanaimà*, and the utter dissolution of the person produced by *iupithatem* completely terminates and erases ontologically the individual, who becomes the food of the gods. Given that this role sustains cosmological relations, it is no wonder that, just as with the *kanaimà*, there is a reluctant acceptance of the necessity for such dark shamans among the Warao. The *kanaimà* as shamans of Makunaima, creator of all animals and plants, are likewise responsible for ensuring that the bounty of Makunaima is balanced by a sacrifice of human nourishment that feeds *kaikusi-yumu* (lord jaguar) and nourishes *koumima* (the garden spirit). However, the fact that Makunaima shares responsibility for the cosmic order with his younger brother, Piai'ima, has meant that, as with the Warao, there are other forms of shamanic intercession. Unlike among Warao shamans, there seems to be an inherent tension and competitiveness involved in the relationships of the Patamuna *piya* and *kanaimà*, mythically chartered by the tensions between Piai'ima and Makunaima.

The *hoaratu*, like the *kanaimà*, visit the graves of their victims to criticize their stinginess and suck the corpse's blood through a cane. However, in an important contrast with *kanaimà* the younger *hoaratu* are also curers, whereas *kanaimà* are concerned solely with death, and even the older *hoaratu* are principally concerned with killing outside their own communities. These notions of sociality do not restrain the *kanaimà*, which helps account for the idea of their pervasiveness; however, their importance to the constitution of society is still present, even if not overtly recognized by all Patamuna. In the same way that the *hoaratu* mediate and balance the predatory forces of the cosmos, so the *kanaimà* ensure the continuing beneficence of the creator of plants and animals, Makunaima. Moreover, since dark and light shamanism cannot be easily separated, the mere potential for shamanic action is already somewhat threatening to the fragility of everyday life, even when it is carefully controlled by its modes of ritual enactment, as with the Arara (see Pinto, this volume). Nevertheless, the close connections that emerged between the *kanaimà* and the changing patterns of warfare in the highlands over the last two hundred years are no less part of the current meaning of *kanaimà* (see Vidal and Whitehead, this volume). This historicity relating to shamanic practice in turn raises broader issues regarding the role of shamanism in the social production of warfare and the cultural performance of violence. Wright's work (1998; and this volume) on the Baniwa thoroughly investigates the historical nature of shamanism, witchcraft, and prophecy in the creation of notions of self and otherness, as well as how those ritual practices relate to a broader cosmology in which shamanism itself comes to represent the triumph of human creativity over the destructive forces of witches; a struggle that is similarly represented in Patamuna thought by the contest of the primordial brothers Piai'ima and Makunaima. As with the Warao and Patamuna, the Baniwa also recognize the inevitable existence of dark shamans, *manhene-iminali*, or poison-owners, who are cosmologically connected with the existence of death in the world.

In these ways it becomes apparent that whatever the tragedy, distress, and death that dark shamans and allied ritual specialists may perform on humanity, they are an inevitable, continuing, and even a necessary part of the cosmos. For these reasons dark shamans are not simply vilified and hunted down in the manner of the European witch-hunts of the sixteenth and seventeenth centuries (although they may be: see Heckenberger, Pinto, and Santos-Granero, this volume), but rather can become the source and even symbols of a potent indigenous society and culture that is capable of defending itself against the depredations of the outside world, be that a neighboring village or even the national state (see Vidal and Whitehead and Santos-Granero, this volume). Indeed, in this light the religious wars against witchcraft, in both the New and Old Worlds, can also be seen as part of the establishment of the authority of the state through the priestly manifestations of the church (Griffiths 1996). The close identification of indigenous shamanism, of whatever kind, with "satanic" practices has been an important political tactic of Western evangelism. It is certainly not our intent in this volume to suggest that shamanism is necessarily of this kind, but the abusive ethnology of the evangelists should not inhibit a better understanding of phenomena that loom so large in the cultural practice and imagination of Amazonian peoples.

Dark Shamanism and Assault Sorcery in New Guinea and Africa

The notion of assault sorcery as a way of capturing the variety of practice that is associated with the darker aspects of shamanism is suggested by a parallel literature in New Guinea (Stewart and Strathern 1999). In reviewing the existing literature on witchcraft and sorcery in New Guinea and comparing it to the literature from Africa, Stewart and Strathern stress the way in which these phenomena can be seen as forms of "supernatural warfare," implying that they engage community relations, not just individual fates, to a significant degree. At this level not only warfare but epidemic diseases and the changing settlement patterns induced by colonial contacts covary with the pattern of assault sorcery and witchcraft (see Buchillet, Heckenberger, Pollock, and Santos-Granero, this volume). Sorcery and witchcraft are also united in the common themes of a bodily invasion, both individual and political, that is the mode of such supernatural assault and that concludes either in the destruction or consumption of body parts themselves. This link between the body-politic and individual bodies, in New Guinea as much as in Amazonia, reveals the way in which techniques of dark shamanism may become entwined with the exercise of political power not only within indigenous communities (Heckenberger, this volume) but also even at the regional or state level (Vidal and Whitehead, Wright, and Santos-Granero, this volume). By the same token the execution of "witches" invokes the connection between bodily presence and cosmological power, because the modes of killing child sorcerers (Santos-Granero, this volume) are unusual and cruel precisely to prevent physical resurrection by their tutelary dark shamans or spirit forces.

These approaches allow Stewart and Strathern largely to dispense with a forced distinction between witchcraft and sorcery, as implied by Evans-Pritchard's original definition. It is clear from the New Guinea material that even if there is the potential to make such a distinction based on the varieties of mystical violence that are practiced, to do so inevitably leads to an oppositional typology that cannot then account for intermediate cases. In this volume we show that there are many opportunities to make such a distinction, but also that its general usefulness is limited to the specifics of a given case. As Stewart and Strathern point out (see also Knauft 1985), such typologies are very much snapshots of ritual practices at a given point in time and do not necessarily reflect the changing relationships over time that ritual practices of all kinds undergo.

It has also been suggested that even if the ritual meaning and content of witchcraft and sorcery show historical change, what does not change is the marginal status of such reviled characters. The marginality or illegitimacy of the witch and sorcerer has become the basis of a juridical approach to the definition of these terms in the New Guinea materials (Stephen 1987) that allows the adept and respected sorcerer-shaman who can cause death at a distance to be contrasted with the spiteful and hated witch who might be punished by community outrage, as with the child sorcerers and witches described by Heckenberger and Santos-Granero in this volume. However, generalizing this distinction still begs many questions regarding the possibility for intermediate practices (Lagrou, this volume), even if it may have relevance in Amazonia (Heckenberger and Pollock, this volume). Like Stewart and Strathern and Evans-Pritchard we note the possibility for discrimination among the forms of mystical violence and assault sorcery, but we also see no compelling reason why the sorcery/witchcraft distinction should be considered a universal one.

From their inception, Africanist studies of witchcraft and sorcery have referred to the wider dislocations of colonialism—evangelism, wage labor, migration—as relevant to understanding the incidence and meaning of accusations of mystical violence (Douglas 1970; Middleton 1987; White 2000), and much the same has been noted in other regions (Watson and Ellen 1993; Hoskins 1996). This is important to an understanding of the historicity of dark shamanism generally, because the harsh realities that colonial or neocolonial contacts bring are a vector for both the increase in anxieties about sorcery and the emergence of certain specific forms of occult violence. But it has also become very evident that the occult has emerged as a political idiom of postcolonial national cultures as well, as a mimesis of continuing exploitation and oppression by global capitalism (Ellis 1999; Geschiere 1997; Comaroff and Comaroff 1998), or as an idiom for the suppression of internal revolution (Santos-Granero, this volume). The career of Mandú, the powerful shaman discussed by Vidal and Whitehead in this volume, perfectly exemplifies the conflation of "tradition" and "modernity" that has otherwise perplexed external observers but that in the last decade or so has led to even wider engagements between shamanism and external politics (Conklin 2002). As Stewart and Strathern state: "It is not simply a matter of arguing for an increased frequency of types of action; rather, it is a matter of studying the changing loci of accusations over time" (1999:649). In this way, colonial actors and neocolonial oppressors themselves become the agents and instantiations of dark cannibalistic spirits, even as the boundaries between the all-engorging state and remnant autonomous communities, such as in the New Guinea Highlands or in Amazonia, become uncertain and unclear and seem to threaten a total dissolution of the body-politic, represented as a cannibal consumption of the individual and collective spirit.

Witchcraft and Sorcery in Amazonia

In contrast to Africa, New Guinea, and Europe, native South America has not been the subject of an extensive analysis of witchcraft and sorcery, except perhaps in the Andean region where the interest of the Catholic Church in the suppression of native religious practice produced "witch-hunts" in the manner of Europe, which often were inflected with a similar gender bias (Aigle, de La Perrière, and Chaumeil 2000; Griffiths and Cervantes 1999; Silverblatt 1987). A few early studies of attack shamanism stand out, however; for example, the work of Michael Harner (1962, 1972, 1973) and of Norman Whitten (1976, 1985) among native peoples of eastern Ecuador (the upper Amazon); as well as Lévi-Strauss (1967), Dole (1973), Goldman (1963), and even Napoleon Chagnon's controversial filming of Yanomamo assault sorcery in the 1973 film *Magical Death*. Still, even with the appearance of more recent literature on various aspects of shamanism in general (Brown

1985; Gow 1996; Hugh-Jones 1996; Langdon 1992, 1996; Sullivan 1988; Taussig 1987) anthropological analysis of Amazonian dark shamans is far less extensive than for other ethnographic areas. Witchcraft and sorcery in Amazonia has been treated mostly in a haphazard way, with some excellent ethnographic accounts but no real regional comparisons or broader suggestions as to historical origins and processes. As a consequence, none of the larger questions about ethnological differences or the workings of local variation have been broached. It is our intention here to offer some initial discriminations in the forms of Amazonian shamanism in order to illustrate some of the important features of shamanic practice that are less evident in particular ethnographic accounts.

In general the literature on Amazonia has subsumed the topic of witchcraft and sorcery under the topic of shamanism—reflecting the ethnographic reality that shamans are quite often sorcerers: two sides of the same coin. This often-noted dual capacity of the shaman to heal and to cause harm, frequently referred to as the "moral ambiguity" of the shamans, is also reflected iconographically in the archaeological record where the double-headed bird is associated with shamanic ritual practice (Whitehead 1996). In some societies, shamans also stand in contrast to priestlike specialists whose functions are rarely considered ambiguous and are connected to "legitimate" social reproduction in the cosmological sphere (Thomas and Humphrey 1996). The tendency of the literature on shamanism, as noted above, has been to concentrate on the morally "good" side; that is, the healing function of the shaman as a vital service to the community.

As Michael Brown (1989) pointed out, there has been a marked tendency in the past two or three decades to emphasize the positive, therapeutic, and socially integrative dimensions of shamanism—a trend that shows no sign of diminishing (Harner 1998). This appropriation of native shamanism has been particularly evident among well-educated North Americans, Europeans, and urban Latin Americans, who approach shamanism as a set of magical techniques that can be used for self-realization, for attaining profound or mystical experience, and for alternative therapy, both physiological and psychological. The ethnographic experience of Amazonian dark shamanism pointedly contradicts this imagery and, while issues of the politics of representation cannot be ignored, it is obviously the role of anthropology to provide a more adequate interpretation and presentation of actual Amazonian practices. Although recognized, the "dark" side—the shamans' power to destroy or inflict harm through sorcery and witchcraft—has received little in-depth attention. In several of the most important contributions to the South American shamanism literature in recent years (Langdon 1992, 1996; Sullivan 1988), the weight of the attention is on the shaman's capacities to harness cosmic forces for the benefit of humanity. This is not to say that witchcraft and sorcery have been totally ignored, but rather that some of the more notable extended studies (Albert 1985; Chaumeil 1983) have not been widely read in North America.

Theoretical Approaches

Various schools of thought are currently evident in the anthropology of Amazonia (Rival and Whitehead 2001; Viveiros de Castro 1996). These schools can be characterized as (1) the "political economy of control," as originated in the works of Terence Turner for central Brazilian societies and of Peter Rivière for the Guyanese region, which emphasize the control by certain categories of persons over others as central to the dynamics of native sociopolitical process; (2) the "moral economy of intimacy," first represented in the works of Ellen Basso among the Kalapalo (1970, 1975) and Joanna Overing among the Piaroa (Overing-Kaplan 1972, 1973; Overing and Passes 2000), which focuses on the social philosophy and practice of everyday society in Amazonia; (3) the "symbolic economy of alterity" of the structuralist-inspired ethnologists, which concentrates on processes of symbolic exchange (such as war and cannibalism, hunting, shamanism, and funerary rites) that cross cultural boundaries and thus play into the definition of collective identities; and (4) "historical processes and the cultural production of history" (Hill 1996; Gow 2001; Whitehead 1997, 2002; Wright 1998), which is concerned with a broad range of issues such as landscape, the production of ethnicity, warfare, and the epistemology of historical text. An important emergent theme across these topics has been the mutual production of cultural and social categories between "native" and "colonial" (or national) societies that have come to dominate indigenous communities throughout the region. In this context shamanism has emerged as an important vehicle for the mediation of change.

These analytical styles and theoretical tendencies are not necessarily exclusive. The present volume includes all of these approaches, and thus we have chosen to organize the chapters to reflect these various theoretical emphases as well as cultural traditions. In the latter case it would be premature to make a strict contrast between, say, the Tupian, Arawakan, and Cariban groups discussed in the volume, but certain tendencies do begin to emerge that may well be a useful basis for future research into shamanism generally. Among the Tupian groups shamanic power is persistently threatening, even in its "curing" aspect. Indeed the historical sources refer to the cannibalistic nature of the shaman's rattles (*maraka*) that constantly demanded human flesh, while the imagery of the pet/captive suffuses the notion of shamanic assault. Among the Arawakan groups there seems to be an incipient notion of a "witchcraft substance," not directly inheritable, as in the African case, but nonetheless seen as a distinct penetration of the body, which is simultaneously seen as a disruption and attack on the conviviality / siblingship / hierarchy. In this guise dark shamanism is an attack on specific sets of social relationships rather than sociality itself, suggesting particularly strong links between the exercise of power and shamanism in these societies. In the case of the Warao and the neighboring Cariban peoples, there are hints that there is a far more legitimate role for the dark shaman—for even if the sorcerer is a highly antisocial figure he is so with regard to an evanescent set of social relationships, and his actions may paradoxically ensure the possibility for sociality at all through his propitiatory relationship with the predatory cosmos that might otherwise consume humanity and destroy the beneficence of the earth. In this sense the dark shaman enables, but does not aid, the construction of sociality.

The essays by Pollock, Lagrou, and Pinto in this volume focus on the implications of sorcery for the ethics of conviviality in each of the societies studied. Another essay, by Mentore, partly expresses this analytical focus by analyzing close, even familial, relations among the Cariban Waiwai, but also looks to the political economy of power and the role of shamanic voice and ceremonial chant in creating the space of death in life—a theme also present among the Parakanã (see Fausto's essay). Mentore thus creatively combines a number of the broad approaches described above. Santos-Granero's contribution, sharing this theoretical orientation, grapples with the difficult question of the apparent contradiction between an ethic emphasizing "the power of love"—the title of his monograph on the Amuesha of the Peruvian Amazon—and the killing of children accused as sorcerers. It is precisely this ambivalent or even positive evaluation of the role of dark shamanism, along with the existence of culturally different ways of evaluating the meaning of pain, sickness, and death, that form a central challenge in the anthropological interpretation of assault sorcery and its consequences.

Yet it is apparent, as illustrated by Vidal and Whitehead, that dark shamanism produces its own kind of legitimacy, especially where it acts as a mediating force in relations with a threatening alterity—be that either enemy sorcerers from among other native peoples or the very presence of the colonial or national state. In Vidal and Whitehead's essay, as well as Wright's, there is a strong emphasis on historical analyses—that is, investigating the relations between the expressions of sorcery that are the consequence of situations of contact and articulation with nonindigenous societies, as well as internal social, political, and ritual processes. Through its regional and comparative approach, Vidal and Whitehead's contribution especially demonstrates the interaction between shamans, sorcerers, and religious cults with regard to regional and national (even international) politics.

The structuralist-inspired "symbolic economy of alterity" approach is clearly presented in Fausto's analysis of Parakanã warfare, hunting, and shamanic symbolism, focusing on the predominance of predation as central to social and political dynamics. But Fausto goes beyond this ethnographic analysis to provide a reflection on its radical differences relative to the neo-shamanistic movement of Western society.

One of the initial objectives of this volume was to understand the connections between the symbolic relations of aggression in mythology, cosmology, and shamanism and the social and political dynamics of witchcraft and sorcery. Another objective was to understand, through case histories, the sociological and political contexts of conflicts and aggression based in witchcraft and sorcery accusations—that is, to identify the types of sorcery and/or witchcraft that occur within communities, between communities, and between distant "enemy" groups. Further, we wished to direct attention to the acts of performing witchcraft and sorcery as parts of a sequence of events immediately prior to (e.g., omens or other premonitions, dream symbolism) and following (inquests on vengeance killings) the infliction of harm. Finally, we wished to present native exegeses on the various forms of sorcery and witchcraft: more specifically, how these are distinguished in terms of their efficacy and techniques of application; what metaphors or physiological imagery are used to represent the different forms of magical action; and the rules or norms governing the exercise of these acts, or their representation as a form of uncontrolled or illegitimate aggression.

The essays herein thus give primary attention to these questions by presenting in-depth discussions of methods and techniques of sorcery (Buchillet, Lagrou, Wright); in some cases by an examination of previously little-known societies, such as the Parakanã (Fausto) or the Arara (Pinto); in others, by offering fresh approaches to well-known societies (Pollock on the Kulina; Vidal and Whitehead on Arawakan and Cariban groups). All of the essays seek to relate sorcery and witchcraft to social and political processes, particularly relating to questions of power (Heckenberger, Mentore, Santos-Granero, Vidal and Whitehead), where the contradictions of egalitarian societies in which inequalities, whether or not produced by external contacts, become the crux for witchcraft and sorcery accusations (Wright, Buchillet). By the same token, many of the contributions demonstrate how sorcery accusations may represent forms of discourse about tensions in intervillage and interethnic relations, and may be structured by the idiom of kinship (consanguinity and affinity) and village hierarchy (Heckenberger). It is more likely that other communities, other societies, are to be held responsible for sorcery, and it is equally unthinkable that kin would ever resort to sorcery or witchcraft as a form of action. Such discourse shapes social action, as is demonstrated in several of the case histories in this volume. It is also apparent that dark shamanism becomes an idiom for wider interethnic relations and engages with other occult traditions, such as obeah (Vidal and Whitehead).

Ethics in Anthropological Research on Witchcraft and Sorcery

A number of contributors to this volume expressed anxiety over the possible consequences of even contemplating its subject matter, as Santos-Granero neatly states: "The challenge for me, as well as for all the contributors to this book, is to find ways of talking about cultural practices that are odious to Western sensitivity without either making enemies out of those who practice them or providing their enemies with arguments to deny them their rights."

However, close and long-term ethnographic engagement with societies where shamanism is practiced shows that shamanic power is deeply, if ambiguously, involved in all community affairs. As a result, and as this volume argues, shamanism inevitably is concerned with dark shamanism, aggression, warfare, and the struggle for political and economic power. In fact, many scholars have written about the healing systems of indigenous peoples showing how no one becomes ill and dies without human agency. That agency is evil, and it comes from spirit attacks directed by a shaman or attack sorcerer. Although anthropologists have understood this and the significance of dark shamanism more generally, the scholarly literature, particularly where it is likely to reach a wider audience, has recently tended to downplay these aspects of shamanic practice. This is evident, for example, in the presentation by Luis Luna of the depictions of the "ayahuasca visions" of Pablo Amaringo, a Quechua shaman (Luna and Amaringo 1991). Amaringo's paintings clearly show attack sorcery, and the artist himself explained to the anthropologist how "evil shamans tried to kill the person who is counteracting their evil doings by throwing magical darts, stealing the soul of their victims, or sending animals to bring harm" (1991:13). Nevertheless the presence of attack sorcery in the text is depicted as marginal and the result only of personal maliciousness, although the paintings themselves belie this because the figure of the dark shaman is very evident throughout the collection.

In light of recent events[1] the urge to downplay dark shamanism is intelligible even if self-defeating. Not because there is no issue to be addressed here but rather because the issue itself has been with us since the initial reports on the New World were sent back by Columbus and his contemporaries. Within European cultural tradition, Rousseau's "noble savage" emerged in opposition to the notion of presocial Hobbesian brutes, and these stereotypes have proved to be remarkably persistent in the popular and professional literature alike. But, as Fausto comments in his essay herein: "Understandably enough, the predatory act is the lost fact in modern, urban, middle-class shamanism, which purged the phenomenon from all its ambiguous attributes. It is thus no wonder why the jaguar, although a recurrent figure, is depicted as an endangered species and not as a dangerous predator. Neoshamanism subjects others' thoughts to Western thinking and moral standards: there must be good and bad, both a light and a dark side, and a clear-cut frontier in order to demarcate a basic contrast of ethic. There is no such dichotomy in South American shamanism, which thrives on ambivalence."

This volume does not represent dark shamanism as something else, as an aberration or an error, nor does it glorify the violence and suffering that the activities of dark shamans can cause. Rather, this volume offers only ambivalence, shifting perspectives, shadowy possibilities, and the necessity for the active, participatory relationship with the cosmos that is at the heart of shamanic ritual practice. In this way we intend to more properly represent the spiritual realities of Amazonian peoples which, if they are strongly marked by the violence and predation of a hostile world, should cause us to reflect on the sources of that aggression, which are as much the legacy of our own cultural presence in Amazonia as they may be the product of an ancient vision of cosmological order.

If the Ashárinka identify "child sorcerers," against whom violent acts are then carried out to preserve community harmony, then it is well to remember, lest we judge the Amuesha to be Hobbesian brutes, that we similarly demonize our children as "gang-bangers" and "school shooters." Our response to this issue may be medical rather than spiritual, for the drug Ritalin is widely prescribed for children throughout the Western world, but is it more or less appropriate or credible than the responses of the Amuesha? We do not attempt to answer that question in this volume, but it is our intention that it serve to illustrate why we should be asking it. The notion of satanic abuse that led to witch-hunts in the United States and Europe against parents thought to be suborning their children into the practice of satanism might therefore be compared to the child sorcery of the Amuesha in a new and informative light—we may not assail our children with antisorcery measures, but the disruptive and different are no less condemned among ourselves. The futility of sanitizing the violence of others lies not in the short-term nature of the intellectual comfort this may bring, but rather in the fact that it simultaneously encourages a blindness to the deep history and unacknowledged social value of our own violence toward others and ourselves.

The ethnographies presented throughout this collection seek to document and analyze such cases in order to understand the motivations, processes, symbolism, mechanisms, and dynamics involved. To intervene (i.e., to take action) in any of these cases is another question altogether, and here we emphasize that by the simple fact that in one case the victims are children doesn't make the case any more critical in terms of "human rights abuses" than any of the others. In nearly all cases, it is documented that the societies in question have their own mechanisms and norms for dealing with such cases, and in no way does the anthropologist have a responsibility to intervene. If any case demonstrates clearly the impact of nonindigenous societies as being responsible for a triggering of sorcery accusations or witch killings, however, then we agree it is the anthropologist's obligation to act on his or her own society. Thus we limit our comments here to the point that the study of assault sorcery in native societies frequently reveals the nature of violence at work in state societies. Any larger discussion of ethics would demand another volume and would include other practices that historically have "horrified" the West, such as cannibalism, headhunting, warfare, and torture—which likewise plague our own societies.

Notes

1 "Recent events" refers here to the continuing controversy over the publication of Patrick Tierney's *Darkness in El Dorado* (2000), which accuses anthropologists of having been complicit in medical experimentation on Amazonian peoples and of having seduced them into lewd and destructive behaviors. Ironically Tierney's only other published work (*The Highest Altar*, 1989) concerns "child sacrifice" in the Andes, and his current journalistic foray (2000) is avowedly something of a penance for past wrongs.

References

Aigle, Denise, Bénédicte de La Perrière, and Jean-Pierre Chaumeil. 2000. *La politique des esprits: Chamanismes et religions universalistes*. Nanterre: Société d'Ethnologie.

Albert, Bruce. 1985. "Temps du sang, temps des cendres: Représentation de la maladie, système rituel et espace politique chez les Yanomami du sud-est (Amazonie brésilienne)." Ph.D. diss., Université de Paris-X (Nanterre).

Basso, Ellen. 1970. "Xingu Carib Kinship Terminology and Marriage: Another View." *Southwestern Journal of Anthropology* 26: 402–16.

———. 1975. "Kalapalo Affinity: Its Cultural and Social Contexts." *American Ethnologist* 2 (2): 207–28.

Brown, Michael F. 1985. "Shamanism and Its Discontents." *Medical Anthropology Quarterly*, 2 (3): 102–20.

———. 1989. "The Dark Side of the Shaman." *Natural History* (November): 8–10.
Butt-Colson, A. 2001. "Kanaima: Itoto as Death and Anti-Structure." In *Beyond the Visible and the Material*, ed. Laura Rival and Neil L. Whitehead. 221–34. Oxford: Oxford University Press.
Campbell, A. 1989. *To Square with Genesis: Causal Statements and Shamanic Ideas in Wayãpi*. Edinburgh: Polygon.
Chaumeil, Jean-Pierre. 1983. *Voir, savoir, pouvoir*. Paris: EHESS.
Comaroff, J., and J. Comaroff. 1998. *Occult Economies and the Violence of Abstraction: Notes from the South African Postcolony*. Chicago: American Bar Foundation.
Conklin, Beth A. 2002. "Shamans vs. Pirates in the Amazonian Treasure Box." *American Anthropologist* 104 (4): 1050–61.
Dole, G. E. 1973. "Shamanism and Political Control among the Kuikuru." In *Peoples and Cultures of Native South America*, ed. D. R. Gross. 294–307. New York: Natural History Press.
Douglas, Mary. 1970. *Witchcraft: Confessions and Accusations*. London: Tavistock.
Ellis, Stephen. 1999. *The Mask of Anarchy: The Destruction of Liberia and the Religious Dimension of an African Civil War*. New York: New York University Press.
Evans-Pritchard, E. E. 1937. *Witchcraft, Oracles and Magic among the Azande*. Oxford: Clarendon Press.
Fausto, Carlos. 2000. "Of Enemies and Pets: Warfare and Shamanism in Amazonia." *American Ethnologist* 26 (4): 933–56.
Geschiere, P. 1997. *The Modernity of Witchcraft: Politics and the Occult in Postcolonial Africa*. Charlottesville: University Press of Virginia.
Goldman, Irving. 1963. *The Cubeo Indians of the Northwest Amazon*. Urbana: University of Illinois Press.
Gow, Peter. 1996. "River People: Shamanism and History in Western Amazonia." In *Shamanism, History, and the State*, ed. Nicholas Thomas and Caroline Humphrey. 90–114. Ann Arbor: University of Michigan Press.
———. 2001. *An Amazonian Myth and Its History*. Oxford: Oxford University Press.
Griffiths, Nicholas. 1996. *The Cross and the Serpent: Religious Repression and Resurgence in Colonial Peru*. Norman: University of Oklahoma Press.
Griffiths, Nicholas, and Fernando Cervantes. 1999. *Spiritual Encounters: Interactions between Christianity and Native Religions in Colonial America*. Lincoln: University of Nebraska Press.
Hamayon, Robert. 1982. "Des Chamanes au Chamanisme." *L'Ethnographie: Voyages Chamaniques Deux* Tome LXXVIII, numéro 87/88: 13–48.
Harner, Michael J. 1962. "Jivaro Souls." *American Anthropologist* 64 (2): 258–72.
———. 1972. *The Jívaro: People of the Sacred Waterfalls*. Berkeley: University of California Press.
———. 1973. *Hallucinogens and Shamanism*. New York: Oxford University Press.
———. 1998. *The Way of the Shaman with Michael Harner*. Berkeley: Thinking Allowed Productions; San Rafael, Calif.: Intuition Network.
Hill, Jonathan, ed. 1996. *History, Power, and Identity: Ethnogenesis in the Americas, 1492–1992*. Iowa City: University of Iowa Press.
Hoskins, Janet, ed. 1996. *Headhunting and the Social Imagination in Southeast Asia*. Stanford: Stanford University Press.
Hugh-Jones, S. 1996. "Shamans, Prophets, Priests and Pastors." In *Shamanism, History, and*

the State, ed. Nicholas Thomas and Caroline Humphrey. 32–75. Ann Arbor: University of Michigan Press.

Knauft, Bruce. 1985. *Good Company and Violence: Sorcery and Social Action in Lowland New Guinea Society*. Berkeley: University of California Press.

Langdon, E. Jean. 1992. *Portals of Power: Shamanism in South America*. Albuquerque: University of New Mexico Press.

———, ed. 1996. *Xamanismo no Brasil: Novas perspectivas*. Florianópolis: Editora da UFSC.

Lévi-Strauss, Claude. 1967. The Sorcerer and His Magic. In *Magic, Witchcraft, and Curing*, ed. John Middleton. 23–42. New York: Natural History Press.

Luna, Luis E., and Pablo Amaringo. 1991. *Ayahuasca Visions: The Religious Iconography of a Peruvian Shaman*. Berkeley: North Atlantic Books.

Middleton, John. 1987. *Lugbara Religion*. Washington, D.C.: Smithsonian Institution Press.

Nimuendaju, Curt. 1932. "Idiomas Indígenas do Brasil." *Revista del Instituto Ethnológico de Tucumán*. Universidad de Tucumán, Tomo II: 543–618.

Overing, Joanna, and Alan Passes, eds. 2000. *The Anthropology of Love and Anger. The Aesthetics of Conviviality in Native Amazonia*. London: Routledge.

Overing-Kaplan, Joanna. 1972. "Cognation, Endogamy, and Teknonymy: The Piaroa Example." *Southwestern Journal of Anthropology* 28: 282–97.

———. 1973. "Endogamy and the Marriage Alliance: A Note on Continuity in Kindred-Based Groups." *Man* 8 (4): 555–70.

———. 1985. "There is no End of Evil: The Guilty Innocents and their Fallible God." In *The Anthropology of Evil*, ed. D. Parkin. 244–78. Oxford: Basil Blackwell.

Rival, L., and N. L. Whitehead. 2001. *Beyond the Visible and Material*. Oxford: Oxford University Press.

Silverblatt, Irene M. 1987. *Moon, Sun, and Witches: Gender Ideologies and Class in Inca and Colonial Peru*. Princeton: Princeton University Press.

Steinen, Karl von den. 1942 (1884). *O Brasil central: expedição em 1884 para a exploração do rio Xingú*, 3rd ed. São Paulo: Companhia Editora Nacional (Col. Brasiliana).

Stephen, Michele, ed. 1987. *Sorcerer and Witch in Melanesia*. New Brunswick: Rutgers University Press.

Stewart, P., and A. Strathern. 1999. "Feasting on My Enemy: Images of Violence and Change in the New Guinea Highlands." *Ethnohistory* 46 (4): 646–69.

Sullivan, Lawrence E. 1988. *Icanchu's Drum: An Orientation to Meaning in South American Religions*. New York: Macmillan.

Taussig, Michael. 1987. *Shamanism, Colonialism, and the Wild Man: A Study in Terror and Healing*. Chicago: University of Chicago Press.

Teixeira-Pinto, Márnio. 1995a. "Entre Esposas e Filhos: Poliginia e Padrões de Aliança entre os Arara." In *Antropologia do Parentesco: estudos ameríndios*, ed. E. Viveiros de Castro. 229–64. Rio de Janeiro: Editora da UFRJ.

———. 1995b. "Histórias de Origem e Relações Ambíguas: notas comparativas sobre um simulacro da questão étnica no Brasil." In *Brasil em Perspectiva: O debate dos Cientistas Sociais*, ed. M. A. Gonçalves. 192–213. Rio de Janeiro: Relume/Dumará.

Thomas, Nicholas, and Caroline Humphrey, eds. 1996. *Shamanism, History, and the State*. Ann Arbor: University of Michigan Press.

Tocantins, Antônio M. G. 1877. "Estudos sobre a tribu Mundurucu." In *Revista Trimensal do Instituto Histórico Geográphico e Ethnográphico do Brasil*, 73–161. Rio de Janeiro: Garnier Livreiro e Editor, Tomo XL.

Viveiros de Castro, Eduardo. 1996. "Images of Nature and Society in Amazonian Ethnology." *Annual Review of Anthropology* 25: 179–200.

Watson, C., and Ellen, R., eds. 1993. *Understanding Witchcraft and Sorcery in Southeast Asia*. Honolulu: University of Hawaii Press.

White, Luise. 2000. *Speaking with Vampires: Rumor and History in Colonial Africa*. Berkeley: University of California Press.

Whitehead, Neil L. 1996. "The Mazaruni Dragon: Golden Metals and Elite Exchanges in the Caribbean, Orinoco, and the Amazon." In *Chieftains, Power, and Trade: Regional Interaction in the Intermediate Area of the Americas*, ed. C. H. Langebaek and F. C. Arroyo. 107–32. Bogotá: Universidad de los Andes.

———. 1997. *The Discoverie of the Large, Rich and Bewtiful Empire of Guiana by Sir Walter Ralegh*. (Edited, annotated and transcribed). *Exploring Travel Series Vol. 1*, Manchester: Manchester University Press and, *American Exploration & Travel Series Vol. 71*, Norman: Oklahoma University Press.

———. 2001. "Kanaimà; Shamanism and Ritual Death in the Pakaraima Mountains, Guyana." In *Beyond the Visible and the Material*, ed. Laura Rival and Neil L. Whitehead. Oxford: Oxford University Press.

———. 2002. *Dark Shamans: Kanaimà and the Poetics of Violent Death*. Durham: Duke University Press.

Whitten, Norman. 1976. *Sacha Runa: Ethnicity and Adaptation of the Ecuadorian Quichua*. Urbana: University of Illinois Press.

———. 1985. *Sicuanga Runa: The Other Side of Development in Amazonian Ecuador*. Urbana: University of Illinois Press.

Wilbert, Johannes. 1972. "Tobacco and Shamanistic Ecstasy Among the Warao Indians of Venezuela." In *Flesh of the Gods: The Ritual Use of Hallucinogens*, ed. P. Furst. London: Allen and Unwin.

———. 1993. *Mystic Endowment: Religious Ethnography of the Warao Indians*. Cambridge: Harvard University Press.

Wright, Robin. 1998. *For Those Unborn: Cosmos, Self, and History in Baniwa Religion*. Austin: University of Texas Press.

 *The Order of Dark Shamans among the Warao*

Johannes Wilbert

According to the Warao of northeastern Venezuela, the universe contains a world ocean encompassed by a chain of soaring mountains.[1] At the cardinal, intercardinal, and solstitial points of sunrise and sunset this range incorporates twelve towering columnar peaks that brace a bell-shaped cosmic vault. Below the dome's zenith, and in the middle of the ocean, there floats a disklike earth comprised of the Orinoco delta, the Warao's traditional swampy homeland. Bundles of twirling energy rising from the center of the ocean floor transpierce the earth-disk and a small discoidal tier close to the summit of the sky, conjoining nadir and zenith as a world axis (figs. 1 and 2).

Populating the peripheral and axial regions of this cosmic landscape are divine powers that interact with humankind in various ways. They either visit earth from time to time or make their earthly presence known by proxy. Although humans originated in the sky world as disembodied beings, after their descent to earth the Lord of Death destined them to be of corporeal existence, unsuited for celestial life. The cosmic landscape and its powerful constituents, therefore, are inaccessible to common human beings and only reachable by shamans and shamanic artisans capable of ecstatic trance.

The Warao recognize several different orders of shamanism, usually distinguishing between junior, senior, and veteran members. In some instances practices among same-order ranks vary such that outsiders erroneously perceive them as categorically distinct from one another. Still, there exist as many as four different orders of shamanism in Warao society, including priest-shamanism, light shamanism, weather shamanism, and dark sha-

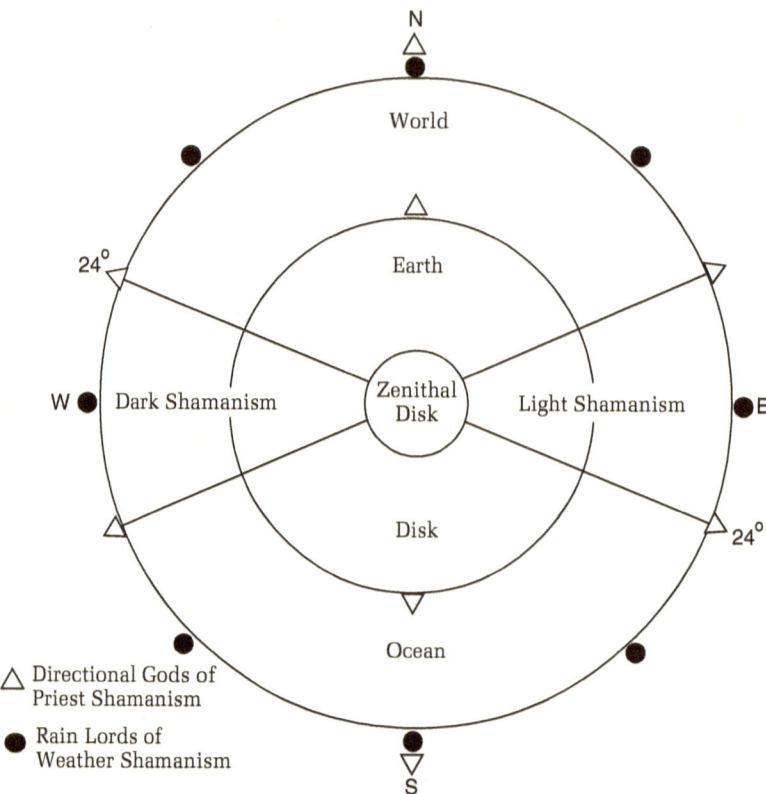

Figure 1. Warao cosmology and shamanic domains, showing directional gods and priest-shamanism, the rain lords of weather shamanism, light shamanism, and dark shamanism. (Drawing by Werner Wilbert)

manism. Whereas in this essay I address primarily dark shamanism, I offer a brief description of the other types to help clarify the difference between Warao shamanism and sorcery as well as to situate both practices within respective cosmological domains. Although shamanism and shamanic crafts are primarily reserved for males, women may also practice these arts, except that of boatbuilding. However, I have known but few practicing female shamans and am aware of none who were ecstatics who were initiated, like male shamans, by resorting to tobacco (nicotine) as a medium of trance.

Priest-Shamanism

The order of priest-shamanism derives its power from "our ancients" (*kanobotuma*), residing on world mountains at the extreme cardinal points (other than the western) and at the solstitial corners of the universe. Lesser deities by that name live on hills at earth's edge, opposite the southern and the northern mountains, as well as at the zenith and the nadir. The two southern and two northern gods are mirror images of each other, even though the distant members of the pairs rank higher than the near ones. Highest-ranking of all ancients is the god of the far south (see fig. 1).

The name *kanobotuma* translates also as "our grandfathers," designating the primal forebears of the Warao. Jointly with their retinues of deceased priest-shamans, they constitute a hidden but important segment of the population. By frequenting pathways that connect their cosmic stations, the ancients traffic with each other and with humankind, remaining well disposed toward their mortal kin as long as they provision them with food (tobacco smoke) and with rejuvenating water (sago). Thus, there exists a covenant of compelling mutuality between humans, on the one hand, and ancestral gods and late priest-shamans on the other: protection of terrestrials by celestials depends on propitiation of celestials by the earthbound.

The priest-shaman, a trance-initiated ecstatic who mediates between the parties, is responsible for humankind's compliance with this pact. Instatement to his office follows weeks of rigorous asceticism, nicotine habituation, and instruction in the knowledge of priest-shamanism, leading to the candidate's empowerment as a "master over pain" (*wisiratu; wisimo* is the plural form). The mentor hands the candidate a three-foot-long cigar prepared with six wads of tobacco that, on ingestion, enter the pupil's body as his sons, or tutelary "pains," and accommodate themselves, in pairs, on both sides of his throat, chest, and abdomen. On his initiatory journey, the neophyte follows a psychopomp through life-threatening situations and past deadly creatures. He contemplates a pile of bones left by unfortunates who failed to clear a dangerous passage of rapidly opening and closing doors.

Figure 2. Profile of the Warao bell-shaped universe.
(Drawing by Werner Wilbert, after Noel Diaz)

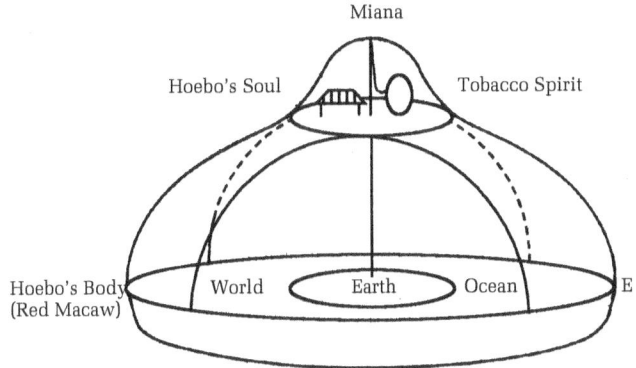

Only after making it safely through these crushing gates does the apprentice, finally, behold a huge horned viper balancing a bright red ball on its protruding tongue. The enlightened novice finds himself on top of his sponsoring ancient's mountain, where he is assigned a house where he can stay on future visits and then reside forever at the end of his career as a priest-shaman.

From the time of his instatement, the priest-shaman functions as a healer of patients suffering from febrile illnesses (*hebu*), which, like most diseases, originate ultimately with spirits in the sky who were prevented by primordial Warao from following them to earth. In their anger these spirits transformed themselves into physical disorders and diseases, pledging to afflict their terrestrial kin in perpetuity. Pains are sent by disgruntled ancients, by priest-shamans who request the gods to send them, or by the ancients' proxies in the shaman's body. Priest-shamans take offensive action by blowing pains from their bodies into victims who, by their behavior, threaten the integrity of the covenant with the ancients. Individuals whose misconduct poses a threat to themselves and to the community at large prompt illness caused through intervention of a priest-shaman. Generally speaking, however, priest-shamans do not practice sorcery with evil intent. Of course, the chastisement they mete out will hardly be perceived as particularly benevolent by the patient. But, once aware of their offenses, *hebu* patients become contrite and, if old enough, confess transgressions as part of the therapeutic process. Most patients seen by a priest-shaman healer are children and adolescents who, particularly during the annual rainy seasons, feel the wrath of the ancients castigating the community for delays in feeding them or for propitiating them insufficiently with sago. A priest-shaman healer expects to be compensated for his efforts by a child's father or by a recovered adult male as long as the patient is not a member of his nuclear family. A man unable to provide compensation mortgages his body by sitting back to back with the shaman, pledging to be his lifelong *neburatu* (servant).

Whereas, quite evidently, Warao priest-shamanism bears the trademarks of near-universal shamanism, its veteran practitioners also act as priestly leaders in religious rituals on behalf and with support of their congregations. Hierarchically organized like the ancients, priest-shamans of sub-tribal populations are ranked according to their statuses. Highest ranking among them is the *kanoboarima*, "father of our ancient one." In early times, distressed by the amount of illness that prevailed among his people, the founder of priest-shamanism visited the supreme spirit of the south in order to negotiate the noted contract of reciprocal assistance. In exchange for a one-time sacrifice of ten persons, he was granted one of the god's own sons in the form of a rock crystal, and he accommodated the idol in a basket within the village shrine. From the time of this inaugural event, priest-shamans are cofathers to the *kanobo*'s son and kinsmen of his father, engaging the paternal spirit as the divine patron of their subtribal communities.²

Much of an ordinary priest-shaman's life is spent consulting ancestral spirits about the causes of his patients' illnesses and propitiating the *kanobos* with tobacco. He makes his inquiries and pleas by plaintive chant, accompanied by a sacred rattle that contains a family of tutelary spirits in the form of quartz pebbles. When applied to a patient's body, these helpers leave the rattle and effect a cure inside the ailing person. However, in addition to his healing functions, the veteran priest-shaman, ranking as the father of the ancient one, as noted, has also important priestly obligations. Intermittently throughout the year, he invites the ancients from around the world (except the western one) to join his people's patron spirit in the shrine. In the course of ceremonial dancing under his auspices, the gods receive an offering of *moriche* (*Mauritia flexuosa*) starch, or sago — their rejuvenating water and the Warao's staple food. Symbolically, the Warao recognize ritual sago flour as semen, the fundamental font of human life (Briggs 1992:344). Old Spider Woman placed it in the form of silk into the stem of the primordial palm, after the god of the noon sun had fashioned her from the bleached bones of ancestral Warao. Ever since, seminal *moriche* starch serves as sacramental food for human participants in the ritual and as the fountain of youth for participating deities, who immerse themselves therein.

Light Shamanism

The order of light shamanism is generically known as *bahana* and its practitioners as *bahanarao* (*bahanarotu* is the singular form), meaning those who "smoke" or "suck." Extending from the solstitial sunrise corners to the zenith and the center of the earth, its cosmic center is a two-story ovoid structure, located on the upper-world plain, northeast of the world axis (see figs. 1 and 2). Light shamanism is identified with the plenipotent sun of high noon and the avian God of Origin, residing on the world mountain at equinoctial sunrise. This supreme lord is the father of the swallow-tailed kite (*Elanoides forficatus*), the Tobacco Spirit, who, in primordial times, emerged from a cave in the mountain. From there he tracked the sun to the brightest region in the sky, where he built the egg-shaped house near the top of the firmament (see figs. 2 and 3). The house connects with the apex of the world axis via a rope bridge that conveys a beam of power down to earth and to the nadir of the universe. The bridge is bordered on both sides by flowering tobacco plants, whose leaves were harvested by the architect of the cosmic egg to convert them into the thickened smoke of which the bridge, the house, its inventory, and its residents are fashioned. In addition to housing the Tobacco Spirit and his consort, the building's upper floor is

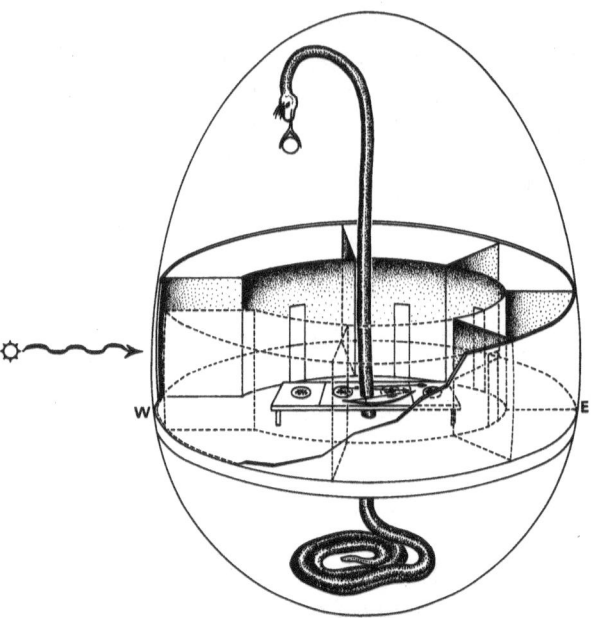

Figure 3. Zenithal house of the Tobacco Spirit.
(Drawing by Noel Diaz)

home to the very first light shaman and his wife, as well as to four insect men and their families. A plumed serpent lives on the structure's lower level. Periodically, the insects gather around a gambling table on which they move specific counters to invade each other's spaces according to an arrow dice cast by the Spirit of Tobacco. On completion of a game, the snake erects itself above the gamblers, jingles the chromatic feathers on its head, and presents an orb of radiant light on its forked tongue. Depending on which gambler wins, someone will live or die on earth. Thus, the stakes are high in the celestial gambling game.

The construction of the cosmic egg, and with it the beginning of light shamanism, occurred in primordial times when plants, animals, and humans, although qualitatively equivalent, became subject, nevertheless, to the fundamental law of mutual predation that governs the zoological world. *Bahana* shamanism is conditioned by this existential necessity because the natural epiphanies of the Tobacco Spirit and his houseguests are linked in an ecological food chain. In his earthly guise, the building's owner manifests as the swallow-tailed kite. The insects materialize as a honey bee (*Trigona capitata*), a stingless bee (*Trigona hyalinata branneri*), a wasp (*Stenopolybia fulvofasciata*), and a termite (*Nasutitermes corniger M.*), while the serpent is modeled on a blind snake (*Leptotyphlops* sp.). By natural design, these species raid or even raze each other's living spaces, decimate each other's progeny, and take each other's lives. Both bees eat the nectar and pollen of the tobacco flowers along the rope bridge; the wasp feeds on the broods of the bees and the termite; the snake eats the larvae of the termite and the wasp; and the kite, at the top of the pyramid, lives on the bees' and wasps' honey and eggs, as well as on the flying insects and the snake. The state of preordained intrusive hazardry pervading the birthplace of light shamanism is what potentiates *bahana* spirituality. Essentially neither good nor evil, it simply constitutes a baneful element of telluric life.

The first light shaman—now residing in the cosmic egg—was only four years old when he surmised that, compensating for the dark world in the west, there had to be a light world in the east. After fasting for four days he fell asleep, and, with the surging heat of virgin fire beneath his hammock his spirit levitated via the world axis to the zenith. From there, a psychopomp conducted him northeasterly to the oval house of smoke. Inside the house, its owner regaled the youth with bow and arrows, while the four insect men gave him four different gambling-board counters, consisting of a crystal, a ball of hair, quartz pebbles, and a puff of tobacco smoke. The board, the dice, and the four counters are referred to as the *bahana* game, and the young light shaman became its first full-fledged earthly owner (*kotubuarotu*). Before leaving the house with his precious gift, the youngster witnessed the snake erect itself over him, its feathers chiming. The boy began manifesting a halo around his head, and the radiance of the serpent's glowing orb filled him with instant knowledge of all things *bahana*.

Back on earth, the youth remained for four days in a trancelike state, ingesting nothing but cigars made of four wads of tobacco. This was to nurture four young insect replicas (the two bees, a wasp, and a termite), that now lodged in his chest. They had become his sons and began opening a lumen in each of his arms, ending in exit holes at the base of each of his fingers (other than his thumbs). At age sixteen—on reaching spermatogenesis—the young man wed a bee girl and, cohabiting with her, introduced her to his spirit wards. Eventually, as noted, the couple took up residence in the Tobacco Spirit's house, where the wife changed into a frigate bird (*Fregata magnificens*) to become the first white shamaness, specializing, like her human successors, in curing nicotinic seizures. Once the Warao began populating the earth, the first light shaman shot two gambling tokens—the termite's quartz pebbles and the stingless bee's puff of tobacco smoke—into a young man's upper body. He did this to perpetuate light shamanism on earth, albeit in diminished form, based on the weaker pair of insects in the primordial shaman's breast. Although referred to as *kotubuarotu* (master of the game), just like the first light shaman, modern practitioners proved incapable of retaining the complete set of gamblers in their bodies. Instead, they carry only one tutelary spirit (termite) in their right torso and one (stingless bee) in their left, requiring but a single exit hole in the palm of each hand.[3]

Among his kind of bird spirits, the swallow-tailed kite ranks supreme, while three of his avian peers represent medium-level light shamanism and, three further ones, lower-level light shamanism. A similar hierarchy prevails among contemporary light shamans of the Warao. At their own initiative, and after eight days of isolation, instruction, fasting, sexual abstinence, and heavy smoking, they follow the example of the first light shaman and become enlightened in the Tobacco Spirit's house. Soon after their initiation, they begin practicing within their families and, by accompanying established healers, on nonfamily members. With growing expertise, the shaman takes on cases singly, treating pains of sudden onset, highly contagious diseases, and, particularly, gynecological problems precipitated by a hostile opposite number. He massages the patient's hurting body part and applies oral suction to bring the sickness-causing object to the surface. Depending on which of the two possible pathogens are diagnosed as implicated, he lays on either one of his hands, the right for termite, and the left for stingless bee. The appropriate tutelary spirit travels through the healer's arm and hand, extracts the pathology, and inserts it into an object the shaman keeps ready for this purpose. Should a light shaman's helper spirits be too "young" to overpower those of older counterparts, the healer acknowledges defeat and defers the patient to a more accomplished colleague. However, if one of the two celestial gamblers (not represented in the chest of the light shaman) wins the game, the patient dies. Light shamans expect payment from their patients. Should they be unable to pay their healer, they offer their bodies as remuneration to serve him as a lifelong "son" or "daughter."

As the number of therapeutic failures increases throughout their careers, senior light shamans come under suspicion of being no longer willing to treat patients or of causing illnesses themselves. In his offensive role, a light shaman is referred to as *hatabuarotu*, "master of (magic) arrows," or *mohokarotu*, "he who discharges through the hand." Acting either on instruction of an ancestral shaman or on his own accord, he swallows an arrow in the form of a small object. His internal helper spirits "play" with the projectile to establish whose token's identity (termite's pebbles or bee's smoke ball) the projectile is destined to adopt. The winner stores the missile in the shaman's (right or left) elbow or wrist, waiting for him to fumigate the openings in his hands and to dispatch the projectile into the victim.

Senior light shamans are adamant that, while perfectly fit to do so, they never practice sorcery of this sort in their home communities. To demonstrate their loyalty to the group, they sometimes play a dangerous game at nightly séances, letting their helping spirits fly like sparks throughout the house. The spirits are believed to be particularly partial to such playfulness, and the shaman comments on their trajectory, as only he and, possibly, other participating light shamans can see them wafting gingerly from person to person without touching or landing on anyone's head. However, commoners are less approving of such frivolous sport that might result, for them, in illness or in sudden death. Instead, they are relieved when light shamans recall their "playing sons" by blowing at them with tobacco smoke.[4]

Veteran light shamans, on the other hand, are, first and foremost, sorcerers. Highest ranking among light shamans, they are known as *daunonarima,* "fathers of the wooden figurine." The effigy in question is a twelve-centimeter-high and two-centimeter-thick sculpture in the round, fashioned either in the stylized form of the swallow-tailed kite's head and neck or in a naturalistic rendering of a young person of undetermined sex, wearing a neckband to which two parrot feathers are attached as wings (J. Wilbert 1975a:67, plate 66). The shaman keeps the effigy in a small calabash bowl and basket in the sanctuary. Also stored in this container are three quartz pebbles, representing the elite of the kite's avian companions.[5] This foursome, comprised of the God of Origin's son (kite) and his senior vassals (pebbles), possesses devastating power that veteran light shamans employ not just to cause pain, as normally inflicted by their junior colleagues, but to kill. Veteran light shamans' sorcery is assault sorcery deployed to settle intercommunity conflict or to conduct extratribal warfare (Lavandero 2000: 28), liquidating a large portion of a target population, especially its children. Thus, not all light shamans are also fathers of the figurine. At most, there exists only one *daunonarima* per regional subtribe, and possession of an effigy seems to run in families. Because masters of the figurine are not inclined to liquidate their own group's offspring, tolerating them in their midst assures villagers of the most powerful deterrent to assault *bahana.*

To perform assaultive sorcery, the master relies not on his insect helpers but on the kite itself and on its most eminent associates. The owner awakens the effigy by fumigating it with tobacco smoke and makes it stand and sway on the palm of his cupped hand. Suddenly, the figurine lifts off with the roar of a hurricane and flies to the targeted village, whose residents can hear the missile approaching but not see it. Only the local white shaman beholds the flying image and warns the people of the dying days that lie ahead. When in the air, the quartz pebbles surge in a triangular formation closely followed by the figurine. Hovering over the village, and in true *bahana* spirit, the intrusive foursome selects its victims, swoops down, and kills the enemies one by one in quick succession. The pebbles tear into their bodies like an arrowhead, allowing the effigy to penetrate deeply into its victims. The siege may last for four days, until many have succumbed as if to an attack by epidemic pestilence or a war party.

Returning to its owner, the figurine's head and body are smeared with blood. While cleaning it with water, the sorcerer inquires about the success of the raid and the number of people killed. If there were more than five, he promises to prepare a gift of tobacco and sago flour. With this, the effigy is usually satisfied and rests in its basket until the sorcerer arouses it again, the reason for which might be to launch a new attack or simply to use the missile's roaring presence to warn the enemies and neighbors of what will happen if they won't desist, mend their ways, or improve their conduct vis-à-vis the sorcerer (J. Wilbert 1979).

Weather Shamanism

Weather shamanism is at home in the mansions of the rain lords, situated on top of the mountains at the cardinal and intercardinal ends of the world (see fig. 1). Known as the *kabo arotutuma*, "masters of the night sky," the rain lords, except for large flaring heads, are of ordinary humanoid appearance, wearing white robes during the dry seasons and black ones during the wet seasons. They also don spectacles and sandals and smoke elbow pipes. The rain lords occupy hierarchical positions in their assembly of one female and seven male associates. During the dry seasons, the doors and windows of their mansions, facing toward earth, are shut, while in the rainy seasons they remain wide open. Particularly after months of seclusion during the long dry season, the lords burst out of their houses to urinate. On earth, it rains profusely and rivers overflow and flood the land.

Men with the ascribed ability to influence precipitation are referred to individually as *naharima*, "father of rain." I have known only one (postmenopausal) woman who was recognized as *naharani*, "mother of rain." It is peculiar to weather shamanism that all duly initiated practitioners are of mature age, ostensibly because the younger set cannot be entrusted with its power. Personal initiative rather than supernatural call is what motivates the individual to apprentice himself to a competent master, seeking empowerment through instruction and trance initiation. The study period may last from six to twelve weeks, depending mainly on the physical and mental fortitude of the student. The gradual increase of tobacco consumption by smoking long cigars subjects the novice to a nicotine-induced inhibition of hunger pangs that culminates in physical distress and the mental symptoms of intoxication. Through this eminently didactic experience, the candidate becomes aware that weather shamanism regulates hunger and starvation. Whether in the form of soft rains or torrential downpours, precipitation determines human survival. Over slow-moving and soft rains, weather shamans exercise only defensive control by diverting them from their communities. Over stormy rain, however, they wield the power both to redirect and to attract the rain, thereby ruling over people's lives and deaths.

What raises this statement above mere hyperbole is the connection that exists between precipitation and the reproductive cycle of the sago palm *moriche*. Traditionally the mainstay of Warao economy, weather-dependent sago provokes frequent episodes of seasonal hunger and periodic famines. As the equatorial trough passes over the Orinoco delta twice in a single year, it produces a four-season pattern of equinoctial dry and solstitial wet weather. During the intermittent shower activity of the dry seasons, sago is abundant, or at least reasonably plentiful. However, in the wet seasons, slow-moving disturbances can cause continuous rainfall of up to ten or more hours at a time, triggering inflorescence in *moriche* palms across wide tracts of land and inhibiting sago production in their stems. More typical of rainy seasons are fast-moving storms of violent but localized downpours, generally accompanied by thunder. Instantaneous, random, and sporadic, they restrict flowering to much-smaller areas and reduce sago production in *moriche* stems to insignificant amounts or even none. This interrelationship between precipitation and sago production is the crux of Warao weather shamanism: anybody purported to control the rain in *moriche* groves is, ipso facto, empowered to control local hunger or regional famine among *moriche* sago eaters like the Warao.

To acquire this climatic power is precisely the intent of someone who aspires to become a weather shaman. After weeks of learning, fasting, and tobacco smoking, the emaciated candidate prepares for the event of initiation. He points three or four two-foot-long cigars successively into the directions of the rain lords around the world, and by smoking the cigars by hyperventilation he offers them tobacco smoke. This puts him into an ecstatic state in which he meets a manifestation of the supreme rain lord in the form of a waterspout or a tornado. Lifted up and swallowed by the colossal spirit, the novice journeys through the lord's serpentine physic of water, thunder, and resplendent lightning, receiving instantaneous and total knowledge of the masters of the night sky and their ways. On leaving the twister spirit (via the rectum), the new weather shaman has aged precipitously, and the rainbow, the lowest-ranking rain lord, takes up residence in his chest to give him titular status as rain lord and serve as his familiar.

On rainy days throughout the year, weather shamans admonish people to be generous with their food and share it with their neighbors, especially with the aged. They hint at possible chastisement for unseemly stinginess and they practice their skills to keep the rain at bay. In the Orinoco delta with its nearly 200 cm average annual precipitation, the rain falls often, even in the dry seasons. To prevent rain from adversely impacting the *moriche* groves, weather shamans blow between the joined palms of their hands, thrust their arms skyward, and, uttering brief spells, command the clouds to dissipate. Besides staving off hunger, weather blowing also serves the purpose of forestalling numerous diseases (rheumatic, respiratory, gastrointestinal) caused by rain that is believed to be the urine, sweat, and tears of sky people. Like hunger, climatic health conditions are the weather shaman's weaponry, and hinting at its possible deployment provides sufficient stimulus to coax the people into generous and congenial behavior.[6]

Generally speaking, precipitation has a negative connotation for the Warao. Were it not for sundry ill-intentioned spirits and the weather shamans, however, rain would pose less of a problem to survival in the world. Acting either to protect their people from the rain or to subject them to it, weather shamans do not cure but rather are primarily involved in sorcery. For, if not falling of its own accord, without their intervention, the precipitation against which weather shamans protect their groups is caused by other weather sorcerers who inflict it on them. Especially during the long rainy season, when climatically related suffering is at its peak, weather shamans are not merely respected but are deeply feared as capable of enforcing their demands for resource sharing with the elderly (themselves included) by conjuring up the specters of ill health, hunger, and starvation. All shamans, and even commoners, can blow against up-coming storms, albeit with varying promise of success. But people think of the weather shaman primarily as a sorcerer whom they might hear practicing his witchcraft against their neighbors or their own community. A good part of the initiatory curriculum of weather shamanism is dedicated to the learning of necromantic chants, aimed at inciting the ire of the rain lords, individually, in groups, or all at once. Infuriated by the provocative and violent imagery contained in these lengthy evocational recitations, the rain lords stride with pounding heels to congregate on the celestial plaza below the top of the cosmic vault, where they perform a dance. Their stomping thunders through the clouds, the impact of their walking staffs sparks sky-rending lightning and their sweating causes heavy rainfall, while bellowing alligators dialogue with them in the sky. In fact, weather shamanism, serving the masters of the night sky, is akin to dark shamanism, in that slow-moving climatic disturbances that provoke widespread famines every four to five years are caused by alligators, the naguals (animal doubles) of dark shamans, providing weather shamanism with its most lethal weapon.

Dark Shamanism

Dark shamanism pertains to the land of darkness, which extends from the zenith and the center of the earth to the solstitial sunset corners of the universe (see fig. 1). The ruler over this domain is Hoebo, the Ancient One, residing on the western mountain of the setting equinoctial sun. In fact, the sun sets daily in the very mansion of this god, keeping it and the entire precinct in perpetual darkness. Only two small lights—one white, the other yellow—illuminate the central site and cast a bone-white hue on its surroundings.

Hoebo's binary and lesser opposite is Miana. He occupies a house located on the world plane near the zenith, west of the world axis, and is considered the soul of Hoebo (see fig. 2). This is the region where the sun starts its descent and moves across the threshold of the land of darkness. As his name indicates, Miana suffers from dimmed vision and favors soft crepuscular light; broad daylight dazzles him and causes him to squint. Nevertheless, despite his eye condition, Miana travels unimpaired between his home and Hoebo's place at the world's end in the west.

The land of darkness and its ruler have existed since the universe began. And when, in early times, the Lord of Death decreed that spiritual humans were henceforth to become embodied mortals, Hoebo manifested as the red macaw (*Ara chloroptera*) and claimed the new terrestrial species as his and his relation's staple food. In time, the parrot people built a settlement of humble houses near macaw's colossal iron (or aluminum) mansion, and they gathered there with their lord to drink of human blood from a thirty-foot canoe and feast on human flesh from well-stocked larders. The blood container, like the parrots' houses and their furniture, is made of human bones. A gagging stench of putrefaction saturates the air, and blowflies carpet the environs, sodden with coagulating blood. Wind instruments of human tibias and skulls are playing, and partakers in the banquets are attired in their feather coats adorned with necklaces of human costal bone.

Originally, Miana was responsible for providing the denizens of this netherworld with their fare. To procure sufficient blood he used a hosepipe (*hoa ahutu*) that was fastened to a high-rise structure near the drinking trough. The line ran up the cosmic vault to reach a place halfway between Hoebo's and Miana's stations, from where it dangled over the encampment of the newly formed Warao. The duct was furnished with a brilliant headlight, which helped it find, at night, the heads of unsuspecting sleepers. When activated by Miana's chant, the blood duct pierced the people's skulls and entered their hearts to start the draining. The caterer, however, did not permit the robot hose to bleed its victims dry. Instead he saved them, in their weakened state, for likely future tapping. When meat was needed in the netherworld, Miana aimed his lethal chant at one or more such damaged persons and waited until they died to carry their corpses to the land of night.

The supreme macaw constitutes the quintessential morbus of Warao spirituality. Whereas individual priest-shamans stand to lose their body and their soul (bones) between the clashing gates through which they must pass on their initiatory journey, no ancient one, except macaw, threatens all humanity with such complete annihilation. Throughout their oral history, the Warao have sought to strike some kind of modus vivendi with this awesome predator. There are, for instance, those who tame macaws and make them pets, part of their families. However, to avoid extreme aggressiveness, and thus injury from hacking beaks, they choose the blue-and-yellow species (*abuhene; Ara ararauna*), representing subordinate members of the netherworld, over the red-and-blue macaws (*abahera*) that stand for the divine macaw himself and his close kin. In turn, there were macaw girls who attempted to bring humans into their families as husbands. As ranking members of their predatory community, however, the macaws, instead of keeping men as mates, took them for food and ate them, triggering an all-out war that nearly wiped out both peoples. Traditional spirituality has taught the Warao that peaceful coexistence between humans and macaws is more than likely unattainable, so long as both are proximal sequential members in a food chain. Some mitigating manner thus was needed to make coincident survival possible for both species, and it is the nature of dark shamanism to be this existential compromise.

Dark shamanism takes its origin precisely from the last attempt at rapprochement between macaws and human beings. It all began when the macaw god's son—named Abahera, like his father in his avian form—started courting a beautiful Warao. On frequent visits to his girlfriend's village, the couple did indeed enjoy each other's company and lived as if they were already married. Alas, the woman also continued relations with a previous lover, Miana's son, called Hoebo like the ancient one. While neither of the men had any knowledge of the other, the maiden's elder brother reprimanded her because of her promiscuous dealings. During an upcoming festival, he insisted, she was to take no notice of her second wooer, the macaw, and socialize exclusively with Hoebo.

The timing of the fiesta coincided with the day on which Miana had agreed to take Hoebo on a visit to the land of the supreme macaw. The father had already taught his son the chant that activated the celestial blood duct. Now, however, the young man wished to see the drinking trough into which the siphoned blood was pouring and get to know the god and all his distant kinfolk in the land of darkness. Reaching the halfway point of their journey (where the artery hung down from heaven to the human village), the travelers heard the parrots' musicmaking in the netherworld. They also saw the white and yellow lights projecting through the darkness and heard the humming of the blood duct as it conveyed its vital cargo. Young Hoebo knew this place from earlier experience, when he had come that far en route to meet his paramour. But now that he observed the people and his girlfriend dancing below him in the village plaza, he decided to forgo his visit to the netherworld and glided down the duct, head first, to join his woman and the merrymaking crowd.

Meanwhile, Abahera, the Warao girl's other lover, had also been approaching the festivities while playing, as courting bachelors do, a variety of flutes to announce his arrival. Instead of regular flutes, however, made of wood or deer bone, his instruments were of the kind macaw men play; that is, of human skeletal parts that sound like earthly aerophones but carry messages that are foreboding to the human ear. In fact, the woman's brother trembled when he heard their eerie sound, and he warned his sister to beware and heed his counsel. This time, the courting flutist would arrive prepared to take her as his wife.

As Abahera reached the village, Hoebo was about to jump onto the plaza from above. But when the parrot realized that his intended wife recoiled from him in favor of this other man, the jilted suitor stepped into the middle of the dancing guests, reached up with his machete, and sliced his rival horizontally in half. A thunderous noise resounded through the universe as the halves of Hoebo's body fell to the ground and as the blood duct, which Abahera's knife had simultaneously severed, snapped westward to its moorings in the land of darkness. The headlight of the duct, which had been seen above the village like a small-sized moon, crashed with Hoebo's body to the dance floor.

It had been Abahera's intention all along to cut the blood duct of the netherworld and rid humanity of this scourge. But he had also wished to keep the orb of light in his possession to benefit his wife's community and humanity at large. He had infused the light globe with his breath by chanting over it incantations of his own invention. This would enable the light globe to function under his control as a new link between macaws and humans. But now, although the food chain was forever severed, the fallen orb had shattered and its light dispersed across the earth like wind. The scattered light had turned into a myriad of pneumatic agents (*hoa*) that entered all components of the objective world. Villagers who witnessed the momentous transformation felt a sharp pain in their chests and became nauseous as the miasmal air entered their bodies, debilitating everybody as if the blood duct were still working. Nobody knew of the pneumatic agents and their function, because their creator had rejoined his people in the netherworld and Hoebo's body parts had moved, one half to the western region and the other half to the eastern region of the earth, where everybody learned of *hoa* pneuma and its workings. Thus, while perhaps of only qualified success for its avian instigator, the last attempt at peaceful coexistence between macaws and humans was of immense importance to Warao of later ages. It broke the ironclad conditions of macaw predation, supplanting it with the more moderate regime of *hoa*, controllable by *hoarao* (*hoarotu*, singular), that is, dark shamans.

Having lost his body to a rival's jealous ire, Hoebo's soul rose to his father's (Miana) place west of the zenith. This is the classic location of Warao dark shamans, where all practitioners of the order go to be empowered. Young men embarking on this quest do so of their own accord and not in answer to a higher calling. Together with their chosen teacher, they retire for a week to an isolated hut and start the process of initiation. During the first phase of this arduous procedure, the candidate abstains from food and drink, smokes tobacco incessantly, and internalizes a repertoire of chants: *miana* chants to secure victims for the netherworld and *hoa* chants to prevent patients from being sacrificed.[7] Toward the end of this initial period, the master takes the burning end of a two-foot-long cigar into his mouth and blows a *hoebo* spirit into it. He hands this magically endowed cigar to his anxious ward and asks him to inhale its content deep into his chest. On performing the same task for a second time (with a brother of the first *hoebo* spirit), the student levitates in narcotic trance to the zenithal house, where he comes face-to-face with Miana's son, Hoebo, the guardian of dark shamanism.

Hoebo's house is similar in construction to the macaw god's mansion, albeit somewhat smaller, perhaps, but black like it and built of metal. The furniture includes benches made of human bone and skin and hammocks fabricated of curdled blood. Hoebo occupies this reeking house together with his wife and their son. The child is only one year old and lies in a hammock in which his mother swings him gently in his sleep. For, when awake, the boy cries constantly from pain, prompting his father to console him with a cradle song. This is the very song that Hoebo once learned from his father, Miana, to activate the blood duct of the netherworld in search of sleeping humans. And this is why trainees must come here to receive the singing power that activates the sucking snare (*kaidoko*) that they will receive as a proboscis in replacement of the inoperative celestial blood duct. Looking like a man with long, blood-matted hair, Hoebo bids the novice to enter his dark house and sit before him on a bench. He then inspects the young man's chest, hands, lips, and tongue and, if found adequate, inducts him as a novice shaman. He lets him keep the two fraternal *hoebo* spirits in his upper body and implants a wound-up snare of *hoebo* power in his chest, below the sternum.

Waking from his ecstatic maiden voyage, the candidate begins the second phase of his initiation, which will take a full month to complete. Because he needs to nurture the fraternal *hoebo* spirits in his chest and make his nascent lariat grow longer, he fasts and smokes incessantly until the tendrils of this bifid sucking snare emerge from the corners of his mouth each time he chants Miana's song or speaks ceremonially in a loud voice. As the ordeal of his induction draws to an end, the neophyte becomes increasingly emaciated and displays the symptoms of severe nicotine intoxication conducive to confirming the tenets of dark shamanism. He suffers from a smoker's throat that makes the act of swallowing most painful. But, because his hunger pangs are quieted by nicotinic action he shows no interest in food or drink. Chances are that as the drug transports him deeper into Miana's world, the neophyte experiences tobacco amblyopia (dimness of vision) and color blindness, which allow him to discern only white and yellow. His world takes on a bone-white, silverish hue, and he sees better in crepuscular light than in the open sunshine. As neurotransmission becomes progressively impaired, the candidate assumes a deathlike state, which in some cases stops him temporarily from breathing.[8] In this acutely liminal condition, the novice meets a demonic spirit who beats him on the neck with a heavy cudgel. The spirit comes a second time and places him into a wooden dugout coffin. The fearsome demon then manifests a third and final time to entomb him in a sarcophagus that reeks of putrefaction. Near death, the neophyte beholds a beam of sunlight entering a crack in the coffin wall. Enlightened, he escapes and is reborn a new dark shaman.

Dark shamans are members of the terrestrial cohort of the zenithal Hoebo, which includes vampires and bloodsucking insects like mosquitoes and sundry species of pestiferous flies. Vampires descend from a nocturnal tribe of people who ate children and who acquired their present form through a promiscuous bat woman. Blood-sucking insects stem from a young man who preyed on his sleeping wives and other members of the population by sucking their lifeblood through a straw. Both etiologies share characteristic features with the origin of dark shamanism and, as explained below, with its current parasitic practices of bleeding people. Dark shamans and their cohort constitute the living body of the zenithal Hoebo's soul, just as the latter is the soul of the red macaw, and Miana that of the ancient Hoebo's body. Thus, as with light and weather shamanism, the spiritual home of dark shamanism is located near the zenith, where its practitioners' souls assemble every night while their bodies remain sleeping in their hammocks on earth. To prove that they continue nurturing their *hoebo* spirit pair and *kaidoko* snare through ceaseless smoking and tobacco chewing, dark shamans, on their nightly visits, repeatedly present their paling yellow chests, tremulous hands, black lips, and furring tongues, which distinguish them as active *hoarotu*. These nicotine-related characteristics pertain to them, as do their fusty body odor and pronounced halitosis, ostensibly because they frequent Hoebo's fetid place and smoke cigars of curdled human blood at their nightly meetings.

One other item continuously monitored by the zenithal Hoebo is the rate of human sacrifice, because the difference between the new and old regimes of netherworld-humanity relations is one, respectively, of autonomous and contingent manners of predation. No longer can the animated blood duct be employed to transport human blood directly to the parrot's place. Because it was severed, the zenithal Hoebo and his cohort are the only means of contact between the denizens of the netherworld and humanity. The ancient one of the west, whether in his preepiphanic form of Hoebo or in the guise of red macaw, can no longer come to the earth in person. However, as in earlier times, the zenithal Hoebo continues in his role as steward of the macaw's world, only now the rate and timing of predation depend entirely on him and on his kind. While fully capable of traveling between the celestial and terrestrial worlds himself, he usually relies for help on mature dark shamans and on the power of the proboscidean snares he has implanted in their chests.

The difference between a mature and an immature dark shaman is one of respective growth and practical experience. Although he knows the rudiment of his art, a young *hoarotu* nevertheless must allow sufficient time to let the spirit children in his breast grow up and his sucking snare grow long before he qualifies to serve as Hoebo's hunter. Only in exceptional cases is a young shaman to practice killing people, as when, soon after his initiation, the Macaw appears to him in his dream, requesting human flesh. Intimidated by the commanding apparition, the novice shaman may agree to snare a weak older person or a child. However, the initiation master warns his pupil not to defer to the macaw again, lest, as his tutor, he become obliged to divest the novice of his powers. Mature dark shamans are usually older men, referred to as hoa fathers (*hoarima*). To attain this rank, they are required to possess the tools and techniques of their trade, as well as to have mastery over *hoa*, the pneumatic agent of sickness and death.

An accomplished master of *hoa* is essentially different from a beginner. Physically, as noted, long-time and copious tobacco use has changed his appearance and engulfed him in a nicotine-effected atmosphere of pungent percutaneous odor and chronic fetid breath. He has become infused with the miasma of the netherworld (marsh methane) that, since the light globe of the blood duct shattered, pervades the earth and all life on it with a latent stench of putrefaction. Originating with the exhalations of the jilted parrot lover, this pneuma is considered to be a disease-carrying emanation that forms the basis of Warao dark shamanism in particular, and of the group's pneumatic theory of illness as a whole (W. Wilbert 1996). Mentally, as will be explained, the veteran *hoarotu* became the top predator of humankind and a lycanthrope who assures the survival of the macaw people, while leaving continued human existence in the hands of younger colleagues.

When, in the course of maturation, the time has come for the dark shaman to begin his service to the netherworld, the zenithal Hoebo takes the shaman there to present him to the divine macaw. The visitor looks around to see how the macaws are living. He sees the blood canoe with its inactive duct. He also sees the house in the village of diseased dark shamans (*hoarao*) that he will occupy on future visits and will dwell in permanently after death, when he assumes, like all his predecessors, a chimeric form that is half-parrot and half-human with a simian tail. But when the supreme macaw offers him a meal of human blood and roasted human flesh prepared with peppers, garlic, and onions he must decline,[9] thereby demonstrating that, while the macaw's ally, he is a mortal and not in food competition with the macaw people. Several nights later, a gratified macaw appears to the shaman begging him for food. If the zenithal Hoebo—in whose company the shaman spends his sleeping hours—should consent, the approached dark shaman will target, stalk, and kill a person at the next best opportunity.

The ancient Hoebo (as red macaw) and his parrot retinue have an insatiable appetite and keep asking for human fare. They do this mostly via the dark shaman's spirit sons, who appear to him in dreams. However, according to the new regime of contingent predation, the shaman stalls and propitiates them at least four times with palm starch and tobacco before agreeing to comply. But when the spirit children appear a fifth time to demand their proper food, he can no longer turn them away unsatisfied. He selects a person who might already have been compromised by the climatic sorcery of a weather shaman, or any other vulnerable member of his own or of a neighboring community.

Sitting alone in his boat or somewhere in the forest, the sorcerer smokes five or six cigars to image and sequester the *hoa* of a particular object in the world around him, usually a plant or animal. Once identified, he draws the fetid agent into himself so that it lodges in his throat. He blows his spirit sons into the final cigar and makes them linger just below the knot that ties the wrapper. Focusing his attention on the head of his intended victim, the sorcerer intones Miana's ancient song to activate the snare below his sternum: Miana, *warao akuamo saba* ("dimvisioned, going for a person's head"). With this, his proboscis begins unwinding and emerging from the corners of the conjurer's mouth. Potentiated by the spirit sons, its bifid ends travel near or far to find their target and, once at their destination, wind themselves around the victim's neck. This is the moment when the sorcerer takes another deep draught from his cigar, turns it about, and, holding the fire in his closed mouth, blows forcefully into it. Wafting from the distal end come ribbons of tobacco smoke that now transport the appropriated *hoa* across rivers and over tree tops to its intended target. It enters painfully below the victim's rib cage and, with a final exclamation of the sorcerer's song, "*miana!*" the snare asphyxiates the victim as the *hoa* penetrates the heart.

It takes the entire next day for the sucking snare to contract and completely return to its owner. And it may take several additional days or even weeks before this magic murder will materialize. Meanwhile, though, the people are well aware of what is going on. The sorcerer had left the village unaccompanied and, soon thereafter, someone began complaining of strong chest pain. This someone will soon face complete annihilation and pass the final hours haunted by the specter of nothingness.

Shortly before expiring, moribunds are often urged to identify their killer. The naming of the sorcerer provokes great fury among bystanders, who may revile and physically maltreat the culprit. The cadaverous pallor of his chest is seen as evidence of his culpability, as are his deeply nicotine-stained lips that resemble the macaw's black lower beak, with which he breaks his victims' skulls and necks. If nothing else, the mourners want the sorcerer quarantined for several days and scrutinized to see if he will suffer pain or issue blood by mouth or from his body. For when a *hoa* penetrates a person's heart, the blood starts flowing through the proboscis into the sorcerer's body. Furthermore, the morning after the interment, the sorcerer visits the aboveground tomb to criticize the dead person for having refused to give him food, payments, or gifts (such as a machete, boat, or woman). In voicing his complaints, he bends over the covered coffin and sucks the rest of the corpse's blood out through a cane. The blood exchange between the victim and the sorcerer can also be observed in a spillage in the stools of patients, especially *hoa*-stricken children succumbing to dysentery; in the sputum of victims dying from *hoa*-mediated pulmonary tuberculosis; or from still other hemorrhagic specialties of dark shaman sorcery.

Because of all these indications of occurring blood transfusion, quarantined sorcerers are expected to become soiled with blood or to leak excess blood from their bodies, thus determining their fault and fate. They may be banned from their communities to lead a lonesome life accompanied only by a wife or daughter. However, even ostracism cannot prevent a sorcerer from causing further harm. No matter how isolated he may be from other people, his snare is never out of reach, and his macaw folk will keep prodding him for sustenance. Thus, with compulsive intermittent regularity, the veteran dark shaman must continue carrying blood (within his body) and corpses to the netherworld, dangling them head down on his back, their heads knocking against his heels with every step he takes in spiteful mockery of his victims.

The first part of the carcass-bearer's road leads up the world axis to the zenith. Even though he is supported in this effort by his *hoebo* sons, the climb is strenuous and often aggravated by the victim's friends, who placed a red-hot coin into the dying person's mouth or else mutilated the corpse in order to hurt and handicap the murderer using sympathetic magic. From the zenithal Hoebo's house the sorcerer carries his victim to the netherworld, following the blood-sodden road along the firmament. After emptying the blood into the trough, the victim is butchered and cooked to feed the shaman's *hoebo* sons and local denizens, reserving the heart and liver for the supreme macaw. Four days later, the sorcerer returns to earth, where his family prepares a gift of palm starch to compensate the *hoebo* children for their help in slaying and transporting the body. Should the sorcerer's kinfolk fail to produce an adequate amount of sago, the spirits will get angry and demand a further human victim.

Sometimes sorcerers fall ill or die soon after they have killed. That happens when, at dawn or dusk, male relatives of the deceased take up positions near the gravesite to surprise the stealthy bloodsucker. Occasionally, they hear the sorcerer taunt the corpse, deriding his or her pathetic lot. To get impressions of his footprints, they place a layer of damp clay on the coffin. To injure or to kill the visitor, they shoot at him with a bow and arrow (or a shotgun) and find his blood or his dead body in the morning. If the sentries wound the visitor, the sorcerer will soon contract a hemorrhagic illness or will sustain a laceration. But if they kill him, they will find the sorcerer's body in its nagual form of alligator (*Crocodylus acutus*) or, more rarely, *teju* lizard (*Tupinambis nigropunctus*) of blackish color with yellow bands across its back.

The Warao consider alligators and sorcerers as qualitatively equivalent with interdependent fates, simultaneously suffering injury or death when either part is harmed. To dream of an alligator is to be confronted with the reptile's *hoa*, about to strike through magic action. If the alligator bites, the dreamer will fall sick or die. Should the dreamer take up weapons against his attacker, the alligator shape-shifts and reveals itself as a well-known sorcerer. Alligator and sorcerer share several characteristics that make them fitting as doppelganger. Both are night stalkers, for example, whose eyesight is best adapted to crepuscular light. Both identify themselves to friend and foe by a fusty body odor, the shaman on account of excessive nicotine absorption and the alligator because of distinctive glandular secretions. Most important, alligator and sorcerer are fiercely aggressive to the point of cannibalism and vampirism. As the life-devouring man snatchers they are said to be, they strike their victims indiscriminately whenever they get a chance to drag their prey into the netherworld to die. Thus, dark shaman sorcerers are shape-shifting were-alligators, feared and loathed by the Warao for their cunning savagery.

As a rule, only veteran dark shamans function as sorcerers, while junior practitioners, owing to retarded metamorphic growth, as noted, practice as dark shaman healers. Even once matured, some dark shamans say they rarely feel inclined to practice sorcery, remaining focused instead on protecting their community from attacks by their malignant others. There are great battles raging between dark shamans of adjacent communities, each side claiming that if it were not for their predacious opponents, survival rates would be much higher in their land.

As soon as adults or children suffer from sharp pain in their bodies or experience internal bleeding as evidenced in stool, vomit, or sputum, people send for a dark shaman healer to cure them of what they presume is *hoa* sickness. Sitting near the patient's hammock, the attending healer smokes cigars, washes his hands with balsam water, and begins singing a therapeutic *hoa* song without calling on Miana. In diagnosing the disorder, he lets himself be guided by the degree of pain the patient manifests and by a comparison of the case before him with others he has treated previously. While chanting about the etiology of the sickness and about the patient's identity and nature, the healer speculates which of the countless *hoa* might be responsible for the suffering. *Hoa* pertaining to large and hard things cause greater pain than those of smaller and softer objects. Further complicating the diagnosis, patients are frequently afflicted with multiple pneumas, and some require intervention by several dark shaman healers at the same time. While narrowing the options to a likely cause, the healer feels the *hoa* taking shape under his massaging hands. It may feel, for instance, like a tapir, snake, or palm stem, and this "knowing in his hand" enables him to identify the *hoa*. To extract it from the patient's body, he releases his *kaidoko* snare to pry it loose and fling it into space. Should multiple *hoa* be involved, he repeats the treatment, hoping that the patient will eventually recover. If not, the family consults another healer who, if successful, will cast suspicion on his unsuccessful colleague. He is, presumably, no longer interested in healing but rather anxious to advance in his career as caterer to the supreme macaw. Dark shaman healers are rewarded for their efforts unless the recovered patient is a member of their own close family; family members are not expected to pay for treatment. If patients or their kin are unable to raise the needed compensation, the healer receives them in quasi peonage.

Guardians of Society

A detailed discussion of Warao shamanism in a New World, Asiatic, or overall circum-Pacific context is beyond the scope of this essay. Its constituent orders, as enumerated elsewhere, contain critical elements of the shamanic experience that are of near-universal distribution (J. Wilbert 1972:81). Also beyond the scope is a detailed telling of the layered quality of Warao shamanism, featuring sections and, possibly, entire orders of diverse ethnic origins. Readers familiar with South American ethnography will have realized, for example, that in the absence of wild and cultivated nicotianas, ecstatics among nonagricultural Warao must be beholden to aboriginal farmers around the Orinoco delta. Light shamanism, in particular, centering on the Tobacco Spirit, appears to be inspired by northern Carib, of whom contemporary groups picture similar religious landscapes, image the same principal protagonist, and conceptualize identical techniques of shooting pathogenic projectiles (via a lumen in the arm and openings in the hands of sorcerers) as do the Warao (J. Wilbert 1993:183–218, for the Yekuana; Butt-Colson 1977:55–56, for the Akawaio; Gillin 1936:172, 140, for the Barama; Civrieux 1974:55, for the Cariña).

The order of dark shamans in turn contains elements of Mesoamerican religion and ritual. Lethal Warao *hoa* cut into victims just as Aztec flint knives once opened the breasts of sacrificial victims in order to tear out their hearts. And, in both cases, human hearts are or were fed the gods to give them strength. Furthermore, the scarlet macaw was the Maya sunbird, and sun gods featured *kaidoko*-like tendrils in the corners of their mouths and a triangular toothlike projection in the center, resembling the frontal view of a macaw's beak. Anthropomorphic bat demons had long ribbons emerging from their mouths that were associated with boring into or sucking from the head (Barthel 1966). Most striking is the belief that Maya temples were built by a race of dwarfs in complete (*miana*) darkness. The rulers who lived on top of these mountainous structures received their nourishment in the form of blood through an animated hollow rope that hung suspended in the sky. For some unknown reason, the blood duct was later cut and the artery disappeared forever (Tozzer 1907:153; Furst, in J. Wilbert 1993:129; cf. Looper and Guernsey-Kappelman 2000). Further discussion of these ethnohistorical parallels as well as others, such as the apparent relationship of *bahana* gambling to Mesoamerican *petolli* and ball games, must await a future opportunity. What does bear highlighting in the present context, however, is the power that shamans and sorcerers exercise in matters of Warao personal, social, and spiritual survival.

Veteran ecstatics of the Warao form a group of prestigious elders (*idamotuma*). They stand apart from junior members of their respective shamanic orders, as well as from nonecstatic men (*nebu*), especially young ones (*neburatu*). Whereas nowadays elders reside within local bands pertaining to their subtribe, in the not-too-distant past they purportedly lived in ceremonial centers apart from the bulk of the population. Veteran shamans occupied separate houses grouped around a shrine or temple and a dance floor. In their houses they sat on wooden stools (*duhu*) and smoked ritual tobacco (*kohoba*), communicating with the pantheon of celestial powers.[10] Food was catered to them by their sons-in-law and by other rank and file, and most of their further needs were taken care of by former patients who had mortgaged their bodies in compensation for a healing they had received. In the course of their career as curers, elders acquired four or more such servants through the institution of voluntary bondage known as *ateho wabia*, "sacrificing" or "betraying one's body." They were male and female debtor patients who were called, respectively, *neburatu*, "servant," and *ukatida*, "daughter." Even today when ceremonial centers no longer exist, this institution of healer bondage continues to prevail among the Warao, and elders maintain the lifestyle, assume the rights, and exercise the powers of former center residents.

Traditionally, the assembly of elders includes the "fathers" (*arimatuma*) of the ancient one (priest-shaman), of the wooden figurine (light shaman), of rain (weather shaman), and of *hoa* (dark shaman), plus an occasional old shaman of lesser rank. Young practitioners do not qualify for membership because they are considered immature and nonestablished, that is, lacking bonded patients. In contrast, elders not only rely on the services of indebted patients but also secure their personal survival through the control of women in their communities. Allotting each other their daughters (engendered or awarded), nieces, and granddaughters as plural wives (Heinen 1972:332), they aspire to increase their female progeny and acquire additional sons-in-law who are obliged to render bride service for the lifetime of their spouses. Insofar as their rights include privileged access to pubescent girls, elders stand in competition to male adolescents who dare not challenge them for fear of spiritual retribution. Intergenerational polygynous marriages of elders to girls of descending generations inadvertently impinge on the male-female ratio of unwed adolescents that, for this and other reasons, may be as low as one to four. This unnatural demographic imbalance rightly causes great concern among boys anxious to find a marriage partner of their own generation within the (exogamous) bands of their (endogamous) subtribe. Finally, with advancing age, elders cease engendering further children and probably die sooner than their younger spouses, seriously curbing the latter's reproductive potential and thwarting the personal and social unfolding of these prematurely widowed women.

As constantly preoccupied with maintaining a balanced society within a universe in equilibrium, elders justify satisfying their personal demands at public expense in terms of their role as guardians of society. They constitute their congregation's spiritual center, where cosmic pathways meet and life and death become imbued with existential meaning and purposeful adaptive order. In their protective roles, elders shield their people from destructive forces that threaten to tear down their lives. Attack by pathogenic agents is one such force that throws communities into disarray by decimating or, possibly, dissolving them completely. Ideally, however, elders become involved as healers only in severe cases or when the community is overwhelmed by sickness as, for instance, during primary rainy seasons. Ordinarily, healing is essentially left to younger shamans, female herbalists, and even to lay persons. Elders go on the offensive against sickness-causing forces and preempt aggression by proactive measures. Rather than healers, therefore, elders are sorcerers who use their powers to maintain the balance of the universe.

As noted, most pathogenic agents are of supernatural origin and are free to afflict humanity at will, and sorcerers are empowered to engage this lethal force to launch retaliatory attacks against their neighbors. Thus, sorcerers are the interface between their own community and all others, waging intercommunity warfare to protect their congregations from attrition and extermination. Priest-shaman sorcerers engage mainly the southern mountain gods and allied febrile diseases, including measles, typhoid fever, and malaria, that figure among the principal infectious diseases and/or causes of death among contemporary Warao (W. Wilbert 1984). Light shaman sorcerers harness the power of the zenithal tobacco spirit, who has direct access to earth via a rope bridge and the world axis and whose gambling cohort provoke cases of sickness and death. But when the sorcerer deploys the supreme spirit himself, residing with him in the guise of the wooden statuette, he subjects his enemy to the full force of sudden and rapidly spreading infectious diseases, such as whooping cough, influenza, cholera, and dengue, scoring especially among small children with whooping cough and influenza and among the general population with cholera and dengue. Similarly, the lords of rain need no help from humans to spread sickness across the world. However, when incensed by the spell of the weather sorcerer, rain gods bear down with force. They cause hunger in the sorcerer's neighboring communities and famine across the delta, provoking weather-related illnesses of the eastern and the northern mountain gods, including gastroenteritis, diarrhea, influenza, and pneumonia, that claim more than half of the fatalities attributed to eleven principal causes of death in the delta (W. Wilbert 1984). Finally, dark shaman sorcerers retaliate against outside attack by mustering the western god's allied diseases. Demographic studies show that prepuberty mortality among subtribal bands amounts to 49 percent and that nearly half of children's deaths are attributable to dark shaman sorcery (J. Wilbert 1983; 1993:104). Large numbers of enemy children succumb to hemorrhagic diseases like amoebic and bacillary dysentery, and many blood-coughing neighbors die of consumption.

In short, the Warao separate young shamanic healers from old shamanic sorcerers. Young shamans lack the power and qualifications to practice sorcery. They function as their group's defense in stemming assaultive sorcery. In contrast, old shamans serve primarily as offense, attacking hostile outsiders. The practitioners of both sides interact with one another in dissimilar complementarity; one team's defense presumes the other's offense, and vice versa. Ideally, neither side of the contenders counts with shamans who, for practical purposes, would be at once benevolent and malevolent. Instead, one's own healers and sorcerers are generally held as good; those of others are all evil.

The mutual fear of sorcery and the dread of contagion had significant ramifications for Warao survival during the colonial bottleneck. Soon after discovery and throughout the colony, native populations of the Caribbean and northern South America were ravaged by pandemics of Old World pestilence. Warao traders, seeking iron tools and tobacco, witnessed the devastation that previously unknown disease wreaked on their indigenous neighbors. In the eighteenth century, Warao escapees from European missions and Criollo towns had become well aware of precipitous population declines (50 to 60 percent), as well as the disorganization and extinction of autochthonous cultures on the Orinoco plains and in the Guianas (Morey 1979; J. Wilbert 1993:40–45). Occasional crossings of the epidemiological frontier like these also brought exotic epidemic diseases into the Warao heartland, but disease flare-ups there rarely encountered populations large enough to sustain infectious chains.

Experience has taught the Warao to live apart from one another in small bands of "true Warao" (less than 50 persons); to mix only with relatively close subtribal "Warao relatives" (less than 200 persons); and to avoid all other Warao and foreigners. Subtribal boundaries are maintained by dialectical variations in language, kenning, marriage rules, allegiance to subtribal patron deities, and fear of contagion (J. Wilbert 1975b). In integrating the new diseases into the tribal shamanic and cosmological order the Warao wisdom tradition mythologized their etiologies, placing them, like earlier endemic diseases, into the hands of directional gods and sorcerers (J. Wilbert 1983). Thus, native awareness of disease etiology reinforced subtribal boundaries and bolstered the people's faith in their divine patron and in their elders. Under their protection, subtribal bands are safer from pathological spirit intrusion, precisely because, unlike sedentary village farmers and wide-ranging traders in their neighborhood, Warao migratory forager groups were traditionally small, dispersed, and fairly isolated from the outside world, thus offering relative immunity through the dual process of the elimination of most susceptibles from successive generations and the selection of less virulent strains over lethal ones, which die with their hosts (Murdock 1980). Unfortunately, things are not always as clear-cut as they might have been. At times, sorcerers act as healers and curative shamans are suspected, like sorcerers, of unleashing virulent diseases on their own kind. Least feared are priest-shamans, followed by light shamans then weather shamans. But dark shamans become abhorred as enemies from within and may be chastised, beaten, and/or banished from the community.

One frustration frequently expressed by the Warao is that were it not for dark shamans there would be little illness in this world. It is true, of course, that through proactive action by practitioners of other orders, patients may feel less helpless and more empowered to remedy or even to prevent bad health. Thus, patients asked by the priest-shaman to recognize their transgressions contribute to their own healing by confessing their failures. Similarly, weather shamans place illness into the moral sphere by making people accept personal responsibility for altruistic behavior as well as for the consequence of ignoring it. While sorcerer-mediated attacks by pathogenic forces can always be reckoned with, this moralizing paradigm of disease and disease prevention turns patients into healers' helpers and lends a degree of causative order to supernatural capriciousness (Pagels 1988:145–47). However, the Warao's main problem with dark shamanism is that unlike pathogenic spirits handled by practitioners of other orders, the macaw god of the western mountain is completely blocked from reaching earth by himself. His sole access to humanity is via the dark shaman: without the dark shaman's cooperation the terror of *hoa* suffering and dying would not exist at all.

This leads me to refer, in closing, to a second outside force—aside from illness—from which elders are expected to protect their community: warring enemies. For centuries, regional groups in the lower Orinoco delta must have battled intrusive parties encroaching on their respective sago groves. However, at the beginning of the Christian era, Carib-speaking groups from northeast Amazonia spread down the Orinoco to the western edge of the delta. Contemporary Warao refer to their descendants as "red faces" and "warriors" and speak with horror of their practices of enemy mutilation, trophy taking, and cannibalism. Whereas accounts of their violence reverberate ruefully throughout Warao traditional history and lore, the arrival of the red-painted cannibals on the western outskirts of the delta may well have triggered the western mountain god's epiphany as the red macaw, claiming the Warao as his staple food. Like their cannibalistic enemies of the past, this divine denizen and his cohort dismember their victims, annihilating them body and soul by eating their flesh and converting their life-bearing bones into flutes and body ornaments (cf. Whitehead 1984, 1988).

And herein lies the fundamental bane of dark shamanism. Instead of decimating their enemies and keeping them at bay like light shamans do with their devastating idols, dark shamans collude with the insufferable enemy and carry destruction into their own camps, or at least that is how it strikes ordinary Warao who don't hesitate to vent their anger at dark shamans.

However, upon sober evaluation some traditionally enculturated Warao also volunteer that in facing an enemy of catastrophic power dark shamans had no choice but to settle for a more moderate modus vivendi. In order to uphold the primordial covenant of contingent predation they must abide by its imperative to balance the existential needs of the celestial and terrestrial parties involved. The fact that in the process *hoa* fathers became empowered to ration the macaw people's food supply and manage their survival is certainly of great (psychological) benefit to humans and makes tolerating dark shaman sorcerers in their midst more bearable. Further, to the Warao it is equally redeeming that predation by the netherworld is reigned in even more through the healing power of dark shamans, conversely ensuring the survival of humanity.

Notes

1   The data in this chapter were gathered in the course of repeated visits (since 1954) to the Winikina subgroup of the Warao. While I use the generic ethnonym Warao, it is well to bear in mind that regional variations in culture patterns do exist and that the present information pertains primarily to the Winikina. Furthermore, over the past half century, spirituality has changed among the younger set of Winikina; described here are religious ideas I acquired mainly between the 1950s and the 1980s.
2   Regional subgroups may be allied with different supreme spirits either of the south, the north, or the east.
3   One natural model of the cosmic egg is the human body, with its torso and two lungs separated by the diaphragm from the abdomen and the viscera.
4   Nicotine, the principal active ingredient in tobacco, is the most potent insecticide in nature; the Warao are well aware of its effect on bees, wasps, and termites. The wisdom of the Tobacco Spirit in choosing tobacco smoke as the construction material for his sky house lies precisely in the narcotic's hold on insects. Nicotine is the secret magical power that suspends the natural law of predation innate in the residents of the cosmic egg and enables them to join in *bahana* games on earth and in the sky.
5   The aforementioned senior companions of the swallow-tailed kite form a hierarchy among themselves comprising a governor, a chief, and a deputy; that is, the highest political officers of postcolonial regional and local subgroups.
6   Weather shamans have no direct technique for dispatching pathogenic projectiles into individuals. Instead, their sorcery aims at debilitating victims indirectly through exposure to hunger, famine, and inclement weather conditions—exposing them to the machinations of malevolent shamans.
7   The Warao distinguish between three different kinds of *hoa* chants: those used to inflict illness; those used to cure illness; and those used to cure injuries and lesser pains. Dark shamans mediate the first two kinds, but the third kind falls outside the purview of ecstatic shamanism and can be sung by anybody, including shamans and patients themselves. Nonshamanic curing chants are called pain-blowing (*ahitemoi*), and some individuals (*ahitemoi arotu*) are considered better at it than others. As a genre, these *hoa* chants pertain to the pain-blowing complex of wide distribution

in native South America and elsewhere, variously entailing chant-blowing, breath-blowing, and spit-blowing techniques. The latter two therapies are often accompanied, respectively, by tobacco smoke or nicotine-laden saliva, with significant antipyretic and analgesic effects (Briggs 1994; Olsen 1996; J. Wilbert 1987).

8 I have personally not witnessed cases of tobacco blindness and/or nicotine-induced respiratory arrest. The description of Shamanism by dark shamans leaves little doubt, however, that these conditions do occur and that tobacco pharmacology served the complex as a blueprint among the Warao and possibly elsewhere. Needless to say, the symptomatology of toxic amblyopia and acute ganglionic impulse inhibition are not experienced in their totality at any one time. Instead, dark shamanism as a religious institution represents the cumulative experience of generations of shamans that culminated in a comprehensive understanding of the symptomatology and its application to this exacting shamanic belief system.

9 Traditional Warao, especially shamans, don't eat these particular vegetables. Their appearance in the present context only underlines the radical otherness of the course and provides a link between the strong odor of these vegetables and the fetid pneuma of *hoa*.

10 The stratification of Warao society into elders and commoners is reminiscent of the Taino culture of the Greater Antilles. Other parallels include the occurrence of shrines, incense burners, ceremonial centers, rock idols, village gods, ritual dance grounds, as well as ceremonial benches and tobacco use. The designations for superior (*idamo/nitaino*) and inferior (*nebu/naboria*) statuses appear to be cognate. The terms for ceremonial bench (*duhu*) and tobacco (*kohoba*) are identical in both languages, and the so-designated objects represent loan items in Warao ergology. This constitutes an additional example of culture borrowing in Warao shamanism.

References

Barthel, Thomas. 1966. "Mesoamerikanische Fledermausmotive." *Tribus* 1: 101–24.
Briggs, Charles, L. 1992. "'Since I Am a Woman, I Will Chastise My Relatives': Gender, Reported Speech, and the (Re)production of Social Relations in Warao Ritual Wailing." *American Ethnologist* 19 (2): 337–61.
———. 1994. "The Sting of the Ray: Bodies, Agency, and Grammar in Warao Curing." *Journal of American Folklore* 107 (423): 139–66.
Butt-Colson, Audrey. 1977. "The Akawaio Shaman." In *Carib-Speaking Indians: Culture, Society, and Language*, ed. Ellen B. Basso. 43–65. Tucson: University of Arizona Press.
Civrieux, Marc de. 1974. *Religión y magia Kari'ña*. Caracas: Universidad Católica Andrés Bello.
Gillin, John. 1936. *The Barama River Caribs*. Cambridge, Mass.: Peabody Museum of American Archaeology and Ethnology, Harvard University.
Heinen, H. Dieter. 1972. "Adaptive Change in a Tribal Economy: A Case Study of the Winikina-Warao." Ph.D. diss., University of California, Los Angeles.
Lavandero Pérez, Julio. 2000. *Noara y otros rituales*. Caracas: Universidad Católica Andrés Bello.
Looper, Matthew and Julia Guernsey-Kappelman. 2000. "The Cosmic Umbilicus in Mesoamerica: A Floral Metaphor for the Source of Life." *Journal of Latin American Lore* 21 (1): 3–54.

Morey, Robert. 1979. "A Joyful Harvest of Souls: Disease and the Destruction of the Llanos Indians." *Antropológica* 52: 77–108.

Murdock, George P. 1980. *Theories of Illness: A World Survey*. Pittsburgh: Pittsburgh University Press.

Olsen, Dale A. 1996. *Music of the Warao of Venezuela: Song People of the Rain Forest*. Gainesville: University Press of Florida.

Pagels, Elaine. 1988. *Adam, Eve, and the Serpent*. New York: Random House.

Tozzer, Alfred M. 1907. *A Comparative Study of the Mayas and Lacandones*. New York: Macmillan.

Whitehead, Neil L. 1984. "Carib Cannibalism: The Historical Evidence." *Journal de la Société des Américanistes* 70: 69–87.

——. 1988. *Lords of the Tiger-Spirit: A History of the Caribs in Colonial Venezuela and Guyana, 1498–1820*. Dordrecht: Foris Publications.

Wilbert, Johannes. 1972. "Tobacco and Shamanistic Ecstasy among the Warao Indians of Venezuela." In *Flesh of the Gods: The Ritual Use of Hallucinogens*, ed. Peter T. Furst. 55–83. New York: Praeger.

——. 1975a. *Warao Basketry: Form and Function*. Los Angeles: Museum of Cultural History, University of California.

——. 1975b. "The Metaphoric Snare: Analysis of a Warao Folktale." *Journal of Latin American Lore* 1: 7–17.

——. 1979. "Gaukler Schamanen der Warao." In *Amerikanistische Studien*, 2 vols., ed. Roswitha Hartmann and Udo Oberem. 2: 294–99.

——. 1983. "Warao Ethnopathology and Exotic Epidemic Disease." *Journal of Ethnopharmacology* 8: 357–61.

——. 1987. *Tobacco and Shamanism in South America*. New Haven: Yale University Press.

——. 1993. *Mystic Endowment: Religious Ethnography of the Warao Indians*. Cambridge: Harvard University Press.

——. 1996. *Mindful of Famine: Religious Climatology of the Warao Indians*. Cambridge: Harvard University Press.

Wilbert, Werner. 1984. "Infectious Diseases and Health Services in Delta Amacuro, Venezuela." *Acta Ethnologica et Lingüística, 58*: 1–117.

——. 1996. *Fitoterápia Warao: Una teoría pnéumica de salud, la enfermedad y la terápia*. Caracas: Instituto Caribe de Antropología y Sociología.

Dark Shamans and the Shamanic State:
Sorcery and Witchcraft as Political Process
in Guyana and the Venezuelan Amazon

Silvia Vidal & Neil L. Whitehead

The democratic, or would-be democratic, political process is perhaps the touchstone of the maturity of the modern state. Yet participation in such a political process through the norms of democratic action favored in Europe and the United States (i.e., TV campaigns, media interviews, sponsor dinners, public meetings, and caucus committees, etc.) is not generally a significant part of the political culture of other countries. On the one hand, this allows the "progressive" West to devalue the political processes of postcolonial societies through the rhetoric of liberal democracy because of the lack of Western forms of political institution and practice. On the other hand, the absence of such cultural idioms leads to forms of political engagement that are culturally opaque to Western observers. This is not to suggest that properly democratic political process is irrelevant or unachievable in such postcolonial contexts, but it does imply that, as in other realms of sociocultural life, cultural difference needs to be interpreted and understood rather than taken as a marker of primitiveness or lack of development. Such interpretation might then suggest that the absorption of the word democracy into a local lexicon of words and ideas that are cast as necessary for progress, such as "democracy," "participation," "globalization," "biodiversity," reveal a mimetic process at work, in which "democracy" is regarded as an exogenous social good, yet also one that is distinctly underproblematized in the local context. In the case of Guyana it is common to hear that "they [the developed countries] have it; we have [depending on whom you talk to] had it since 1992; it's a good thing for us." Democracy is, of course, no less a problematic concept in countries with a long history of democratic political process.

In this essay we analyze and compare the role of sorcery and witchcraft in contemporary local and regional politics in Guyana and the Venezuelan Amazon in order to illustrate the way in which occult forces have been incorporated into the regional and national political process. In general terms this has recently been the subject of study by both Taussig (1997) and Coronil (1997), who in different ways consider how the "magic" of the Venezuelan state is established through its association with occult powers, particularly the popular spirit cults. In a broader frame of reference it is evident that voudoun has played a similar role in the establishment of the Duvalier regime in Haiti (Diedrich 1970; Ferguson 1989), and we suggest here that Obeah has also been used to enhance the political potency of the Forbes Burnham regime in Guyana. However, although we may have elegant and informative studies of the forms of ideology that the ruling elites have deployed to gain consensus for their projects of modernization and development, we have little sense of how those processes played out in the margins of national political culture, or what broader cultural forms are harnessed in the process of occult government, in particular those that invoke indigenous powers or indigeneity in general. Thus Taussig (1997), for example, discusses the ideological power of the Tres Potencias but does so through an exclusive consideration of the Spirit Queen, and the latent and darkly mysterious spirit force of El Indio is left without commentary. This essay is in part intended to correct Taussig's lack through a consideration of how native dark shamanism, by *kanaimàs*, *pitadores* (poisoners), and false prophets has fed the political imaginary and practice of postcolonial Guyana and Venezuela.

Shamanic Forces and Colonial Rule

From the sixteenth to mid-seventeenth centuries, the Warekena, Baré, and Baniwa were part of the peoples belonging to the macropolitics of the Manoa and Omagua (Oniguayal) areas of the Río Negro region. (Vidal 1993; Whitehead 1993, 1994, 1999a, 1999b). These macropolities were multilingual, multiethnic social systems with an internal interethnic hierarchy led by a paramount chief and a powerful elite of secondary chiefs. Internal sociopolitical contradictions and conflicts and the demographic decimation of the Amerindian populations through disease and enslavement after the European colonization of the region combined by the end of the seventeenth century to produce radical disruptions in these macropolities. These disruptive processes caused the regrouping of many indigenous peoples such that by the early eighteenth century in the Río Negro region new less-hierarchical and more-confederated sociopolitical formations emerged (Vidal 1993). Such confederacies were flexible and varied in their ethnic membership and were led by charismatic chieftains whose political power was based first on their ability to build a personal following (kinfolk, in-laws, and allies) sufficient to generate military capacity, as well as on their skills as regional traders, especially of European goods, and on their shamanic knowledge and power. During the eighteenth century there were as many as fifteen such confederacies led by the forefathers of the Warekena, Baré, and Baniwa groups.

By contrast, to the east in the Guyana region the proximity of the Atlantic coast meant that interactions with the colonial regimes in the area were early and intense, leading to the co-option of some Amerindian groups into the structures of colonial power—principally as an informal militia to defend the colony externally against other European powers and internally to control the black slave population. The aboriginal macropolities of this region, Huyapari and Aruaca, were thus undermined by European intrusion and their leaders either co-opted or conquered (Whitehead 1994, 1998). In their place, due to the nature of colonial policy toward the native population in this region, an implicit system of ethnic ranking emerged with regard to the colonial administration, which baldly promoted the favored "tribes," such as the Caribs and Arawaks, to the detriment of other inland and coast groups, such as the Akawaio, Makushi, Warao, and Yao (Whitehead 1996).

These ethnic formations were, however, inherently unstable and often evanescent, owing to their dependence on European weapons and manufactures and their increasing integration with the colonial commercial networks of European goods. This colonial integration led to fierce competition and internecine conflicts among the leading groups as well as with those excluded by the colonial co-option of particular tribes and confederacies. Thus, the European colonial system itself and interactions among Europeans and Amerindians were decisive for the creation, transformation, and extinction of these ethnic sociopolitical formations of the eighteenth century (Whitehead 1990, 1999c).

By the early nineteenth century the Arawakan groups of the Río Negro region were often led by shaman-chiefs, who conducted important rituals according to a shamanic tradition known as *kúwai*. Such cosmologically adept leaders were thus able to both consolidate clan and group identities and lead military actions against the colonial regime. In the period 1831–1851 these groups were still celebrating important multiethnic rituals and religious ceremonies in the areas of Vaupés, Isana, and Negro rivers (Chernela 1993; Spruce 1996; Wallace 1969; Wright 1981), and, during the second half of the nineteenth century, panindigenous messianic movements had also emerged (Hill and Wright 1988; Wright and Hill 1986). These messianic movements, led by Arawak- and Tukano-speaking shamans and prophets promising the means to material survival and the persistence of community, laid a basis for regional relationships and the formation of the political-religious hierarchies that are present today. As a result, during most of the nineteenth and twentieth centuries the Arawakan peoples were an important factor in the formation of urban and rural Criollo cultures in this region, particularly those in Manaus, Puerto Ayacucho, and Puerto Inírida. These influences included most of the practices for daily diet and cooking, fishing, hunting, and agricultural, for the exploitation of natural forest resources, and, most significant, for spiritual and ritual beliefs and practices.

In the Guyana region the process of contestation with colonialism was deflected by the way in which the more powerful indigenous leaders were co-opted by colonial policy. Indeed, open antagonism to the colonial authorities in British Guiana was classically more a symptom of isolation and marginalization from the perceived benefits of alliance with the colonial authorities than a token of antipathy to the colonial projects of development and evangelization. Comparatively speaking it is important to note the almost simultaneous emergence of prophetic and millennial-style cult leadership among the Amerindians of Guyana and the Río Negro in the latter half of the nineteenth century. However, although in both cases this was rooted in the sociopolitical challenges that colonial intrusion created to "traditional" modes of ritual and political action, in the Guyana region such prophetic movements were directed toward securing, rather than resisting, the attentions of colonial development (see Whitehead 2002).

For this and other reasons there are important differences in postcolonial political culture as it emerged in Venezuela and Guyana. Most important to appreciate is the fact that Guyana was not decolonized until the 1960s, some 150 years after Venezuela. This time difference clearly limits the way in which the postcolonial political processes of the two countries can be compared as a matter of political science. However, it is relevant to observe that models of democratic action, as defined by Western politics, could not be wholly and simply transposed to settings where the political history of colonialism itself was so distinct, as argued in the introduction to this essay. The invention of radical new political norms in the wake of decolonization thus provoked in both Guyana and Venezuela the development of alternative models of political association that had more or less overt "occult" associations—*francmasonería* (freemasonry) in Venezuela and *óóbeah / óóbia* (obeah) in Guyana. It was not so much the content of these beliefs as the fact that they were shared among an emergent and self-defining elite political class of rulers that made them important initially. But over time the exercise of power through such potentially occult forms made such political systems responsive, even vulnerable, to shamanic influence, as was notoriously the case in Duvalier's Haiti.

Arawakan Shamans, Witches, and Sorcerers

Amazonian shamans have extensive spiritual-political and economic power in their societies because their ritual knowledge is crucial to the reproductive processes, in both biological and sociocultural terms, of the local group. The religious beliefs and ritual powers of Arawakan shamans of the northwest Amazon are thus strongly preoccupied with collective death, the rebirth of individuals and groups, and the continual processes of cosmic destruction and renewal.

The Warekena, Baré, and Baniwa are three Arawak-speaking groups living in different cities, townships, and riverine environments of the upper Guainía, upper Negro, and upper Orinoco basins.[1] These peoples share with other Arawakan groups the shamanic and prophetic tradition of *kúwai*, *kuwé*, or *katsímánali* ("the voice of the creation"), which first made the world. *Kúwai* is also present as a monstrous, primordial human being (Hill 1993:xvii), master of all visible and invisible beings (Wright 1993), who controls the sky and the universe through his powerful knowledge and who came to this world to teach people his sacred ritual powers, which men secretly learn during initiation or puberty rites. The ritual system associated with *kúwai* is divided into mythical cycles, with each cycle consisting of a corpus of narratives in the form of stories, myths, chants, songs, prayers, and so forth. Together with other kinds of ritual knowledge, the "teachings of *kúwai*" comprise a coded symbolic and pragmatic repertory of great significance that strongly influences and orientates indigenous ways of living, in both the ritual and secular sphere. Among the Arawakan groups of the northwest Amazon, political leadership is closely associated with the religious and ritual system (Vidal 1993). Many of the great native leaders of the past were also powerful shamans and experts in facing and manipulating the occult world, and these qualities were precisely those that supported their regional political power. The importance attributed to shamanism and ritual specialization to validate and strengthen leadership thus stemmed from the centrality of occult idioms of power in both daily existence and elite regional relationships.

Initiation into shamanic practices, including witchcraft and sorcery, is complex and arduous and requires a significant personal motivation involving sexual abstinence, a strict dietary regime, and exhaustive physical endurance. These practices are intended to bring out the special supernatural powers of the individual as shown in the capacity to rapidly memorize songs, prayers, and the names and formulas for medicines and poisons, and in a physical ability to deal with the ingestion of psychotropic drugs. Such initiation involves five levels of shamanic specialization, knowledge, and practice that could be interpreted as a hierarchy of ritual knowledge and power to mediate between the natural and the supernatural worlds (Vidal 1993:92–93).[2] These specializations, from the lower to the higher levels, are the *biníji* or the one who prepares medicines with plants and water; the *makákana* or the blower who cures by means blowing tobacco smoke; the *uyúkali* who cures by means of sucking the ill parts of the body; the *sibunítei* or the dreamer who cures by means of divination and dreams; and the *hniwakali* or the one who knows more, or dreams more knowledge. Those of this ultimate level dominate all the other specializations and also know numerous ancestral ritual songs and prayers. In the seventeenth and eighteenth centuries, great chiefs or captains were shamans who possessed the *hniwakali* level of ritual power and specialization. These indigenous political leaders thus organized men in their sacred rituals and festivals, in their economic activities and commerce, and in wars.[3]

Shamanism is also associated with the continuing relationship that the Arawak-speaking groups established between the *inépe mikí náwi* (first ancestors) such as Kuwé, Nápiruli, Purúnamínali, and Dzúli, and the *pjénawjí* (living elders). *Pjénawi* or *péinjli-náwi* are living adult individuals with great wisdom and important historical, mythical, ritual, and practical knowledge. Most of these elder men and women perform the sacred songs, chants, and prayer formulas for the curing of illnesses and other spiritual needs, using tobacco and plants as remedies. Some of these remedies and curing powers are known as *pusanas*, which are used as magic potions to gain sympathy or love, or to improve fishing and hunting success. These *pusanas* are thus comparable to the spell and charms used by the owners of *talen* magic, discussed below. However, as with *talen*, there are some who are devoted to the use of poisons and the other resources of dark shamanism to harm others. These "poison-owners" (*dañeros* and *pitadores* in Spanish) are men and women who use traditional shamanic and botanical knowledge, including songs and prayers, to kill and injure. These *pitadores* are pictured as naked with their bodies painted black who wander at night through the forests or towns to search out their enemies in order to eliminate them.

Dark Shamans in the Politics of the Venezuelan Amazon

The role and impact of the Arawakan shamans in the local and regional politics of the Venezuelan Amazon derives in large part from three key characteristics of Arawakan societies generally: the practice of exogamy and the way the resulting system of marriage alliances closely links to commercial activities and political alliances; the tradition of *kúwai* and its role in local and regional political systems; and the adoption of Arawakan cosmological and shamanic idioms by Criollo and European populations.

Many Arawakan marriage systems are mainly focused on widening alliances in order to incorporate other groups that are not part of their traditional affinal kin (Vidal 1993, 1999). The system of marriage networks has an enormous potential for regional alliances because it includes as kin a large number of population segments—both at a regional level in the category of siblingship (we / us) and in the spread of alliance networks among affinal kin of diverse groups (they / others). These cultural characteristics have strongly influenced forms of leadership, the control and expansion of political and commercial alliances, and the emergence of interregional political alliances and multiethnic sociopolitical formations.[4]

Since the first European expedition to the Río Negro basin, European men have often been enmeshed in this Arawakan style of marriage alliance through formal marriage to indigenous women or by informally taking them as concubines (Vidal 1993; Wright 1981). This custom allowed Amerindians to treat these Europeans as their affinal kin (brothers-in-law) and commercial partners. According to Arawakan tradition, the strongest alliances were those between two or more political groups that were also affinal kin, or practitioners of *kúwai* and / or commercial partners as well. By the eighteenth century, these kinds of alliances produced ever-closer relationships between the Baré, Warekena, and Baniwa groups as well as with their European / Criollo commercial partners and affinal kin. However, this also meant that Amerindian populations were more closely involved with the colonial regime, which eventually resulted in a dramatic loss of their political and economic autonomy, to the point of outright enslavement and political oppression.

By 1850 many groups, such as the Warekena, Baré, Wakuénai, Baniwa, and Tukanoans, found a powerful form of expressing their oppression through millenarian movements whose ideas invaded both the festivities of Catholic saints and traditional Amerindian ceremonies (Wright 1981). One of these millenarian movements was led by Venancio Camico (Hill and Wright 1988; Wright and Hill 1986), a Wakuénai shaman married to a Baniwa woman from the Aki River in the upper Guainía basin. Camico, also well known as the God of Mane, exercised a great authority among the Amerindians of the Guainía and Negro basins until his death in 1902. According to Tavera Acosta (1927:146), Venancio Camico knew the healing properties of many plants and made surprising cures among both the Amerindians and Criollos of the Venezuelan Amazon. Acosta also mentions that Camico spoke Portuguese, Spanish, and several indigenous languages of the region. A contemporary of Venancio Camico was Joaquín Bolívar, a Baré shaman and political leader who was famed as a healer and expert on plant magic. Although Bolívar was not a leader of millenarian movements he was widely known and respected as a shaman to both indigenous peoples and the Criollo populations of the Negro, Casiquiare, and Guainía rivers (Tavera Acosta 1927:146; González Niño 1984:137; Henríquez 1994). His popularity among the Criollos, especially politicians, was due to his ability both to cure the victims of poisoning and to restore the health of those who suffered the assault sorcery of the *dañeros* and *pitadores*. Bolívar is also remembered as the founder in 1873 of the town of Santa Rosa of Amanadona on the upper Río Negro.

It is evident, then, that during this period a significant number of non-Amerindians had become involved with the shamanic traditions and rituals of the indigenous peoples of the Río Negro (Wright 1981:169; Chernela 1993). The Criollo population, especially the politicians and those working for the government authorities, had adopted important shamanic ideas deriving from the Arawakan groups. This process was not confined to the Amazon region: most of the politicians of renowned national political parties in Venezuela had personal shamans and seers to heal and protect them from their enemies and from supernatural forces. The ritual traditions of these shamans were influenced by both Amerindian and Afro-Venezuelan cultural traditions. For example, it is currently part of the popular oral tradition that Rómulo Bethancourt, president of Venezuela from 1958 to 1963 and also known as the "father of the Venezuelan democracy," had a personal shaman who had made his pipe into a magical amulet. It is believed that this amulet and his shaman's powerful magic saved Bethancourt's life and protected him from injury during a bomb attack by leftist guerrillas. According to Martín (1983:64), these popular beliefs in Venezuela are part of an ideology based on the magical forces of the political powers of national and regional authorities; this ideology forms part of and is represented in the cult of Simón Bolívar, the Venezuelan liberator and founding father of the republic and the Gran Colombia (an argument recently further elaborated by Taussig [1997]). In the later nineteenth century the infamous rubber barons who controlled the extraction of raw latex from forests in the Amazon regions of Peru, Colombia, and Venezuela, also utilized shamans and continued with the earlier tradition of marrying indigenous women or of having them as concubines (Iribertegui 1987:302–3).

As a result, by the early twentieth century there were several widely renowned shamans in the Río Negro region, such as Hilario Bolívar and Hilario Maroa. Bolívar was a Baré Amerindian from Santa Rosa de Amanadona and the son of Joaquín Bolívar, mentioned above. He learned his shamanic knowledge and skills from his father, and his fame as healer and powerful shaman soon extended to other areas of Venezuela and even to neighboring countries. He was also a favorite of some of the rubber barons. Hilario Maroa (Maroita) was also a famous Baré shaman who lived in Santa Rosa de Amanadona, the town founded by Joaquín Bolívar. His fame as a powerful sorcerer not only extended across Venezuela, Colombia, and Peru but also among local and regional politicians, as well as medical doctors practicing in San Carlos de Río Negro and other cities of the Venezuelan Amazon. In fact, Maroita was one of the first Amerindian shamans to share patients and to maintain professional relationships with Criollo medical doctors (Anduze 1973:167). Maroita and Hilario Bolívar were also famous for countersorcery: curing people of the diseases, poisoning, and other forms of assault sorcery caused by *dañeros* and *pitadores*.

Kanaimà, Alleluia, and Millennial Prophecy in the Guyana Highlands

Although the politics of Arawakan exogamy strongly mark interethnic relations in the Río Negro, exogamous forms of marriage alliance were also used extensively by the Cariban peoples as well as Arawakans of the Guyana region, especially to form alliances with both blacks and whites. The key difference with the situation just described for the Río Negro was the disposition of the British, Dutch, and French colonial regimes. In Guyana evangelization was not the conquest of souls but an absent-minded afterthought (Rivière 1995), part of the efficient and beneficent administration of a colony primarily interested in the plantations and mines of the coastal regions. The hinterland remained a vista of exotic opportunity rather than threatening alterity, and the evangelical effort was concomitantly relaxed. As a consequence of this relative disinterest, especially because in earlier times the alliance of the native population had been so critical (Whitehead 1988), the peoples of the hinterland were doubly marginalized. This led to repeated attempts by the groups of the interior to entice both missionaries and other possibly potent whites to settle among them.

The unresponsiveness of the coastal colonial authority thus provoked native political practice to attempt to find other ways of attaining the manufactures, both material and immaterial, of the colonial world. On the one hand, new forms of shamanism, known collectively as *alleluia*, were invented as a means of offsetting the lack of missionary activity and finding a uniquely Amerindian route to Akwa (God). On the other hand, a number of individual prophet-shamans emerged with visions of both the imminence of earthly destruction and promises of material bounty. Among these prophets was also a white man named Smith, in apparent imitation of the Mormonism of Joseph Smith, who in the early 1840s announced his status as Amerindian savior.[5] Amerindian prophet-shamans were thus interstitial figures between the native and colonial world. Often basing themselves in the authority of "tradition" they proffered a vision of engagement with a "modernity" that seemed to offer the spiritual and material bases for a new kind of life in which ideas of redemption and material plenty figured strongly. As a result there were also examples of native visions of redemption and material advance that competed with those of the white shamans, be they the false prophets like Smith or the official missionaries of colonial modernity. For example, the English missionary William Brett wrote: "A Warau woman of singularly weird appearance was employed to spread a report that she had seen ... [in] Kamwatta ... the figure of a white man on horseback, *riding through the air*, who promised to give money and other valuable presents to her, and to all of her tribe who would assemble at that spot and dance from early morning to early afternoon" (1868:250–51). Those already baptized were excluded, and despite the efforts of the missionaries to break up the gathering, when they arrived near the place and saw the preparations "neither the men nor the women would give the least information." There are still similar prophet-shamans today, and Patamuna people remember a false prophet from the 1950s. She, like Smith, called on everyone to join her there, saying that "the Lord will not come if you keep planting" (Whitehead 2002:154).

However, there were also darker aspects to these shamanic visions that eerily prefigure forms of millennial vision that became notorious in Guyana in more recent times. In the case of Smith, also know as the "Impostor" in the writing of his missionary rivals, his call to come to a place in the highlands and await the arrival of a new age of material plenty was certainly answered and many hundreds went to his encampment. In fact the settlement there lasted over a year and eventually failed only due to a lack of provisions. But the would-be disciples of Smith had also been instructed to bring guns and ammunition to the camp, and among some of the early recruits were certainly groups known for their military prowess such as the Karinya and Akawaio. Smith earlier had also led physical attacks against the missions on the Demerara River, which suggests that more was intended than a simple watch for the advent of a new age.

Contemporary with these events in the upper Mazaruni, in the Kukenaam Valley to the west of Mount Roraima, was the emergence of an Amerindian shaman-prophet, Awacaipu. He founded a settlement, named Beckeranta, and called on all the Amerindians of Guyana to join with him there where they would learn how they could become equals to the whites.[6] Awacaipu had been employed by Robert Schomburgk, and in Karl Appun's (1871: vol. 2, 257–64) account he suggests that this may have inspired Awacaipu in his millennial quest for equality with the whites. As in other of these millenarian movements, great emphasis was put on continual singing and dancing accompanied by *cassiri* beer and the renunciation of existing material goods in the hope of greater reward in the future. Like the prophet Smith, Awacaipu also handed out pieces of inscribed paper, apparently sheets from the *Times* that Schomburgk had previously used for his plant specimens, as tokens and charms. Awacaipu even promised that his followers would get white skin, marry white women, and have guns instead of bows. However, what was notably new and sinister in the prophecy of Awacaipu—and what grimly anticipates some "modern" cult activity—was the suggestion that those who wished to have these benefits must first die: "All who wanted to obtain these advantages would have the opportunity between that night until the one after the morrow, but those who followed this course must die during one of these three nights, at each other's hands. The night after the full moon the bodies of those killed would rise from the dead and come down the slopes of Roraima to meet with their families, in color and disposition they would become equal to the whites, and rule over the other brown men who had not undergone this ordeal" (1871: vol. 2, 260).

Appun continues that in order to encourage the others Awacaipu immediately clubbed two or three individuals standing next to him, who then fell into a large *cassiri* container. As their blood and brains spread into the liquid, Awacaipu drank and then offered some to the others. There then followed an "orgie" of killing, which lasted three nights and resulted in nearly four hundred dead. The survivors waited two weeks in vain for the resurrection of the dead and their descent from Mount Roraima in newly acquired white skins. On the fifth night after the appointed moment Awacaipu was clubbed to death by the father of Wey-Torreh, who later narrated the events to Appun.

Awacaipu claimed that his vision of how the Amerindians could gain equality was received from the creator-being Makunaima, who is also central to the practice of *kanaimà* assault sorcery. *Kanaimà* as a shamanic practice centers on the relationship of exchange between the *kanaimà* adept and Makunaima, creator of plants and animals, and this interrelation of affinity, cannibal predation, and exchange forms a triad in other Amazonian cosmologies (see, e.g., Viveiros de Castro 1992; Fausto 2001). This exchange of the mutilated human victims of *kanaimà* assault for the beneficence of Makunaima underlies the logic of *kanaimà* ritual practice. This ritual practice enjoins precise mutilations of the victim's mouth and rectum in order to produce a lingering, painful, and inevitable death. The corpse is then sought out after burial in order to use the *maba* (literally "honey") or juices of putrefaction produced by the rotting of the cadaver as a ritual "food." *Kanaimàs* thus emerge as another dark shamanic force active under the conditions of radical change induced by colonial contacts in the nineteenth century. The antiquity of *kanaimà* is probably much greater than this, but it is first consistently documented from the 1820s onward. As such it is in part a response to the colonial modernities of mining, evangelism, and interior "exploration." The pattern of killings by *kanaimàs* in the later part of the nineteenth century thus shows that it was explicitly understood as a means to resist and reject the white man's materiality and spirituality, unlike *alleluia* and the other forms of shamanic prophecy discussed above. For example, Brett mentions that the "clan of Capui" had a "blood-feud which had begun in the days of their fathers, but had then been lying dormant for many years," but that the "heathen sorcerers" revived this feud because of their opposition to Capui and the evangelical movement he played a central role in (1881:210–11). Capui's son, Philip "the Evangelist," was therefore a repeated target for attacks through poison or *kanaimà* mutilation, only escaping from one such attempt by repeatedly clubbing his attacker with the butt of his gun and leaving him for dead. Apparently this event as well as lingering disabilities due to repeated poisoning "affected the mind and conduct of Philip for a time, and probably shortened his days" (1881:211). Brett also narrates the killing by *kanaimàs* of the brother of one of his recent converts: "They found him on the ground, with his back and neck bruised, but not bleeding," his tongue had been pierced. Brett held this to be "in fulfillment of a threat of the heathen sorcerers, to 'kanaima' in detail all the Acawoios and others who dared to attend Christian instruction" (1868: 269–70). The very substance of political engagement had thus become assimilated to the ritual practice of dark shamans, whose assault sorcery became effective in a way that traditional village leadership no longer was. Village leadership, like the military leaders who were disarmed by the colonial administration, progressively succumbed to the evident power of the missionaries as potential interlocutors with the threatening world of modernity, and the breaking of the shamanic rattles of village shamans became the overt and public token of that submission to colonial authority.

Kanaimà sorcery, secretive and panethnic, thus challenged colonial domination in a more diffuse way. The symbolic and ritual force of the relentless pursuit and violent mutilation of its victims became no less potent in the imagination of the colonial official than it was for Amerindians themselves, and this, as much as the tally of possible victims, accounts for the ambiguous acceptance of *kanaimà* up to the present day. As with the Arawakan shamans discussed earlier, overarching cosmological notions, in this case Makunaima and the way in which local and regional politics were embedded in ideas of ritual action, as well as the close intertwining of the spiritual notions of the Amerindian and their colonizers, meant that certain forms of Amerindian sorcery and prophecy become politically significant. However, unlike the Río Negro region, which was part of a newly independent nation, Guyana was still a colony of Britain in the nineteenth century, and these kinds of local politics had less visibility on the "national" political scene. The colonial political agenda was largely set by the metropolis and its interests, and the forms of political patronage were originated in London not Georgetown. Nonetheless, as we shall see, with independence from Britain local forms of political culture have become significant on the national, even international, stage.

As in the case of the Río Negro dark shamans, *kanaimà* is not the only form of assault sorcery that might be practiced. At a more mundane level *talen* (blowing) magic can be used to harm as well as charm and cure others. The kind of injury that might be achieved through *talen* is certainly far less than that involved in *kanaimà* assault, but it illustrates that assault sorcery is possible even for those without shamanic initiation. *Talen* magic tends to be the exclusive property of families and is handed down within the familial unit. Through it one might create charms (*bina, murang*) that can influence others, particularly to limit them in the harm that might be done to an individual one. However, the very accessibility of these kinds of magical forces only serves to enhance the cultural force of the practice of deadly assault, such as *kanaimà*.

Arawakan Shamans and Politics since 1958

With the democratic elections after the fall of Pérez Jiménez's dictatorship in 1958 many political parties sought the votes of the indigenous peoples of Venezuela's state of Amazonas, including the three main national political parties: Acción Democrática, Unión Republicana Democrática, and even Copei, the party of Catholicism. This party political contest gave rise to the contradictory images and ideas of Amerindians that have persisted in political culture right up to the last elections in 1998 and 2000. On the one hand, Amerindians are seen as naive and ignorant persons whose votes can be bought in exchange for money, food, electric plants, gasoline, and other basic articles of consumption. On the other hand, "Indians" are considered unreliable and incapable of political loyalty, because they are thought to whimsically change their opinions according to passing political circumstance and short-term economic interests, although this is not unlike how politicians view voters everywhere.

By 1958–1959 the Río Negro shamans were known for their abilities in preparing both love potions and poisons, including substances that produced such illnesses as *edári* (*pica-pica* in Spanish), a fatal affliction that causes great pain and even death. However, precisely reflecting the ambivalence of shamanic power, such shamans were also known for being able to cure *edári* in both Criollos and Amerindians, even if medical prognosis had already condemned them to die. Many persons so afflicted went to see Maroita, mentioned above (Anduze 1973:82). Arawakan shamans also possess other abilities that are highly valued by Amerindians and Criollos alike, particularly divination, potions, and chants to obtain and hold onto political appointments or other employment in the public administration of local and state governments.

Estado Amazonas (state of Amazonas) of Venezuela was the Territorio Federal Amazonas (Amazon Federal Territory) until 1992 when the National Congress passed a law transforming it in the twenty-second state in the country. Territorio Federal Amazonas had a governor appointed by the president of the republic and was politically divided in four districts (Atures, Atabapo, Casiquiare, and Río Negro), each of which was ruled by a prefect directly appointed by the governor. Until 2000 the governor's position was occupied by Criollo politicians, mainly party loyalists from Acción Democrática, Unión Republicana Democrática, and Copei. From 1958 until 1970, the prefect's positions were also in the hands of Criollos who came from other regions of Venezuela, or they were mestizos born in different cities of the Territorio Federal Amazonas.

The 1970s were a crucial period for the Amerindian populations of Venezuela, particularly in Territorio Federal Amazonas. During the presidency of Rafael Caldera (1969–1973) a new expansion of socioeconomic and political frontiers into indigenous lands began, particularly in the region south of the Orinoco River. This neocolonial process was aptly dubbed *La conquista del sur* and the national government began an aggressive development policy geared toward the integration of indigenous peoples and territories into the national economy and culture (Arvelo-Jiménez and Scorza 1974; Arvelo-Jiménez 1980). The idea behind this "conquest of the south" was that the Amazon region was underdeveloped due to the economic backwardness and sparse settlement patterns of indigenous people, and the whole region was represented as being practically "uninhabited"; indeed, according to the plan Territorio Federal Amazonas needed new immigrants with new economic development projects to properly occupy and develop it. This national policy opened up the Río Negro region and its surrounding areas to the invasion of a number of developers, who then began to occupy key locations in the Guainía, Casiquiare, and Negro basins.

At the same time the Declaration of Barbados in 1971, recognizing indigenous rights and signed by Venezuela, had a great influence in the reorientation of the official politics of national and regional governments toward a more active participation by indigenous peoples in national political life. In 1972 various regional indigenous federations and the Confederación Indígena de Venezuela were founded. Several indigenous leaders were chosen to occupy important positions inside these organizations, including the Federación Indígena de Amazonas (FIA). Although the idea of reorganizing the existing national indigenous movement through these external organizations did not originate with indigenous peoples, many Amerindian leaders and their communities saw in the federations a political alternative to participation in the "democratic" Venezuelan political system.

The conquest of the south thus brought an invasion of new settlers as well as public and private institutions into Territorio Federal Amazonas, which in turn provoked various responses among the Amerindian population, including a reorganization of the indigenous groups in the defense of their lands; the employment of many natives as salaried, dependent workers for the national and regional governments; and an increasing participation by indigenous individuals and groups in the major political parties. However, indigenous participation in the official political parties was offset by the growing importance that indigenous federations were winning among local communities and ethnic groups, primarily as legitimate alternatives to the usual means of interaction with the regional and national government authorities. These developments also increased the popularity, among both Amerindians and Criollos, of the Arawakan shamans, because their occult powers enabled individuals to get and maintain jobs in public administration, to obtain financial credits from national agencies, to win or lose national election campaigns, and to predict the future in order to know which party and candidate were going to win the presidency of the country. Among these shamans were such individuals as Carlos Menare (Warekena), Lino Yuri-yuri (Warekena), Pancho Guaca (Kurripako), Rosendo Da Silva (Baré), Horacio Camico (Baniwa), and Mariana Evaristo.

This shamanic intervention in the political process created an opportunity for many Amerindians to achieve important political positions in the local and regional governments, as, for example, with Hernán Camico, a member of Copei. Camico was appointed as the first Amerindian prefect of Maroa from 1970 to 1973. During his period in the prefecture of Maroa, Camico, grandnephew of Venancio Camico, the famous shaman-prophet of this region, hired many indigenous people of the area as workers. He also made Baniwa, his maternal tongue, the official language for the daily affairs of the prefecture. However, from 1975 until the mid-1980s various sociopolitical changes occurred in Territorio Federal Amazonas. Changes in the national government (from Acción Democrática to Copei and vice versa), competition among political parties to control Amerindian votes, and confrontations among indigenous leaders over control of the FIA generated many divisions among the region's ethnic groups. It should be noted, however, that this situation also helped to strengthen Amerindian political movements and allow new forms of leadership and political participation for Amazon's indigenous peoples to emerge (Vidal 1977).

In this same period Bernabé Gutiérrez began to emerge on the political scene in Territorio Federal Amazonas as a national and regional leader of the Acción Democrática political party. A Criollo, Gutiérrez was born in Caicara del Orinoco (Bolívar State), but lived since his infancy in Territorio Federal Amazonas, first in the Warekena township of Guzmán Blanco and then in Puerto Ayacucho. Due to these bonds with the region, Gutiérrez became a key figure in the electoral campaigns there. His success in these campaigns allowed him to consolidate his position of growing influence on the central committee of Acción Democrática, both in Caracas and in Puerto Ayacucho, as well as to make his support indispensable for those individuals who aspired to obtain a position and / or a permanent job in the public administration of Territorio Federal Amazonas. Officially and politically Piñerúa Ordaz, one of the founders of Acción Democrática, and other prominent members of the Acción Democrática central committee, backed up Bernabé Gutiérrez's political power. However, in the minds of people in Amazonas his political power was also based on his consultations with dark shamans from the Río Negro. Many of his party allies and friends made reference to Gutiérrez's visits to Río Negro to consult with dark shamans, and they predicted that Acción Democrática would win the next national elections and that Gutiérrez would be governor. Indeed, after the elections of 1983, won by Acción Democrática party, Bernabé Gutiérrez was appointed governor of the Territorio Federal Amazonas.

During his governorship, Bernabé Guttiérrez appointed Enrique Zandalio Camico, a Baniwa, as prefect of Maroa. Zandalio, after just a few months in office, began to draw sharp criticism due to his negligence and abuse of official powers and to the corruption in the handling of the resources of the prefecture. As a result, complaints against Zandalio were made to Governor Gutiérrez. He was asked to pay a visit to Gutiérrez in order to explain his behavior, but before traveling to Puerto Ayacucho, Zandalio went to see Horacio Camico, a famous Baniwa shaman. When Zandalio returned from his meeting with Gutiérrez in Puerto Ayacucho to the prefecture in Maroa, he told the people that he had been reaffirmed in his office by Gutiérrez. A while later he began to threaten his political enemies with the use of assault sorcery. However, Bernabé Gutiérrez himself was then also accused of corruption and abuse of power, and as the presidency of Jaime Lusinchi was coming to an end new election campaigns were in progress by 1988.

The electoral campaign of Gutiérrez and his associates was characterized by fulsome promises of positions in the public administration, by the distribution of gifts and money to voters, and by the claim that many sorcerers were predicting that the Acción Democrática candidate for the presidency of the republic, Carlos Andres Pérez (formerly president of Venezuela, 1974-1979) would win for certain. Indeed, Carlos Andrés Pérez did win the presidency of Venezuela, and that same year he passed Decree 625 wherein the Guainía-Negro basin was declared to be a tourist area, giving free access to all "visitors." The region thus was opened up to development through various infrastructure projects and the encouragement of national and international tourism. Legally this also meant that the region lost its status as an "indigenous zone," which had given it special protection. As a result, the indigenous peoples lost their ancestral rights to their territories, and invasions of Amerindian lands were encouraged throughout the area.

Also in 1988 the famous Hohodene (Baniwa do Isana) shaman Manuel (Mandú) Da Silva arrived at the Río Guainía. Part of the reason for his visit was to seek the aid of the resident Guahibo dark shamans in his struggle against the sorcerer Emi, who made a series of shamanic assaults against Mandú's family. At this time Mandú was the chief-leader (*capitao*) of the town of Uapui Cachoeira ("center or navel of the world" for the Arawakan peoples), located on the Río Aiary, an important branch of the Río Negro. Mandú was considered by the Arawakan groups of Venezuela as one of the truly powerful shamans of the Negro and Guainía basins. During his visits to different places, Mandú received many people of different ethnic groups who made requests to consult with him. This alerted him to the fact that many individuals were using the teachings of *kúwai* and the wisdom of their ancestors in malicious and incorrect ways. Mandú went to Maroa and other towns to speak with people, especially the old men and women, to warn them about the negative consequences of using poisons, chants and prayers, and supernatural powers with selfish purposes or to harm others—a subject on which he had tragically personal experience. Mandú gave the names of numerous men and women who had used poisons to kill their enemies or used assault sorcery to harm and waste the life of many people. He publicly recalled that these were the errors that had caused the destruction of the world in past times and the disappearance of the "ancients" who had once populated the earth. He pointed out that by using assault sorcery they themselves were going to be ruined and that they would have nothing but bad luck. Whole families had been devastated by shamanic attacks and the Criollos were then able to dominate the Amerindians as slaves and take their lands from them. Mandú nonetheless emphasized that it was necessary to continue with the teachings and healthy customs of the ancestors because these traditions were the guarantee of cultural survival and continuity for all the followers of *kúwai*. Needless to say, the warnings and advice of Mandú had a slow but significant impact on the political and cultural life of the indigenous peoples of the Río Guainía.

In 1995 the former Electoral Supreme Council of Venezuela opened the national and regional campaign for the election of governors, mayors, and municipal counselors, each of which have a term of three years. In the gubernatorial campaign, Bernabé Gutiérrez ran as the candidate for Acción Democrática and Nelsón Silva for Copei. The candidates for mayor and municipal counselors included a number of candidates from the Criollo, Amerindian, and Mestizo populations. In the municipality of Guainía, mayorial candidates included Antonio Briceño Querebi for Copei and Angel Angulo Briceño for a joint ticket of Acción Democrática and Convergencia (a small political party created by Rafael Caldera in 1993). Briceño Querebi is a merchant of Baniwa descent, and Angel Angulo is his nephew. In his electoral campaign Gutiérrez deployed all the economic and political influence of his party. On a trip to San Carlos de Río Negro and Maroa he visited two Baré and Tariana shamans, who told him he was going to be the first governor elected by popular votes. Indeed, the winners were Bernabé Gutiérrez as governor, and Antonio Briceño Querebi as the first mayor of Guainía. However, in December 1996 the Supreme Court of Justice annulled the regional law regulating the election and ordered that, after a lapse of three months from the date of that decision, the Legislative Assembly, together with now-Governor Gutiérrez, should dictate and promulgate a new law, and then devise a new electoral process to choose the mayors and other municipal authorities. In the event the result was the ratification of the already elected mayors and municipal counselors.

In 1995 indigenous leaders from Amazonas were proposed for political and governmental positions at the local, regional, and national levels, and today they occupy positions in the municipalities, constituent assembly, governments, legislative assembly, and the national assembly. With the exception of the municipality of Atures, where the state capital, Puerto Ayacucho, is located, in Amazonas most of the candidates for government positions were Amerindians. However, Gutiérrez and Acción Democrática remained in firm control of two of the municipalities—Alto Orinoco and Río Negro. Gutiérrez again won the elections of 1998, but this time he did not have central government support because the new president, Hugo Chávez, considered him a corrupt politician. Further, in February 1999, Chávez promulgated a decree that ordered a national referendum so that "the people" (or "the sovereign people of Venezuela," as Chávez terms it) could decide whether or not to name a constituent national assembly that would create a new national constitution. In that decree, Chávez ordered that the indigenous peoples of Venezuela would name three representatives before the constituent assembly, who could be chosen by themselves in their own traditional ways. Guillermo Guevara (Hiwi or Guahibo), Noelí Pocaterra (Wayúu), and Jesús González (Pemón) were chosen. Two additional Amerindian representatives to the assembly were chosen in national elections: Atala Uriana (Wayúu), representing the state of Zulia, and Liborio Guaruya for the state of Amazonas.

In the elections of July 2000 the candidates for governor were Bernabé Gutiérrez, Liborio Guaruya, Nelsón Silva, and Freddy Borro. Gutiérrez was supported by Acción Democrática, Copei, ORA (a party of the evangelical churches), Proyecto Venezuela (a right-wing movement), and OPINA (a movement of the extreme right wing). Gutiérrez's theme for the electoral campaign was that he was the "governor of the prosperity," while Guaruya promised a "true change with Amazonian feeling" and was supported by various left-wing parties such as PPT, PUAMA, PCV, Bandera Roja (a movement of the extreme left wing), MUPI, and ORPIA. Nelsón Silva was the official candidate of president Chávez's party, MVR, together with MAS, POPA, and other regional and local organizations. Borro was supported by the democratic left and by Francisco Arias Cárdenas's followers (another of the leaders of the abortive coup d'etat of 1992, and former candidate to the presidency of Venezuela in 1998). With the exception of the municipality of Atures, where all the candidates were Criollos, all the other candidates for mayors and counselors were Amerindians or Mestizos. Nonetheless, in some areas several indigenous leaders became candidates on their own initiative because of the support of sympathetic local people, although they received little back-up from the main political parties or organized movements. For the municipality of Maroa the candidates were Angel Angulo Briceño (Acción Democrática, Copei, ORA, OPINA), Antonio Briceño Querebi (MAS, POPA, MVR), and Valdemar Reverón (PPT, PUAMA, MUPI).

These elections were one of the most aggressive and hard-fought in the history of the Venezuelan Amazon, not least because most of the electorate was against Gutiérrez but knew that he could use his official position and even outright fraud to win. Indeed, Gutiérrez used all the power and economic resources at his disposal as governor of the state to ensure his victory. He also appealed for the support of several Arawakan shamans from the Negro and Guainía rivers as well as shamans from other areas and ethnic groups. Gutiérrez also dedicated his electoral campaign to debate with Silva, whom he considered his only "real" opponent, and totally ignored Guaruya as a contending candidate. Silva based his campaign on his previous struggles against Bernabé Gutiérrez and his corrupt government, but in that strategy he counted on President Chávez's support. However, President Chávez never visited the state of Amazonas to give Silva his support.

Guaruya, besides emphasizing the "outsider" status of Gutiérrez and his proven administrative corruption in the government, centered his electoral campaign on the indigenous population, whom he considered the single largest voting block in the electorate, and which therefore held the balance of power in the coming elections. He also highlighted his political connections with the charismatic President Chávez. However, Guaruya's main electoral strategy was based on his own indigenousness—his identity as a Baniwa Amerindian—and he therefore characterized his confrontation with Gutiérrez as a struggle between two different cultures—albeit coexisting in an indigenous region. He also appealed for the support of the Amerindian shamans and other ritual specialists as representatives of the powerful forces of traditional wisdom. Guaruya is quoted in a press interview saying, "Criollos are men and women that are in passing" (Morillo Ramos 2000), meaning that he considers the majority of Criollos as not having strong bonds or roots in the region or with indigenous peoples.

For the indigenous peoples of Río Negro, Guaruya's call for unity among Amerindians as a strategy to gain political power had a strong impact. Also, many Arawakan shamans and ritual specialists of the area remembered the advice given to them in 1989 by Mandú Da Silva on the abuse of occult powers, and they began to have dreams and visions that Gutiérrez would finally be defeated in the elections. During his electoral campaign, Gutiérrez went to San Carlos de Río Negro to visit a famous Baré sorcerer, Nieve Cabucuare, who informed him that she had seen in a dream that he would lose the elections, and that all the indigenous groups of Río Negro knew this. Cabucuare also mentioned that a period of big changes was coming for all the people in the Venezuelan Amazon. These visions meant that some local candidates, such as Antonio Briceño, went downriver to Sao Gabriel das Cachoeiras in Brazil to see the Baniwa and Baré shamans there with the purpose of guaranteeing their own reelection.

As it turned out Briceño was reelected mayor of Maroa again, and Gutiérrez was reelected governor, apparently beating Guaruya by just 221 votes. However, the day following the elections Guaruya denounced Gutiérrez and Acción Democrática for electoral fraud, and he invited in the Consejo Nacional Electoral to recount the votes and possibly repeat the elections (Cortez 2000). Gutiérrez immediately denied fraud, but by mid-September the Consejo Nacional Electoral and the Tribunal Supremo de Justicia had found enough evidence to annul several voting records and to order that the votes be recounted in some places. At the end of September both candidates traveled to Caracas, accompanied by some of their followers, in order to present their cases before the Tribunal Supremo de Justicia (Pérez Rodríguez 2000).

While the judges heard the allegations of each of the candidates, outside the doors of the tribunal two different indigenous factions faced off in a ritual duel. On the one hand there were Amerindians who supported Gutiérrez and wanted him to continue in government. They danced and sang a traditional ceremony called the Dance of the Death, which is used to exhume the bones of deceased relatives. On the other hand, those who supported Guaruya also performed a traditional ceremony that in the Piaroa language is called Warime. This is usually performed after a shaman has a vision and is used to reestablish the balance between man and nature, between the mythical world and the real world. The purpose of this Warime was to reestablish the political order by a repeat of the elections so that Guaruya could become governor of Amazonas. A week later, the Consejo Nacional Electoral decided that Guaruya had won by seventy-nine votes, and they ordered that Guaruya be proclaimed as the new governor of Territorio Federal Amazonas.

The popular rumor was that there was not anything as powerful as the magic of the sorcerers of Río Negro, the "relatives" of Guaruya,[7] and for that reason Bernabé Gutiérrez had lost the elections, especially since the dark shamans of the area had abandoned him to support the Amerindian Guaruya. However, by December the Tribunal Supremo de Justicia ordered the Consejo Nacional Electoral to repeat the elections in those areas where it had been demonstrated that serious doubts existed for the results obtained in the last elections of July. Consequently a provisional governor was named (the president of the Legislative Council) and they proceeded to rerun the electoral campaign in five different areas of the state. On February 11, 2001, the elections were repeated and this time the winner, without any doubt, was Liborio Guaruya.

Guaruya was proclaimed the new governor, and he is the first Amerindian ever to be elected by popular voting in Venezuela. However, perhaps the most important aspect of these political events was that his electoral victory vividly demonstrated the importance of the occult powers of the famed Río Negro shamans. As it is said in the Criollo political world, "the sorcerers they fly, they fly," meaning that one has to respect powerful sorcerers and shamans if one wants to remain safe and in good health.

Occult Politics in Guyana since Independence

The influence of Amerindian shamanisms on the politics of Guyana has not proved to be as widespread or as consistent as in Río Negro. Two factors may account for this. First, the direct involvement of Amerindian people in the political system of Guyana is relatively recent—Guyana having only become an independent country in 1966. Moreover, demographically the Amerindian population of Guyana is a far smaller segment than that in the Río Negro region, so that even where the Amerindian population becomes politically engaged by national politics it is still marginal to the coastal areas where the majority of the population lives.[8] Second, the ethnic composition of Guyana itself means that there are already traditions of occult power firmly in place, in particular obeah, deriving from Africa. The emancipation of black slaves in the mid-nineteenth century led the British authorities to recruit a vast number of indentured laborers from the Indian subcontinent in order to undermine the market in free black labor. Not only did this set up an enduring basis for conflict between the free blacks and indentured Asians, it also ensured the marginalization of the Amerindian population which, insofar as it had acted as a bush police against the plantation slaves, was seen as a tool of the colonial authorities. In short, there was not the same social and economic basis for intermarriage between the Amerindian and non-Amerindian population in Guyana as there was in the Río Negro region of Venezuela.

Sorcery, then, is not used to advance and control the processes of political election and brokering per se, but does operate in a wider framework to mark off and delimit the scope of Amerindian political action in other spheres. In particular the Amerindian practice of *kanaimà* has created a cultural field of external imagination, as well as internal ritual practice, in which the dark shamanism of the Amerindians provides a form of protection from the depredations of both the state and rapacious individuals, such as the diamond and gold miners. This theme is directly present in the novel *Canaima*, written by Romulo Gallegos in the 1930s. Significantly enough for a political system already inured to the reality of spirit forces, Gallegos went on to briefly hold presidential office at the end of World War II and his novel became required reading in Venezuelan schools. At the same time it must be recognized that the practice of African-derived shamanism in the form of obeah is not culturally sealed off from other occult or spiritual practice, so that there is a synergy between the cultural significance of *kanaimà*, obeah, and other ideas of the priority and possibility of magical action.

Thus, while in Guyana there has not been the kind of intense and sustained social and cultural interchanges that produced the situation in Río Negro, there is nonetheless a widespread appreciation of the potential of Amerindian magic for curing purposes, just as Amerindians will also make use of obeah or, in the Brazilian border regions, the related complexes of *santeria* and *candomblé*. There is an eminent pragmatism in the way in which people will use whatever system or form of magical action that seems to offer the best hope for effective results (Riley 2000). In this way, just as the possibility of *kanaimà* acts to empower Amerindians generally in the relationship with outsiders, so too the practice of obeah by national political leaders can be seen as culturally significant beyond those who may share a preeminent belief in the effectiveness of obeah magic.

In just this way the political power of Linden Forbes Burnham, president of Guyana during the 1960s and 1970s, was augmented by his association with obeah practice. Although much of what passes for fact on this matter may be nothing more than mythology, that in a sense is the very meaning of the association of political power with magical potential. Moreover, the popular legacy of Burnham still very much alludes to this aspect of his political regime. According to a Letter from Emile Mervin in the *Stabroek*

News on July 12, 2001: "Burnham's personal status was supremely elevated throughout the land. They [the People's National Congress] had developed a fear and a sense of awe among many people. Some people still claim he had a 'presence,' whatever that means. But it was the apparent high, worshipful esteem, he harbored from people that made him feel it was okay to push ahead with his initiatives knowing, if he failed, he was answerable to no one, and could readily blame others." Burnham certainly had an obeah adviser, Mother Monica, and even appears to have acted out his obeah on the international stage. Once on a visit to London for a Commonwealth heads meeting he sent for one-hundred-year-old Chinese eggs, which he solemnly devoured, averring that they would increase his potency. Another time, when out shooting ducks on the Abary River with Shridath Ramphal, secretary general to the Commonwealth, he would have the ducks brought to him, stick his hand up their backsides and pull out any eggs he might find, and proceed to drink them raw—again claiming they enhanced his power. Burnham was certainly credited with strange powers, and noticeably neither of the houses he once inhabited, his country house at Belfield as well as the presidential residence in Vlissingen Road, was inhabited after he died—it was said that the obeah was too strong. The presidential residence is now Castellani House, home of the national collection of art, and Belfield is a storage place for the reconditioned car import business, but is still treated with some fear as a site where *jumbies* (spirits) might be encountered.

Even in death Burnham seemed mysteriously powerful and the bizarre happenings surrounding his eventual burial had much to do with these occult connections. His body was flown to Moscow for embalming, as was done with Lenin. But some months later, when the body eventually came back to Guyana, it was poorly embalmed because it had already become too decomposed for proper embalming. As a result Burnham was eventually buried above the ground at the Seven Ponds Monument in Georgetown. Some Guyanese believe that all subsequent national troubles flow from this above-ground burial. Certainly the mausoleum structure and his tomb are the site for the practice of animal sacrifice, indicating a continuing interest in the residual supernatural powers of the dead president. It is also believed that a monument to Cuffy (the slave who led a famous rebellion in the Berbice River in 1763) with Burnham's face carved at the back of Cuffy's head is a sacred object with powers. The monument, created by the Berbician artist Philip Moore, is even now not without controversy, as its detractors—from all ethnic groups—accuse Moore, an ardent spiritualist, of invoking African witchcraft in his work. Moore admits to addressing elements of African animism but obviously resists the suggestion that his work glorifies Afro-Guyanese obeah.[9]

This addition of Burnham to the monument of Cuffy and his general association with "science" (obeah) suggests also a strong ethnic dimension to the use of obeah. Indeed, in the riots that followed the 1997 elections, some of the People's National Congress (PNC) stalwarts were said to be doing "science" on the effigy of an Indo-Guyanese anthropologist, Janette Forte. Certainly it is widely held that those who were opposed to Burnham, or who had crossed him in some particular way, were subject to obeah assault sorcery. Victims of such sorcery are known as "Burnham's people," or in Guyanese-English (creole) "Burnham people them." They can be encountered quite often in Georgetown, and one is advised to "not worry after them" because they have been deranged by assault sorcery and are therefore not really harmful or in need of physical help. Typically, such individuals are extremely emaciated Indo-Guyanese women and men who walk the streets of Georgetown at night asking for very small, almost worthless sums of money—no more than GY$10 or $20 (US10 or 20¢)—so that conventional begging seems not to be the motive here. Although there are others who do not fit this ethnic / gender profile, such as an older Afro-Guyanese man familiar on the main streets of Georgetown, they are still called Burnham's people. Such individuals are widely believed to have been deranged and damaged by obeah either ordered by Burnham or personally "sent" by Burnham because they were dangerous elements in the opposition or had somehow crossed him or his government. Not unlike other assaults by dark shamans, the actual victim did not have to be the offender but could be a relative. One taxi driver who regularly sees such people in the course of his work even went so far as to say that Viola Burnham (his widow) could call these people to her to do work if she wanted, and that they were clothed and fed by sympathetic Burnhamites or by employees of his estate. It is also said that "they can't remember their family, even if they get them" or "they na mess with them once they be deranged."

In general terms many (if not most) people in Guyana believe that Burnham must have invoked some sort of occult force or he would not have been able to bind people to him as he did. Moreover, obeah was not the only occult force politically associated with the Burnham regime. For example, a cult called the House of Israel was established by an American fugitive—David Hill, also known as Rabbi Edward Washington—who arrived in Guyana in 1972. The cult was nominally influenced by Judaism but was essentially a black supremacist movement. The House of Israel claimed a membership of over eight thousand and had a daily radio program in which it preached that Africans were the original Hebrews and needed to prepare for an imminent racial war. Opponents of the Burnham government claimed that the House of Israel constituted a private army for Guyana's ruling party, the PNC. Certainly, members of the House of Israel were an effective and brutal force in street demonstrations. During one antigovernment demonstration, a House of Israel member murdered a Roman Catholic priest, Father Darke, who was on the staff of a religious opposition newspaper, the *Catholic Standard*. The House of Israel also engaged in strike-breaking activities and disruptions of public meetings on behalf of the PNC. In short, House of Israel members apparently acted with impunity (if not overt immunity) during the PNC government of Forbes Burnham.[10]

There was a similar association to that of Rabbi Washington and Forbes Burnham that further underlines the nature of the PNC "occult" regime: the Reverend Jim Jones, leader of the People's Temple. These connections, however, were not mere "spiritual" or "inspirational" associations but, quite evidently, ones that had pragmatic material benefits in the politics of postcolonial Guyana, especially on the international stage. During the 1970s, Guyana was very isolated politically as it moved further to its own brand of socialism as a "co-operative republic." It should not be forgotten, then, that Jim Jones declared himself both shaman and socialist: "I come with the black hair of a raven, I come as God Socialist" (quoted in Reiterman 1982: 56). But, as Reiterman suggests, the raven is a shamanic familiar in the Western imagination: "Prophet! Said I, 'thing of evil!—Prophet still, if bird or devil!' (Edgar Allan Poe, *The Raven*)" (56).

The Temple thus distinguished itself from other cults of the times by its overtly political, leftist ambitions. Cult members had won a surprising degree of political acceptance among socialists and radicals in the United States, and they translated that radical socialism into a convincing program of development and human investment for the purposes of winning the agreement of the Guyanese government for the relocation of the group to Port Kaituma in the northwest district. In particular Emerson Mitchell, under the orders of Ptolemy Reid, the deputy prime minister, met with Jones personally at the proposed Temple location in late 1973. There were a number of advantages that the Guyanese government saw in letting Jones relocate his group to Kaituma: foremost was its possible role in the development of the interior region, but also the mere fact of its presence in this border area meant that it was unlikely that Venezuela, with an outstanding claim to this Guyanese territory, would choose to provoke any incidents that might involve "endangering" Americans.

However, as it transpired it was not the Venezuelans who were endangering U.S. citizens but Jones himself. Allegations of atrocities by commune leaders and charges that the commune was holding people against their will led a U.S. congressman, Leo Ryan, to go to "Jonestown" at Kaituma to investigate the allegations of abuse. Fearing that Congressman Ryan's report on the commune would bring unwanted publicity and restrictions on his operations, Jones had the congressman shot as he was boarding an airplane to return to Georgetown. The U.S. government immediately asked

Guyana to send in its army, but before the Guyana Defense Force could reach Jonestown, Jones had coerced and cajoled 913 members of the commune, already habituated by repeated "suicide drills," to commit murder and suicide in what he called a "White Night." Jones killed himself with a bullet to the head.

Certainly there is no direct historical connection between the end of this dark shaman in a White Night and that of Awacaipu at Beckeranta, the Land of the White, but both movements share the cultic, messianic hope for material improvement through spiritual redemption. Just as Awacaipu played off the relative deprivations of the interior Amerindians with regard to the colonial economy, so, too, were the social origins of Peoples' Temple members, many of whom were poor blacks from California. At the geographical and social margins of the Guyanese coastal world dark shamanic prophecy thus emerged with eerily consistent consequences over a space of 130 years.

Conclusion

Obeah, like voudoun and other spiritual systems deriving from the African slave experience, have always had strong political associations (Suttles 1971), including, first, as social structures and cultural idioms within which resistance to the colonial mastery might be covertly organized and expressed; second, as an idiom, with the decline of slavery, for the struggle against colonialism; and finally, as a popular and widely understood expression of power and potency with the advent of postcolonial government. In short, the political has become firmly entwined in broader cultures of spiritual significance. Western forms of government and politics are, of course, no less shaped by the politics of a "Christian" experience, so the key issue is not that shamanism and other occult forms are part of postcolonial politics but rather to what extent the control of the darker forces is particularly relevant to the exercise of power. If the state is indeed the Leviathan of the Hobbesian political imagination, then its monstrous appetites can only be satisfied by a continual sacrifice of the individual to the body-politic. In this frame of reference Aztec human sacrifice is equivalent to the European theater of public punishment and execution. Is it any wonder, then, that the exercise of state power should so often carry with it the association of a ravenous and all-consuming deity whose priest-shamans (politicians) mysteriously produce and control the forms of propitiation? If the Western political imagination can invent "the prince" of Machiavelli, then how very appropriate it becomes to view the political process as the individualized conflicts of the powerful, conducted by whatever means necessary. In this sense the conjunction of the occult and political power in Guyana and

Venezuela might culturally confound us, but the politics of individualized assassination and defamation are hardly novel in the West either.

Amerindian shamanism has always the ambiguous aspect of being a force for both good and evil—a force that is very much in the hands of the individual shaman to control. This in itself would tend to promote a close association of power and individuality that plays easily into the kinds of postcolonial political contexts that have been outlined here. More broadly this allows us to appreciate aspects of shamanism's darker side that are missing in accounts of personal curing and particular allegations of sorcery. To some extent anthropology in Amazonia has already recognized that social and political dimension of witchcraft (Rivière 1970), but only recently has this recognition come to focus on the intimate connections between shamanic ideas and the forms of political action, as in the case of *kanaimà* (Butt-Colson 2001; Whitehead 2001). Equally, while general questions about how shamanism, as a typically personalized and noninstitutional form of spiritual action, might have been harnessed to or suppressed by the state (Thomas and Humphrey 1996) have been considered in a number of global contexts, the way in which occult forms of ritual action become the *accepted* processes of the state has not yet received the attention it deserves. This need for closer attention to the shamanic aspects of state power and authority does not arise just because it happens to be an interesting issue of political science, but rather because it is a key cultural difference between ourselves, who supposedly are practitioners of a rational and spiritually neutral political process, and others, who are seen as immured in a superstitious past. Moreover, unlike some commentators on this theme (Comaroff and Comaroff 1993, 1998; Coronil 1997; Taussig 1997), we do not just see the role of the spirit world as providing a "local" idiom for the work of a transnational or "global" capitalist ideology but rather as a unique idiom and understanding of power that is part of an original and independent postcolonial political condition, as Moore and Sanders (2001) suggest for contemporary African contexts. It is this use of dark shamanism as a legitimate expression of political power that has thus been the focus of this essay. We hope also to have shown that, as this volume demonstrates more generally, dark shamanism is integral to the cosmological understanding of Amazonian peoples.

Notes

We would like to thank Rupert Roopnaraine, Terence Roopnaraine, Stephanie Huelster, George Simon, and Christian Feest for their invaluable assistance in researching and commenting on the materials for this essay.

1   There are about 600 Warekenas, 2,000 Barés, and 2,500 Baniwas in Venezuela, all of whom are part of a regional sociopolitical system with some other 40,000 Tukano-

ans, Makuans, and Arawakans of the northwest Amazon region of Venezuela, Brazil, and Colombia. The main characteristics of this regional system are extensive multilingualism and exogamy, and the tradition of *kúwai* (Wright 1981, 1993; Jackson 1983; Hill 1983, 1993; Chernela 1993; Vidal 1993, 1999). Internally, the Warekena, Baré, and Baniwa groups are organized in several patrilineal, localized, and exogamic phratries; each consisting of two or more sibs ranked according to the birth order of the ancestral mythic brothers. Exogamy clearly enhances the possibilities for Arawak-speaking groups and subgroups to associate with each other and other societies. Hierarchy is not only the criterion to classify people and place them in a given status, it also influences intra- and intergroup alliances. Each phratry and sib is identified with a specific area within its group's territory. Localized phratries and sibs exercise political and economic control over rivers, sacred places, and natural resources of their territories. However, this territorial control can be negotiated through economic bargaining and political alliances among phratries and groups.

2 These levels of shamanic specialization, and the terms for the ancestors and elders (used below) are expressed in the Baré language and derive from Baré shamanic practice, but they are also known and used by the Warekena and Baniwa.

3 Although male shamans are mostly mentioned in anthropological sources, indigenous myth, and other oral literatures, there are a significant number of female shamans among the Arawakan groups of the Río Negro.

4 From the eighteenth to the mid-twentieth century the influence of Arawakan groups and societies on the urban cultures of northwestern Amazonia (i.e., in Puerto Ayacucho, Manaus, San Fernando de Atabapo, Puerto Inírida, etc.) was very important (Vidal and Zucchi 1999:127). This influence is manifest in daily diet, spiritual practices and beliefs, agricultural activities, and particular ways of exploiting forest resources.

5 Mormonism pictures itself, through Joseph Smith's revelation from the angel Maroni of the location of inscribed plates of gold (the textual basis for the Book of Mormon), as being connected to more ancient forms of knowledge possessed by the native inhabitants of the Americas.

6 The source for this information is Appun (1871), who visited the Kukenaam Valley in the 1860s and heard this story from the son of the man who eventually killed Awacaipu. The term Beckeranta is an Amerindian form of a Creole-Dutch term meaning Land of the White, according to Appun. Appun also used this incident as the basis for a piece of popular fiction, *Der Zauberer von Beckeranta: Erzählung aus dem Inneren Guianas*.

7 In the state of Amazonas, Amerindians are referred to among themselves (and by the Criollos) as "relatives" (in Spanish, *parientes*), even though there are no biological or affinal ties among them.

8 For example, Matteson Williams was the member of Parliament for region 8 as a member of the Working People's Alliance. Notably the major political parties, the People's National Congress and People Progressive Party, have no indigenous representatives in Parliament but have co-opted Amerindian individuals in various government capacities. However, few ministerial or high-level appointments, even in areas that affect Amerindian people directly, are made.

9 One observer suggested, from a meeting with Philip Moore on the occasion of his birthday party around the monument, that "[Moore] has that rather 'regal African aura' around him. He sits on a 'throne' of his own devising that looks like many of his other

sculptures [which usually involve many shape shifting animal / human forms and/or more color than the bronze monument to Cuffy]. Although Moore is much revered by art lovers, he is on this 'throne' as much because he is elderly and rather fat, for comfort perhaps more than symbolism. However, there is a palpable sense of awe and respect surrounding his person, but whether that is from his popularity and fame [which would appeal to many Guyanese] or to his mastery of obeah is an open question" (S. Huelster, personal communication). Others would strongly deny this depiction of Moore, and see it simply as an expression of anti–People's National Congress PNC prejudice (G. Simon, personal communication).

10 However, under Hugh Desmond Hoyte, Burnham's successor, Rabbi Washington and his key associates were arrested on a long-standing manslaughter charge and then imprisoned.

References

Anduze, Pablo. 1973. *Bajo el signo de Máwari*. Caracas: Imprenta Nacional.
Appun, Karl Ferdinand. 1871. *Unter den tropen Wanderungen durch Venezuela, am Orinoco, durch Britisch Guyana und am Amazonenstrome in den jahren 1849–1868*. 2 vols. Jena: H. Costenoble.
Arvelo-Jiménez, Nelly. 1980. "Autogestión y concientización." In *Indigenismo y autogestión*, ed. Andrés Serbín and Omar González Ñáñez. 225–37. Caracas: Monte Avila.
Arvelo-Jiménez, Nelly, and Juan V. Scorza. 1974. *El integracionismo y sus modalidades de acción en el indigenismo venezolano*. Paper presented at the 41st Congress of Americanists, Mexico City.
Brett, W. H. 1868. *The Indian Tribes of Guiana*. London: Bell and Daldy.
———. 1881. *Mission Work in the Forests of Guiana*. London: Society for Promoting Christian Knowledge / E. & J. B. Young & Co.
Butt-Colson, A. 2001. "Kanaima: Itoto as Death and Anti-Structure." In *Beyond the Visible and the Material*, ed. Laura Rival and Neil L. Whitehead. 221–36. Oxford: Oxford University Press.
Chernela, Janet. 1993. *The Uanano Indians of the Brazilian Amazon: A Sense of Place*. Austin: University of Texas Press.
Comaroff, Jean, and John L. Comaroff, eds. 1993. *Modernity and Its Malcontents: Ritual and Power in Postcolonial Africa*. Chicago: University of Chicago Press.
Comaroff, John L., and Jean Comaroff. 1998. *Occult Economies and the Violence of Abstraction: Notes from the South African Postcolony*. Chicago: American Bar Foundation.
Coronil, F. 1997. *The Magical State*. Chicago: Chicago University Press.
Cortes, Adriana. 1999a. "Ante relaciones interiores y congreso: Indígenas denuncian corrupción en Alcaldía del Alto Orinoco." *El Nacional* (April 8): n.p.
———. 1999b. "Dejan sin efecto medidas contra responsables por hechos de corrupción en Amazonas." *El Nacional* (February 27): 7.
———. 2000. "Denuncian fraude de AD en gobernación de Amazonas." *El Nacional* (August 3): 10.
Diederich, Bernard. 1970. *Papa Doc: The Truth about Haiti Today*. London: Bodley Head.
Fausto, Carlos. 2001. *Inimigos Fiéis: História, Guerra e Xamanismo na Amazônia*. São Paulo: Edusp.

Ferguson, James. 1989. *Papa Doc, Baby Doc: Haiti and the Duvaliers.* Cambridge, Mass.: Basil Blackwell.

González Niño, Edgardo. 1984. *Historia del Territorio Federal Amazonas.* Caracas: Ediciones de la Presidencia de la República.

Henríquez, Manuel. 1994. *Amazonas: Apuntes y crónicas.* Caracas: Ediciones de la Presidencia de la República.

Hill, Jonathan D. 1983. "Wakuénai Society: A Processual-Structural Analysis of Indigenous Cultural Life in the Upper Negro Region of Venezuela." Ph.D. diss., Indiana University.

———. 1993. *Keepers of the Sacred Chants: The Poetics of Ritual Power in an Amazonian Society.* Tucson: University of Arizona Press.

Hill, Jonathan D., and Robin Wright. 1988. "Time Narrative, and Ritual: Historical Interpretations from an Amazonian Society." In *Rethinking History and Myth: Indigenous South American Perspectives on the Past*, ed. Jonathan D. Hill. 78–105. Urbana: University of Illinois Press.

Iribertegui, Ramón. 1987. *Amazonas: El hombre y el caucho.* Puerto Ayacucho: Vicariato Apostólico.

Jackson, Jean E. 1983. *The Fish People: Linguistic Exogamy and Tukanoan Identity in Northwest Amazonia.* New York: Cambridge University Press.

Martín, Gustavo. 1983. *Magia y religión en la Venezuela contemporánea.* Caracas: Ediciones de la Biblioteca Universidad Central de Venezuela.

Moore, Henrietta, and Todd Sanders, eds. 2001. *Magical Interpretations, Material Realities: Modernity, Witchcraft and the Occult in Postcolonial Africa.* London: Routledge.

Morillo Ramos, Morelia. 2000. "PPT y MVR apuestan a reducir ventaja adeca en Puerto Ayacucho." *El Universal* (May 16): 11.

Pérez Rodríguez, Solbella. 2000. "Durante acto de rendición de informe: CNE admite errores en registro electoral de Amazonas." *El Nacional* (September 26): 4.

Poleo Zerpa, Willmer. 1999. "Investigan presuntos hechos de corrupción: Fiscalía y PTJ allanan gobernación y alcaldías de Amazonas. *El Nacional* (July 7): 7.

Reiterman, T., with John Jacobs. 1982. *Raven. The Untold Story of the Rev. Jim Jones and His People.* New York: Dutton.

Riley, Mary. 2000. "Measuring the Biomedical Efficacy of Traditional Remedies among the Makushi Amerindians of Southwestern Guyana." Ph.D. diss., Tulane University.

Rivière, Peter G. 1970. "Factions and Exclusions in Two South American Village Systems." In *Witchcraft: Confessions and Accusations*, ed. M. Douglas. 245–56. London: Tavistock.

———. 1995. *Absent-Minded Imperialism: Britain and the Expansion of Empire in Nineteenth-Century Brazil.* London: I. B. Tauris and Co.

Spruce, Richard. 1996. *Notas de un botánico en el Amazonas y en los Andes.* Quito: Abya-Yala.

Suttles, William C. 1971. *Voudoun and Conjuring as Ideologies of Slave Rebellion.* Ann Arbor: Center for Afro-American and African Studies, University of Michigan.

Taussig, Michael. 1997. *The Magic of the State.* New York: Routledge.

Tavera Acosta, Bartolome. 1927. *Rionegro: Reseña Etnográfica, Histórica y Geográfica del Territorio Amazonas.* Maracay: Estado Aragla.

Thomas, Nicholas, and Caroline Humphrey, eds. 1996. *Shamanism, History, and the State.* Ann Arbor: University of Michigan Press.

Vidal, Silvia M. 1977. "Antecedentes e historia de la destrucción de un movimiento indígena: El caso Amazonas." Manuscript.

———. 1993. "Reconstrucción de los procesos de etnogénesis y de reproducción social entre los Baré de Río Negro (siglos XVI-XVIII)." Ph.D. Thesis. Centro de Estudios Avanzados-IVIC.

———. 1999. "Amerindian Groups of Northwest Amazonia: Their Regional System of Political-Religious Hierarchies." *Anthropos. 94: 515-28.*

Vidal, Silvia M., and Alberta Zucchi. 1999. "Efectos de las expansiones coloniales en las poblaciones indígenas del noroeste Amazónico (1798–1830)." *Colonial Latin American Review 8 (1): 113-32.*

Viveiros de Castro, Eduardo Batalha. 1992. *From the Enemy's Point of View: Humanity and Divinity in an Amazonian Society.* Chicago: University of Chicago Press.

Wallace, Alfred Russell. 1969. *A Narrative of Travels on the Amazon and Rio Negro, with Account of the Native Tribes.* New York: Greenwood Press.

Whitehead, Neil L. 1988. *Lords of the Tiger-Spirit: A History of the Caribs in Colonial Venezuela and Guyana, 1498–1820.* Dordrecht: Foris Publications.

———. 1990. "Carib Ethnic Soldiering in Venezuela, the Guianas, and Antilles: 1492–1820." *Ethnohistory* 37 (4): 357–85.

———. 1993. "Historical Discontinuity and Ethnic Transformation in Native Amazonia and Guayana, 1500–1900." *L'Homme* 28: 289–309.

———. 1994. "The Ancient Amerindian Polities of the Lower Orinoco, Amazon, and Guayana Coast: A preliminary Analysis of Their Passage from Antiquity to Extinction. In *Amazonian Indians. From Prehistory to the Present*, ed. A. C. Roosevelt, n.p. Tucson: University of Arizona Press.

———. 1996. "Ethnogenesis and Ethnocide in the Settlement of Surinam." In *History, Power, and Identity: Ethnogenesis in the Americas, 1492-1992*, ed. J. Hill. 20–35. Iowa City: University of Iowa Press.

———. 1998. "Colonial Chieftains of the Lower Orinoco and Guayana Coast." In *Chiefdoms and Chieftaincy in the Americas*, ed. E. Redmond. Gainesville: University Press of Florida.

———. 1999a. "Native Society and the European Occupation of the Caribbean Islands and Coastal Tierra Firme, 1492–1650." In *A General History of the Caribbean*, vol. 3, ed. C. Damas and P. Emmer. 180–200. New York: UNESCO.

———. 1999b. "The Crises and Transformations of Invaded Societies (1492–1580): The Caribbean." In *The Cambridge History of Native American Peoples*, vol. 3, ed. F. Salomon and S. Schwartz, 864–903. Cambridge: Cambridge University Press.

———. 1999c. "Tribes Make States and States Make Tribes: Warfare and the Creation of Colonial Tribe and State in North-eastern South America, 1498–1820." In *War in the Tribal Zone*, ed. R. B. Ferguson and N. L. Whitehead. 27–50. Oxford: SAR Press.

———. 2001. "Kanaimà: Shamanism and Ritual Death in the Pakaraima Mountains, Guyana." In *Beyond the Visible and the Material*, ed. Laura Rival and Neil L. Whitehead. 235–46. Oxford: Oxford University Press.

———. 2002. *Dark Shamans: Kanaimà and the Poetics of Violent Death.* Durham: Duke University Press.

Wright, Robin. 1981. "History and Religion of the Baniwa Peoples of the Upper Rio Negro Valley." Ph.D. diss., Stanford University.

———. 1993. "Pursuing the Spirit: Semantic Construction in Hohodene Karidzamai Chants for Initiation." *Amerindia* 18: 1–40.

Wright, Robin, and Jonathan D. Hill. 1986. "History, Ritual, and Myth: Nineteenth-Century Millenarian Movements in the Northwest Amazon." *Ethnohistory* 33 (1): 31–54.

*The Wicked and the Wise Men:
Witches and Prophets in the History
of the Northwest Amazon*

Robin Wright

It is widely recognized that the ethnology of lowland South America has dedicated relatively little attention to what Michael Brown (1989) has called the "dark side" of shamanism. In comparison with other ethnographic areas of the world, the literature dealing with witchcraft and sorcery has been rather thin: a few early studies still stand out as classics, such as Lévi-Strauss (1967), Dole (1973), and Goldman (1963), and there have been some more recent discussions deriving from the continuing interest in the nature of shamanism (Gow 1996; Hugh-Jones 1996; Langdon 1992; Taussig 1987; Wright 1996, 1998). Recognizing this lack, and inspired by the research of Johannes Wilbert (1993: 92–125), the works of Whitehead (2002) and, in part, our work have sought to develop innovative perspectives on the question.

It is also evident that there is a far richer bibliography on the "light" side of shamans—that is, their healing and curing activities—including that of the more powerful and prophetic "world-healers" or, as they have often been called, "messiahs," and the socioreligious movements led by them throughout the history of contact and across the South American continent (see, for example, the discussion and bibliography in Sullivan 1988). Furthermore, various native accounts of such movements have been published that frequently present the miraculous and victorious struggles of such leaders against the violence used by the state to suppress their leadership (Turner, in Hill 1988, has labeled such narratives as "messianic myths"). The northwest Amazon is one area where such narratives abound (see Wright and Hill 1986), and native peoples there have experienced centuries of contact with the agents of Western society (missionaries, merchants, the military).

Historical prophetic movements are often marked by the ways in which native peoples have appropriated Christian symbols, practices, and representations of authority, often independently of any kind of missionary interference. Christian missionaries, for their part, have frequently been surprised by the manner in which native peoples have converted en masse to the religions they have introduced—sometimes with the same enthusiasm with which they have followed prophetic leaders. Anthropologists have sought to explain conversion movements as solutions to two kinds of problems faced by native societies, the first of which is external, referring to the multiple ways in which nonnative societies have disorganized and destructured native societies. Such disorganization is frequently manifest through a rise in witchcraft and sorcery accusations. Conversion offers moral reform, which enables native peoples to control witchcraft and regain their integrity vis-à-vis intruders. The second problem is internal, having to do with dilemmas inherent to cosmologies and inherited from primordial times; for example, the ontological status of affinal groups and their perceived threat to the continuity of consanguineal or descent groups; the challenges of harnessing dangerous shamanic power for the purposes of social reproduction; and so forth (see, for example, the essays in Wright 1999).

Rarely do we find in the literature native accounts of prophetic figures who, through their connections to primordial powers, have sought to combat the devastating effects of witchcraft and sorcery perceived as inherent to the nature of the world and as the legacy of the chaotic primordial world. In this essay I present one such account that represents the dialectical tension between dark and light consciousness, manifest as two historically opposed forces: witches, or those who practice witchcraft in order to kill; and prophets, those with direct access to the sources of creation. Both are represented symbolically in mythical consciousness and both are necessary, the tradition seems to say, to the dynamics of cosmological and historical existence, illustrating what we have observed elsewhere, that "the deep mythohistorical presence of dark shamanism, contemporary with, if not actually preceding, the original emergence of persons and shamanic techniques, indicates that dark and light, killing and curing, are complementary opposites not antagonistic possibilities"; and that "whatever the tragedy, distress, and death that dark shamans and allied ritual specialists may perform on humanity they are an inevitable, continuing, and even necessary part of the cosmos . . . [and] can become the source and even symbols of a potent indigenous society and culture that is capable of defending itself against the depredations of the outside world, be that a neighboring village or even the national state" (Whitehead and Wright, this volume). In fact, in numerous religious traditions throughout the world, the two faces of the sacred—light and dark, good and evil—are seen as integral parts of human existence in history. What I seek to show here is the nature of this dynamic as the Baniwa perceive it.

The Baniwa of the northwest Amazon in Brazil have experienced a long history of engagement in prophetic movements (Wright and Hill 1986; Wright 1998), and in fact their mass conversion to evangelical Christianity beginning in the 1950s may be understood as a modality of such engagement (Wright 1999). Immediately prior to conversion, and even concomitant with it, they followed prophetic leaders who, according to narrative accounts, sought to eradicate witchcraft and, in so doing, reform the foundations of living together in society. Despite the historical evidence, which clearly shows that the Baniwa at that time were traumatized by the devastating effects of rubber and other extractivist industries, the narratives deny the destructive power of the whites over prophetic leaders and point to the internal problem of witchcraft as the true source of evil. Posed in this way, the problem of evil is thus susceptible to the actions of prophets, who are uniquely capable of keeping it in check.

The first part of this essay thus explores the nature of witchcraft, its mythical foundations and sociopolitical contexts. I contrast witchcraft with sorcery and describe the institution of shamanic vengeance used to destroy witches.[1] I also explore the extent to which exogenous influences have exacerbated levels of witchcraft accusations. In this essay's second part I present a lengthy oral history that demonstrates how prophets, or "wise men," constantly waged battle against wickedness, witches, and the white man. While prophets demonstrated their superior knowledge over the white man, they succumbed to the implacable evil of the wicked, enemies within their own society. Even the mass conversion of the Baniwa to Protestant evangelicalism in the 1950s and 1960s did not succeed in erradicating the evil and witches from this world, as converts had hoped. Yet the wisdom of the prophets survives to the present day, and their followers continue to journey to their graves to request their protection.

Dark and Light Consciousness in the Baniwa Cosmos

To represent the dialectical tension between light and dark consciousness it is necessary to discuss briefly how the universe is perceived and human existence evaluated by those who are most directly concerned with such questions in Baniwa society, the shamans.

In my fieldwork in 1997–2001, one of the most knowledgeable shamans of all the Baniwa in Brazil elaborated at my request his understanding of the structure of the universe. In his view, the universe is organized into an enormous vertical structure of twenty-five layers, or worlds (*kuma*), with twelve layers below "This World" (Hliekwapi) of humans and twelve above. As a master shaman, he had experienced all of these levels including the highest and most difficult-to-reach world of the creator/transformer and father of all Baniwa, Nhiãperikuli or "Dio," whom he called the "Illuminated One," whose body shines "like a brilliant mirror," and who is "eternally young." The sun is considered to be a manifestation of Nhiãperikuli's body.

The twelve worlds below ours—collectively known as Uapinakuethe—are inhabited by different types of beings or "tribes of people." With the exception of the people of the lowest level and one other, all other peoples are considered to be "good" and assist the shaman in his search for the lost souls of the sick. The worlds above ours—collectively known as Apakwa Hekwapi, the "Other World"—are in large part defined by shamanic qualities and have to do with sickness and curing. With the exception of levels five and six, which are inhabited by the spirit "Owner of Sickness," Wamundana or Kuwai (who is Nhiãperikuli's son), and his "secretary," the white sloth (*tchitamali*), all other levels are likewise inhabited by "good people." Some may "deceive" or "lie" to the shaman, but only the Owner of Sickness possesses death-dealing substances used in witchcraft. All other spirit-beings are considered "good people."

By contrast, This World of humans is considered to be irredeemably evil. Thus, of all the layers in the universe, four are considered to be comprised of wicked people. It is remarkable how, in the context and from the perspective of the most elaborate cosmic structure thus far recorded among the Baniwa, the theme of evil in the world of humans clearly stands out. In shamanic discourse about the qualities of the universe, This World is frequently characterized as the place of evil, *maatchikwe*; place of pain, *kaiwikwe*; and place of rot, *ekúkwe*, in contrast to the world of Nhiãperikuli, which is notable for its sources of remedies against the sicknesses of This World, which is considered to be contaminated by the existence of sorcerers and witches. Both cosmogonic myths and the shamans' discourse repeatedly emphasize that the human world is intrinsically flawed by evil, misfortune, and death.

Shamanic powers and cures, by contrast, are characterized in terms of the protective, beneficial, and aesthetically correct: "to make the world beautiful"; "to make This World and the people in it better and content"; "to not let This World fall or end" (meaning, to be covered in darkness and overrun by witches); "to retrieve lost souls and make sick persons well"—are all phrases that appear in shamanic discourses about their journeys to the Other World. In all phases of this journey, the beauty, goodness, unity, order, and truth—in a word, light—of the Other World (with the exception of the places of Kuwai) stand in contrast with This World of multiple pain and evil. In one sense, then, the shaman's quest would seem to be one of "beautifying" This World by seeking to create order and preventing the darkness of chaos. With this background, I now turn to the practices of witchcraft and sorcery in This World and the sorts of remedial actions individuals can take against these practices.

The Nature of Witchcraft and Sorcery

Manhene (witchcraft). The word I translate as witchcraft, *manhene*, literally means "one does not know," which is an accurate reflection of the extreme secrecy associated with its practice. The Baniwa translate the word into Portuguese as *veneno*, poison (and in *lingua geral* as *marecaimbara*), and use the word to refer not only to poisonous substances but also to the act of secretly putting such substances (plants, resins, ash, berries, thorns) in the food, drink, personal objects, or bodily orifices of an enemy with the intent to kill him or her. Various forms of poisoning can produce such severe reactions (high fever, vomiting blood, diarrhea with blood) as to result in sudden and instant death, while others provoke a process of chronic sickness that slowly weakens the victim, leaving him or her pale, thin, anemic,[2] and sometimes with behavioral disturbances characterized by the adoption of animallike behavior and an incapacity to perform the normal activities of daily life.[3] For all Baniwa, *manhene* is the most serious and frequent form of traditional sickness and explanation for death.[4]

The importance of *manhene* can be estimated by the fact that the first death in the primordial world was caused by poison. According to the myths of origin (see ACIRA/FOIRN 1999) Kuwai, the son of the creator/transformer Nhiãperikuli, left all forms of poison in this world as vengeance for his own killing. Nhiãperikuli gathered up this poison in a pot and hid it in his house, but a tribe of ancestral monkey-spirits, called Eenunai, stole this poison and became powerful witches, or "poison-owners" (*manhene iminali*). They poisoned one of Nhiãperikuli's younger brothers, who then became the first person to die. After this, Nhiãperikuli succeeded in regaining the poison from the Eenunai, wrapped it in a bundle, and threw it on top of several hills located in southern Venezuela, where witches today may still go to get it. It is noteworthy that in their efforts to explain why Nhiãperikuli left poisonous plants in This World shamans use the simple statement "in order to kill people." Although seemingly odd, this statement reflects no more than the complementary opposition of killing and healing, which are inherent to cosmological dynamics and historical existence.

In contrast to other indigenous societies of Amazonia, Baniwa shamans do not double as witches; in fact, although shamans do have the power to kill, they adamantly deny that they use poison and affirm that their principal function is to cure *manhene*.[5] While all adults know about poison killings and are capable of occasionally using witchcraft, not all can become poison-owners, for this requires, among other things, the acquisition of specialized knowledge having to do with the location and preparation of poisons and their antidotes—an extensive knowledge judging from the wide range of poisons known.[6] In addition, a poison-owner is someone who is considered to be "no longer like a person," for "his only thought is to kill": the bodily form of such a witch differs from that of normal people. The poison-owner's body, according to shamans who "see" their true nature, is that of a monkey, like the mythical Eenunai. Shamans see them with fur all over their bodies, especially on their arms and hands. Moreover, the poison-owner's soul is, according to shamans, a spirit of the dead, *inyaime*, which inhabits the periphery of This World. They say that when a poison-owner enters a house, first *inyaime* goes in, then the body of the poison-owner, that is, of a monkey, enters.[7]

Only shamans are capable of curing *manhene* through sucking out the poison, the visible representation of which is usually monkey or sloth fur; there are, however, no spells or chants powerful enough to reverse the effects of poison given by poison-owners. Besides extraction, shamans usually recommend plant medicines (various types of roots that counteract the gastric effects of the poison). While the Baniwa have also discovered a number of white man's remedies (liquid vitamins, for example) that help in cures for poison, they still seek the cures of shamans first for cases of *manhene*.

What motivates a person to practice witchcraft or, even, to become a poison-owner? The most compelling reasons cited were: vengeance (*lipuamina* or *liuma likuada*, "he seeks exchange") for the death of a kin who is believed to have been poisoned or killed by sorcery—in this case, the person may either seek vengeance through the Guahibo shamans (see below), or take vengeance personally, for the dying person "tells" who is responsible for his or her murder; envy (*nakhemakan* or *maatchi likapakan*, "he looks with evil") at the success, prosperity, and well being of others, relative to one's own situation: debt, rejection, isolation and continued misfortune may fuel a person's desire to "ruin" the lives of those more successful and prosperous; resentment (*maatchi likaale*, "his heart is wicked, bad"), for example, when a person does not live up to his or her part of an exchange (e.g., marital), thus producing an inequality, or when someone is known to have spoken malicious gossip, one's heart turns against that person which may result in poisoning; (d) the loss of control over one's thought and emotions (*manhekada lima*, a state or condition of being in which a person acts without thought). This latter reason is perhaps the most dangerous of all motives, for it implies that the person no longer has any control over emotions such as hatred, anger, or envy, and lets these feelings dominate his or her thoughts. In such cases, the person becomes an asocial being, for living in society implies "thought" (*ianheke*, the negative of which is *manheke*; in its least harmful aspect this may mean stupid or ignorant, but even so such a state may result in fatal errors), and the importance of remembering the counsel of the elders at initiation to "treat one's kin well, share one's food, never fool with poison," etc. In the past there were other motives for swift killing by poison related to ritual transgressions, such as exposing the sacred flutes and trumpets to women.

What are the social correlates of witchcraft? That is, are certain types of social relations more subject, or vulnerable, to it? My initial idea, based on counting known incidents, was that it is said to occur more frequently among affines than among consanguineal kin, which would be consistent with mythical and historical narratives. Yet, when I pressed the Baniwa about this, they would not agree. "One doesn't know, one can't know," one man said, "it could be anyone, sib-brother, cousin." People agree that there is never witchcraft among members of a nuclear family, but as the circle of kin widens to include parallel cousins, sib-brothers, and at the extreme, affines (*imathana*) and potential affines (*itenaaki*), the probabilities become ever greater. With "enemies" (*ipuunda*)—socially, geographically, and linguistically distant peoples—warfare (*uwi*) was waged in the past, but with the abandoning of warfare, affines and potential affines have in fact come to represent the greatest perceived threats to kin groups.

What means do communities have for preventing outbreaks of witchcraft? One such mechanism has to do with the deliberate shaping of a community sentiment that downplays any and all discussions of, or references to, witchcraft and its transmission.[8] Baniwa from a very large and prosperous community on the upper Aiary River, for example, insisted that there were few cases of witchcraft in their community because the elders "only spoke of good things," such as dance festivals and music, happiness, etc., and frowned on discussions having to do with witchcraft incidents. In contrast, another community was plagued with problems of witchcraft because there the elders had let it get out of control.

In this regard, it is of great importance to note that the oral histories I cite later in this article point to the control of witchcraft and poisoning as one of the most important powers of the historical prophets and messiahs. Such figures preached against poison and sought to eradicate its use by publicly accusing those whom they knew possessed it. Again, their efforts worked in the direction of creating community unity and repressing whatever would provoke misunderstanding and conflict.

Hiuiathi (sorcery). These are evil spells sent by persons who desire to cause harm to their enemies.[9] They can be done by shamans, chanters, or common people who know their contents. These spells use a logic similar to that of their symmetric opposites, curing chants; they name things that are considered dangerous (e.g., biting insects, snakes, scorpions, spiders, poisonous fruits, spirits of the dead, etc.), seeking to cause harm to the victim.[10] In performing these spells, the sorcerer speaks the names of aggressive beings in a low, almost inaudible, voice, over his cigar, then blows the spell into the air with the smoke. The sorcerer may also leave the rest of his cigar, enchanted by the words of his spell, at a place where the victim will pass or stay. The spells can also be blown on the clothes or hammock of the victim, or even on houseposts. A powerful sorcerer may as he speaks the spell, simply spit on a place where the victim will pass, or even just stare at his victim while remembering the spell in his mind (a sort of evil eye) in order to produce the desired effect. Spells may be done to provoke sickness, but also to cause discord, misunderstanding, and fights within communities.

There are numerous types of *hiuiathi*, but the special group of sicknesses and abnormal conditions related to women and reproduction should be highlighted because it is more common than others.[11] Postpartum hemorrhage, excessive menstruation, abortions, death at childbirth, infertility, lack of maternal milk, or milk that produces vomiting and diarrhea in the newborn are all conditions that are said to be produced by sorcerers' spells that seek to "ruin" the woman, generally because of jealousy or anger from slighted would-be lovers. Unmarried women and pregnant women are thus a high-risk group for sorcerers' attacks. In the past, it is said, these spells would be spoken during the male initiation rituals when women could not be present. But while these forms of *hiuiathi* are often due to problems in love affairs more generally, the social sphere that defines this type of aggressive action against other humans is gender relations, regardless of any other associations (sib or phratry membership, kin or affinal relations) that the sorcerer might have with the victim.

All of these forms of sorcery likewise began with Kuwai who, according to myth, taught Nhiãperikuli and humans how to chant at initiation rites and how to cure; but he taught *hiuiathi* to Nhiãperikuli's younger brother Eeri who, thinking that they were to do good, transmitted them to humans. Other versions say that in the great fire that marked Kuwai's death, he passed on all his knowledge about *hiuiathi* to the spirits of nature called *iupinai*; for this reason, they are the true sorcerers, or *hiuiathi iminali* (sorcery-owners) in the world today. In both versions, Kuwai, the "owner of sickness," began all forms of *hiuiathi*. Other spirit-beings and humans learned and transmitted this knowledge over the generations. Thus, in curing, a chanter must identify correctly the form of sickness and its specific spirit origin in order to name and counteract the effects of the sorcery.

Shamanic vengeance (iupithátem). The practice of shamanic vengeance appears to be very ancient among the Baniwa and specifically links them with various indigenous peoples of the llanos in Colombia, especially the Guahibo of the Vichada River, who are known to be powerful shamans capable of killing at long distances. What underlies the practice is that Baniwa shamans themselves, while perfectly capable of undertaking vengeance, even at a long distance, say they do not do so out of "fear" of reprisals against their families by witches. Thus they seek other, distant, non-Arawak-speaking peoples whose power to kill in order to avenge is held to be as strong or stronger than their own.

Perhaps the first reference to this practice is found in Theodor Koch-Grünberg's report (1967 [1909]) of his ethnographic travels on the Aiary River at the beginning of the twentieth century. His principal interlocutor, a shaman, told him that sometime after a person's death, the relatives of the victim take an article of clothing and the "poison" that the shaman had extracted to "a people in the northeast," whom they request take vengeance on the murderer by "magical action at a distance." Koch-Grünberg understood that these people lived in large roundhouses on the Vichada River and were called Pidzári. The "magical action" consisted of placing the article of the deceased inside a circle traced on the ground over which the shaman pronounced a spell to "call the murderer," whereupon he burned the poison. In an instant, in the ashes, the shaman found and killed the "distant enemy" responsible for the death.[12]

Shamans whom I interviewed in the 1970s and 1990s confirmed that the Guahibo, or Wanhíwa, were still sought to perform this service. Cubeo and "true" Baniwa shamans could even produce more rapid results,[13] but the Hohodene preferred the Wanhíwa because even though Hohodene shamans know who is responsible for a death or a series of deaths in their communities they will never reveal it publicly nor, they say, will they take direct action for "fear" of reprisal from the witch against their own families or because they know that the witch is a sib-brother against whom no action can be taken.[14]

The Hohodene shamans' descriptions of the ritual performance reveal some variations from the accounts cited above. Known as *iupithátem* (a word I am unable to translate), the hair or "filth" (*hiuidamakáthi*) or even a piece of clothing is taken by the deceased's relatives, sometimes years after he or she has died (although it is collected immediately after the person's death, it is kept wrapped in a bundle), and they pay (*lidauanátaka*) the Wanhíwa shaman to take vengeance (*liuma likuada*, "he seeks exchange"). It should be noted that *iupithátem* is performed not only in cases of death by *manhene* but also *hiuiathi*. Since *hiuiathi* is done secretively and by anyone, the family of the victim has no way of determining who was responsible and may thus seek the services of the Guahibo.

The Wanhíwa shaman places the hair of the deceased on the ground in front of him, together with the payment, a bucket of water, and a stone that is said to be the shaman's soul.[15] The shaman takes the hallucinogenic *niopo* (snuff) and begins to sing, "looking for the soul" of the murderer. When a butterfly, or small bird, or "whatever little thing" appears before him, this is the murderer's soul and the shaman takes the stone and "bites it," killing it instantly. The shaman may even "hear its death-cry."

At that time, or later, he sends a great wind to where the intended victim is, and the victim begins to go mad (*ikaka*). According to various reports, he begins to eat ashes from the fire, sits on hot coals but doesn't burn, eats his fingernails "for his hands don't know what they are doing," runs after women and attempts to rape them, and rips off his clothes and runs about in circles—sometimes into the forest. The madness subsides but, several days later, the Wanhíwa sends another great wind with thunderclouds and lightning. The victim does the same as before but now he confesses, revealing the names of everyone whom he has killed. He bites his lips and tongue so that he won't tell who has killed him. He rips off his clothes, mutilates his genitals, and finally dies. Numerous eyewitness accounts of *iupithátem* confirm the efficacy of this vengeance killing.[16]

Urban sorcerers (macumbeiros). In the late 1970s, new forms of sorcery were introduced into the municipal capital of São Gabriel da Cachoeira, located a short distance from Baniwa territory. Brought by Afro-Brazilian and *mestiço* migrants from Manaus, Belém, and other areas of northeastern Brazil, who came by the thousands to work on the construction of the northern perimeter highway (BR-210), and later in the 1980s by gold panners from Roraima, these new forms, known as *macumba*, became incorporated into the already-existing repertoire of ritual specialists, or *benzedores* (spell-blowers), usually Baré and Tukano Indians, or Mestizos of the city. Further research is needed on these forms of sorcery, and here I only wish to note that for Baniwa shamans, *macumba* refers to the practice of killing through sorcery or evil spell-blowing at a distance, and it is thus, they say, "like *iupithátem*," as done by the Wanhíwa.

I have noted the ways in which community elders may actively prevent witchcraft from taking hold by reinforcing a community sentiment of "happiness" while also downplaying discussions of witchcraft incidents. The great Baniwa prophets of the past, on whom I focus in the next section, centered their messages and actions precisely against witches and sorcerers who provoked discord, revealing their nefarious intentions in public—

thus reshaping community sentiment toward a much-desired harmony and unity.

Baniwa Prophets

Kamiko, or Venancio Anizetto Kamiko, was the greatest prophet in the history of the Baniwa, if not of all other movements that have arisen in the northwest Amazon region since the mid-nineteenth century (see Wright 2002 for a complete listing). He was of the Dzauinai phratry, which inhabited the middle Içana and upper Guainía rivers. His power and fame extended throughout the northwest Amazon region during the second half of the nineteenth century, and he was known as the "Christ of the Içana." There are numerous histories told about him by the Baniwa, Tariana, and Desana of the Brazilian northwest Amazon, and also by the Wakuenai, kin of the Baniwa, in Venezuela. There are various anthropological publications about Kamiko, based on analysis of written documents from the mid-nineteenth century and on the oral histories.

The tradition presented here was told to me in July 2001 by João Fontes, a Hohodene elder of the large Hohodene village of Ucuqui Cachoeira on the upper Aiary River. It was narrated in Baniwa and translated to Portuguese by the narrator's son, Albino Fontes. The tradition is about two prophets—Kamiko and his son Uétsu Mikuiri (the term *mikuiri* is used to refer to deceased persons). According to the calculations that I and the narrators made, Uétsu lived in the first half of this century. Kamiko, according to historical records, died in 1903.

Never before has a tradition about Kamiko's son been recorded. In fact, I began researching oral histories about Baniwa prophets in 1976, but at that time and until 2002 the Baniwa never told me anything about Uétsu; rather, they recounted pieces of stories about other powerful shamans of the past, including Kamiko. When I asked them why they never told the tradition before, knowing my interest in their histories, they responded that in the 1970s the story was still being organized and constructed, and the experience with Uétsu was too recent to have elaborated the narrative. A generation later, the narrative had become fully elaborated. Both prophets were considered messiahs whose powers and knowledge surpassed various attempts by the white men to kill them. Most important, both utilized their powers of clairvoyance gained from the visions produced by the use of *pariká*, shamanic snuff (*Virola* sp.), and the hallucinogenic plant *caapi* (*Banisteriopsis caapi*), as well as their wisdom to control, if not eradicate, the practice of witchcraft in Baniwa communities. Both, however, suffered great losses in the process as a result of the treachery of their enemies.

My transcription of the tradition is given below; I include my questions and other information in brackets.

Kamiko was a *pajé* [shaman] of the Dzauinai tribe [phratry]. He lived long ago. He could see well; he could see everything [referring to the shamanic power of vision, clairvoyance]. He lived in Tunui [on the middle Içana]. He saw who had poison, *manhene*, and ordered them to throw the poison away. He ordered whoever had poison to take it out of where it was hidden, and he could tell people, "you have evil stuff." [Q: He knew who had it?] He knew. He would arrive in a community. Then at night, his knowledge would show him where people had poison buried. His knowledge would indicate who had it and where it was buried. He already knew in his dream at night. If it was hidden in the water [stream], at a meter's depth, he knew where the poison was. Everything, he already knew. Then he would join everyone from the community together and communicate to them everything, indicating the people who had poison. The people who didn't have poison wouldn't appear in his dream. Those who had it, even if it was hidden in a really difficult place in a stream, he would order them to find and dig it up. After, he would put it altogether in the center of the village. Others that he indicated would go and dig up their poison. One after another until he found all the poison. Then, he would get everyone together to give them advice. Only those who had poison, for those who didn't have poison had nothing to do with what he had to say.

Then... he went to various communities doing the same things. He would come to a community, and in his dream, his knowledge would show who had poison and where it was. The next day, he would order people to make a drinking fest. Then after the fest, he would speak to those who had poison, "you have it, in such-and-such place you are hiding it." Then he would call another and say, "you have poison, in such-and-such a place you are hiding it."

He would go to other communities, like Nazaré, then farther downriver. ... There, it seems, someone made a complaint against him to the whites saying that Kamiko was calling himself a saint. The white men came, captured, and took him prisoner to see whether he really was resistant, if he really was a saint. They prepared a coffin, put Kamiko inside the coffin and threw him into the river. He stayed one whole night inside the coffin at the bottom of the river. Next day, they took the coffin out of the river, opened it, and he was inside, but still alive. During the night, his soul had gone out of the coffin and went wandering about. Then they believed that Kamiko really was a saint.

Kamiko cured various sicknesses, he did shamanism, always curing the sick. Then, later, he died. [Q: How did he die?] The white men took him and sent him away. Those who had poison were angry with him and complained about him to the whites requesting that they remove him from the area. And so it was, the white man made this decision. The whites took him far away, way beyond Manaus, and he died there. The saint said, "I will not seek to avenge myself. I will go away, I will seek to die as Jesus died," Kamiko said that. And that was the end.

[Q: Did Kamiko say he would come back one day?] No, he died there among the whites. [Q: And did he have children? Or grandchildren who are alive today?] He had one son. His son's tomb is on the Ake river, Kamiko's son. Today, people always go there. His name was Uétsu. He was also captured by the whites. And the whites did exactly the same things to him as they did with his father. They came, took him prisoner, made a coffin, made him get inside the coffin, and threw him into the river. After an hour, they took the coffin out of the river, opened it, and he was alive, holding a Bible in his hand. The white man did exactly as he did with his father. Learned men from Caracas came to do that to him. They thought he was deceiving, lying to the people. So, they came to prove whether he really was a saint. Two people came, learned men from Caracas. There they asked him, "is it true you are a wise man? A saint? God?" "No, I am not God," Uétsu replied. "Because most people say that you are God, that you cure, do everything. We are going to prove whether you are a saint or not. We are going to make a coffin and put you in the river for an hour." "Alright," Uétsu replied and gave himself up. They made the coffin, made the lid of the coffin, put him inside, and tied it up. But before closing it, Uétsu's soul left his body. They put the coffin in the river for an hour at two meters' depth. After an hour, they took it out, opened it, and he was fine.

Then Uétsu said, "now, you did it to me. It's my turn to do to you what you did to me. So our Lord ordered, you are learned men, let's prove whether you have knowledge equal to mine. So our Lord ordered." Seeing that he was right, one of the learned men got in the coffin. They did exactly as they had done to him. After an hour, they took the coffin out, and that learned man was already dead. The other learned man who was there with him became frightened. He was afraid because it was true what they had told him. He said, "see how this one is dead and the other is fine." Then the learned man went away, he was afraid of Uétsu.

[Q: Where did Uétsu live, in which village?] On the upper Río Negro, on the Guainía, but he didn't have a fixed community. He lived almost like a nomad. He lived in one place for three months, another two months. Thus was his life, he didn't have a fixed community.

The learned men ended up believing that he really had knowledge, that he was a saint. And people spread the word of his fame, saying, "there, there is a man who is a saint, who has knowledge, who is a diviner." They began spreading word of his fame, saying that he was a good *pajé*. There people began believing that he was a good saint.

He went around making festivals. And the fests, the elders didn't know when these fests would happen. He would go in the midst of the people and announce, "tomorrow there is going to be a fest. Prepare for it, with *caxiri* [manioc beer]. Our heavenly Father will also make a fest with his angels. We also are going to make a fest. Let's imitate him." After, he would go to another community and do the same thing.

He attracted a lot of people, many people followed him. During the fest, he would call each person and give them counsel, "you have wickedness, you have a bad thing that kills people. Don't do that. Throw away the bad stuff that you have so that we can live well together, in tranquillity." If they came happily, he would say nothing, but if a person came with the thought to do evil, he would tell them, "throw that evil stuff away, let's live as one family." If a woman came with the thought to cause harm to a man with *pussanga* charm,[17] he would say, "that *pussanga* causes harm, don't do that." He would advise, "this advice is not made by me"; he would say, "our heavenly Father has sent me to give counsel to you. Throw that evil stuff away so that we can live well." His objective was to bring people together and to give them counsel.

[Q: How did he get so much power to do this? How is it that he knew how to see everything?] Because he was a *pajé* he used *pariká* [shamanic snuff], even the *pariká* of the Wanhíwa.

One day, people began to disbelieve in him, saying, "can it really be that this man is a saint?" Then, they started poisoning Uétsu's sons. He performed the *pajé*'s ceremonies to cure them, but his first son ended up dying. So he called the people together to get rid of the evil that they had done, but people said, "why is it that he didn't cure his son, if he is a saint?" The people became revolted with him. His wife remained silent. Later, they poisoned his second and third sons. He performed the *pajé*'s cures on them, with *pariká* and everything else, but even so, they ended up dying.

Then his wife began to disbelieve him. She complained, "so many times you have said you are a saint, counseled these people, seen the wickedness of each one, yet you didn't even cure our son. You are false, you are speaking nonsense." She disbelieved in him, she was revolted with him. She ordered him to get his shaman's rattle and said, "throw this away. This is not the truth. You don't cure." Then he said to her, "I will die with *pariká*." She was revolted, but he said he would die with *pariká*. He began to snuff. He called his wife, "look, blow [*pariká*] for me, for me to die." His wife blew *pariká* for him and he fell, unconscious. From ten in the morning until five in the afternoon, then he got up. He was fine. And thus he increased his knowledge of the world more and more. With *pariká*, you don't really die, there is no way to really die with it. It only makes you more intelligent, know the world more. After, he said, "now I am going to use the *caapi* [plant] of the Wanhíwa, with *niopo* [*pariká* of the Wanhíwa]." Then he prepared the *caapi*, a gourdful of it, drank it, and fell unconscious again. They said he was dead, but *caapi* is like *pariká*. He remained unconscious until five in the afternoon when he got up again. While he was unconscious, he walked on the vine [that is, his soul journeyed on the *caapi* vine] until the end of the vine, then came back.

So each time he took it, he deepened his knowledge. He came to know the angels, he saw all those people who had died, his father, his mother, his brother. All those he saw, he even conversed with them. That is the consequence of *caapi*. The dead sent messages to people who were still alive, and he would pass on the messages, their remembrances. He conversed with the dead and each time, he passed on messages. And so he deepened his knowledge, really showing that he saw the dead.

Then one day he went fishing, downriver. At a certain point, he stayed still, fixing his fishing line, when suddenly he heard a noise of people behind him. He turned around to see, and it was his deceased sister. The more she approached him, he felt her presence until he fell unconscious in the canoe. His sister came close to him, passing her perfume over him. The other dead gave him medicine and the world opened more for him. The dead took him to the world of the dead. "We live here, that other family [of the dead] lives here. There is the house of the Lord. This here is the house of God"—which shone—"God, the house of God"—very beautiful, brilliant, resplendant, just as the sun when it rises, like gold. Then, after they showed him, they came back and said, "here is where we live when people die."

Then, they say, Uétsu conversed with God, with our Lord, who said, "look, from now on, you really will be a saint, you can already say this to people. You will get to your house. When you get to your house, don't tell about what you saw. Not even news about your sister, that perfume that she passed over you, nothing that you saw. Act as though you had seen nothing."

Then he went back to his house. And he didn't tell anything. From then on, he would always see our Lord. When he slept, they say that he would wake up in his dream and sing, "Gloria, Gloria Jesus." Every time he would sleep, he would sing this song. In his dream, he would wake up, awaken to the other world. Then his wife got tired of hearing those words, "why are you singing that when you sleep? What's the matter with you, what do you feel?" "No," he answered, "I am dreaming, God sent this dreamwork." "It's too much!" she complained.

Wherever he went, he always met up with that sister of his and those dead people, his deceased father and mother. The dead people waited for him and would tell him, "it will be like this, people will come who want to poison you." They informed him, alerting him, "people will come wanting to poison you. Tell them to get rid of that wickedness and live well." They always guided him.

From that time on, he became "authorized" to say what he saw. He came back and told his wife, "I have seen your dead father, the time has come to say that I have seen the saints and the dead." He told this to his wife. Thus the word spread. His wife told other women, "look, my husband is like this," and they told other women. She went around telling.

And the people who had bad omens, Uétsu knew how to see and explain [the meaning of the bad omens]. Everything that a person saw in those bad omens, he would fix and advise, "I saw such and such." He didn't have to wait for night, he would just roll himself up in his hammock, then the spirit would come and stay just a short while, not even an hour. Then he would get up and say, "you saw that bad omen? Somebody is going to poison you. But our Lord has left it so that nothing will happen to you." Thus he was showing his capacity.

So because of these consultations that people made with him, he began attracting more people. More people came. They wanted him to turn into a king for them, a chief. There were those people who rowed a canoe for him like a king, a chief, a president. He had rowers, he had people who gave food to him, he had people who accompanied him. Even the people wanted him to be king. But he didn't want this. Our Lord gave him orders, but ones that didn't allow that he put himself as chief. He wanted to be equal to the other people. Equal—neither superior nor inferior.

In this work of attracting people, he went up the Içana and Aiary rivers. He traveled a lot on the Aiary river, from Jandú [near the mouth of the Aiary] to Seringa Rupitá [at the headwaters of the Uaraná, a tributary stream of the upper Aiary]. He went to live with Hohodene kin, the deceased Pedro Fontes [grandfather of the narrator]; he was Pedro's brother-cousin [i.e., of the same phratry but different sibs].[18] He was an *Adzanene* [younger sib-brother to the Hohodene, of the Hohodene phratry], but he was an elder brother because of his mother, he was the son of an elder brother. He traveled all over the Içana area and its tributaries, all the Río Negro. He spoke many languages: Venezuelan, Baniwa, Curipaco, Werekena. He held many, many fests in the communities of Nazaré, Ambaúba, Taiauassú, Tucunaré—all on the lower Içana.

[Q: What happened to him?] Well, after he became a wise man, when people came with the thought of poisoning him, during the night, in his dream, he was advised, "that person is bringing poison for you, so watch out for him." He would greet the person and say, "look, you have the bad intention to poison me." He was really proving that he already knew that others were wanting to destroy him, to do evil.

Until there came a time when God didn't advise him anymore. Because the time for him to leave this world had come. Then, people poisoned him. God himself didn't say anything to him, for it was already time for him to leave this world. [Q: But who poisoned him?] Pará thayri, Paráthana. The land of the Paráthana lies below [the rapids of] Ambaúba, on the Pará stream. So he went back to the upper Guainía, because he always traveled there. But there, many people came together, and in order for there not to be so many people he went to another place. But in each place, people came together. [Q: Where was he buried?] On the Guainía. His tomb is on the Ake River. But his body was divided in two. One part was buried in Macarenta on the Ake; another part in Yauitá in Venezuela. [Q: Why was it divided like that?] Because he really was a saint. Today, people pray to him. His tomb serves as a place for people to come to consult him. When a person sees an evil omen, people ask that he bless and protect them. And it has worked, the tomb is working even today.

He said that he himself would return six days after his death. His wife took care of his body. Six days passed and she took care of it. Then it began to rot, dripping water. His wife let the water drip into a pan. Then the people who had poisoned him, his enemies, spoke to her, "you're suffering with this dead, let us take care of him." His enemies said. A day before he would come back to life, she left him, she put his body in the hands of his enemies. Then the day came. Those who were keeping watch over him began to scream because he made an omen. That was the end of his life. If he had come back to life, he would never again die. He would be immortal. Like Jesus. He wouldn't die. That ends this story. After him, there was never again another person like him.

Interpretation of the Tradition of Kamiko

Witchcraft and sorcery, as we have seen, are critical questions for the Baniwa. In another study (1998), I have shown how witchcraft accusations within a community reflect actual interpersonal conflicts and explosive tensions in intercommunity relations, producing a discourse that attributes all occurrences of witchcraft—real or suspect—to designated individuals marked as witches. If poison and witchcraft have the potential to literally destroy a community, even from within, what are the means that the Baniwa have to protect themselves against it or even to prevent outbreaks of witchcraft? One of these certainly is the shamans' cures through which, in the encounter with the Owner of Sickness and poison, Kuwai, the shaman can request the medicine necessary to cure the cases of poison in This World. Another mechanism is to prevent people from using poison—that is, to discover who has poison within the community and wage a campaign to eradicate it. Again, it is the *pajés* who, through the clairvoyance that *pariká* gives them, know who has poison and where it is hidden (either buried or at the bottom of a stream). This was the way Kamiko and Uétsu initially controlled witchcraft in Baniwa communities.

In order to prevent future outbreaks, however, they had to shape community sentiments against the use of any substance that might ruin the health and well-being of the people. Thus, they counseled the people against poison and they organized fests to encourage the collective sentiment of happiness among the members of a community or, in other words, of *comunitas* among an "assembly of believers" (Sullivan 1988). The prophets took advantage of the fests to preach and to act against those who had poison by exposing them in public and giving them advice. In short, both prophets sought to create a sentiment of community unity and "throw away" everything that could provoke misunderstanding, conflict, envy, jealousy, resentment—all motives for practicing witchcraft.

The two prophets were messiahs, or saints in the terminology of Amazonian popular Catholicism, for, as the story relates, they resisted the attempts of the white man to kill them by suffocation, thus demonstrating the superiority of their knowledge over that of the two "learned men" (*doutores*) from Caracas (a characteristic of many messianic myths). The irony of history, however, is that what ended up destroying the two prophets did not come from outside but from among their own people. It was the reaction (*revolta*) against them of the poison-owners and those who practiced witchcraft, for having exposed them in public. In the case of Uétsu, witches killed three of his sons; and, inexplicably, he was unable to avoid their deaths by poisoning. Revealing, advising, and seeking to create a collective sentiment proved to be insufficient to combat or prevent the treachery of the witches.

Uétsu then adopted a more radical stance than that used by his father who, victimized by the witches, simply went away and like Christ didn't seek to avenge himself. Uétsu sought "to die" by taking the very potent mixture used by the Wanhíwa (Guahibo) Indians of the *llanos* of Colombia, which combines *caapi* with *pariká*. In shamanic language, "to die" means to go farther in shamanic journeys to the Other World in order to acquire deeper knowledge. As a result Uétsu developed the power to foresee, not just to reveal and advise as before. This new power was acquired through communication with the souls of the dead and with Dio (God) himself. Thus Uétsu could foretell when a person was about to suffer an attack from a witch, and he could change what most afflicted and terrified people—evil omens, signs of inevitable death.

In order to avoid being a victim of peoples' envy and sure poisoning, Uétsu refused to be considered a "king, chief, or president," as people wished; that is, he refused to solidify a hierarchical position of centralized authority among the people, although it is evident that he had many followers who accompanied him from village to village and took care of him, and that he was capable of attracting many people to his fests and ceremonies. His power came from his knowledge and not from an accumulation of political prestige, goods, or force. There is thus no basis for sustaining the argument, suggested by some anthropological analyses, that prophetic movements represent periodic efforts to install chiefdoms; to the contrary, the tradition of Uétsu supports the idea that prophetic movements were more in line with states of egalitarian *comunitas*.

Both prophets, however, were inevitably subject to the determinations of destiny. The Baniwa say that the times of coming into this world and leaving it are predetermined, or "marked." Uétsu stopped receiving divine messages and was poisoned; and once again wickedness and weakness prevailed, preventing him from returning and becoming immortal (had his wife resisted his enemies and gathered all his mortal remains, as he instructed her, he would have revived). Nevertheless, his "knowledge," or wisdom, remained in this world, together with his mortal remains at his tomb, in order to be able to help his kin and those who requested his protection following his burial.

Uétsu's body was "divided" into two parts (a reminder of dismembered Catholic saints, or even further afield, the myth of Inkarri, whose body was quartered and buried in separate places) both of which continue to protect his people. The significance of the division of Uétsu's body, however, is still not yet clear to me: the other traditions that I am aware of say that Kamiko's tomb is on the Ake River but say nothing about the tomb of his son in Yauitá. Furthermore, different from most of the other traditions of Kamiko, this says that the prophet was "removed from the area" and sent far away, "beyond Manaus," which requires further clarification.

In comparing the mortal deaths of each of the prophets with others who have arisen after them, Kamiko sought to die "like Christ"—that is, revive in another place but without seeking vengeance, another reform in Baniwa ethics—but for many Baniwa he continues to be a protector. It was the same way with Uétsu, who would have died and revived "like Christ," although he sent an evil omen against his enemies, implying that they inevitably died shortly afterward. Many Baniwa visit Uétsu's tomb because they still consider him a "saint," and they leave coins and other items on the tomb to ask his protection. This prophetic consciousness (in both belief and practice) is reflected in the respect with which the Hohodene today have for another powerful *pajé* who died in the 1970s. He was the father of one of my shaman-teachers and the master of various other *pajés* who considered him a prophet, a "wise man." According to what one of his exapprentices explained to me several years ago, Guilherme (or Kudui) was of the Hohodene phratry; he was an exapprentice of the master-*pajé* Kumadeyon, of the Dzauinai phratry, who in turn was exapprentice of the *pajé* Heriwaipe, a disciple of Kamiko. In the mid-1950s, Kudui already had considerable fame among the Baniwa, and he advised his followers before dying that, "when I die, my soul will leave my body, but I will remain with you still." That is, his body was buried (significantly on the island called Warukwa, the mythical home of the creator/transformer Nhiãperikuli), but "his thought [that is, his wisdom] still continues alive." His "soul" made the normal journey of the souls of the dead, but later "it came back and entered his body again, so that he could explain things for us," an exapprentice explained. People today also leave payments (coins) on top of his tomb and ask for his protection against sicknesses, evil omens, etc., as they do with Kamiko, Uétsu, and all other wise men or prophets. In all these cases, we see a prophetic consciousness (in an earlier work [1998] I called it "millenarian consciousness," which perhaps is too Western in its connotations). The prophets, it is worth repeating, are not just any *pajés* but rather only those who have reached a superior level of knowledge, and whose knowledge—acquired through the constant use of *pariká* and *caapi*—transcends mortal time.

Baniwa conversion en masse to evangelical protestantism in the 1950s and 1960s was thus nothing more than a dejá vu experience for many. Recall that Kamiko and Uétsu counseled the people to "throw away" poison and to live in peace and harmony. Several times in the past in Baniwa oral histories, practices and institutions have been abandoned with the objective of producing a desired change. For example, Baniwa sibs "abandoned" the institution of warfare because it was leading to the end of their society—that is, warrior sibs were "finishing off with people." With the objective of reconstructing social alliances and guaranteeing a prosperous future, they "threw away" all of their weapons of war into the river and forgot them. In the same way, the prophets counseled the people of various communities to "throw away" poison and abandon the practice of witchcraft. Later, Sophie Muller, the North American missionary who sparked Baniwa conversion to evangelicalism told them to abandon their practices of drinking *caxiri*, smoking tobacco, and celebrating the ancient rituals. She told the *pajés* to "throw away" their instruments (rattles, stones, crystals, etc.—many of which are considered the shamans' weapons) into the river.

There is also a notable similarity in the way in which the practices considered to be highly secret (witchcraft, shamanism, sacred flutes, and trumpets) are exposed in public before being abandoned. Kamiko and Uétsu publicly indicated the people who had poison as well as their hiding places for it, making these people pile up their poison in the central plaza of the village, where he then counseled them before ordering them to throw the poison away. The converted disciples of Sophie Muller likewise went around to villages where they told the men to pile up the sacred flutes and trumpets—considered highly secret and prohibited from the sight of women and children under pain of death by poison if exposed in public—on the central plaza of the village before they threw them away or burned them. In the dialectical tension between states or conditions of human existence that are perceived to be threatened by the real existence of evil or a catastrophic end—that is, the predominance of the dark side of consciousness—and those of harmony, unity, and prosperity—the light side of consciousness—then the means by which society takes the first step to restore order is to "throw away," abandon, or provoke a rupture with the instruments or material of destruction and then reshape peoples' consciousness.

Final Considerations

Together with their campaign to eradicate witchcraft, Kamiko and Uétsu sought to create a new religious order by incorporating Christian ritual practices such as baptism, marriage, and Christian names with fests celebrated in the traditional styles of the *pudali* drinking fests. They sought to create a new mode of consciousness and a new way of living together—in short, a utopia—free from what most ruined peoples' lives: witchcraft. In relation to the white man, there was never any question from the beginning that the prophets' wisdom could overcome the efforts of the "learned men" to destroy them.

In a similar way, Sophie Muller left the control of evangelicalism in the hands of the pastors and deacons she trained, thus producing the means by which evangelical knowledge could be transformed into the basis for the production of a new generation of believers who, from then on, would reproduce this process. As I have argued elsewhere (1999), the Baniwa understood that conversion would reestablish their communitarian way of life, drastically disorganized by the extractivist regime. To be sure, the marginal period of transition to the new religion was marked by intense conflicts, above all because what was being "left behind" (such as the *pudali* drinking fests) had traditionally served to administer intercommunity relations and create solidarity among affines, while the new order imposed another opposition between believers and nonbelievers, thus realigning already-existing political divisions into religious ones but without the means to administer this opposition. Thus, hostilities and (possibly) witchcraft accusations increased initially among groups as a result of the shifts produced in community political alignments. Furthermore, neither the explanations offered by the evangelical missionaries for deaths nor the means for overcoming lethal sicknesses proved to be adequate, unlike the "knowledge" of the prophets that survived their deaths and that had a built-in guarantee of protection against evil omens. Thus, even evangelical *crentes* (believers) continued visiting their tombs long after Protestant conversion had solidified.

Both utopias were instigated and plagued by the same destructive force: witchcraft. In the same way that the wise men suffered losses due to the revolt of their enemies, from the beginning the Baniwa detected weak points in the utopia of the evangelicals. The problem of evil and wickedness continued to exist, but because converts had "thrown away" nearly everything that was capable of combating witchcraft (except medicinal plants, antidotes to poison, and curing spells) there was no way to go back to them, and everything indicates that today among the *crentes* the abuse of witchcraft is increasing due to new forms such as *macumba* introduced by the Mestizos of the city of São Gabriel. Even so, the majority of the Baniwa continue to profess the *crente* religion and are also converting to the newer pentecostal religions such as the Assembly of God and Seventh Day Adventism. At the same time, however, they continue to visit the tombs of their wise men, nourishing the hope that perhaps through discipline and a rigorously ordered life, or through the immortal knowledge of the wise men, the problem of evil—even if it can never be eradicated because it is inherent to the nature of existence—can at least be controlled.

Notes

The research on which this paper is based was conducted in 1976–1977 for my doctoral dissertation; and in 1997, 1999, 2000, and 2001 with the generous assistance of the Harry Frank Guggenheim Foundation, and as collaborator of the Socio-Environmental Institute (ISA) / *Institut pour Récherche sur Développement* (IRD) in the project "Socio-Cultural and Economic Risk Factors for HIV and Tuberculosis in the Region of the Upper Río Negro (Brazilian Amazon) (1998–2000)." I am grateful to the Hohodene shamans and elders of the Aiary River who have always taught me with great patience and wisdom.

This essay was first prepared for presentation at the session of the Society for the Anthropology of Consciousness and the Society for Latin American Anthropology during the annual meeting of the American Anthropological Association, New Orleans, November 2002.

1   I am here distinguishing witchcraft from sorcery in a way that is different from the definitions used by Evans-Pritchard in his classic study (1937). For the Zande, witchcraft refers to a substance in the body of certain persons that emanates from that person causing injury to health and property (9); sorcery is magic that is considered illicit or immoral and involves bad medicines and/or spells. For the Baniwa, I use witchcraft to refer to the *manipulation* of poisonous substances (in contrast to the *emanation* of substances from the witch) for the purpose of killing. Sorcery, on the other hand, is the use of evil spells to harm or kill; anyone can practice either or both, although individuals may specialize in certain kinds of spells or in poisoning.

2   Various people drew attention to the idea that *manhene* "affects the blood" of the victim; "sucking the blood" inside the victim's stomach and thus producing anemia.

Others observed that victims vomit so much blood that they have difficulty in recovering from the loss; hence the body "dries out." This is why tuberculosis is considered by traditional Baniwa to be a form of *manhene*.

3 In my research I was able to determine fourteen different kinds of *manhene*; space limitations, however, do not permit presenting them here. In Goldman's research (1963:268–69) with the neighboring Cubeo of the Querary and Cuduiary rivers in Colombia he was able to determine a number of plant poisons equivalent to those the Baniwa knew.

4 In this, they demonstrate patterns that are similar to the Cubeo. In his classic monograph, Goldman writes that "the arts of killing or of causing serious illness are to the Cubeo mind extraordinarily well developed. As the Indians see it, most deaths, illnesses, and misfortunes are products of human malevolence. . . . All . . . live in dread of sorcery" (1963:266).

5 In the early 1950s, the Brazilian ethnologist Eduardo Galvão also noted that there were three specialist roles in Baniwa society: the *maríri*, or shaman, who uses *maracá* rattles and snuffs the hallucinogenic *pariká* to perform cures; *dzuri*, or chant-owner, who uses primarily orations and tobacco, *mutawari*; and the *mah~eminare* (equivalent to the *manhene iminali*, poison-owner), who are the sorcerers, or *matiára* in *língua geral* (Galvão 1954:164–66). My definition of sorcerer differs from that of Galvão, being restricted to the blowing of spells to inflict harm and not the use of poison to kill. On Baniwa shamanism, see Wright 1992, 1996, 1998; on chanters, see Hill 1993.

6 For the Cubeo, Goldman distinguishes between the methods of killing undertaken by the *yaví* (jaguar) shamans, and the "nonprofessional sorcerer" whom the Cubeo feared even more: "The arts of sorcery, which include the arts of poisoning, are known to all men and are believed to be used by all men" (1963:266).

7 Dreams often serve as warnings in Baniwa culture. Thus, if one dreams of a monkey or sloth, or of being drunk on *cachaça*, these images refer to the danger of being poisoned by *manhene*.

8 Here one is reminded of Overing's analysis of the "aesthetics of conviviality" (Overing and Passes 2000).

9 I use the word "spell" and not "chant" to distinguish these speech forms from those used in curing, which may be chanted, and the special set of initiation chants called *kalidzamai*. Given their very nature, these spells are never chanted but rather spoken, or thought, in secrecy. The word "oration" likewise is not an accurate description, referring more to the speech of community leaders.

10 As with *manhene*, dreams may reveal to a person if she or he should be aware of possible sorcery attacks. For example, if a person dreams of many snakes, or of electric eels, or of *tocandira* ants—all of which have poisonous bites or stings—these are signs of impending *hiuiathi*.

11 In the research I have been conducting since 1999 with Dr. Luiza Garnelo of the *Universidade de Amazonas*, we have identified some twenty different conditions classified under the category of *hiuiathi*.

12 Goldman makes some very interesting observations on Cubeo *yaví* shamans, among which he describes the method of "dirt killing" (identical to *iupithatem*) which the *yavís* had learned from "Indians from the Rio Negro in Venezuela" (1963:266–67).

13 A more complete account is found in *The Call of the Curassow and the Land of the*

Guahibo Indians (1990), the diary of two adventurers and filmmakers, Felix DiGiovanni and Paul Beer, who in 1940–1941 traveled to the llanos of southeastern Colombia to make a documentary film on the Guahibo of the Vichada. According to the authors, the Guahibo were "held in high esteem" for their "occult powers" to avenge deaths and were frequently sought to perform such services by the Baniwa of the Atabapo River, "to circumvent their enemies and appease the death of their loved ones.... It is their belief that a person dies because an enemy has cast a potent spell over him, from which he is unable to recover. It follows, therefore, that it is the duty of his kinsmen to avenge his death" (107–9). Morey and Metzger's 1974 monograph on the Guahibo includes further observations that refer to the shaman's capacity to undertake vengeance at a distance, although they suggest that the sorcerer is often "of another band" of Guahibo: "In most cases, the sorcery is attributed to another Guahibo (although almost never to a close consanguineal), emphasizing the lack of specific fears of other, foreign tribes" (111). The ethnographers make no reference, however, to services performed for other peoples, such as the Baniwa.

14 The response "fear of reprisal" was what the shamans repeatedly offered to me when I pressed them to find out why they themselves, knowing that a certain witch had killed numerous people in a village, didn't simply eliminate him. Because, they said, if they themselves took vengeance, then the family of the victim could take the dirt to the Guahibo, who would then tell who was responsible and send a counterattack against them and their family. If it is the shaman of another distant group (and not everyone can or is willing to make the long and dangerous journey), the question is dislocated to the outside, to shamans who are considered more powerful than their own. And the victim of the Guahibo shamans, besides confessing the names of all those whom he has killed, "will bite his tongue" and not tell who it was that paid the Wanhíwa to take vengeance against him. It is an effective system, even more so because *iupithatem* is like certain kinds of witchcraft poisoning or *manhene* (remembering that a literal translation of this word is "one does not know") in that it leads to madness and there is no way of bringing it under control or of curing it by orations or shamanic extraction.

Baniwa shamans, however, do admit to having the power to attack other shamans at a distance and even to kill them. They say they also have the power, if paid well, to eliminate whole villages with a single blow of lightning. Thus their powers are not limited to curing, although in relation to *manhene*, they insist that they do not get involved but rather seek the Guahibo to undertake vengeance. Finally, I think that it is consistent with the Baniwa ethos (as it is to many other South American peoples) to attribute greater shamanic powers to outside or other groups. In the history of Baniwa prophetic movements, for example, the most powerful prophets were from the outside, or distant Baniwa phratries to the north. As mentioned, the Baniwa also believe that the most potent poisonous plants come from the hills of southern Venezuela.

15 In Morey and Metzger's 1974 monograph, they clarify the nature and power of the Guahibo shaman's rock: "The shaman also has his magic rock (*wánali*), a piece of crystalline rock which defracts light, said to have been given to him by *kúwai* or one of his familiars. The light from the crystalline mass is believed to have a deadly effect. Supposedly it is only necessary for the shaman to wave it in front of, or point it at, his victim, to induce sickness or death. The rock is also used in the interests of justice. One ceremony involving the discovery and punishment of the party responsible

for a death is as follows: the shaman cuts off the little finger of the left hand of the corpse and boils it in a specific type of tree sap, all the while chanting the appropriate formula. The rising vapor is said to flow to where the guilty sorcerer is and force his *húmpe* [spirit] to leave his body and come—whereupon it is cut up and destroyed by the shaman wielding his magic rock (1974:113).

16. The Baniwa relate that the Guahibo acquired these extraordinary powers in the following manner: In ancient times, there was a shaman called Huiti Uanakale who looked for shamans' powers, or *malikhai*. He obtained much power but began to lose control and to kill people. He transformed into an enormous black jaguar. After he had killed many people, he went on to kill his own family: his wife's father and mother, his own wife, children, and other families. As he became more and more of a menace, his kin got together and killed him; it was Huiti Uanakale himself who recommended that they kill him. He instructed them to burn his body, but instead they simply cut off his head and threw it into the river. The head floated downriver still with its brains and the knowledge of how to cause all sicknesses and also how to cure them.

    When the head reached a place a bit above Juívitera (on the Içana River), the Guahibo shamans called Dzauinaikada got the head, took out the brains, and got all the shamanic powers in them, thus learning all sorts of evil things. After the Guahibo had taken out the brains, the head continued on downriver, but already empty. In that time, the Guahibo shamans were of a people called Padali (note Koch-Grunberg's reference to the people called Pidzári), who were affines of the Baniwa of the Aiary River. After they had learned all these things, they began to transform into jaguars, forest-spirits, and other animals; they threw sickness-giving spirit darts onto people and ate people.

    The story goes on to tell of a man who secretly overheard four Guahibo jaguar-shamans planning to kill and devour the people of his village. The man forewarned the people who eventually killed the four shamans. Nevertheless, other Guahibo had succeeded in getting their power to kill.

    This story reveals that the Guahibo were ancient dwellers of the Aiary, affines to the Baniwa. They obtained extraordinarily dangerous powers to transform and kill from an ancestral jaguar-shaman, who had lost control over his powers, and they thus became true "jaguar-shamans" or, as the Hohodene today say, *pariká* jaguars (*dzato dzauika*), permanently roaming on the edges of this world, seeking to kill and devour their victims. The Baniwa were able to get rid of the Guahibo as immediate and internal threats, although these jaguar-shamans continue to be owners of dangerous powers to kill at a distance.

    I am grateful to Dr. Luiza Garnelo for referring me to this story, which she obtained in her fieldwork with the Baniwa of the Içana River in Brazil.

17. The *pussanga* charm comes from a thin, crawling vine called *munutchi* that produces a powerful perfume. Girls who wish to cause harm use the leaf on boys, which causes strong headaches: "They start to go crazy, as though drunk, they want to run away, to flee." In the same way that a man who is jealous of a woman can ruin her life with poison, women can ruin a man's life by using *munutchi*.

18. The narrator said that, during the fests, Uétsu would perform marriages and baptisms. He even gave the narrator's elder brother his name, which means that he was at the height of his power when the narrator's elder brother—at that point around sixty-five years old—was born in the 1940s. The narrator's father, who in the 1970s was around seventy years old, served as a rower for Uétsu.

References

ACIRA (Associação das Comunidades Indígenas do Rio Aiari) and FOIRN (Federação das Organizações Indígenas do Rio Negro), eds. 1999. *Waferinaipe Ianheke: A sabedoria dos nossos antepassados. Histórias dos Hohodene e dos Walipere-dakenai do Río Aiari*. São Gabriel da Cachoeira, AM: ACIRA/FOIRN.

Brown, Michael F. 1989. "The Dark Side of the Shaman." *Natural History* (November): 8–10.

Carneiro, Robert. 1977. "Recent Observation of Shamanism and Witchcraft among the Kuikuru Indians of Central Brazil." *Annals of the New York Academy of Sciences* 293: 215–28.

Chaumeil, J. P. 1993. *Voir, savoir, pouvoir: Le chamanisme chez les Yagua du Nord-Est Pérou*. Paris: Éditions de l'École des Hautes Études en Sciences Sociales.

Di Giovanni, Felix. 1990. *The Call of the Curassow and the Land of the Guahíbo Indians*. Jamaica, N.Y.: Paula Di Educational Enterprises.

Dole, Gertrude. 1973. "Shamanism and Political Control among the Kuikuru." In *Peoples and Cultures of Native South America*, ed. Daniel R. Gross. 294–307. New York: Doubleday.

Evans-Pritchard, E. E. 1937. *Witchcraft, Oracles and Magic among the Azande*. Oxford: Clarendon Press.

Galvâo, Eduardo. 1951–54. Unpublished field notes. Library collection of the Museu Paranse Emílio Goeldi, Belém do Pará.

Goldman, Irving. 1963. *The Cubeo Indians of the Northwest Amazon*. Urbana: University of Illinois Press.

Gow, Peter. 1996. "River People: Shamanism and History in Western Amazonia." In *Shamanism, History, and the State*, ed. N. Thomas and C. Humphrey. 90–114. Ann Arbor: University of Michigan Press.

Hefner, R. W., ed. 1993. *Conversion to Christianity: Historical and Anthropological Perspectives on a Great Transformation*. Berkeley: University of California Press.

Hill, Jonathan. 1988. Rethinking History and Myth. Urbana: University of Illinois Press.

———. 1993. Keepers of the Sacred Chants. Tucson: University of Arizona Press.

Hugh-Jones, Stephen. 1996. Shamans, prophets, priests and pastors. In *Shamanism, History, and the State*, ed. N. Thomas and C. Humphrey, 32–75. Ann Arbor: University of Michigan Press.

Langdon, Jean, ed. 1992. *Portals of Power: Shamanism in South America*. Albuquerque: University of New Mexico Press.

Lévi-Strauss, Claude. 1967. "The Sorcerer and His Magic." In *Magic, Witchcraft and Curing*, ed. John Middleton. 23–42. New York: Doubleday.

Morey, Robert V., and Donald Metzger. 1974. "The Guahibo: People of the Savanna." *Acta Ethnologica et Linguistica* 31.

Overing, Joanna, and Alan Passes, eds. 2000. *The Anthropology of Love and Anger: The Aesthetics of Conviviality in Native Amazonia*. London: Routledge.

Sullivan, Lawrence E. 1988. *Icanchu's Drum: An Orientation to Meaning in South American Religions*. New York: Macmillan Press.

Taussig, Michael. 1987. *Shamanism, Colonialism, and the Wild Man: A Study in Terror and Healing*. Chicago: University of Chicago Press.

Turner, Terence. 1988. "Ethno-ethnohistory: Myth and History in Native South American Representations of Contact with Western Society." In *Rethinking History and Myth:*

Native South American Perspectives on the Past, ed. Jonathan Hill. 235–81. Urbana: University of Illinois Press.

Whitehead, Neil L. 2002. *Dark Shamans: Kanaimà and the Poetics of Violent Death*. Durham: Duke University Press.

Wilbert, Johannes. 1993. *Mystic Endowment: Religious Ethnography of the Warao Indians*. Cambridge: Harvard University Press.

Wright, Robin. 1992. "Guardians of the Cosmos: Baniwa Shamans and Prophets." In *History of Religions*. 32–58, 126–45. Chicago: University of Chicago Press.

——. 1996. " 'Aos que vão nascer': Um etnografia religiosa dos Índios Baniwa. Livre Docência." Thesis presented to the Department of Anthropology, IFCH, UNICAMP.

——. 1998. *Cosmos, Self, and History in Baniwa Religion: For Those Unborn*. Austin: University of Texas Press.

——. 1999. "O tempo de Sophie: História e cosmologia da conversão Baniwa." In *Transformando os deuses: Os múltiplos sentidos da conversão entre os povos indígenas no Brasil*, ed. Robin Wright. 115–216. Campinas: Editorial Unicamp.

——. 2002. "Prophetic Traditions among the Baniwa." In *Comparative Arawakan Histories: Rethinking, Language, Family, and Culture Area in Amazonia*, ed. Jonathan D. Hill and Fernando Santos-Granero. 269–94. Champaign: University of Illinois Press.

Wright, Robin, and Jonathan D. Hill. 1986. "History, Ritual and Myth: Nineteenth-Century Millenarian Movements in the Northwest Amazon." *Ethnohistory* 33 (1): 31–54.

Sorcery Beliefs, Transmission of Shamanic Knowledge, and Therapeutic Practice among the Desana of the Upper Río Negro Region, Brazil

Dominique Buchillet

Since the pioneering work of Evans-Pritchard (1937) on Azande concepts of witchcraft and sorcery and their connections with social relationships, the importance of beliefs in sorcery and witchcraft as explanations for misfortune, illness, and death has been widely reported from different parts of the world. Anthropologists have analyzed these beliefs from various theoretical frameworks—as a reflection of social structure and relationships and as a functional regulator of social equilibrium—or have examined their use in political and moral questions and/or in changing gender relations, or even have shown how witchcraft and sorcery beliefs and practices are the product of social and cultural change (Dole 1973; Douglas 1991; Lyons 1998; Marwick 1965; Turner 1957; Zelenietz 1981).

The "theory of the unity of knowledge" (Douglas 1991)—that is, that "those who can cure can also kill," and the resulting ambivalence of shamanic power are well documented in many Amerindian societies (Brown 1988; Buchillet 1990; Crocker 1985; Hugh-Jones 1994; Overing-Kaplan 1975; Vilaça 1999). Crocker (1985:237), for example, depicted the Bororo shaman as an "ambiguous, suspicious personage" and Brown (1988:104), after alluding to the "dubious social status" of the Aguaruna shaman, illustrated how, during the curing session, he strove to show his zeal in curing as a way not to be suspected of trying to bewitch the sick.

For the Desana Indians of the upper Río Negro region, the great majority of illnesses that affect people today are attributed to sorcery.[1] There are various forms of doing sorcery, one of which is based on evil spells that are cast in the direction of the future victim. Evil spells, along with their counterparts, therapeutic spells, are part of the current shamanic repertoire of one category of traditional healer (the *kumu*). As I have shown elsewhere (Buchillet 1990), the *kumu*'s abilities to cure and to kill derive from the same source: they are two complementary and intersecting developments of the same creative mythic speech. It remains, however, to explore the implications of this conception for the transmission of shamanic knowledge and for the *kumu*'s therapeutic practice. In this essay, I focus on the Desana's beliefs about poisoning and sorcery, seeking to clarify the social contexts in which sorcery suspicions occur as well as to show their importance in indigenous cosmology and mythology. I address the implications of these beliefs in one form of sorcery—the harm produced by evil spells—for the transmission of shamanic knowledge and the *kumu*'s therapeutic practice. I show that, in a certain way, sorcery beliefs impose some heavy limitations on the *kumu*'s work and on the dissemination of shamanic knowledge in this indigenous society.

The Desana of the Upper Río Negro Region

The Desana Indians, or ~~Umu~~koho masã, "People of the Universe," are a Tukanoan-speaking people who live with other groups of the same and/or other (Arawak and Maku) linguistic families in the upper Río Negro region of the northwest Amazon (Brazil) and in the Colombian Vaupés.[2] Numbering approximately 1,460 individuals in Brazil, they are divided into some sixty local communities along the Uaupés River[3] (a tributary of the upper Río Negro) and its two main tributaries, the Tiquié and the Papuri, and also along some of their navigable streams—in particular, the Umari, Cucura, and Castanha rivers of the Tiquié and the Urucu River of the Papuri.

The eastern Tukanoan peoples claim a common origin and history and form a homogeneous sociocultural group, whose main characteristics include: a common identity established in mythic history (until the dispersion in the Uaupés region of the various groups' ancestors) and in ritual practices and representations; the use of languages belonging to the same linguistic family; and a system of kinship and marriage founded on linguistic identity. Within this homogeneous system, the group is subdivided into exogamous units of patrilineal filiation, differentiated by language, territory of historical occupation, and a specialization in material culture. Members of the group are related to the other peoples of the region through a complex system of matrimonial alliances and/or ceremonial and economic relations. They are sedentary and their subsistence is based on shifting cultivation of bitter manioc (*Manihot esculenta* Cranz) combined with fishing, hunting, and gathering (fruits, insects).

This apparently homogeneous system should not hide, however, several differences among the various groups of the region or even between the sibs of the same language group. There are, for example, gradations in shamanic knowledge and also different attitudes concerning the shamans' knowledge and practices. In fact, the distribution of shamanic knowledge is unequal in the region. Certain groups, like the Desana, are acknowledged by others (as they recognize themselves) as specialists in matters of therapeutic or evil spells. Others, like the Arawakan Baniwa, are renowned for their extensive knowledge of poisonous plants and plant remedies. There are also differences in relation to certain aspects of the *kumu's* therapeutic practice between the linguistic groups (for example, spells are recited either silently or sung, or may be considered secret or not).

Like many other indigenous groups of lowland South America,[4] the Desana distinguish among various categories of traditional healers according to the source and nature of their power and knowledge and curing practices: the jaguar-shaman (*yee*) and the blower of spells (*kumu*). The *yee*, who derives his power from direct contact with spirits during a trance induced by the ingestion of hallucinogenic snuff (*Virola* spp. and/or *Anadenanthera peregrina*), is said to have the ability to transform himself into a jaguar in order to accomplish his goals and, in ways similar to the classical shaman as described in the ethnographic literature, effects cures by means of blowing tobacco smoke, massage, and sucking out pathogenic objects from the body and spitting them away. The *yee* is described as being able to see the illness inside the patient's body and to divine the cause of the evil, a capacity strictly associated in Desana thought with the inhalation of the hallucinogenic snuff. By contrast, the *kumu's* skills and reputation stem from his great knowledge and mastery of mythology and of spells to protect, cure and/or harm. Their curing ritual consists of the inaudible recitation of highly formalized therapeutic spells over the opening of a gourd (*Lagenaria siceria* Mol.) containing a liquid (water, boiled manioc juice, manioc flour gruel, or fruit juice, etc.) that is later given to the patient to drink, or over a plant that the *kumu* then rubs onto the patient's sick body-part. This liquid or plant gives the spell a material support and transfers it to the patient (Buchillet 1990, 1992).

In the past, these shamanic specialists had complementary functions: the *yee* effecting the diagnosis through a visionary or ecstatic state and through the sucking out from the patient's body harmful objects that symbolize the disease substance: the *kumu* "undoing" (as the Indians say) the disease process and restoring the bodily integrity of the patient through specific spells. These two functions, traditionally reserved for men, could be assumed by a single individual if, evidently, he had been trained in both practices. Among the Tukanoan-speaking groups, the *yea* (plural form of *yee*) have virtually disappeared as a result of the intolerant campaigns waged against them by the first Catholic Salesian missionaries. Since their installation in the region in the beginning of the twentieth century, these missionaries denounced shamanic practice as "charlatanism," destroyed the ancient communal households, robbed the *yee*'s diagnosing and curing instruments (gourd rattles, wooden darts, quartz crystals, snuff tubes, etc.), broke the pots of hallucinogenic drugs, etc. They are, in other words, responsible for the gradual disappearance of the jaguar-shamans, whom they perceived as the principal obstacles to Christian influence and as the main opponents to their presence and authority.

Whereas some *yea* fled from the missionaries to the lower Río Negro, others, considering that there was no chance for traditional culture to survive, refused to pass on their knowledge to apprentice shamans and also eventually abandoned their practice. Certain features of the *kumu*'s curing session—for example, its private and silent character—probably explain why this specialist survived missionary intolerance. As we have seen, the *kumu*'s practice is essentially based on the inaudible recitation of spells. Unlike the classic shamanic curing session, it does not require any public ceremony which must, or may, be attended by others. It is a solitary ritual. As I have shown elsewhere (Buchillet 1992), there is nothing to hear or even see. For this reason, the curing session is not thought of as a means of acquiring shamanic knowledge, as is usually the case in indigenous societies. Moreover, it is not a way for the *kumu* to demonstrate his knowledge or his skills to others in order to assert his reputation.

Exogenous Pathogenesis as Etiological Category among the Desana People

According to the Desana, the majority of traditional (or indigenous) illnesses are the result of exogenous aggression. This emphasis on exogenous pathogenesis is explicit in the vernacular term most commonly used to designate "illness": *doreri*. As a substantive form of the verb *dore* ("to send to," "to give an order to," "to command"), *doreri* qualifies the way the ailments that are imputed either to aggressions of aquatic and forest spirits (or animals) or to human malevolence are transmitted.[5]

In the first category (*wai [yukɨ]-masã doreri*, literally "sicknesses of the water and forest peoples"), illnesses are the result of an error of the sick person (dietary transgression, breaking rules concerning the cooking of game animals, abusive use of hunting charms, excessive hunting, etc.) and/or of others (the *kumu*'s involuntary forgetting of animal or spirit names during the recitation of protective spells in the life cycle rites or during the shamanic ritual to decontaminate food, for example). Illnesses attributed to aquatic or forest animals and spirits generally appear in an ambiguous fashion through a set of imprecise symptoms: headaches, fevers, nausea, digestive disorders, vomiting, nightmares, nonanxious recurrent dreams, muscular pains, back pains, sores, and so forth (see Buchillet 1983).

In relation to the second category, it should be noted that the indigenous languages of the region possess various terms to refer to sorcery—that is, to the conscious and intentional act to cause harm to a specific person or community, depending on the identity of the person who practices it and/or on the means used to do it. Sorcery has great importance as a cause of illness and death in sib genealogies, and it is one of the main causes of disorders that affect human beings today. It can be done through a variety of means, some of which presuppose a high degree of specialized knowledge of evil spells, or a special knowledge of poisonous plants.

Nima tɨɨãri refers to the common form of sorcery using cultivated or wild vegetal poisonous substances that are secretly put in the victim's food or drink and/or applied or rubbed onto an object that he or she uses. It is generally practiced during community drinking parties (widely known in the region by the *língua geral* term of *caxiri*, referring to a mildly fermented beverage made from manioc mixed with seasonal fruits) or during intercommunity ceremonial exchange festivals, known as *dabucuri*, in which food or objects are exchanged. The effects of these poisonous substances, which are said to work rapidly, are quite varied depending on the nature of the plant used, but they frequently include digestive disorders, coughing, spitting blood, appetite and weight loss, etc.

The more serious ailments, which can eventually result in death, are supposedly cured only by specific counterpoisons. The use of poisonous plants to cause harm, misfortune, or injury is accessible to anyone and is not reserved to one sex: men or women who know about some plants can make use of them against others. In contrast to the Baniwa, there is no specialization in the use of poisonous plants (the "poison-owner," as described by Wright in this volume); nor does this form of sorcery require a high degree of esoteric knowledge or skill. To manipulate poisonous plants is, however, considered dangerous. For this reason, there are protective rules that are to be followed by the person who makes use of them. In particular, he or she must be careful not to touch the plants with his or her hands in order not to be poisoned. Several deaths recorded in sib genealogies were actually interpreted as a consequence of the failure to respect this simple precaution. According to several Desana, there is a special place in Baniwa territory replete with poisonous plants. This place is located near the Uapui rapids on the Aiari River, the mythical birthplace of all the Arawakan-speaking peoples of the region. There, Kuwai, the mythic hero of the Baniwa and Tariana peoples, was burned to death because he "killed" young boys who were being initiated. All the plants that later grew on this spot are said to be poisonous.[6] As a precaution, everyone who goes there today to get poisonous plants must put the liquid of specific plants in his or her eyes in order to avoid being poisoned.

Dohari refers to the harm caused by evil spells that are silently cast, by a *kumu* or by someone who knows evil spells, in the direction of a person when he or she is nearby, or on a cigarette when he or she is spatially distant. It is said that the smoke of the cigarette transports the evil spell to the intended target. Spells can also be blown on a cigarette butt left by the victim and then buried in front of his or her house. Through the use of specific spells, the *kumu* can introduce into his victim's body objects, plants, substances, or animals, making them develop inside the body and/or causing the body part affected by the foreign element to deteriorate. Plants and objects can also be manipulated by the kumu so that they affect a person through simple physical contact, provoking illnesses.

Dohari is a form of specialized sorcery that is based on acquired knowledge, the access to which is limited to certain specialists. It can inflict all kinds of diseases, varying in severity, which can either be easily cured or are highly resistant to therapy. The victim will either recover fairly quickly or die. This depends on the intent of the *kumu* who may choose to send an illness that the sib or the language group of the victim does not know how to cure. In this case, the victim will die. Some of the ailments are localized, affecting a determined part of the body as, for example, inguinal tumor with no sores or wounds, breast tumor, local swelling, menstrual colic, etc. However, some wasting away and/or chronic illnesses, which produce persistent weight loss (such as tuberculosis), are also attributed to *dohari*. It can also be the cause of various kinds of misfortunes, as, for example, making a good worker turn into someone who does not want to work anymore, or making a person turn into an alcoholic or addict to coca-powder or tobacco; making a woman barren, abort repeatedly, die in childbirth, give birth to dead or defective children, or have a difficult delivery; cause unpleasant dreams; prevent a person from marrying another; and so on. But an evil *kumu* can equally intervene in cycles of nature by, for example, destroying crops or affecting the fertility of plants and animals. He can also provoke floods, thus preventing people from going to their manioc gardens or to fish, and making trees and plants weep (see discussion below). Illnesses attributed to spell-blowing are only curable by the sorcerer or by another *kumu* if he knows its mythic origin (i.e., how the mythic hero brought the illness into being) in order to reverse the disease process.

Yee-weheri refers to sorcery practiced by the jaguar-shaman through the projection of a pathogenic object (dart, thorn, tuft of hair, tiny stone, quartz crystal, fur, piece of cotton, etc.) into the victim's body, thus provoking various kinds of physical disorders such as, for example, rheumatic pains, local swellings, or tumors. It is also said that he can throw an illness onto his victim's body like a garment.

Birari refers to collective assault sorcery effected either by the *kumu* who recites an evil spell on a cigarette that he buries at a definite spot at the entrance of a village, or by a *yee* through a lightning bolt. It differs from individual forms of sorcery in the dimension of the attack and from epidemics attributed to contact with the whites and their objects, on the basis of spatial and temporal contiguity: whereas collective assault sorcery affects three or more persons of a single community at the same time, the epidemics attributed to contact with the whites disseminate from a starting point, gradually affecting all the communities of the same river (see Buchillet 1995). Various epidemics of fevers (possibly of malarial origin) and of diarrhea reported in the region were attributed to collective assault sorcery. *Birari* is a strong motive for members of a village to abandon it because it is "too poisoned."[7]

Biá-soariñe is the term used to refer to countersorcery, which consists in sending aggression back to the sorcerer. There are different techniques for doing this, but the most usual consists in taking remains of the deceased's body (hair, nail clippings, bodily excretions, facial or bodily dirt) that are then cooked in a pot with pitch and various kinds of peppers. The ritual is performed secretly, in an isolated place, in order not to be seen. When the content of the pot starts to boil, it is said that the sorcerer begins to suffer from stomach and abdominal pains. From time to time, the *kumu*, or a member of the victim's family who uses this technique of countersorcery, goes back to his community to verify if someone is complaining of pain. If the presumed sorcerer lives in another community, the *kumu* supposes that he is suffering. Then, he decides to continue or not. If not, he takes the pot off the fire and the presumed culprit is relieved of his pains. If he decides to continue, he lets the pot boil for a long time until the alleged sorcerer dies. It is said that when the sorcerer's identity is discovered, a bee falls into the cooking pot. In reality, it is the *kumu* who strikes at a nearby bee and then throws it into the pot. The bee is said to represent the spirit/heart of the sorcerer. When it falls into the pot, the pains in the sorcerer's stomach and belly increase, he begins to puff and blow, bloody foam comes out of his nose and mouth, and he dies. Some Desana say that the *kumu* can also blow a spell onto a cigarette. The smoke of the cigarette serves to unite the heart/spirit of the sorcerer and then takes it back to the *kumu*. The heart/spirit arrives in the form of a bee that the *kumu* strikes and throws into the cooking pot. This is the technique of countersorcery generally used by the *kumu* who, unlike the *yee*, does not have the visionary power that allows him to divine the identity of a sorcerer and to kill him through a lightning bolt or the projection of disease onto his body. At the same time that it permits the identification of the sorcerer, this technique sends the aggression back to him, killing him. It is considered to be an infallible means for finding the culprit. In other words, it is not necessary for the alleged sorcerer to admit his guilt: his very death reveals it. Various deaths in Desana genealogies are imputed to countersorcery and several people admitted that they may use this technique of retaliation in specific circumstances.

It is no exaggeration to say that the great majority of the adult population of the upper Río Negro region has relatives or friends who believe that they have been the victims of some form of the sorcery attacks described above. In the following sections I examine the beliefs and practices related to *dohari*, the form of specialized sorcery practiced through evil spells that are cast on a person or on an object that he or she uses.

The Social Context of Sorcery Suspicions and the
Origin of Envy and Sorcery in the World

The Desana are rarely at a loss to explain why someone would want to cause harm to local group members or to anyone else with whom the relationship is close. Their explanations invariably center on envy, jealousy, revenge for conflicts over theft in the manioc gardens, refusal to give or to lend something, meanness, insults, anger, or vengeance for some harm or injustice done by the victim. All these are motives for the desire to harm another or to suspect someone of using sorcery against another. Faced with an ailment, the sick person will examine his or her relations with relatives and neighbors in order to identify in his or her recent or past conduct the signs of an enmity that could possibly explain the sorcery attack.

Sorcery suspicions can also arise between persons not related and even belonging to different language groups but in close contact with each other. For example, one man was suffering from rheumatic pains in one knee that he attributed to an evil spell cast on him by a Maku Indian after a conflict with him. According to him, the Maku used to steal coca plants (*Erythroxylon coca* var. *ipadu*) from his manioc garden to make coca powder for his own use. One day he scolded him, accusing him of stealing the coca plants. The Maku Indian responded furiously that he would never again eat his coca powder. Later on, this man began to suffer pains in one knee which he immediately attributed to an act of sorcery by the Maku Indian, thinking, "he is doing harm to me because I scolded him." According to Koch-Grünberg (1995 [1903–1905]:277), sorcery suspicions against Maku Indians were in the past a strong motive to lead an attack on their houses and steal their women and children.

The Tukanoan-speaking peoples frequently use Maku people as a scapegoat. If a Tukano Indian dies from a mysterious illness, the ritual healer tries to divine the identity of the enemy who bewitched the deceased and, very often, the suspicion falls on a Maku Indian. The family of the deceased goes to revenge the "crime" and attacks the culprit and robs women and children to sell later to the whites.

Competition over women, frustrated love affairs, or personal rejection are also strong motives to harm people. The refusal of a matrimonial union by a woman or by her parents can lead to a sorcery attack as a kind of revenge of the type "if she can't be mine, she won't be anyone else's." Depending on his intent, the sorcerer can send a mild or a lingering illness to the woman. He can also send a disfiguring illness to make her ugly as a way of preventing her from marrying someone else. After she has married, he can interfere with her ability to give birth, making her abort repeatedly or causing her to give birth only to females. Many women's illnesses, such as barrenness, difficult childbirth, stillbirth, and recurrent miscarriages have been associated by the *kumua* (plural form of *kumu*) with the refusal of the parents to give their daughter as a spouse to someone.

Prestige, status, wealth, or success (material or political, for example), however temporary or qualified (i.e., depending on the person's work), inevitably arouses envy and ill will among neighbors, close kin, and others not so lucky or successful. Because of this, a prudent person will never boast of his accomplishment or wealth so as not to arouse the envy and resentment of others. Such resentment often leads to evil desires that result in actions performed either by the man or the woman harboring the antipathy or jealousy toward the person—if he or she knows how to do it—or through a specialist hired for this task. But, unlike what seems to happen, for example, among the Kuikuru (Dole 1966) or the Aguaruna (Brown 1988), sorcery suspicions rarely lead to public accusations or result in overt violence or confrontation against the alleged sorcerer that may eventually lead to his homicide. They circulate, above all, in malicious gossip and/or in private conversations. Should vengeance be sought it will be in secret, via countersorcery. Nevertheless, veiled suspicions and accusations have sometimes obliged the presumed sorcerer to disappear from the community, going to live temporarily or permanently in another village. In such cases various *yea* or *kumua* suspected of being responsible for several diseases in their own community were thus obliged to flee and take up residence elsewhere.

Sorcery is not solely used against common people, nor are envy or jealousy sentiments experienced only by common people. A headman or a political leader with great visibility, a *yee* or a *kumu* known for his frequent successes in therapy or even a master of dances and chants (*bará*), can also become the object of envy, resentment, and other antisocial sentiments. One man well known for his great ability to chant related to me how during a festival in another village he suddenly lost his voice, then immediately blamed the headman of the other community for putting sorcery on him because of the headman's jealousy of his great knowledge. He then threatened the headman with retaliation if he didn't recover his voice, which, fortunately, he regained a few days later. This ever-present possibility of being bewitched generally prevents the *kumu* from talking about his knowledge to someone else. In fact, in contrast with the shamans of other indigenous societies, such as the Warao (see Wilbert 1996), for example, who gain their status and reputation by demonstrating their talents and skills, the *kumu* avoids speaking about his knowledge and power to another *kumu* or even to members of his own community. He would never openly assert, for example, that he knows mythology perfectly well, that he is the only one who knows a certain potent therapeutic or evil spell, or that he is the only one who is able to cure a serious illness. He should not be obligated to demonstrate his talents or enter into a kind of dispute or competition of power and knowledge with another *kumu*—a situation that will only produce illnesses and deaths in the community. The following narrative was told to me by the *kumu* Américo, from Cucura River:

"One day, in a moment of tension and enmity, during a discussion, one *kumu* began to boast of himself by saying he is very knowledgeable and that he is able to steal the heart/spirit of a person. Another *kumu* answers that he too is very knowledgeable. In the heat of the discussion they decide to show to each other their knowledge, their shamanic power. They begin to insult each other, and one says 'You don't know anything! I will show you how to do this' [i.e., how to steal the heart/spirit of a person]. Furious, the other casts a spell in his direction or against other people, causing illnesses.

According to some Desana, in the past there were power disputes between *kumua*, mainly over questions of hierarchy; but the correct way of being a shaman prohibits these kinds of struggles, which can only provoke various kinds of bodily disorders and deaths. Nevertheless, it is necessary to point out here that, as a way of preventing conflict with another person if he refuses to teach him or her a special spell (for example after a curing session), the *kumu* can resort to some subterfuge based in mythology. In the Desana myth of the origin of night in the world, Ñamiri masu, the "Master of the Night," who did not want to teach the primordial ancestors of humanity the rituals to install the alternation of day and night in the world, made them fall asleep during his explanations by making them fix their attention on the designs of the benches on which they were seated. Today, the Desana *kumu* can make use of this stratagem when he is explaining a spell to a sick person or to a member of his or her family who is not a direct relative in order to prevent him or her from listening attentively to it. It is important to specify here that, for the Desana Indians, spells are secret—they constitute the property of specific sibs and, traditionally, can only be taught by the father *kumu* to one of his sons.

A lack of respect for a very knowledgeable man (a headman, a *yee*, or a *kumu*, for example) or even the simple refusal to give him something he requests, are also said to be strong motives for sorcery. Various epidemics of malaria or diarrhea that, in the past, devastated specific communities of the region were attributed to the ill will of a *yee* or of a *kumu*, who was angered because he felt that he had not been shown respect or because a member of his own family refused to give him something he asked for.

Finally, sorcery can be used as a way of calling attention to the disappearance of a very important man and, at the same time, serves as a form of retaliation for his death. In 1993 a man from the Cucura River, Dorvalino, related to me how his grandfather made it rain for ten days after the death of Garafa, a very knowledgeable *kumu*: "Garafa was very old. He walked entirely bent over. His family didn't treat him well. They didn't give food to him. When he died, my grandfather was so furious that he made it rain without stop for ten days. He did this to take revenge on the family of Garafa (who did not treat him well when he was alive) and also to call attention to the fact that a very knowledgeable person, a great connoisseur of mythology, was dead. He made it rain for ten days. People could not go to the manioc gardens because of the rain. They could not go to fish or to hunt because of the rain. It seems likely that the trees, the termite nests, were weeping. All of nature was crying. One day, after a reunion, various community headmen asked my grandfather to make the rain stop."

This form of revenge for the death of someone important, which can put human survival itself at risk, is well documented in mythology. The Desana myth of Baaribo, the "Master of Food," shows how he wept for the death of his youngest son, who was killed by his elder brother because he had sexual relationships with his sister-in-law: "*Baaribo* was weeping for his son. To accompany him in his weeping, he made it rain. He invited also the birds, the animals, the fishes, the stones, the trees, the trunks, the termite nests ... to weep with him for the death of his loved son. He wept for the death of his son with the whole world. ... He made it rain and he wept with the entire world. He wanted to sink into the earth with all the plants. Because of the death of his son, he wanted to punish all of humanity" (Fernandes and Fernandes 1996:83). Based on this passage of myth, there is a spell that is used to weep for the death of an important person or for someone who during his life was disdained by members of his own community: "For example, the son of a headman, angered because of the death of his father, does as *Baaribo* did in this myth. [As in the myth] summer ends. When someone goes to the forest, to fish or to the manioc garden, he only meets animals weeping. Afraid of this, the persons who do not know where to go anymore, die of hunger" (Fernandes & Fernandes 1996:83).

Indigenous political leaders are also subject to envy and jealousy because of their greater visibility. Two indigenous leaders in the region died recently of very strange and debilitating illnesses that, in one case, Western medicine couldn't diagnose properly. Another one was, at various times, strongly warned to stop his work as a leader if he didn't want to be killed (i.e., to be poisoned or bewitched). As in many other societies characterized by an egalitarian ideology, greater visibility, prestige, wealth, or knowledge—even when acquired by much work—are not tolerated. In fact, envy, jealousy, and the desire to poison or bewitch another have always existed in the world, and there is general agreement in the region that Bupu, "Grandfather Thunder," is responsible for this state of affairs. He is considered the creator and master of harm, the master of evil intentions and deeds,[8] and a myth credits to him the first act of evil in the world. Angered because *Boreka*, the principal Desana ancestor, and his younger brother *Toaramu-yee*, did not consult him before undertaking the transformation of humanity, Bupu, who wanted to be the master of the universe, magically put a poisonous snake (*Bothrop* sp.) under the tree that the two brothers intended to use to make the transformation canoe that would serve to transport the primordial humanity to the upper Río Negro region.[9] The snake bit *Toaramu-yee*, who then died, but *Boreka* brought him back to life through a therapeutic spell (see Buchillet 1983). This was the first evil act in the world, and it is considered to be the origin of sorcery.

Various Desana myths clearly depict the ambivalence in relationships among mythic ancestors and, above all, the sentiment of envy (*iãturiri*). Once introduced into the world, envy became a malignancy that grew by itself. Today, people are said to do harm to others if they are seen to work well, fish well, have numerous sons, have high-yielding manioc gardens, etc. Envy, the desire to do harm, and illnesses are considered to be the heritage left by the mythical ancestors and, today, they constitute an ever-present threat or possibility.

*The Mythical Origin of the Illnesses
That Affect Humanity Today*

According to indigenous ideology, all illnesses which are imputed to evil spell-blowing (*dohari*) have a mythical origin.[10] Some are the consequence of the disregard of a cultural rule by some mythical ancestor. The Desana myth of the introduction of the *pupunha* palm fruit (*Guilielma speciosa* Mart.) into the human world is, for example, one of the origin myths of inguinal tumor and localized swellings. According to this myth, the Desana culture hero, married to a woman of the water-people world, wanted a *pupunha* pit, which belonged to the water people, in order to plant it in the human world. Because his father-in-law refused to give him one, the Desana culture hero took advantage of the moment when the *pupunha* fruits were cooking,[11] in order to get the pits that he then hid in various hollows of his body (groin, armpit, mouth, anus, behind the knee, etc.) to prevent his father-in-law from recovering them. Today, swellings may occur in every part of the body where he concealed the fruit pits. In reality, this myth is essentially about matrimonial alliances and dietary categories. The creation of the inguinal tumor refers to the antisocial attitude of the Desana's father-in-law, who broke the rule of food exchange between affines by refusing to give to his son-in-law the fruit pit that symbolizes his own world (see Buchillet 1983). Other myths also associate the creation of a determined illness with some transgression. In all of them, the creation of a determined illness—which was inherited by humanity—establishes, by contrast, the social, ritual, or cultural norm transgressed. It is, in a sense, the symbol or the metaphor of the infraction of a specific rule.

The creation of an illness can also result from the attempt by a mythical hero to try out his knowledge in order to test its efficacy. One myth recounts how, for example, Butari gõamʉ involuntarily created numerous ailments when he wanted to verify the positive (therapeutic) and/or negative (illness-producing) potency of the various therapeutic and evil spells he knew. In a sense, these myths constitute an *a posteriori* validation of the real efficacy of the spells that form the current repertory of any *kumu*. But they also illustrate a fundamental point in indigenous thought about the reversible character of therapeutic spells; that is, that the use of a therapeutic spell out of context runs the risk of reverting its power, transforming it into a pathogenic weapon.

The mythical creation of an illness can also result from a joke or game of some specific mythic hero. For example, the ailment known as *wʉmãrãrõ*, a kind of throat inflammation that continues today to affect the Desana people, is the consequence of the two mythical brothers called Diroá chewing various kinds of peppers in order to make a cord with their spiced saliva. This illness is the product of their game.

In fact, every illness has one or more specific myths that recount how it was created in mythical times. In this sense, each ailment and also each symptom are the physical expression of a specific mythic event. In the context of illness, myths are known as *bayiri pagʉsʉmã* "the fathers of the spells"; that is, they are the "trunk" or the "root" of the spells (Buchillet 1990). The relation between mythic narratives and the origin of illnesses is a form of esoteric knowledge. Outside of the specific circumstances of a *kumu*'s training, the narrator of the myth does not specify that a specified action of a determined mythic or cultural hero gave rise to a particular disease. The knowledge of the etiological dimension of the myth is traditionally reserved to the *kumu*, being part of his training. To know the origin of a specific illness (i.e., how it was formed during mythical times) gives the bearer of this knowledge the power to cure it. But this knowledge can also be used for aggression.

In fact, the revelation of the mythic foundation of an illness reveals its essence. As the *kumua* frequently say, "only the one who knows how a specific illness was created in mythology is able to cure it" or, alternatively, "to cure a specific illness you have to know how to provoke it" (Buchillet 1983, 1990). It is important to point out, however, that in order to cure or cause a specific illness, the *kumu*'s knowledge must not be limited to the mythology of its origin.

According to Américo, "to put sorcery on someone or to succeed in curing someone you have to know the mythology very well, not only the myth related to the specific illness you want to cure or to provoke, but all mythology. Every word of a specific spell has many senses, it has also many correspondences with other myths."

Therapeutic and evil spells are constructed around the actions of mythic heroes or ancestors that were sanctioned by (or led to) the creation of specific illnesses imputed today to the blowing of evil spells. The disclosure of the points "where one pushes out the spells" (Beksta 1968; Buchillet 1983) as that of the mythic origin of the illnesses, is an essential part of the *kumu*'s apprenticeship. A true *kumu* knows how to cure as well as kill. The intimate relationship between therapeutic and evil spells is well attested by the shamanic denomination of the latter: *bayiri pera maarã* "the companions of the (therapeutic) spells" (Buchillet 1990). Spells are the essence of the *kumu*'s power. They constitute—like the darts, crystals, arrows, etc. of the *yee*—his defenses and his weapons. As we have seen, like magical darts, they can be shot into the victim's body and cause various ailments. In other words, spells are efficacious in themselves, and they may affect the intimate experience of the individual.

*The Consequences of Sorcery Beliefs for the
Transmission of Shamanic Knowledge and
for the* Kumu*'s Therapeutic Practice*

It seems likely that the knowledge of the means to cure and to harm was not widespread in the past. According to the Desana, therapeutic and evil spells were first taught by Boreka to other Desana ancestors, who later on passed on their knowledge to the ancestors of certain Tukanoan groups as part of their cultural patrimony, before their dispersion in the Uaupés area.

Américo states: "In Ipanoré [on the middle Uaupés river], the ancestors of humanity knew nothing [i.e., how to cure and how to do evil]. After Boreka descended from the sky, he began to teach the other Desana ancestors the means to cure and the means to do sorcery. . . . He explained to them, as we are doing with you: 'this mythology provoked this or that illness.' The learning lasted a long time. It is Boreka who created the therapeutic and evil spells. As he was very old, he knew exactly what happened [in the world], he knew perfectly well how all these things [illnesses] were created. This was not the case of the *Pamɨri* masã [name of the primordial ancestors of humanity] who were totally ignorant when they arrived in Ipanoré. Later on, our ancestors began to divide their knowledge with some other language-groups ancestors.

It is for this reason that the Desana are recognized as specialists (as they acknowledge themselves to be) in matters of therapeutic and evil spells. Since their transmission by Boreka, spells have been passed down almost virtually unchanged[12] through the generations along the patrilinear line, from a *kumu* to one of his sons.[13] A spiritual line binds the actual *kumua* to the first ancestors holding this knowledge and, according to indigenous ideology, this shamanic genealogy is essential to the efficacy of the spells (see Buchillet 1983, 1992).

Spells that belong to a specific sib cannot be passed on to members of other language groups or even to other Desana sibs.[14] They are, along with the sets of personal names, songs, musical flutes and trumpets, body paintings, and weaving designs, the ritual property of the sib, a symbol of its identity. For this reason, ideally, each sib (and, *a fortiori*, each language group) has a specific knowledge in matters of therapeutic and evil spells and also of the mythic origin of the illnesses.[15] However, such strong emphasis on spiritual genealogy by the Desana *kumua* must not be taken too literally. In fact, it does not preclude them from teaching a cousin, a nephew, or even a son-in-law (who is always of another group, according to the rule of language-group exogamy among the Tukanoan-speaking peoples) some therapeutic spells that might help them face certain family problems (difficulties in delivery or minor ailments). But they will never teach them evil spells, the knowledge of which is traditionally restricted to a son. Needless to say, the *kumu*'s cousin, nephew, or son-in-law are in no way considered as *kumua*, and their skills for curing are limited to the family sphere.

At the same time that they point out the importance of the spiritual genealogy that binds the actual *kumua* to their ancestors, old Desana *kumua* complain of the frivolity of their colleagues of other language groups who agree to teach therapeutic spells for specific illnesses, including the corresponding evil spells, to anyone. This critique is well-founded. For some of the other language groups of the upper Río Negro region—as, for example, the Arawakan Tariana peoples, with whom I have been working since 1999—therapeutic spells are not secret and, theoretically, they can be taught to anyone interested in them. However, given local beliefs about the prevalence of sorcery, Tariana *kumua* think that it is better for a person who is interested in knowing a spell not to learn it with someone of another language group. This is to prevent an innocent man from being taught an evil spell, instead of a therapeutic one, without him suspecting it. This, according to one Tariana *kumu*, actually happened in the past, with the result that the man who learned the spell killed, without him understanding why, his own sick kin during a curing session.

The importance of sorcery beliefs in Desana society also has consequences for the *kumu*'s therapeutic practice. In order not to be suspected of intending to bewitch a sick person, he will never propose to attempt to heal him or her, even if he knows the illness. In this way, he can even let the sick person die. According to Américo, "the *kumu* is very afraid of explaining to others [an unrelated person] his knowledge. . . . He prefers to let the others die than to be forced to say and show what he knows. If he is invited to cure someone, he must accept to do it, but he will never say first that he knows how to cure a specific illness, in order not to be obliged to explain afterwards what he did, which spell he used."

This is something that health professionals who work in the upper Río Negro region have great difficulties understanding: it is too distant from their own ideology based on Hippocrates's oath, which claims the right and the obligation to treat any sick person, even against his or her own will. For the Indians, the sick, or his or her family in case he or she is very ill, has to ask the *kumu* to treat illness, and in this case he can't decline the demand. The household that requested his service will then prepare the object (part of a plant or liquid) on which he will recite the spell. Generally, after the curing session the *kumu* explains more or less precisely to the patient or to a member of his or her family the spell he used against the illness. This is to protect himself from being suspected of having bewitched his patient in case the illness worsens. However, the preciseness of his explanations greatly varies according to his proximity with the patient. For the Desana *kumu*, only a member of his own biological family has the right to know exactly the text of the spell used. For relatives and/or nonrelated patients, he will simply give the name of the spell he used and make a rapid summary of what he did through the spell: "I did this," "I took this or that," etc.[16]

Are the Kumua Morally Ambiguous?

It remains now to examine whether the intimate relationship reported between therapeutic and evil spells is a motive for doubting and fearing the power of the *kumua*. In other words, do they use their knowledge in harmful ways against others? In fact, all *kumua* with whom I have worked are convinced that sorcery is something very dangerous. As Raimundo from Umari River explained to me in 1985: "Sorcery is like the coca-powder calabash: it always goes back to the sender. For example, I am seated here with my coca calabash: I pass it to my neighbor who passes it to his neighbor and so forth, until the calabash returns to me. It is the same for sorcery: I put something [through evil spells] inside the body of someone else. One day, this thing will be returned to me and I myself will be bewitched. This is the danger of sorcery!"

Because of this latent danger of sorcery, and of the specific reasons related to the *kumu*'s training, the Desana *kumua* with whom I have worked admitted that they will only make use of evil spells for one highly justified reason: to retaliate the death from an illness induced by sorcery of a family member (parents, wife, or child). With the exception of this circumstance, all affirmed that they never intend to make use of their knowledge against others, even when they are invited to do so by someone with payment. Such conviction expressed by my informants in a way has to do with the *kumu*'s training itself.

As I have shown elsewhere (Buchillet 1990), therapeutic and evil spells are taught in two separate phases of learning. Myths and therapeutic spells are taught first. When the father decides that his son understands perfectly well both the spells as well as the multiple dimensions embodied in myths, the neophyte is initiated into the world of evil spells. In the second phase, the training is closed by a ceremony, performed by the father for his son, which has two main purposes: first, it prevents the novice from being spoiled by the evil spells he has learned; second, it leaves the two forms of knowledge dormant in separate parts of his body. It is as if this ceremony, which highlights the dangerous character of the shamanic knowledge of the *kumu*, conferred to him the power of oblivion, and the knowledge is only supposed to be remembered in a concrete situation (the curing of a sick person, for example). Whereas the therapeutic spells are put into his brain, the evil ones are placed in his belly, where they are covered and maintained at the bottom by numerous calabashes and/or baskets. This ceremony is said to prevent the novice from an untimely use of his knowledge. It protects him from the dangers of experimenting "just to see," which would do nothing but provoke needless illnesses. As described earlier, the dangers of testing the knowledge out of context are well illustrated by a number of myths. The ceremony also prevents the two kinds of spells from getting mixed during the curing session—the *kumu* remembering at the same time both the therapeutic and the evil spells—thus involuntarily worsening the state of his patient. Finally, it exercises a kind of inner control over the *kumu*'s own emotions, thereby preventing him from reacting aggressively in a moment of tension, enmity, or anger. According to Raimundo: "With this ceremony, the *kumu* does not worry anymore about what he knows; he will not speak about his knowledge or even think of experimenting with what he has learned. It is just when he meets a sick person that he will remember the therapeutic spells. . . . If he does not have this protection, he suffocates. The two knowledges stay on top of his tongue, the evil spells disturb his thoughts. When he wants to cure a sick person, the therapeutic spell gets mixed with the evil one, and the sick person worsens. When he has this protection, he only remembers the therapeutic spell, the evil one stays at the bottom of his belly . . . When he has this protection, he does not even think of bewitching someone in a moment of anger, of tension."

Conclusion

The data examined in this paper show that, as in many other societies, indigenous or others, sorcery suspicions arise mainly in contexts of envy, jealousy, resentment, or situations of inequality, etc., and are frequently attributed to disturbed, problematic, or alienated relationships. But suspicions, as we have seen, may remain vague and unformulated, and accusations are seldom made in public. If we attempt to analyze the material on harm through evil spell-blowing in the context of the distinction established by Evans-Pritchard (1937) between witchcraft and sorcery, it can be seen that, a priori, the distinction has no precise counterpart in Desana thinking. This is the case for four specific reasons: first, evil presumes a deliberate and conscious action; second, the cure must be addressed to a specific person (or community, in the case of *birari*) in order to be effective, and in this way the cure presupposes a clear idea about the identity of the person against whom the evil deed will be directed; third, evil spell-blowing is considered to be a learned skill; and fourth, because of the mythic origin of illness, aggression, and cure, the *kumu* may choose which kind of bodily disorder or misfortune he wants to provoke. In this way, for the Desana Indians evil depends above all on a malefic intention and a certain knowledge about the means to do it.

As we have seen, however, evil spells, the knowledge of which is said to have been strictly reserved in the past to the *kumu*'s son as apprentice, are made dormant in a part of his body so that he does not have to worry about them. At the same time, old Desana *kumua* today complain of the high incidence of illnesses associated with the blowing of evil spells. In 1986, Feliciano, from the Tiquié River region, told me that "in the former times, there were not as many illnesses as today: the *kumua* knew how to defend [people] against them, how to undo the process of illness . . . Nowadays, everyone wants to do it, everyone wants to recite a spell without being prepared to do it. The one who is not well prepared tries immediately to exercise his knowledge; he attempts to prove [the efficacy of] what he knows, provoking, in this way, numerous illnesses for other peoples. The one who was well prepared by his father—that is, the one who passed through this ceremony [that leaves the shamanic knowledge dormant]—does not do this. He does not even think about this!" Another example was given to me in 1992 by Wenceslaw, from Urucu River: "There are some *kumua* [i.e., the pseudo-*kumua*], the ones who go here and there, who try to learn something with one or with another, who were not trained by their father. Once they know something, they want to experiment to see if it works. The *kumu* who has learned with his father does not think this way. The one who has learned here and there wants to experiment his knowledge to see if it works. Doing this, he creates numerous illnesses, he ruins children, he ruins old people, he ruins women."

The region's high incidence of illnesses that are commonly associated with the sorcery of the *kumua* is, in reality, based on the carelessness or irresponsibility of people who, after learning some spells (be they therapeutic or evil), want to experiment with them, thus causing numerous illnesses and deaths. In fact, the question is not to know if the *kumua* are, like the Bororo shamans (Crocker 1985), morally ambiguous and strongly suspected of doing sorcery by members of their own local groups. Unlike the Aguaruna shamans (Brown 1988), they don't have to emphasize before others their efforts at curing as a way of repelling suspicions of their supposedly malevolent intents. What I have tried to show here is that, given the prevalence of sorcery beliefs in indigenous society and the nature of shamanic knowledge, Desana culture itself has imposed specific rules related to the *kumu*'s training and therapeutic practice in order to restrain the dissemination of shamanic knowledge in indigenous society. It is to prevent its use out of context, or by a "wrong" person (i.e., one who does not belong to the shamanic genealogy), or by a person with a malefic intent who would do nothing but provoke needless illnesses. It seems likely that, just as for the Piaroa (Overing-Kaplan 1975) or the Wari' (Vilaça 1999), illnesses grow above all out of the lack of control and mastery of a knowledge that has to do with the creation of the world, and thus is so dangerous that it needs to be contained and left dormant in the *kumu*'s body so that he will forget it.

Notes

1   The data on which this article is based were collected between 1980–1981 and 1984–2000, in my fieldwork with the Desana shamans (*kumua*), of the upper Río Negro region (Brazil). My work in 1980–1981 was financed by a doctoral grant from the French

Foreign Office, and in 1984–2000 by IRD (ex-ORSTOM, Research Institute for Development) and the Brazilian CNPq (National Council of Scientific and Technical Research) under a scientific agreement between France and Brazil. I would like to express my profound respect for the great knowledge of the *kumna*, as well as, my gratitude and thanks to them for their patience and interest they always demonstrated in teaching me. I also thank Robin Wright for his useful comments on the first version of this essay.

2 G. Reichel-Dolmatoff worked almost twenty-five years with the Tukanoan peoples, including Desana Indians, of the Colombian Vaupés, and published numerous articles and books on shamanism, cosmology, ritual, oral tradition, and so on. On the Desana Indians, see, for example, Reichel-Dolmatoff 1971, 1976, 1978, 1979a, 1979b, and 1989.

3 In Brazil, the word Vaupés is written as Uaupés.

4 See, for example, Crocker 1985 for the Bororo, and Wright 1998 (and this volume) and Hill 1993 for the Baniwa/Wakuenai peoples.

5 There are two other terms for illness. The first one (*puriri*, "pain") refers to common illnesses that "come by themselves" and cannot be attributed to a malefic intention. Named as umuko puriri "illnesses of the universe," they have existed since the beginning of the world, and they may happen at any time and affect anybody without anyone knowing why (e.g., vomiting, diarrhea, headaches, insensibility of the legs, malaria). The second gloss (*behari*) has two connotations: "transitory" and "that passes from one to another" (i.e., contagious). It is the term used to refer to illnesses associated with contact with the whites and their objects, the characteristics of which are their strong virulence, their sporadic character, and their highly contagious character (e.g., smallpox, measles, influenza; see Buchillet 1995). These illnesses, related to certain characteristics of manufactured objects (including food), are not conceived as the result of white malevolence against the Indians because the Indians do not know how these were created by the whites. This is why *doreri*, which carries the notion of an exogenous aggression, cannot be used to designate these illnesses.

6 According to the Desana as well as other indigenous groups of the region, it is because they live near the place where Kuwai was burned to death that the Baniwa peoples have a highly developed knowledge of poisonous plants and herbal medicines, including counterpoisons.

7 See Brandhuber 1999 on the consequences of beliefs in sorcery (i.e., abandonment of villages, migration) among Tukanoan-speaking peoples.

8 Thunder is also the master of the hallucinogenic snuffs used by the *yee* to induce a visionary and ecstatic state.

9 According to Desana mythology, the ancestors of humanity embarked on the transformation canoe at the mouth of Milk Lake (which the Indians associate today with the Baia de Guanabara in Río de Janeiro) and, after ascending the Brazilian coast and descending the Amazon River, they began to ascend the Río Negro and some of its tributaries before returning to Ipanoré, on the middle Uaupés River, where they put their feet on the earth for the first time. During their subaquatic journey, they stopped in numerous places where they performed special ceremonies. Each place is associated with a phase of physical growth and human development (for two Desana versions of the origin myth, see Lana and Lana 1995, and Fernandes and Fernandes 1996).

10 Part of this section makes use of Buchillet 1990.

11 The *pupunha* palm fruit must be boiled in order to be consumed.

12 Except for newly introduced elements, such as manufactured objects.
13 It is not clear to me which Tukanoan ancestors were taught by the first Desana ancestors and how the ancestors divided their knowledge between them, because, theoretically, the knowledge of each sib and language group is unique (i.e., the existence of specific ideas concerning the mythic origin of diseases and, as such, of specific spells).
14 The knowledge of one *kumu* is relatively closed and limited in scope because, ideally, it can only be passed on to one of his sons. Nevertheless, it is important to note that *kumua* can exchange potent therapeutic and evil spells between them, diversifying in this way their very knowledge.
15 It is important to keep in mind that the "same" illness (according to Western medicine) can have various mythic origins depending on the sib and/or language group. Moreover, as we have seen, the *kumu*'s knowledge is traditionally restricted to that of his sib. For this reason, he may not know other mythic origins of a specific illness and may not be able to cure it.
16 Spells consist of, first, a list of the names of objects, spirits, animals, and substances associated with the mythic creation of the disease that the *kumu* wants to cure or to provoke; second, of a description of the neutralization by the *kumu* of their harmful characteristics; and, finally, of a representation of the restoration process of the patient's bodily integrity through the activation of beneficent animals, plants, and powers. To neutralize the dangers represented by some plants, substances, animals, and spirits, and to activate the positive characteristics of other plants, animals, objects, and spirits constitutes the basic structure of any therapeutic spell. All the verbs in the spell refer to the actions of the *kumu*, who says what he is doing to each part of the plant or animal considered harmful, or beneficent, to his patient: "I break," "I put into pieces," "I pull out," "I chew," "I wash," "I refresh," etc. In this way, both therapeutic and evil spells should be understood as performative actions in Austin's sense (1962): they do not describe actions but constitute, through their correct utterance, the doing of these actions (see Buchillet 1990, 1992).

References

Austin, J. 1962. *How to Do Things with Words*. Oxford: Clarendon Press.
Beksta, C. 1968. "Comunicação sobre as idéias religiosas expressas nos mitos e nos ritos dos Tukano." Manuscript.
Brandhuber, G. 1999. "Why Tukanoans Migrate? Some Remarks on Conflict on the Upper Rio Negro (Brazil)." *Journal de la Société des Américanistes* 85: 261–80.
Brown, Michael F. 1988. "Shamanism and Its Discontents." *Medical Anthropology Quarterly* 2 (2): 102–20.
Buchillet, Dominique. 1983. "Maladie et mémoire des origines chez les Desana du Vaupés brésilien." Ph.D. diss. University of Paris-X (Nanterre).
———. 1990. "Los poderes del hablar: Terapia y agresión chamánica entre los indios Desana del Vaupes brasilero." In *Las culturas nativas latinoamericanas a traves de su discurso*, ed. E. Basso and J. Sherzer. 319–54. Quito: Abya-Yala; Rome: MLAL.
———. 1992. "Nobody Is There to Hear: Desana Therapeutic Incantations." In *Portals of Power: Shamanism in South America*, ed. G. Baer and J. E. Langdon. 211–30. Albuquerque: University of New Mexico Press.
———. 1995. "Perles de verre, parures de blancs, et 'Pots de paludisme': Epidémiologie et

représentations Desana des maladies infectieuses (haut Rio Negro, Brésil)." *Journal de la Société des Américanistes* 81: 181–206.

Crocker, Jon C. 1985. *Vital Souls: Bororo Cosmology, Natural Symbolism, and Shamanism.* Tucson: University of Arizona Press.

Dole, Gertrude E. 1966. "Anarchy without Chaos: Alternatives to Political Authority among the Kuikuru." In *Political Anthropology*, ed. M. J. Schwartz, V. W. Turner, and A. Tuden. 73–87. Chicago: Aldine Company.

———. 1973. "Shamanism and Political Control among the Kuikuru." In *Peoples and Cultures of Native South America*, ed. D. R. Gross. 294–307. New York: Doubleday.

Douglas, Mary. 1991. Witchcraft and Leprosy: Two Strategies of Exclusion. Man (N.S.), vol. 26, n. 4, pp. 723–736.

Evans-Pritchard, Edward E. 1937. *Witchcraft, Oracles, and Magic among the Azande.* Oxford: Clarendon Press.

Fernandes, A. C. (Diakuru), and D. M. Fernandes (Kisibi). 1996. *A mitologia sagrada dos Desana-Wari Dihputiropõrã: Collection of Myths Organized and Presented* by D. Buchillet. Cucura: UNIRT; São Gabriel da Cachoeira; FOIRN.

Hill, J. 1993. *Keepers of the Sacred Chants: The Poetics of Ritual Power in an Amazonian Society.* Tucson: University of Arizona Press.

Hugh-Jones, Stephen. 1994. "Shamans, Prophets, Priests, and Pastors." In *Shamanism, History, and the State*, ed. N. Thomas and C. Humphrey. 32–75. Ann Arbor: University of Michigan Press.

Koch-Grünberg, Theodor. 1995. *Dos años entre los indios: Viajes por el noroeste brasileño 1903/1905.* 2 vols. Bogotá: Editoral Universidad Nacional.

Lana, F. A. (Umusi Pãrokumu), and L. G. (Tõrãma Kehíri). 1995. *Antes o mundo não existia: Mitologia dos antigos Desana-Kehíripõrã.* São João Batista: UNIRT; São Gabriel da Cachoeira; FOIRN.

Lyons, D. 1998. "Witchcraft, Gender, Power, and Intimate Relations in Mura Compounds in Déla, Northern Cameroon." *World Archaeology* 29 (3): 34–36.

Marwick, M. G. 1965. *Sorcery in its Social Setting: A Study of the Northern Rhodesian Cewa.* Manchester: Manchester University Press.

Overing-Kaplan, Joanna. 1975. *The Piaroa.* Oxford: Clarendon Press.

Reichel-Dolmatoff, Gerardo. 1971. *Amazonian Cosmos: The Sexual and Religious Symbolism of the Tukano Indians.* Chicago: University of Chicago Press.

———. 1976. "Desana Curing Spells: An Analysis of Some Shamanistic Metaphors." *Journal of Latin American Lore* 2 (2): 157–219.

———. 1978. "Desana Animal Categories, Food Restrictions, and the Concept of Colour Energies." *Journal of Latin American Lore* 4 (2): 243–91.

———. 1979a. "Desana Shaman's Rock Crystals and the Hexagonal Universe." *Journal of Latin American Lore* 5 (1): 117–28.

———. 1979b. "Some Source Material on Desana Shamanic Initiation." *Antropológica* 51: 27–61.

———. 1989. "Desana Texts and Contexts: Origin Myths and Tales of a Tukanoan Tribe of the Colombian Northwest Amazon." *Acta Ethnologica et Linguistica*, n. 62. Vienna, Wien-Föhrenau (Series Americana, 12).

Turner, Victor W. 1957. *Schism and Continuity in an African Society.* Manchester: Manchester University Press.

Vilaça, Aparecida. 1999. "Devenir autre: Chamanisme et contact interethnique en Amazonie brésilienne." *Journal de la Société des Américanistes* 85: 239–60.

Wilbert, Johannes. 1996. *Mindful of Famine: Religious Climatology of the Warao Indians.* Cambridge: Harvard University Press.

Wright, Robin M. 1998. *Cosmos, Self, and History in Baniwa Religion: For Those Unborn.* Austin: University of Texas Press.

Zelenietz, M. 1981. "Sorcery and Social Change: An Introduction." *Social Analysis* 8: 3–4.

The Glorious Tyranny of Silence and the Resonance of Shamanic Breath

George Mentore

This was what made the Atchei savages: their savagery was formed of silence; it was a distressing sign of their last freedom, and I too wanted to deprive them of it. —P. Clastres

By putting our terror in abeyance, we can placate it of any silence perceived in the so-called savage other. The advantage to doing so, with particular reference to the topic of sorcery, would be to grant Amerindian societies the power to produce, and place in prominent positions, a radically different kind of humanity. Thus, we constantly run the risk of misunderstanding how culture and society perform their work of constructing human subjectivity and, of course, how culture and society take on their particular forms in relation to the human subject (Habermas 1987; Rorty 1989). It seems to me that by the tactical procedures of putting terror in abeyance and allowing difference a radical yet positive subjectivity we may more comfortably pose the question as to why, in Amerindian societies, death is invariably interpreted as murder and is to be explained as the work of the dark shaman.

Can we indeed, from such procedures, go so far as to expect and to accept without fear an altogether different interpretative space for the killer savage? That is, given our beliefs about subjectivity, can we fearlessly embrace an intellectual terrain that does not reduce murder to a "moral wickedness" and/or to "the most heinous kind of criminal homicide" (Little, Fowler, and Coulson 1980:1374)? It could certainly be argued that it has been our prejudice toward homicidal violence—orientating from the knowledge that its source can only be attributed to a universal autonomous subjectivity—that has for so long forced us to ignore the shaman of the dark void and instead place most of our scholarly efforts into analyzing the shaman associated with the light of life.

For analytical purposes, let me push further through my hypothetical aperture to assume that, in our Western tradition, our desire to speak and to be heard stems from a very specific understanding about being. At the cultural and historical foundations of our notions about existence, we have cultivated the firm if not easily retrievable belief that "to be" (in general for all kinds of existence, but more specifically for human existence) is "to be as presence." Through our confidence in being as presence, we interpret, among other things, how various modes of silence operate as a form of terror. The tyranny of silent modes works precisely because, in our understanding, silence threatens our ideas about being as presence.

We clearly attribute some elements of absence to silence. Having done so, and having also associated absence with a lack of being, we place certain modes of silence in the same category as nonbeing. The ways in which we intellectually fuse the notions of silence and absence with, for example, death, exemplifies how the meaning of nonbeing may emerge. The various modes of silence transform into extremely capable forms for controlling the tactics of terror.

Within the various institutionalized modes of silence such as, for example, the monastery, the isolation cell, or even the experiential field site of the anthropological fieldworker, our Western ideas about the autonomous self receive their exposure to the ritual processes of being as presence. Such exposure actively engages the ritualizing processes of transformation supplied by silence. Here the initial movement to silence, by the self, mimics death, but only to achieve the further transformation of a ritual rebirth or a return of presence to being. The cultural creation of new social identities often depends on this crucial work performed by silence. Through the silence of self-abnegation, the monk seeks withdrawal from the hectic secular world in order to be "reborn" in the halcyon sacredness of the divine. Through the enforced silence of self-contemplation, the prisoner supposedly imbibes "reform" or "rehabilitation"—that is, from incarcerated delinquent to liberated moral conformist. Through the silence of self-removal (from home to foreign places and from body to text), the anthropologist can usually attain the legitimate credentials of an ethnographic field researcher. In this last mode, note particularly how achieving the legitimacy of the autonomous subjectivity pertaining to the field researcher comes to depend on the presence of the anthropologically researched other.

Take, for example, the ethnographic instance by Clastres (1998) offered in the epigraph above, which appears (at least to me) to demonstrate how his text anxiously attempts to give presence to an Atchei silence of being.

From the wild and chaotic "primitive" spaces of the Paraguayan forest to the tame and ordered pages of his "civilized" anthropological text, Clastres carefully and sympathetically uproots the tyranny of the *iroiangi* (Atchei silence) and literally gives to it the presence of a savagery. In his perhaps romantic view of them, he additionally extends to their savage silence the knowledge of a liberty. He ponders and becomes enlightened by the knowledge that as soon as the silent and free "savage" successfully communicates with us—that is, when such a being acknowledges our presence by breaking silence and becoming present—that being loses its "last freedom."[1] Is it not extremely revealing, however, how the social being of our aspiring ethnographer—having been denied its presence by the silence of the *iroiangi*—anxiously endeavors supplement and transformation into the silent presence of writing?[2]

You may be skeptical. Consider, nonetheless, some of the reasons why we continue to call Amerindian masculine force, Islamic male honor, and/or African patrilineage "terrorism" or "brutality" when they turn against what we consider to be the vulnerable bodies of women. In the mainstream of our culture, these signs of barbarism signal the obvious result of cultures without justice, without democracy, without God, and without statehood's representation of the treasured autonomous self. They exemplify the denial of access to the individual.[3]

Consider also, for the specific purpose of counterposing an alternative interpretation of Amerindian sorcery, the modern notion that every individual possesses the potential for violence—a force capable of rising up from the deep recesses of an unguarded domain to become the orchestrated property of war (Deleuze and Guattari 1987). Every society recognizes this potential of the individual and, in its own particular way, seeks to conscript this forever imminent force into its service. Whenever it works on behalf of institutional forms, the violence of the body usually becomes something other than simply a negative force (Leach 1977; Riches 1986). Certainly it can disrupt such forms, but it can also reinstate them and bring about the known boundaries of social roles and political community. When disruptive and negative, the terrorism and brutality of bodily violence reveals the warrior savage. In this guise, as mentioned, the savage confirms our civilized presence. Could this perhaps be why most of us can reel off the names of modern-day serial killers but cannot remember the name of even a single one of their victims? Our fascination for the killer savage provides the evidential field in which to confirm the actual potency of bodily violence transported from the gaps to the center. On the other hand, our horror of the killer savage also assures us of our anxious moral presence at the center. For us (or at least for those of us in the ideals of bourgeois modernity), our moral presence seeks to be represented by the state with its appropriation of our potential for violence. There at the center, but on our behalf, the state is given the legitimate right to possess and use violence and, as such—that is, in being used as justified force—violence often loses its character of savagery and becomes civilized. Thus from beyond or even from inside the boundaries of our community, the warrior savage provides us with the necessary grounding for our moral presence. Indeed, when we can no longer see the specter of war on the horizon or in our midst, when we no longer hear the roar of battle and, instead, stand facing an empty field of silence, we confront more than a mere dark and formless void. The silent being of the savage denies our civilized presence.

Clastres's tongue-in-cheek use of the term savage when referring to the Amerindian person and/or society places the burden of interpreting on us. At one level we want to understand this savage as the ideal lack or absence in us of barbarism. Savagery and its barbarism are out there, in the forest, hiding behind primordial beliefs. We in fact need them there, on the boundary or limit, as "the visible frontier of our culture" (Clastres 1998:141). They help to bring us into being. Imagine the alternative, imagine their silence and, of course, to our horror, our own lack of being as presence. At another level we seem to want to understand the savage as existing within the confines of our control, within the reservations, ghettos, prisons, and asylums of modernity. Here given the status of "ward of the state" or even that of legal citizen, the savage Amerindian has, by occupying the lower ranks, historically helped to shape the form of our social hierarchies. We are already afraid that they may not be responsible enough to commit to and be loyal to the concept of the nation-state. Hence we give to them an autonomous subjectivity, which should proclaim on its own behalf its own identity, its needs, and its representation in the modern world. Yet, we remain uncertain and fearful. Suppose, alternatively, we were no longer unsure and afraid of the silence of the savage? Suppose, alternatively, we were more secure and courageous in our knowledge and experience of the world? Suppose we were to put in abeyance the glorious tyranny of any silence from the savage? How would we re-interpret Amerindian being—particularly with reference to the dark shaman?

Attempting to Give Voice to Silence

In our relations with and imaginings of the Waiwai—a Carib-speaking people who live in the remote forests of southern Guyana and northern Brazil—we have sought to suture the gaping wound of their silence and bring them and our selves into the substantive modern world. Not, however, without some impositions.

We can certainly say we imagined ourselves as Christians seeking the conversion of pagans bereft of our god's wisdom and divine grace. We sought to be self-sacrificing and generous (as can be attested to by the early work in British Guiana by Thomas Youd of the Church Missionary Society [Rivière 1995:10]). We came from London in 1904 as Jesuit priests (notably, in this case, Father Cary-Elwes), but the Waiwai were on the very furthest boundary of our diocese and it was difficult to maintain missionary activity with them (Butt-Colson and Morton 1982; Bridges 1985). We came from Texas in 1950 (led principally by the Hawkins family of the Unevangelized Fields Mission [Yde 1965:4]) driven by Protestant missionary zeal to uplift the godless Waiwai from their "degradation and decline" (Dowdy 1964:x). We were armed not only with the moral duty of our religious faith but also with the acquired knowledge and discipline of trained linguists (Hawkins 1952, 1962; Hawkins and Hawkins 1953; Hawkins 1998). Our practical mission was to translate the "word of God," to give a literate voice to the Waiwai. For us as missionaries, the Waiwai spoke about their need "to be saved" from savagery; for us as anthropologists, translating the "word of science" the Waiwai spoke instead about an empiricism that could save them from a savagery.

In this particular case with the Waiwai, anthropology confronts what it perceives as an order in human relations and assumes a causal power behind this order, giving to it the identity of a moral politics.[4]

Waiwai subjectivity becomes political, and strangely its character—if not its form—comes to resemble the modern Western soul. Waiwai subjectivity appears to mouth, in the anthropological translation, a rather familiar discourse about autonomy. In this discourse Waiwai subjectivity finds itself expressing a "sovereign political unit" conceptualized and constituted as the residential space of the village.[5] Said to be "an extension of social principles and the kinship system" (Fock 1963:231) the whole Waiwai political system substantiates through an appropriation of the individual by the family and through the subordination of the family to the residential unit of the village.

During our early period of contact with the Waiwai, we missionaries and anthropologists performed the work of salvage—the former wanted to save the lost souls of the savage and the latter wanted to save some remnants of their dying culture. We both targeted what we understood to be an autonomous subjectivity or its indentation as Waiwai culture, and we both found reassurance for our own modern souls in the savage presence of the Waiwai. The strange irony remains, however, that we carried out this work of salvage by imagining and giving to the Waiwai souls of our own making. Consider, for example, my very own role in the affair.

Consider my traditional anthropological attempt to orientate the subject: I have been working since 1971 with a Waiwai community who in 2000 moved from Akotopono or Akomïtu-pono (Mortar Village) to Masakïnaru

(Mosquito Village) on the upper Essequibo River. In 1986, under the leadership of Mawasha, the community moved from their upriver village of Shepariymo (Big Dog Village) to Akotopono. The population of Akotopono in June 1998 was 230: 133 males and 97 females, with 3 males and 3 females under the age of twelve months, 28 males and 19 females between one and five years of age, 29 males and 22 females between six and fourteen years of age, 57 males and 42 females between fifteen and forty-four years of age, and 16 males and 11 females between forty-five and sixty years of age. There are, however, four other separate village communities calling themselves Waiwai who live on the New River in Guyana and on the Río Mapuera, Río Anawa, and the Río Jatapo in Brazil. Shepurïtopon (Howler Monkey Rock Village) on the Río Mapuera is, with a population of 1,147, the largest of all the Waiwai villages.

It is interesting how, in presencing the subject in the text—that is, in seeking to compensate for the physical absence of the Waiwai with the positive reality of our literacy—I attribute to them a territorial and numerical presence based on an assumed individual autonomy. At the same time, notice how I am able to claim for myself an anthropological authorship. But let us not complicate the issue any more than it has been already—let us concede the fact of our humanizing project. Much more pressing questions persist.

What if Waiwai representations of being did not correspond to the more familiar ones we have constructed for them? Indeed, what if the fundamental relation between the formed institutions of their society and the collective ideas of being was such that an incorrect interpretation of one provided a disfigured representation of the other? Even to begin to answer these questions, it seems to me, we would at least have to reflect a little on our own politico-religious intuitions, informed as they are by deep historical notions about "the magician-king and the jurist-priest" (Dumézil 1948; Deleuze and Guattari 1987). For it appears that this privileging of the two "heads of political sovereignty" derives from our preconceived notions about domination over an autonomous and bodily specific subjectivity. In this imagining, the very existence of the political becomes the compliance of the self to the state or, indeed, that of the state within the self.

Resonance, Spiritual Vitality, and the Dark Shaman

Let us not return, however, to the now well-turned issues of the Amerindian society against the state and their definitions of political power (Clastres 1989, 1994; Overing 1983–1984; Rivière 1983–1984; Santos-Granero 1993).[6] Let us in particular stay away from the whole evolutionary question about whether or not Amerindian peoples have any prior knowledge of the state or possess any individual desire for its accumulated power of "rigid segmentarity" (Deleuze and Guattari 1987; Gil 1998).[7] Let us instead first assume "there is no opposition between the central and the segmentary" (Deleuze and Guattari 1987:210), for surely "there are already just as many power centers in primitive societies; or, if one prefers, there are still just as many in state societies" (211). The issue then becomes one of tracking the resonance that operates within and between centers.

We may trace the resonance of political power, in the case of state societies, from a single accumulated primary point at the center of concentric segmentary circles. From this point, power resonates outward from one concentric vibrating segment to another. Made rigid by being appropriated as echoing and reechoing redundancies, the concentric resonating sequences of power can be experienced as the repeated discourses about, for example, social and economic classes and racial and gendered oppositions. These repeating and rebounding sequences behave as if they were the benevolently cared for truths of the primary center. Thus does every resonance of state power sound like the echo and not the source of a percussion of parts.

In the case of the so-called stateless societies of Amerindians we may trace the resonance of political power, from their various supple segments back to their localized independent sequences. Here the resonators of power remain dependent on particular specificities within their own local domains: the various fragments of their universe cannot be made redundant at a single primary point of intersection. The resonators of Amerindian power can and do indeed illuminate by their vibration the "lines between all the points or spirits" (Deleuze and Guattari 1987:211), but this power expresses no rigidity—it is pliant—always susceptible to the countervailing resonance of other centers.

When listening for the sound of shamanic power in lowland South American societies, for example, we do not hear any accumulated resonance at a single primary point; that is, we do not find any high priest or paramount chief whose individual power originates from a fixed and crystallized ritual space of "an office." Like the layered fragments of the Amerindian universe, the segments of shamanic power echo the sounds attributed only to their specific spirit. Each segment emits its own sequence of spiritual power. In this way—that is, as the resonator of a supple segmentary power (or as the sutured wound of a silence)—the shaman can be known through the source of an oscillatory current. Yet, in order to reinforce or prolong its sounds, the percussive movement of shamanic currents has to rely on the adjacent segments occupied and oscillated by other shamans. In other words, shamanic source sequences are assisted in their sound production and yet kept within their own segments by the current from other spiritual resonators. An interesting feature of these "forces from the outside" is the interpretation of their oscillatory current as negative shamanic resonance.

In this regard—that is, as a negative spiritual resonator—the sutured wound of an ominous silence congeals as the knowledge construed about dark shamans. In contrast to the more familiar and positive resonances of the light shaman (Eliade 1989; Wilbert 1972) experienced within their therapeutic and apotropaic spaces, it is instead, I would argue, the strange and negative vibrations of the dark shaman that reveal the most about the supple segments of Amerindian societies. Let me go ahead and propose that, instead of the healing and protective forces of the light shaman, it is rather the deadly and destructive forces of dark shamans—particularly in the role of spiritual hunter/warrior—that operate to sustain the suppleness of segments in Amerindian societies.

A distinctive vitality of being has been attributed to the shaman; such vitality has been recorded as possessing the ability to transcend the corporal body of its host (Crocker 1985; Eliade 1989; Reichel-Dolmatoff 1997; Roe 1982; Sullivan 1988). In what we in anthropology understand as the dream or trance state, the substantive vitality of shamanic being is said to move from the somatic space of the body or the structural space of shamanic practices into alternative domains (Basso 1992; Furst 1972; Harner 1973; Lévi-Strauss 1972; Rouget 1985). The factual evidence of the body remains, sustaining its dreaming or ecstasy in the material substance of the body recognized by all in the local community—"that's so-and-so dreaming in his hammock or swooning in ecstasy." The transcendent vitality, interacting with other beings in the dream or cosmological world, is not hindered by the limitations of corporeality. Its knowledge of cosmological beings and landscapes empowers it or gives to it the capacity to interact or move effectively within such domains. When it heals as the transcendence of the light shaman, it does so by searching, finding, and successfully returning the dislodged vitality to the body of the patient. When it causes affliction and death as the transcendence of the dark shaman, it does so by the very same abilities and knowledge but with the resulting dislodgment and/or permanent loss of the patient's body. Thus do the harmful and deadly conclusions of the dark shaman's resonance echo on the other side of an inverted complementarity. They fit with the positive form of shamanic effects; they resonate off health, well-being, and life. In both instances, however, it is the body that acts as the convincing signifier.

Much of the literature suggests that the individual bodies of shamans and those of their patients or victims have little if any choice in the matter of being occupied or vacated by their vitalities (Crocker 1985; Lévi-Strauss 1972). The eternal mystic source of vitalities radiates a power that gives life to and takes it from individual bodies. Presumably because of the more frequent, distant, and traumatic separations of the shamanic body from its vitalities during a dream or trance, the social category of the shaman receives and sustains an ambiguity of dependency and pity from society. The community depends on the peculiar placement that the mystic vitalities maintain in the body of the shaman. It is, however, also perturbed by the hold these vitalities have on the shaman, for they can send the shamanic body into "seizures of small deaths" where momentarily the local community can no longer communicate with its privileged member. It would be fair to say that while the effect of shamanic power depends on working through the body, the individual shamanic body places no direct claim on such an effect. In Amerindian societies, this power belongs (if this is even the right word) not to vulnerable human beings but to eternal spiritual entities. Shamanic bodies merely conduct the current of spiritual power into the world. When they kill, however, as the bodies of dark shamans, spiritual vitalities frequently take on the deadly resonance of the predator.

The sick are healed and the healthy are afflicted; either way the body becomes the target of a consuming shamanic resonance. The "mystic human causation of affliction" (Crocker 1985:21) needs the body. The body is the site for the echo of health and life, sickness and death. The body is the space for the shamanic apparatus of resonance. In this space, even within the time of the body, life and death echo as the resonance of shamanism. As the space of death and the end of the body the corpse vibrates the dirge and echoes the lethal passage of the dark shaman. The corpse sounds the presence of death and, as "the object of a collective representation" (Hertz 1960:28), floats as the dominant signifier of the dark shaman in lowland South American societies. It is the effect of a surplus of power. In this regard, all death means murder, all murder the malicious work of the dark shaman. Here the dark shaman sutures, with consumptive spiritual vitalities, the cut between the signifying corpse and its signified meaning of death. In the shape and character of the predatory shaman, spiritual malevolence hunts down the body of its prey. It eats the vitality of its victim. Separated from and unable to reclaim its vitality, the body of the victim dies. The corpse, the death, and the dark shaman fuse into a single dreadful scar. Together they resonate the oscillatory trace of a healed wound; they indicate the former condition of a rupture. In other words, the very fact of the vulnerable wound of human mortality is known and has meaning in the predatory work of the dark shaman. At the level of anthropological interpretation, this can explain why, even though the corpse may still be speaking with a shaky voice or staring in quiet pain, the "decomposition" (Descola 1996:365) of the social person often precedes the dying body. Hence the obsequies are more for the social person than the individual body. What the living body does is allow spiritual vitalities to permit the person to invigorate social relations and society itself. But, as the object of the dark shaman's predation—as the effect of a surplus power—the corpse and death provide society with the means to restore and retain social personhood even as the individual rots away.

As hunter and/or warrior, the dark shaman occupies that conceptualized predatory space between the social and the political (or between what anthropology and political science would call the social relations of society and its distributive means of power). The dark shaman resides in the nightly crevices between every segmentary center of Amerindian society and, as such, actively functions against any possibility of a concentrated political power at a rigid center. No repetition of segments can coagulate to form a single rigid center capable of appropriating in the political the shamanic power to kill. The death-dealing arrows of the dark bewitching shaman keeps the social segments supple, never allowing them to accumulate at one point as the surplus of a single entity. Death comes to everyone. It comes in the dark horizon of the west propelled by the bewitching shaman. The redistribution of any surplus power placed into healing by the light curing shaman is, therefore, the energy effect of the dark shaman's complementariness.[8] The surplus can only be forced into its distributive mode by the hostile act of the dark shaman who causes the "little deaths" of sickness as well as death itself to appear in the first place.[9] Without the violence of the dark shaman, there is every reason to believe that the surplus power of the light shaman could transform itself into a rigid segmentarity within the political domain. Without the dark shaman's ability to initiate death, the shamanic power of life—streaming from the east like the blazing light of the sun—could dominate, as the political, all the supple segmentarities of transcendent presence.

The Case Opened

Sunday, June 29, 1993, Akotopono. From the other side of the village, from the tight cluster of huts near the river, a tremulous wave of heart-felt grief kept repeating itself. It lifted me from my hammock, carried me across the open plaza, and placed me unnoticed among the mourners. Around the corpse of Yaymuchi (Little Eagle), the wailing seethed like a stormy sea.

No longer a young man, perhaps in his early fifties, Yaymuchi had belonged to the age-grade of active and respected married men (*porintomo-komo*). The community particularly cherished him for his knowledge of building traditional Waiwai houses, a wisdom teetering on the brink of extinction. He was admired most, however, for his calm leadership in communal work—an almost daily feature of Waiwai village life. Perhaps it was after all this very attribute, of his being able to lead by example through an indomitable will to complete any task he began, that ultimately contributed to his death. He had climbed for his arrow—lodged high in a palm after missing its target of howler-monkey meat—and in doing so he passed through a cluster of caterpillars whose poisonous hairs had brushed against his skin. For three days afterwards he bled from his nose and chest, gasping for air through his swollen throat, but he made it all the way back from the hunt to the village. Signaling to his son and other companions not to assist or follow him, he left the canoe, walked up the embankment to his house, and collapsed dead in his hammock.

From the wood fire by the cold pale body, a dim yellow light glowed feebly. It barely gave form to Yaymuchi's corpse sagging in its hammock. Standing over him, with gourd in hand, his daughter bathed his body with warm water, as if seeking to keep it from death's frigid grip. With each decant, she cried out for him to respond. His son, held up by his weeping wife, swayed from side to side, groaning from the wound of his grief. All around the fire and from the deep gloom beyond a chorus of sorrow kept rising and falling, rising and falling, rising and falling again. Shoulder to shoulder they stood crying, calling, smarting at the sudden loss. His death had broached a question that all in the village sought desperately to answer: who had used deadly spiritual violence to kill Yaymuchi?

Yaskomo: *The "Catcher" of Spiritual Vitalities*

In Waiwai collective ideas about human fatality, all death results from the intentional implementation of spiritual violence. Waiwai interpretation assumes that even though human practitioners cannot strictly own spiritual forces, they work, nonetheless, through their human host and require the moral will of humans to initiate their technical functioning. The corporeal body of a victim dies because its *ekatï*, its life-giving spiritual vitalities, have been permanently removed by mystical missiles deliberately set in motion by the malicious intent of human breath.[10] The victim's body suffers its loss of life from the aggressive actions of an individual killer's chanted words propelled into the wind by puffs of breath. Given through some stolen particle of the intended victim's body (like fingernails or clipped hair) or through some intimate object of its recent contact (a morsel of food or a favorite fire fan), the *ekatï* of the quarry are stalked by *erem*—silent predatory words. Gained from the mystical vocabulary of helping spirits, the deadly words either directly force the *ekatï* of the intended victim out of its corporeal host or further influence some other means to achieve the eviction. The temporary separation of the victim's *ekatï* causes illness; permanent separation results in death. What occurs is a desperate struggle of breath against breath, vitalities vibrating against vitalities. If the grappling vitalities collapse into each other, becoming one with eternity beyond the targeted body, the victim dies. Being ejected and unable to return to the corporeal body of its host, the spiritual vitalities settle with their original collective source in the stratified celestial realms of the cosmos (*kapu*). Here, ideally after death, the distinctive parts of an individual's vitalities reside. The *ekatï* of the human eye, for example, takes up occupancy between the earth and the first stratum (Maratu-yena, Guan-people) of the celestial realm. The *ekatï* of the human chest, if not placated by the vengeance of kinsmen, will angrily roam the earthly stratum in solitary phantom form. It is, therefore, the conspicuous corpse that immediately arouses the speculation of the village community.

Because in Waiwai society everyone can claim access to the death-dealing force of spiritual violence, the specific individual identity of the killer is initially very difficult to ascertain.[11] Either through contract or personal use, and in its accessible form of *erem*, the constant availability of spiritual violence directly contributes to the specific killer's anonymity. As in the case of Yaymuchi's death, open access to and availability of spiritual violence evokes the inevitable question of "who done it?" And yet, because the Waiwai consider *tono* (the ballistics of deadly breath) to be an exclusive part of shamanic knowledge, the profile of the killer is already known. Once implemented and having achieved its result of death, spiritual violence resonates as the echo of deadly words chanted only by a *yaskomo*, the "catcher" of spiritual vitalities.

The Waiwai word *yaskomo* comes from the verb *yasï* (to catch or to hold) and the collective particle *komo*. It has been suggested that *yasï* "means magical power, supernatural gift and medicine man" (Fock 1963:75, n.10). Consider, nonetheless, that when referring to snared prey, the most commonly used verb is *nasiya*. The impression I obtained was that *nasiya* not only referred to the action of successfully capturing game, but also to the distinct substantive corporeality of the meat caught. Whenever speaking specifically about the snaring or catching of spiritual vitalities, however, the Waiwai used the word *yasi* more often. In its shamanic context, *yasi* carries the meaning of a heightened spiritual association with the divine precisely because of the greater familiarity that the *ekatï* of the shaman has with divine domains and entities. Divine familiarity and its consequence of *yasi* identify the shaman more with the spiritual than with the material world. Revealingly, in this regard, the other category of person in Waiwai society to be designated with the collective particle of *komo* is that of child, referred to as *rikomo*.

Waiwai culture provides the understanding that children are not yet fully *toto* (human). That is, in the aspect of their vitalities, children are, like shamans, more of spirit than of matter. The child and the shaman belong as it were to dual communities—the ethereal and the material. With both the child (particularly babies and infants) and the shaman, however, the hold on them seems greater from the community of spirit than from the community of matter. Their bodies are the tenuous materials for the animation of spiritual vitalities that have stronger bonds with their divine sources. The movement of infantine and shamanic vitalities between communities can be dangerous to the more sedentary vitalities occupying the bodies of adults in the material domain. In the case of a newly born child, for example, the members closely related to each other as husband and wife and as new parents to the baby in the material social world have to be vigilant about what enters and leaves their bodies. For instance, still containing the residue of spiritual potency, heavy foods like meat and cassava bread could, if consumed by the parents, attract the volatile vitalities of the baby and, in the process, "catch" the vitalities of the parents and return them to the world of spirit. As part of what anthropology understands as the couvade (Menget 1979; Rival 1998; Rivière 1974), Waiwai restrictions on certain foods during the early period of an infant's life function to protect adult vitalities and to assist them in the social construction of parenthood, which comes out of the spousal category. As part of Waiwai understanding, these food restrictions are practiced precisely because of the collective perceptions about and beliefs in the volatile vitalities of the *rikomo* and *yaskomo*. In their familiarity with both worlds and in their ability to move into and out of the body, as well as between the social communities of humans and spirits, the spiritual vitalities of the child and the shaman echo as the resonance of a divine power capable of ensnaring life itself.

Both *rikomo* and *yaskomo* conceptually signal to the living the fundamental message of human mortality. The birth of a child pushes the categories of husband and wife along the identity trail to take on the role of parent. In becoming a parent, a Waiwai individual sees in ever-closer proximity the dark horizon of personal death. Every son and daughter weaned from the coherent source of divine power confirms and brings closer that moment of contact with the dark shaman. Death and the dark shaman are "knotted" together at the end of the trail and at the end of the day.

In Waiwai, *kamo-yemi-topo-i-a* refers to twilight and the coming of night. It conveys the idea (in free translation) that "the final loop in tying up the sun has been made." The end result of the movement of the sun through the day is the knot of night on the western horizon. Sunlight and mortality always face west; they are like the dawn, *kamo-yepataka-topo-i-a*, "coming directly from the east, facing and moving toward the night." At midday, *kamara-kataw*, "when the jaguar is in between," from where death begins its move into the night, the sun stares fixedly like the eye of a jaguar upon its prey. In Waiwai ideas, just as a jaguar would stalk, kill, and eat its prey and as a hunter would catch and tie up his game, the dark shaman hunts and kills his victim like the night tying up the day. It is a catching and tying up done with the fatal rhythms of shamanic breath.

With the whispered syllables of lethal breath, an approach has been made. A movement has occurred both within the material world from day to night and from life to death, and between the material and the spiritual worlds from *ewto* (the village, "the place where people live") to *kapu* (the celestial realm). The movement of words has a rhythm. The resonance emanating from the chest of the shaman has a cadence, the metrical movement of which reveals not only the location of the shaman but also, in its effect of death, the community of its victim. After the corpse—by dying—exposes the lethal effect of shamanic breath, the relatives of the deceased immediately respond with the unmistakable mournful sounds of grief.[12] Waiwai ritual wailing is the counterpoint to the silent predatory words of *erem*, and in its response to the resonance of the dark shaman it echoes the social solidarity of the community in which the deceased lived. It also seeks to place the dark shaman firmly outside the village community where lethal shamanic rhythms can more reassuringly be identified with other village communities. Like laughter and the shared expression of joy, mournful wailing and its meaning of sadness help to reveal Waiwai ideas about social solidarity. In this regard, it is very much in concordance with their traditional ceremonial dialogue of *oho-karï* (Fock 1963:216), which was performed after every death.

The Waiwai *oho* occurs in various social contexts that give this single genre the impression of producing functionally distinct formal dialogues. The previous ethnographic record states there was *oho* for marriage contracts, trade, communal work, festival invitations, and for the public display of grief (Fock 1963: 216–19).[13] In its traditional structured form *oho* involved only two participants, both seated on low stools facing each other not more than a few feet apart. It was invariably an exchange of dialogue between men, particularly senior men who were not "ashamed" to speak in public and possessed "a deep chest of words" they could use. Women did participate, but normally only with a man. The "*oho*-opener" (Fock 1963:216) or "lead speaker" (Urban 1991) began the dialogue with a single line of speech that ended in a rise of pitch. The lead speaker would continue with these speech lines until ready to pause, whereupon the speech line ended in a noticeable fall of pitch. At this point, the respondent countered with an affirmative *oho*. The declarative speech lines of the lead speaker and the affirmative counter of the respondent comprised a "form-defined cycle" (Urban 1991:127) of dialogue. With the participants alternating as lead speaker and respondent, the dialogue cycles would continue until one of the participants ran out or had "emptied" his chest of words. The overall chanting effect of the cycles sounded more like song than talk, yet their semantic content and "form-defined dialogicality" (Urban 1991:127) conveyed to the audience—by "indexical and iconic" (123) modes (like, for instances, the back channel responses of *oho*)—a parody or caricature of normal, everyday discourse.[14]

Specifically with the death-*oho* or "*oho* of lament," a resident close relative of the deceased must cautiously interrogate at least one representative of every household in the village. Until the public lament for the dead has been performed, everyone beyond the resident close relatives of the deceased is a murder suspect. Particularly beyond the household cluster of the deceased[15] everyone becomes a potentially hostile stranger—a dark shaman waiting to attack the remaining and related spiritual vitalities of the deceased's relatives. The accumulated exchanges of vitalities between members of household clusters make it extremely dangerous for the living when one of their own dies. Tiny particles of vitalities belonging to those with whom the deceased lived get caught, tied up, and carried away along with the dead individual's vitalities. Their capture may make their owners *karipera* (sick), and may even be interpreted as causing the *ñe ewa* (pain) of the grief felt by the living for the recent dead. What the close relatives of the dead want most from those outside their household cluster and from those within their village community is reassurance of amicable intentions toward their being. In other words, they want to be reassured of no further loss of vitalities to themselves from the departure of resident members and, concomitantly, from the hostilities of dark shamanism. Thus, in regard to the form-defined dialogicality of the death-*oho*, the participants do appear to evoke a public display of normal, everyday discourse for the good reason of wanting to resume the regular flow of amicable relations—or at least, in the mimicry, of wanting to suggest that the flow of normal conversation implies the resumption of normal relations.

Often, however, the actual semantic content of *oho* does not cite the normal and the everyday (see Fock 1963:302-12). Yet where the declarative lines of the relative of the deceased mostly question, the affirmations of his partner fill with the entreaties of friendliness. What remains most instructive is that the form-defined dialogicality of the death-*oho* forces the semantic content to conform to a formula—albeit an exaggeration of normal discourse. As such, the formula can successfully serve the function of mediating "in situations that are likely to give rise to conflict" (Rivière 1971:306). The social boundaries, at which hostilities could begin within the village community, apparently occur between the conjugal household clusters where the everyday exchanges of spiritual vitalities seem less reciprocal and hence more vulnerable. Thus, with the death-*oho*, it could be concluded, the icon of normal discourse in ceremonial dialogue seeks to jettison the dark shaman beyond the boundaries of the village community.

As the counterpoint to *erem*, the death-*oho* resonates as the formal opportunity to deny any accusations of personal guilt and to affirm innocence. What is interrogated and displayed in the discourses of lament are the innocence of every village member and the demonstrative sociability of the community. It seems that the ideological Waiwai focus settles on a dual concern for the quality of human mortality and the knowledge of human character with its capacity for violence. Knowing about the emotional disposition of those with whom one lives appears to be of crucial interest. Locating where bad intentions reside, and making sure—when they erupt—to deter them from accessing violence, become the required aspects of social harmony. When this fails, however, even without knowing the murderer's identity, knowledge about hostile intentions remains the leading evidence toward exposing the killer.

The Waiwai configure violence in the same intellectual frame as eating; in their view, the ultimate rational conclusion for all killing has to be for food. This notion contains social, albeit ambivalent, approval when the object of violence carefully confines itself to vegetable and animal life (Hugh-Jones 1996; Viveiros de Castro 1998). In the case of homicide, however, the interpretation of killing in order to eat the victim does not alter significantly, but the question of legitimacy makes the victim's death more problematic. To kill another human being illegitimately is likened to the actions of the solitary, antisocial jaguar devouring its prey: the murderer kills and eats the body of the victim without cooking it and without sharing it: the decomposing body disappears like food into the carnivore's mouth. In converse, to kill legitimately—that is, to hunt or to feud in honorable vengeance—is to behave like a proper social being governed by the moral obligations of society, wherein cooking and sharing of the victim's body locate the hunter and the warrior firmly inside the community. A successful hunter will not only make sure the animal he has killed is transformed into cooked meat before it is consumed, but also goes to some length (even after collective hunts and communal meals) to make sure he never eats the meat of an animal he himself has killed. Likewise, the avenger of a dead relative will, after the cremation or burial of the deceased, take the remaining bones, place them in a hollow bamboo and "recook" them. If the bamboo bursts in the heat of the fire, the murderer will die. While an illegitimate act of violence tends, therefore, to locate the murderer outside of society and, in fact, makes him or her the target of a legitimate use of violence, legitimate violence, on the other hand, succeeds in reaffirming the hunter and the warrior inside society as beings of esteem and prestige. Nevertheless, in both cases it is hostile human intentionality that remains the initial source of violence, while the spiritual force it stimulates contains the actual cause of death. The cannibalism of illegitimate violence always resonates in *erem*. Lethal mystical words, like projectiles from the mouth, can bring about the death of another human, and death, in Waiwai ideas, can only be initiated by ill will for the explicit purpose of illicit consumption.

Only those people motivated by their own ill will actually make use of deadly spiritual force. In such cases, public knowledge and recall about the existing nature of relations between community members provide the resident community of the deceased with the identities of possible suspects. In addition, public perception about past events and about bodies capable of igniting emotions leading to violence also helps to establish the identity of the guilty. The shared and unofficial obligations of the living to the recently murdered victim begin with having to locate and assemble the evidence of the active presence of individual human malice. Such evidence can be achieved with relative ease because the range of expectant emotions assumed to be felt by people with ill intent are generally known to result from specific observable actions. The actions producing the felt emotions, which tend to lead to and govern a matching set of responses, actually expose the presence of the bad intent that activates and uses violence. Recalling and perceiving, for example, that so-and-so had been on the retreating side of a dispute, allows observers to assume that the retreating individual had, for example, felt some *rïwo* (anger) or *ki i* (frustration or emotional turbulence) and became possessed with *ki i ito* (ill will or, more correctly, "to be dangerous") enough to seek retribution against his or her opponent. The subsequent sickness or death of the offending disputant who caused the anger confirms both the bad intentions of the shamed person and the actual effect of the angry person's violent retribution. Taken together, the felt emotions of human malice and spiritual violence cause sickness and death, but they also provide the very clues for answering the question as to the identity of the individual contributing to the ailment and/or fatality.

In Waiwai moral philosophy, everyone should exercise the social responsibility to guard against wrongly arousing one's own destructive desires. The general availability of violence as a weapon and the link between ill will and the actual use of violence seemingly compel collective social harmony to depend on the individual's emotional calm and bodily discipline. Here where violence can only be accessed through human intent and practice, it is, in an analytical sense, the result of an articulation between the attribute of individual human will and the resources of spiritual energy. In this sense, violence is inalienable to the individual, because only the individual can transform its force into the product of destruction. Yet, in being irreducible to the individual, violence is, in its potential, the culminating sum of a culturally built identity. The individual, in becoming a social person, consciously ascribes to the body and the spiritual vitalities an acquired knowledge of ownership over the potential use of violence—a knowledge actually constituting the movement of personhood.

Graphically expressed on the adorned body with traditional signs of adulthood and gender, but also more substantively in the achievement of marriage and the making of children, the emotional base for the will to violence becomes a known property, subject to customary displays of control by the individual. Being able to exhibit constraint over the emotional base to violence expresses both an individual's commitment to society and the affective means toward collective social harmony. It could be said that Waiwai culture has, in such cases, indirectly persuaded individuals to perform, on behalf of society, the fundamental task of managing social turmoil. Here the onus of control does not rest in any rigid, centralized institution of governing, but rather in the supple, overlapping, multifaceted realms of personhood and household clusters. In these social domains—that is, actually through personhood and residence—the individual retains legitimate access to the use of violence. In other words, the individual uses the moral constraints in kinship and marriage to police human intentionality and to secure harmonious residential fellowship. It is, however, precisely because morality becomes meaningful only within these domains that the constant availability of violence keeps individual control and collective harmony vigilant.

The social and cultural requirement of living together offers the opportunity for expressing, monitoring, and managing the amicable relations of collective social life. Without the fact of residence with others, the need for emotional calm, the potential for violence, and the ideal of community fellowship could not find their current form and meaning. For the effect of residence to best perform its tasks, however, the patterned ties of kinship and the institution of marriage must also be active, for they are the very means through which affection can be shared and violence denied. The dominant moral obligations to love rather than hate and to be kind rather than hurtful toward those related to you and toward those with whom you live have to be in constant practice. Yet each individual's capacity for affection is counterpoised by the known potential for violence from the dark shaman. Indeed, as mentioned, the very occurrences of sickness and death confirm the deliberate implementation of spiritual violence and the presence of the dark shaman. Whenever sickness and/or death occurs, the veracity of violence and the dark shaman acknowledge themselves from within the collective substance of social knowledge and, at the same time, reaffirm the open character of their accessibility. While on the one hand it is the access to and availability of violence that directly contribute to the murder's anonymity, and indirectly produce the inevitable demand for suspects, it is, on the other hand, the murderous ill will of somatic emotions that exposes itself to the community of the deceased as the incriminating evidence of guilt and as the definitive means of confirming the identity of the murderer.

The Case Closed

Yaymuchi died because he had incurred the ill will of an individual unable or unwilling to control his or her emotions; the fine virtues of a cultural constraint could not or were unable to restrain the inherent violence of a bodily passion. As far as the members of his village were concerned, this was due in part to Yaymuchi's unnecessary absence from the protective feelings of family and friends. That is, his recent visit to the Trio village, where he was a stranger and an obvious target for feelings of animosity, contributed to his death. Strangers have no grounds for feeling affection toward other strangers and, with this lack, fall into the category of potential murderers. In the minds of his grieving friends and relatives, therefore, Yaymuchi's assailant lived in another village—a malignant shamanic force outside the immediate constraints of residential filial and affinal moral obligations. Thus contrasting with the amicable immediacy of residential relations, it can be argued that, among the Waiwai, death and the dark shaman serve to keep secure the ideological constraint of a supple political segmentarity. In these ideas, violence and shamanism can never be transformed into the rigid repetition of segments; they cannot, for example, be concentrated at a primary or dominant theocratic center.

Parting Remarks

I have assumed throughout this essay that one reason for the difficulty we have in modernizing the savage soul has been our initial incomprehension of its silence. While savage subjectivities sustain a discursive existence—perhaps in an idiom of fractionalized, interactive, dependent being—their statements appear to us not as discourse but as silence. When giving them our voice, we seemingly seek to give to them an understanding of our autonomous and constantly desiring selfhood. In addition, we seemingly wish them to take on the self-assertive work of proclaiming an identity—a subjective being that would willingly search for its own subordination first to the concept of having an identity and, second, to having that identity represented in the world. What, we ask ourselves, is the most ideal citizenry for the modern state? Arguably, for us, it is the assemblage of disciplined souls. There appears to be no greater horror to the modern state than the possibility of a presence that not only refuses to obey but also does not even recognize the command and the voice responsible for giving it. It occurs to me that until modernity takes up a more flexible position—a more supplementary posture with regard to those who may have other ways of being in the world—it will always confront this other as savage, and, indeed, it will never find a positive accommodating space for such otherness in its world. Until such time, the dark shaman of death will remain in the twilight between the dim crevices of society blowing those dangerous mystical words we will never truly hear.

Notes

Parts of the ethnography for this paper were presented in the session "Violence and Population: Bodies and the Body Politic in Indigenous Amazonia" at the annual meeting of the American Anthropological Association, Philadelphia, November 1998, and at the festschrift for Peter Rivière in Oxford in December 1998. A very truncated version of the theoretical parts of the essay was presented at the conference "Indigenous Amazonia at the Millennium: Politics and Religion," New Orleans, January 2001. I wish to thank all those who offered comments on my ideas at these gatherings. I also wish to thank Edith Turner and Christopher Crocker for their reading and comments of early drafts of this essay; I, of course, have to take the final responsibility for its content.

1. As can probably be ascertained from the epigraph quote, I have been particularly fascinated by what to me has been the consistent preoccupation by Clastres with the issue of silence. In his *Chronicle of the Guayaki Indians*, he purposely gives intentionality to Guayaki silence (1998:17); it is the very substance of a "health" and "freedom" (96, 97); and it even metamorphoses into the social "invisibility" of a third gender (293). Again in his more famous *Society against the State*, and in probably his most brilliant essay, "Of Torture in Primitive Societies," the central concept of the marked body as memory can only begin to resonate with full meaning when silence expresses "courage" (1989:184) and "consent" (185). My fascination, however, goes beyond Clastres, for in much more subterranean styles, many other authors have pursued the topic of Amerindian silence. In two very sophisticated examples, the very intellect and imagination of Amerindian subjectivity takes on a "thing-like" cultural presence (Urban 1996: xiii, 65, 71, 173) and "metaphysics of sociality" (Overing and Passes 2000:12), but only, it seems to me, from our shared understanding of a possible uncommunicative silence on the part of the subject.

2. This is yet another reason why we can never safely imagine a being of humanness without an articulated voice—not necessarily a being human without language, but worse, a human being with a language (as in the case of the Atchei met by Clastres) that did not use language to empower its own individual identity.

3. This for me is the clear message I receive from the purposefully horrific opening scenes of *Discipline and Punish*. In understanding myself and my society as just, lenient, and moral, I perform the modern act of identifying as the "true" criminal not Damiens the regicide, but rather his torturers and executioner. We are no longer this barbaric, this uncivilized. We have "progressed" to a more lenient and humane form of punishment. We now offer the body of the condemned more democratic and rational forms of punishment, ones that reduce pain, yet, nevertheless, clearly manifest their external power over the modern soul (Foucault 1979).

4 Think here of the early debates in anthropology about whether or not "tribes" without leaders had any form of government and, indeed, any politics whatsoever (Barclay 1982; Fortes and Evans-Pritchard 1975; Evans-Pritchard 1974; Gluckman 1982).

5 I am quoting Fock 1963:231, but I am also including myself in this category of the author.

6 I should add, however, that in my own interpretations of Foucault's presentations on power, I do not understand him to be following the classic Marxist definition, whereby access to and amount of power possessed are criteria for defining power. In fact, with regard to the "micro-physics of power" he goes out of his way to say, "in short this power is exercised rather than possessed; it is not the 'privilege,' acquired or preserved, of the dominant class, but the overall effect of its strategic positions—an effect that is manifested and sometimes extended by the position of those who are dominated" (1979:26–27).

7 One of Clastres's more daring and penetrating attempts at illustrating what it takes for Amerindian societies to defeat the state can be seen in "What Makes Indians Laugh" (1989:129–50). Here we see that after the distribution of supernatural power to its shamanic location, the Amerindian "kills"—in the comedic genre of myth and with the equally powerful but natural effects of human laughter—the danger of this potential power lurking in the "distant" and "external" spaces.

8 In this regard, the dark shaman is the "sensual code" into which the "floating signifier" of spiritual power becomes thought about and objectified (Gil 1998:93–105).

9 Here, as the means of spiritual violence, the dark shaman is irreducible; shamanic power cannot be reduced to any kind of rigid apparatus of power like that pertaining to the state. In this sense it is "deterritorialized" beyond the zones of enclosed politics (Deleuze and Guattari 1987:351–56).

10 *Ekatï* is thought of as a vigorous spiritual substance whose ability to influence material life stems from being, in origin, the source of all living things.

11 Perhaps here is where the debate between religion and rationality could begin—that is, at the point of intersection between human reason and the mystical. In this regard I admit it becomes somewhat problematic for me to continue using the term "mystical," particularly where the context could infer a meaning of "divine mystery." In the Waiwai case, however, I am, so far, in agreement with the view that "in an inquiry into witchcraft as a principle of causation, no mysterious spiritual beings are postulated, only the mysterious powers of humans" (Douglas 1970:xvi).

12 I find it absolutely fascinating that given what I understand about the greater relevance that the Waiwai place on spiritual being, the marking that "ritualized lamentation" reveals can just as meaningfully be said to mark "a return after a prolonged absence" (Urban 1996:153) not to the living but to the eternal community of spirits. Indeed it makes just as much sense to say in the case of the Waiwai that a "person who has been, for some time, only" phenomenally accessible "is made once again" (153) noumenally real—through death.

13 While not having occasion to see *oho* in its traditional and more structured form, I have many times witnessed aspects of its formal features in different ritual contexts. In its core character and aims, *oho* remains today very much an element of Waiwai social life.

14 Piwa, an old Waiwai when I knew him, once simulated a traditional *oho* for me, playing the parts of both lead speaker and respondent. I have to say the two most notice-

able features of his reenactment were how the *oho* captured the musical aesthetics of Waiwai flute playing and seemingly mimicked the dawn chorus of a flock of *karapa* (horned screamer [*Anhima cornuta*]).

15 I would here like to note the interesting comparison between a Waiwai household cluster (also called "neighborhood" [Howard 1991: 53]) and a Trio village (Rivière 1970). The Trio are the Waiwai's east or northeastern neighbors in Surinam. I would argue that outside of the natal household and in terms of the social relations entrusted to bear the most weight for coresident trust and harmony, it is today's Waiwai household cluster that resembles a traditional Trio village. Marriage brings new households into social existence. The Waiwai prefer and practice uxorilocality. The ideal and usual residential cluster in a Waiwai village would therefore be a core household comprised of one married couple with their unmarried children (and perhaps even a widowed parent) and, in close proximity, other conjugal households headed by men related to the core household as son-in-law and/or brother-in-law. A Waiwai village can be viewed as consisting of clusters of conjugal households bound to one another by relationships of extended kinship and affinity. In other words, what has been called for the Trio an "agglomeration" (Rivière 1970:246, 1971:294) of three to five autonomous villages would be the rough equivalent of a Waiwai village today. I would even go so far as to suggest that this was the case even when Niels Fock first visited the Waiwai at the time when missionary activity had already drawn traditional villages into today's intravillage household clusters. The relevance of these suggestions is that the Trio's *sip sip man* (mild strong talk) of the *turakane* (ceremonial dialogue), spoken only between agglomerates of the same group, and their *nokato* (severe strong talk), spoken only with people who live "further away, in one of the other two groups" (1991:304) of agglomerates, show similar patterns of operation to the Waiwai *oho*. Within Waiwai traditional villages, within today's Waiwai household clusters, and within Trio traditional villages no ceremonial dialogue would have been brought into action. In both ethnographic cases, the so-called function and meaning of ceremonial dialogue—that is, "mediation in situations that are likely to give rise to conflict" (306)—would, I argue, be the same.

References

Anderson, Benedict. 1983. *Imagined Communities: Reflections on the Origin and Spread of Nationalism*. London: Verso.

Anzieu, D. 1989. *The Skin Ego*. New Haven: Yale University Press.

Balandier, Georges. 1970. *Political Anthropology*. New York: Pantheon Books.

Barclay, H. 1982. *People without Government: An Anthropology of Anarchism*. London: Kahn and Averill with Cienfuegos Press.

Basso, Ellen. 1992. "The Implications of a Progressive Theory of Dreaming." In *Dreaming: Anthropological and Psychological Interpretations*, ed. B. Tedlock. 86–164. Santa Fe, N.M.: School of American Research Press.

Bridges, John. 1985. *Rupununi Mission: The Story of Cuthbert Cary-Elwes SJ among the Indians of Guiana 1909–1923*. London: Jesuit Missions.

Brydon, A. 1998. "Sensible Shoes." In *Consuming Fashion: Adorning the Transnational Body*, (ed. A. Brydon and S. Niessen). 1–22. Oxford: Berg.

Butt-Colson, Audrey, and J. Morton. 1982. "Early Missionary Work among the Taruma and

Waiwai of Southern Guiana: The Visits of Fr. Cuthbert Cary-Elwes, SJ. in 1919, 1922, and 1923." *Folk* 24: 203-6.

Cavallaro, D., and A. Warwick. 1998. *Fashioning the Frame: Boundaries, Dress, and Body*. Oxford: Berg.

Chagnon, Napoleon. 1992. *Yanomamö: The Fierce People*. Fort Worth: Harcourt Brace.

Clastres, Pierce. 1989. *Society against the State: Essays in Political Anthropology*. New York: Zone Books.

———. 1994. *Archeology of Violence*. Trans. Jeanine Herman. New York: Semiotext(e).

———. 1998. *Chronicle of the Guayaki Indians*. New York: Zone Books.

Crocker, Jon. 1985. *Vital Souls: Bororo Cosmology, Natural Symbolism, and Shamanism*. Tucson: University of Arizona Press.

Deleuze, Georges, and F. Guattari. 1987. *A Thousand Plateaus: Capitalism and Schizophrenia*. Minneapolis: University of Minnesota Press.

Descola, Philippe. 1996. *The Spears of Twilight: Life and Death in the Amazon Jungle*. New York: New Press.

Douglas, Mary. 1996. *Natural Symbols: Exploration in Cosmology*. London: Routledge.

———, ed. 1970. *Witchcraft Confessions and Accusations*. London: Tavistock.

Dowdy, H. 1964. *Christ's Witchdoctor: From Savage Sorcerer to Jungle Missionary*. London: Hodder and Stoughton.

Dumèzil, Georges. 1948. *Mitra-Varuna*. Paris: Gallimard.

Eliade, Mircea. 1989. *Shamanism: Archaic Techniques of Ecstasy*. London: Penguin.

Evans-Pritchard, Edward E. 1974. [1940]. *The Nuer: A Description of the Modes of Livelihood and Political Institutions of a Nilotic People*. New York: Oxford University Press.

Fock, Nils. 1963. *Waiwai: Religion and Society of an Amazonian Tribe*. Copenhagen: National Museum.

Fortes, Mayer, and E. E. Evans-Pritchard, eds. 1975 [1940]. *African Political Systems*. London: Oxford University Press.

Foucault, Michel. 1979. *Discipline and Punish: The Birth of the Prison*. New York: Vintage Books.

———. 1990. *The History of Sexuality. Volume 1: An Introduction*. New York: Vintage Books.

Furst, Peter, ed. 1972. *Flesh of the Gods: The Ritual Use of Hallucinogens*. London: Allen and Unwin.

Geertz, Clifford. 1993. *The Interpretations of Cultures: Selected Essays*. New York: Basic Books.

Gell, Anthony. 1996. *Wrapping in Images: Tattooing in Polynesia*. Oxford: Clarendon Press.

Gil, Juan. 1998. *Metamorphoses of the Body*. Minneapolis: University of Minnesota Press.

Gluckman, Max. 1982 [1956]. *Custom and Conflict in Africa*. Oxford: Basil Blackwell.

Habermas, Jurgen. 1987. *The Philosophical Discourse of Modernity*. Trans. Frederick Lawrence. Cambridge: MIT Press.

Harner, Michael. 1973. "The Sound of Rushing Water." In *Hallucinogens and Shamanism*, ed. M. Harner. 15-27. London: Oxford University Press.

Hawkins, W. 1952. *A fonologia da língua Uaiuai*. São Paulo: Universidade de São Paulo.

———. 1962. *A morfologia do substantivo na língua UaiUai*. Rio de Janeiro: Universidade do Brasil.

———. 1998. "Wai Wai." In *Handbook of Amazonian Languages*, vol. 4, ed. D. Derbyshire and G. Pullum. 201-11. Berlin: Mouton de Gruyter.

Hawkins, W., and R. Hawkins 1953. "Verb Inflections in Waiwai (Carib)." *International Journal of American Linguistics* 19: 201–11.

Hertz, R. 1960. *Death and the Right Hand*. Trans. R. Needham and C. Needham. Aberdeen: Cohen and West.

Howard, Catherine. 1991. "Fragments of the Heavens: Feathers as Ornaments among the Waiwai," In *The Gift of Birds: Featherwork of Native South American Peoples*, ed. R. Reina and Ken Kensinger. 50–69. Philadelphia: University of Pennsylvania, Museum of Archaeology and Anthropology.

Hugh-Jones, Stephen. 1996. "Bonnes raisons ou mauvaise conscience? De l'ambivalence de certains amazoniens envers la consommation de viande." *Terrain* 26: 123–48.

Lacan, J. 1977. *The Four Fundamental Concepts of Psychoanalysis*. Ed. Jacques-Alain Miller, trans. A. Sheridan. Harmondsworth: Penguin.

Leach, Edmund. 1977. *Custom, Law, and Terrorist Violence*. Edinburgh: Edinburgh University Press.

Lévi-Strauss, Claude. 1972. *Structural Anthropology*. Harmondsworth: Penguin.

Little, W., H. Fowler, and J. Coulson. 1980. *The Shorter Oxford English Dictionary: On Historical Principles*. Oxford: Clarendon Press.

Menget, Patrick. 1979. "Temps de naître, temps d'être: La couvade." In *La fonction symbolique: Essais d'anthropologie*, ed. M. Izard and P. Smith. Paris: Gallimard.

Niebuhr, H. R. 1999. *The Responsible Self: An Essay in Christian Moral Philosophy*. Louisville: Westminster John Knox Press.

Overing, Joanna. 1983–84. "Elementary Structures of Reciprocity: A Comparative Note on Guianese, Central Brazilian, and North-West Amazon Socio-Political Thought." *Antropologica* 59–62: 331–48.

Overing, J., and A. Passes, eds. 2000. *The Anthropology of Love and Anger: The Aesthetics of Conviviality in Native Amazonia*. London: Routledge.

Reichel-Dolmatoff, Gerardo. 1997. *Rainforest Shamans: Essays on the Tukano Indians of the Northwest Amazon*. Devon: Themis Books.

Riches, David. 1986. *The Anthropology of Violence*. Oxford: Basil Blackwell.

Rival, Laura. 1998. "Androgynous Parents and Guest Children: The Huaorani Couvade." *Journal of the Royal Anthropological Institute*. 4: 619–42.

Rivière, Peter. 1970. "Factions and Exclusions in Two South American Village Systems." In *Witchcraft Confessions and Accusations*, ed. M. Douglas. 245–65. London: Tavistock.

———. 1971. "The Political Structure of the Trio Indians as Manifested in a System of Ceremonial Dialogue." In *The Translation of Culture*, ed. T. O. Beidelman. 293–311. London: Tavistock.

———. 1974. "The Couvade: A Problem Reborn." *Man* 9: 423–35.

———. 1983–1984. "Aspects of Carib Political Economy." *Antropologica* 59–62: 349–58.

———. 1995. *Absent-Minded Imperialism: Britain and the Expansion of Empire in Nineteenth-Century Brazil*. London: Tauris Academic Studies.

Roe, Peter. 1982. *The Cosmic Zygote: Cosmology in the Amazon Basin*. New Brunswick: Rutgers University Press.

Rorty, Richard. 1989. *Contingency, Irony, and Solidarity*. Cambridge: Cambridge University Press.

Rouget, G. 1985. *Music and Trance: A Theory of the Relations between Music and Possession*. Chicago: University of Chicago Press.

Santos-Granero, Fernando. 1993. "Power, Ideology, and the Ritual of Production in Lowland South America." *Man* 21: 657–79.
Scarry, Ellen. 1985. *The Body in Pain: The Making and Unmaking of the World*. New York: Oxford University Press.
Sullivan, Lawrence. 1988. *Icanchu's Drum: An Orientation to Meaning in South American Religions*. New York: Macmillan.
Thomas, David. 1982. *Order without Government: The Society of the Pemon Indians of Venezuela*. Urbana: University of Illinois Press.
Todorov, Tvetzan. 1987. *The Conquest of America: The Question of the Other*. New York: Harper.
Urban, Gregg. 1991. *A Discourse-Centered Approach to Culture: Native South American Myths and Rituals*. Austin: University of Texas Press.
———. 1996. *Metaphysical Community: The Interplay of the Senses and the Intellect*. Austin: University of Texas Press.
Viveiros de Castro, Eduardo. 1998. "Cosmological Deixis and Amerindian Perspectivism." *Journal of the Royal Anthropological Institute* 4: 469–88.
Wagner, Roy. 1981. *The Invention of Culture*. Chicago: University of Chicago Press.
Wilbert, Johannes. 1972. "Tobacco and Shamanistic Ecstasy among the Warao Indians of Venezuela." In *Flesh of the Gods: The Ritual Use of Hallucinogens*, ed. P. Furst. 55–83. London: Allen and Unwin.
Yed, Jens. 1965. *Material Culture of the Waiwái*. Copenhagen: National Museum.

*A Blend of Blood and Tobacco:
Shamans and Jaguars among the
Parakanã of Eastern Amazonia*

Carlos Fausto

Shamanism is Siberia's most successful exported product. Humble immigrants who traversed the Bering Strait, tens of thousands of years ago, originally diffused it throughout the Americas, and it is now found all over the world in multiple guises. Typing the word "shamanism" in an Internet search mechanism will uncover a universe of neoshamanic products: vision quest classes, ayahuasca tourism, healing consultancy, shamanistic aerobics, promises of illumination, and spiritual holism. Every Internet site offers some definition of shamanism, generally in the spirit of Mircea Eliade: that is, the ancient technique of ecstasy, the base of all religious phenomena, not itself a religion. All sites draw heavily on the ideas of trance and the soul's journey in order to propose a loving linkage with all beings in the world, a holistic transpecific and multidimensional network.

The notion of auxiliary spirits also appears in some Internet sites. According to one: "Shamanic work is done with the aid of a helping ally of some sorts that the shaman has befriended. They work together as a cooperative team, with the ally being an intermediary between different levels of reality and the shaman, an engineer of altering states of consciousness." Among these allies, animal and plant spirits abound, with a hegemony of felines and narcotics. A praised partner is the jaguar, whose wisdom includes the capacity of understanding the patterns of chaos, of facilitating soul work and empowering the self, of shifting shapes and psychic sights. A cherished vegetal is the ayahuasca, which "focuses and aligns the patient with the archaic essence of spirituality," all the way down to the cellular level.[1]

To a specialist in Amazonian shamanism, the most noticeable fact about this myriad of neoshamanic sites and rites is not its profusion but rather the absence of blood and tobacco. Although hallucinogens are extremely important for shamanic practice in some parts of Amazonia, their consumption is not as widespread as that of tobacco. *Nicotiana rustica*, the most common species cultivated in the tropical forest, is "the principal and nearly universal intoxicant used" in the region (Wilbert 1987:4). Consumed either alone or in combination with other drugs, tobacco is the hallmark of shamanic activity.

The other neglected substance is blood. I do not refer here to the use of human or animal blood in shamanistic ceremonies, which, as far as I know, is absent in Amazonia, nor do I refer to the link between shamanism and cannibalism or, more generally, predation. We know that one of the shaman's functions is to favor hunting and warfare expeditions. We also know that shamans are held capable of magically killing their adversaries and that many Amazonian people do not clearly differentiate the shaman from the witch. These facts are manifestations of a deeper schema, which structures the relationship with all others in the cosmos and connects shamanism to other social practices like warfare and hunting. Elsewhere, I have explored at length this structural correlation, and will only note its demonstration here (see Fausto 1999a, 1999b, 2001a). I will focus, rather, on jaguar symbolism, which may reveal new aspects of this correlation.

The association between the shaman and the jaguar, whose capacity for killing measures only with that of humans, has been known since the first centuries of colonization. Consider that "the [Guarani] magicians, or more properly imposters, who arrogate to themselves full power of warding and inflicting disease and death, of predicting future events, of raising floods and tempests, of transforming themselves into tigers, and performing I know not what other prenatural feats, they religiously venerate" (Dobrizhoffer 1970 [1784]: vol. 1, 63). For the missionaries, the shamans' ability to transform themselves into the feline stood as evidence of their intimate rapport with the devil, the Great Transformer.[2] The priests were also looking for a transformation, but an internal one, which should happen once and for all: conversion. They abhorred native masks and facial painting, manifesting the deep-rooted Catholic suspicion toward the masquerade.[3] In Amazonia, on the contrary, these are central elements of a transformational world (Rivière 1994), in which the key transforming substance is tobacco, and jaguar-becoming is the most common metamorphosis. As Reichel-Dolmatoff writes, "shamans and jaguars are thought to be almost identical, or at least equivalent, in their power, each in his own sphere of action, but occasionally able to exchange their roles" (1975:44). Another author affirms that "if one concept cutting across geographic, linguistic, and cultural boundaries among South American Indians can be singled out, it is that of qualitative identity between jaguars and shamans and accordingly their interchangeability of form" (Furst 1968:154; Wilbert 1987:193).

We also know that the jaguar haunts another important semantic domain and social practice in Amazonia: warfare and cannibalism (literal or symbolic). This is also a well-known fact since the sixteenth century. Consider now that "this same Konyan Bebe had then a great vessel full of human flesh in front of him and was eating a leg which he held to my mouth, asking me to taste it. I replied that even beast[s] which were without understanding did not eat their own species, and should a man devour his fellow creatures? But he took a bite saying, *Jau wara see*: 'I am a tiger; it tastes well,' and with that I left him" (Staden 1928 [1557]:110). In this event, narrated by the German seafarer Hans Staden, a Tupinambá chief identifies itself with a jaguar while savoring a human leg. Perhaps he does it only to tease his unwilling guest (and future food). But there is something else about this odd dialogue—a revealing misunderstanding: Staden thinks of cannibalism as eating the same, whereas Cunhambebe equates it to eating like the jaguar and occupying the position of a predator, not of a prey.[4] Modern ethnographies contain many examples of the identification of warriors with jaguars, and of killing with (symbolic) cannibalism. One may thus ask: What is the common thread that links warfare and shamanism to the jaguar? And what is it to eat like the jaguar?

To address these questions, I will resort to my own data on the Parakanã, a Tupi-speaking people of southeastern Amazonia. Their population totals some eight hundred individuals dispersed in seven villages along the Xingu and Tocantins river basins. They were drawn into state administration in the 1970s and 1980s, but theretofore they practiced warfare and strongly relied on the hunting of big terrestrial mammals. The emphasis on these two activities increased during the twentieth century, especially among the western Parakanã—a fact that may have reinforced the predatory aspect of their shamanism (Fausto 2001a). I do not mean to imply, however, that predation is absent in the shamanism of other Amazonian peoples where warfare is less central a practice or one that went into disuse longer ago.[5] Much to the contrary, I claim that there is an intrinsic link between warfare and shamanism.

A Stench of Blood

Strictly speaking, there are no shamans among the Parakanã, only dreamers. No one attributes this role to himself, and no one is publicly recognized as being a shaman.[6] The difference between a dreamer (*opoahiweté-wa'é*) and a shaman (*moropyteara*) concerns the ability to heal: only the last is held capable of extracting the pathogenic agents that cause diseases, known as *karowara*. Few dreamers admit to having seen one in their dreams, because it is equal to admitting the possibility of being a witch. The stigma is stronger than the prestige, thus discouraging the institutionalization of the shaman's role. This is perhaps one of the effects of the emphasis on predation among the Parakanã: to make the shaman an unfeasible figure.

But what exactly is *karowara*? Why is seeing it equal to being a witch? The Parakanã are not very loquacious on these questions. But we can explore the concept in a comparative way, because it is a very common one among Tupi/Guarani-speaking peoples. Ordinarily *karowara* is associated with cannibal spirits, who cause diseases by eating, from the inside, the flesh of humans. Among the Wayãpi, for instance, it is a synonym for the *anhanga* (the Tupi/Guarani cannibal monster) and one of the shamans' offensive weapons (Gallois 1988). Among the Asurini do Xingu, *Karowara* are anthropomorphic spirits with whom the shaman interacts and who may penetrate a human body and eat it up (Müller 1990).

The best comparative data about the *karowara* are provided by the Asurini do Tocantins, a people very close in language and culture to the Parakanã, who do have shamans in the strict sense of the term. The definitive experience of a novice shaman is the dreaming about the jaguar, from whom he has to extract the *karowara*. Before doing that, however, he is submitted to a test: he has to eat the jaguar's food, which is raw meat full of blood. If he fails, he wakes up vomiting; if he succeeds, he is ready to suck a *karowara* from the jaguar, which he will retain in his mouth as the source of his curing power (Andrade 1992:132–37). During his professional life, he will repeat this act many times, but instead of keeping the *karowara* he extracts from his patients he will spit and inter them.

Before dreaming about the jaguar, the novices are ritually trained by an established shaman. He prepares the teeth of some animals and insufflates them. The teeth start to move by themselves, becoming a *karowara*. The shaman inserts the *karowara* into a long cigar, which the novices smoke during a ritual known as *opetymo* ("eating tobacco").[7] They absorb the *karowara* and have to learn to control it and not be controlled by it—a hard task for a beginner. This is why menstruating women are advised not to attend the ritual: the novice may lose control of himself and, smelling the scent of fresh blood, attack the women (Andrade 1992:128).

In sum, to be a shaman among the Asurini do Tocantins implies eating like the jaguar, and by our (and Cunhambebe's) definition, to be a cannibal. We also begin to see that eating like the jaguar implies a form of cuisine or, better, its absence: cannibalism is equivalent to homophagy and hematophagy, eating raw meat and blood.

Some Parakanã facts support the association between blood and shamanic power that we find among the Asurini do Tocantins. As with the latter, they do not think of the *karowara* as spirits. In fact, they rarely postulate the existence of spirits. *Karowara* are pathogenic objects controlled by shamans, with no autonomous volition but rather only a compulsion to eat human flesh.[8] Although very few people admit to dreaming about the "master of the *karowara*" (*karowarijara*), the Parakanã hold that to acquire a curing power a shaman must suck the *karowara* from this entity, which is variously described as a bat, a capybara, or an anthropomorphic creature. The presence in this series of the capybara, a large vegetarian rodent, may cause wonder, but it is easy to explain. The Parakanã, as do the majority of the Tupi/Guarani, consider the capybara to have the stench of blood. The smell is classified as *pyji'oa* ("odor of blood") whose verbal form is *pyji'o*. All things that *pyji'o* are connected in some way to shamanism, particularly to witchcraft. That is why one should never eat capybara, or even bring a dead one to the village. Nevertheless, there is an animal that has been consumed, despite its smell of blood: the Parakanã cooked selected parts of the giant otter (*Pteronura brasiliensis*) and gave them to young men to make them dream. The giant otter is called *jawataranga*, which I gloss as "the worn jaguar."[9] This otter is a very aggressive predator: it is for the fishes what the jaguar is for the mammals.

The more significant evidence of the association between blood and shamanic power lies elsewhere. Among the Parakanã, the main way for a man to develop his capacity for dreaming is to follow the road of the jaguar; that is, to be a predator (not only of animals, but above all of humans). Killing is conceived as a form of symbolic hematophagy because it is said that it "makes the killer's mouth smell of blood" (*mojoropyji'o*). This stench never disappears: the killer can only resort to the tobacco to "perfume his mouth" (*mojoropi'e*) and counterbalance the taste of blood.[10] However, as we will see, it is precisely this combination of blood and tobacco that potentializes the dreaming, that makes someone have shamanic power.

The Faithful Enemy

Dreaming is a form of interaction with all the entities of the cosmos in their condition as persons—that is, as subjects endowed with intentional agency and perspective. What qualifies an entity to be dreamt about is to have a different perspective from that of the dreamer's. In other words, all oneiric interlocutors are "others" (*amote*), or more precisely, "enemies" (*akwawa*).[11] But in the dream these enemies do not act as enemies but as allies or, better, as a very particular kind of ally: they are termed "pets" (*te'omawa*) and "magic prey" (*temiahiwa*). They are faithful enemies, prey turned into adopted pets that are under the control of the dreamer.

As I have shown elsewhere, this conversion of fierce others into familiars by means of an idiom of adoption is a central feature of both shamanism and warfare in Amazonia (Fausto 1999a, 2001c). In warfare, there is a widespread notion that the killer establishes a privileged relationship with the victim's spirit, which gives him a surplus of agency and creativity. This surplus manifests itself as a capacity to name or rename people, to produce new songs for the rituals, to favor the hunting or even to fertilize the women and produce new children. Shamans also have a special creativity that stems from the relationship with their auxiliary spirits, the majority of which are animal spirits—that is, as kinds of "magic prey," as the Parakanã would term them. The shaman's and warrior's power and job are very similar, although shamanism focuses mainly on the relationship with nonhuman others, whereas warfare concentrates on that with human others.

The interesting fact about the Parakanã is that they have conflated these two operations. A dreamer interacts with all entities of the cosmos, be they humans, animals, plants, stars, natural objects, or artifacts. There is, however, a hierarchy: not all people dreamt about the more powerful others, among whom are human enemies (sometimes described as monstrous), the jaguar, and thunder. The most ordinary dreamt enemies are animals, which the Parakanã call *ma'ejiroa*, a collective noun that designates both a set of objects ("stuff"), and the animals in their condition of prey ("game").[12] Objects and prey can be classed within the same category because they are not credited with much agency. They are at the ground level of a hierarchy whose organizing principle is the capacity for predation. Humans and the jaguar (or jaguarlike beings) occupy the ceiling.

Among the Parakanã, the most powerful dreaming experience is called "bringing in the enemy" (*akwawa-rero'awa*), which is associated with the healing of diseases. Because the dreamers are held incapable of extracting the *karowara* (the pathogenic object), they bring their familiar enemies to perform the cure. This type of dream is composed of two parts: First, the dreamer's double (*a'owa*) meets an enemy people and brings them to the village. Second, he awakes, and interacts with them, as the Parakanã say, "in his real skin" (*ipireté*), that is, in wakeful state. One who has such potent familiars will have a very long and productive life.[13] Whenever ill, he will be cured by them, and will also learn many enemies' names and receive many enemies' songs to give to his kin. He will be at the center of ritual life and kinship, a center from which flows symbolic goods captured in the outside to produce persons and relationships in the inside.

The jaguar occupies a very productive place in this system. The human enemies about whom the Parakanã dream partake of some of the feline's attributes, particularly its alimentary ethics. Consider an example from one well-know dreamer, Koria. He dreamt about the *karajá*, the most terrifying oneiric enemies and the most helpful pets.[14] The *karajá* took Koria to their village when he was ill. Their main shaman, "the one who knows how to make people stand up" (*oporopo'omohowa'é*), came to him, shaking his victim's bones as if it was a maraca. He made an incision on Koria's belly. Then, according to Koria,

> he sucked my blood that was flowing out, ate it up. He cut me again. Ate it up. He pulled out his little cutter. Again, he stuck it in and pulled it out. Then, he sucked for the last time.
> —Come on, stand up!
> I stood up.
> —That is why you come to our encounter, in order for us to cure you, he said.
> He left me. He vomited my exblood. Then he said to his sister:
> —Bring me water to wash my mouth.
> She brought it in a long pot. He drank and let it drop, dropping perhaps completely the stench of my blood (*jerowypyji'oa*).

The curing act is clearly described as a form of hematophagy, although the *karajá* shaman washes his mouth and vomits afterward. When Koria describes the *karajá* alimentary habits, we come to know that they eat a red-tinted flour that makes one fly, as manioc beer does. We may relate this to a Tapirapé dreaming narrative, in which the shaman's auxiliary spirits effectively drink blood as beer: "He [the shaman] refused to drink it, because he understood that the *kauí* was human blood. Ikanancowi saw the spirit drinking from the *kauí* pot and immediately after vomiting blood; he saw another one drinking from another pot and excreting blood" (Wagley 1976:242). Among the enemies that the Parakanã dreamer familiarizes, we count also the *jawararijá*, a monster who sucks people's heart and blood. We could adduce other examples here of auxiliary spirits who are characterized by hematophagy, as is the case of *Titipiur* among the Achuar (Descola 1993:356–57), but it would divert us from our central personage, the jaguar.

The jaguar is, of course, one of the Amazonian shaman's most praised auxiliaries and the source of a very powerful shamanism. Among the Parakanã, dreams about jaguars are always associated with metamorphosis, and sometimes are directly connected to a jaguar killing.[15] Some dreamers are capable of "bringing in" a real jaguar during their oneiric experience and, subsequently, of transforming themselves into one. The metamorphosis is termed *jyromonem*, which literally means "to put a continent on," that is, "to dress." The dreamer brings the jaguar and enters its skin,[16] and, endowed with all its abilities, he goes to the forest to hunt and eat. He may also employ his newly acquired "natural" tools to cure himself or to kill an antagonist, normally a kin. Here is one song that explores this ambiguity of jaguar-becoming:

Ije pota te we'yra
Amoja'a he'ynia-rehe weha
Wepinimohoa-po
Wepinimohoa-po
He he
He he

Will I make my aunt
For her family cry
With my spotted (skin)
With my spotted (skin)?
He he
He he

The song is Iatora's or, better, Iatora's as jaguar, because, as we will see below, the metamorphosis may imply not only an alteration of form but also of point of view. For now, however, let us explore other jaguar facets of Parakanã shamanism. We need to examine them further, particularly in the ritual context, because neither the alimentary ethics of the dreamt enemies, nor the allomorphosis of the dreamer permit us to fully understand the centrality of the jaguar in Parakanã cosmology.

Killing Jaguars

Songs are one of the dreamt enemies' main gifts. For the Parakanã, to dream is equal to receiving songs from the enemy dreamt about. If you say that you have dreamt but do not remember the songs, you are either a very poor dreamer or a liar. The most unspecific term for "song" is *je'engara*, which is formed by the verb "to speak" (*je'eng*) and the agentive nominalizer "*ara*." A song is a special kind of speech, characterized by a surplus of agency. Birds, for instance, do not ordinarily "sing" (*je'engan*) but rather "speak" (*je'eng*), although of course they can sing in dreams, where they appear as persons to the dreamer.

Most of the time, however, the Parakanã employ another word for song: "jaguar" (*jawara*). A common epithet for the dreamer is "master of the jaguars" (*jawajara*). Recall that the enemies familiarized by the dreamer are his "pets" (*te'omawa*) and that the reciprocal of "pet" is "master" (*-jara*). The dreamer is thus both a master of the jaguar songs and of the dreamt enemies. But what is the relation between the songs and the enemy who gives them? Here I argue that the songs are a partible part of the enemies familiarized in dreams.[17] In offering a song, the enemy gives a part of himself, a jaguar-part so to speak. Now, what is a jaguar-part? As I understand it, it stands for the capacity to hold a particular perspective on a relationship; that is, of occupying the position of subject in a relation (see Vilaça 1992:51). The songs therefore are packs of agency, *quanta* of intentionality, that can be transferred from the enemy to the dreamer. Of course, they are not an abstract pack of agency, which circulates as if it was some kind of generic energy. Each song has an owner and a history that starts with the dreaming event and ends with its ritual execution.

The Parakanã conceive the act of singing during the ritual as a "killing" (*ijokatawa*) and designate it literally "to kill" (*joka*). Because masters never slay their pets in Amazonia, a dreamer cannot sing-kill their own songs during the ritual. They have to give it to a third party, who will be the executioner. During the festival, he will sing the jaguar song and bodily represent the dreamt enemy. He thus condenses in his person both perspectives: his own and the enemy's (who may be, remember, any entity of the cosmos). What allows this ritual conflation is the song, that part of the dreamt enemy which is transferred from him to the dreamer, and from the dreamer to the ritual executioner.

Killing a song produces two effects: first, the executioner matures and develops his dreaming abilities, much in the same way as does a warrior after killing an enemy (although in an attenuated form). The jaguar-part permits then the socialization of the enemy's intentionality, which is already part of the dreamer's. The jaguar song multiplies the effects of a homicide, in much the same way as the trophies manipulated in some warfare rituals.[18] The second effect is that the jaguar song dies and, for this reason, cannot be sung again in the ritual but rather only intoned in ordinary situations. It cannot be killed twice. The song preserves the memory of the ritual killing, but after the fact it is void of intentionality. It has been surrendered to the executioner, who will become himself a dreamer (or a more expert one) and will put the ritual machine in motion again to produce new dreamers and capture new songs.

A Scent of Tobacco

The Parakanã ritual during which the songs are "killed" is known as *opetymo*, the tobacco festival. It is also know as *pajé*, which means "shamanic power." It is no wonder that participation in the ritual "makes one dream" (*mo-poahim*); *opetymo* is an initiation into the science of dreams, as much as a warfare ritual.[19] We have seen that among the Asurini do Tocantins this same ritual is explicitly conceived as a way of transmitting the shamans' curing power to the novices. This transference is replicated by the dream about the jaguar, from whom the novice extracts the *karowara* after eating its food. We also saw that there is a close link between acquiring shamanic power and cannibalism. The question I would like to propose now is what does the tobacco have to do with it?

To answer this question, let me start with a commentary about blood symbolism among the Parakanã. How is it conceived when it is out of the body; that is, when it becomes "someone's exblood" (*rowykwera*)? Its most prominent feature is its odor, which is highly contaminating. Someone's exblood affects other people without any physical contact, causing the swelling of the spleen, an intense fatigue, and anal hemorrhage. It is usually men who are affected, either by the victim's blood or by menstrual (and postpartum) blood.[20] That is why menstruating and new-mothering women cannot cook, nor can they sleep with their husband. The victim's blood is even more endangering. During posthomicidal seclusion the killer must drink very bitter infusions made from the inner bark of two species of *Aspidosperma* in order to "extinguish the spleen" (*tomano ipere oja*), and to avoid other deleterious consequences.[21] These infusions are universal blood neutralizers, and preadolescent girls may take them to retard menarche and avoid having children too young.

Although also used by men during posthomicidal seclusion, tobacco has a very different function that has nothing to do with the spleen. The killer smokes it to "perfume the mouth" (*mojoropi'e*), counterbalancing the savor-odor of blood (*pyji'o*). In this olfactory-gustative register the tobacco and the blood have opposed characteristics. Nevertheless, they must be combined to potentialize the dreaming capacity. On the day after having dreamt about the jaguar, the Asurini novice cannot eat food, only smoke tobacco. The same is true of the killer after the homicidal act.

For the Parakanã, as for many other Amazonian peoples (Lévi-Strauss 1966), tobacco is consistently disjointed from honey, which is associated with love, sexual relations, and heaviness; that is, with a state of "earthly" satisfaction that prevents interaction with dreamt enemies. Honey and sweet porridge are at the center of another Parakanã ritual, the flute festival, which inverts every single aspect of the *opetymo*.[22] It is a ritual turned toward the inside, to the relations between the men and the women. In the past, it was also performed for a woman recently captured in a war expedition. By acting out the role of wife and lover, she was introduced into the game of sex and marriage. As the Parakanã say, she was "to put her heart into the flutes" (*toji'omonem takwara-popé*) and stay long with them, menstruating, procreating, and loving.

Blood and tobacco, on the contrary, are outward substances. They cause the necessary bodily and psychic dispositions to meet others, but in two different ways: tobacco makes one light and amplifies one's capacities to see and dream; blood makes one full of powerful intentionality and enhances one's predatory dispositions.[23] In the Parakanã case, I would like to suggest that the tobacco is a sort of white perfumed blood. In the past, whenever they run out of tobacco (a very common occurrence during periods of nomadism), they employed the leaves of a liana to fill the cigars used in the *opetymo*, which are ordinarily made of enrolled *tauari* bark filled with tobacco.[24] This liana is called "blood-liana-alike" (*ipowyrona*), and contains a great quantity of white sap. It is very similar to another liana, which is its prototype: a "blood liana" (*ipowy'a*) that contains a red, bloodlike sap. The red sap is used to fix the charcoal-rich black dye with which the Parakanã paint their lanceolate arrow points, especially those used in warfare. They believe that the mixture of red sap and charcoal causes a lethal hemorrhage. In sum, the Parakanã smoke the leaves of the white-sap-rich liana to dream, and use the red-sap liana to kill their enemies and large terrestrial mammals.

The complementary opposition between red and white liana resonates with that of blood and tobacco during the *opetymo*. The Parakanã while ritually killing the jaguar song, smoke the cigar. Intoxicated with it, the executioner may fall and dream. The Asurini do Tocantins insert a cannibal principle (the *karowara*) into the cigar. Absorbing it the executioner may run crazily, looking for blood.

Although I cannot generalize from the Parakanã and Asurini cases alone, I would like to suggest that in Amazonia the symbolism of blood and the symbolism of tobacco converge in both being "outward substances." As food for future thought, let me allude to some instances that hint at this suggestion. First, there are examples of a direct association between tobacco and the jaguar. The Akawaio of Guiana call a variety of the tobacco plant "tiger tobacco," comparing the mottling of the leaves with the fur of the jaguar. According to Wilbert, "tiger tobacco is of a very special potency, and its effects on the human body relate it to shamanic combativeness and to the shaman-jaguar transformation complex" (1987:151). The link between the jaguar and the tobacco also appears in mythology. The Toba-Pilaga of the Chaco, for instance, recount a myth in which a woman-jaguar is incinerated after having eaten many of her kin. From her ashes, the first tobacco plant sprouts (Métraux 1946:60–62; Lévi-Strauss 1964:107–8).

Second, there are some interesting references to blood in the myths about the origin of the tobacco that are compiled by Lévi-Strauss in *The Raw and the Cooked* (1964:108–13). The Terena myth begins with a woman who poisons her husband by spilling menstrual blood on his food. Informed of her malice, the man gives her honey mixed with the embryos of a snake he had killed. In revenge, she tries to devour him. While chasing him, she falls in a pit that he had dug to trap game. The husband fills up the pit and surveys it; nearby he finds the tobacco plant. The plot revolves around the relationship between predator and prey, with husband and wife alternating these positions. The man who begins as an eater of menstrual blood ends up as a smoker of tobacco leaves.

In a Bororo myth, we find a parallel reference to embryos and the snake. The plot starts with the men coming back from hunting. The women go to their encounter to fetch the game. One of them carries an anaconda, whose blood drips and penetrates into the woman. She gets pregnant. The "son of the snake blood" goes in and out of the mother's belly at his will. Frightened, the mother asks her brothers to kill the unborn baby, which goes out and is killed. The men incinerate the corpse, and from the ashes tobacco and other cultivated plants appear. In this myth, the prey's blood impregnates the killer's wife but the son is not human and has special capacities. Once more the plot starts with blood contamination and finishes with the origin of tobacco.

In another Bororo myth, some men, while preparing newly caught fish for the grill, find tobacco in the belly of one of their prey. They smoke it. The aroma attracts the master of the tobacco, who appears in the form of a bat—that is, of a bloodsucker. He admonishes the men not to swallow the smoke but to exhale it instead. But his request is in vain. For their disregard, the master of the tobacco transforms them into otters. The myth begins with men eating properly cooked food but finishes with their metamorphosis into eaters of raw fish, as a punishment for them having eaten the smoke of tobacco. The spirit who transforms them is both a hematophagous being and the master of the tobacco.

Third, and finally, let me approach blood and tobacco from an axis that organizes this last myth: of transformation. We do not need to dwell on the well-known fact that tobacco is the transforming substance par excellence in Amazonia. But what about the transforming quality of blood? Menstrual blood has a central role here. It is a sign of fertility, it marks that a transformation is going on in a woman's body and implies the possibility of her transforming future people inside it. It is not surprising, therefore, that warfare rites and male initiations thrive on the analogy with the reproductive and transforming power of menstrual blood, and sometimes establishes an explicit connection between the shedding of the victim's blood and menstruation.[25]

Among the Parakanã this analogy has a mythical foundation. Originally, it was the men who menstruate. One day the armadillo shot the moon. The men told the women not to leave the house, but they came out to the plaza and the moon's blood dripped on them. Thereafter they menstruate, and men do not. The men, however, now can shed their victims' blood and can become a dreamer. As dreamers, they can name infants, give songs to adolescents, favor the hunting, and even capture future-infants (*konomiroma*), who they deposit inside the women. The difference between men's and women's creative capacities is that the former have to be acquired, whereas the latter develop naturally.[26]

This fact founds the politics of gender of Parakanã shamanism: women are not suppose to dream, and only exceptionally smoke tobacco. A justification I heard for this disencouragement is that women are too prone to catch *karowara* in their dreams and to use them against people. Fertile women already have a stench of blood, and engaging in shamanism would mean a dangerous hyperconjunction. Significantly, the dreaming activity of post-menopausal women is well accepted.

Mature men, on the contrary, must dream. When a man refuses to go to war and is ashamed of dancing in the *opetymo*, people say he is a child. Taking part in the killing of enemies and songs is essential for maturing. Those who have shame (*jeroji*) cannot familiarize enemies through the dreaming and be fertile in the giving of names and songs to their kin. The stench of blood connotes this fertility and creativity, the capacity for producing transformation. This is the case because Amazonian peoples conceive of homicide as ontological predation; i.e., as a form of devouring some vital constituent of the victim's person and acquiring a surplus of intentionality.[27] The smell of blood that impregnates the killer without any physical contact is a central signifier for thinking about this acquisition. That is why posthomicide taboos focus so much on blood and its stench.[28] As a substantive quality, blood odor expresses an abstract notion in a sensible code; namely, that to kill is to establish a special rapport with the victim, a rapport that implies fertility.[29]

In light of this we can now answer a question posed earlier: What is to eat like the jaguar? It is to consume the victim's activity, of which blood is a strong signifier, without its neutralization by fire. Everyday food, on the contrary, requires the removal of all traces of blood through cooking. Cooking is a technique for eating meat without the danger of being in touch with the subjectivity of the animal eaten.[30] After all, no one can be a jaguar all the time, and not everyone can be a jaguar sometime. This must be a ritualized and controlled activity because being a jaguar is an ambivalent necessity.

Whose Eyes Are Mine?

The Parakanã attribute intentionality to various entities of the cosmos. Some persons, mostly adult men, are capable of interacting with these entities through the dreaming, where they establish with them a special relationship of adoption. As we have seen, the dreamer is the master, the dreamt enemy is the pet. The former seems to control the latter, imposing on the enemy his own perspective. This is fair enough: the enemy familiarized in dreams does not act as an adversary, because he surrenders a part of himself to the dreamer and asks for nothing in exchange. Nevertheless, the actual relationship is much more ambivalent than that, as is the figure of the shaman in most Amazonian indigenous societies. It is not difficult to understand why.

All dream narratives that I have registered concerning the "bringing in of the enemy" contain the following theme: the pets may act as captors and keep their master as a pet, which means adopting and turning him into one of them. In other words, they reverse the sense of familiarization. This is a very common motif in Amazonia, particularly in regard to the notion of "soul loss," a morbid state caused by the undesirable exteriorization of a vital constituent of the person.

In the Parakanã case, the possibility of reversing the relationship between master and pet points to the fact that the dreamer's enterprise is a dangerous one that may result in him surrendering his perspective to benefit the other's. The danger, however, is not only his own because it involves his kinfolk. He may see them with the eyes of the enemies; that is, he may see his kin as if they were others. In some oneiric narratives, the theme is stated explicitly: the dreamt enemy wants to change the dreamer's point of view. Consider the following dialogue extracted from a dream narrative of a man who had been shot in his leg. The wounded dreamer encounters his enemies:

> I was among them. They asked me:
> —Was it your kin who shot you?
> —No. The enemy killed me, I answered.
> —Tell us where your kinfolk are, so that we can kill them all.
> —Ok. Let's go, I said without conscience.

I translate here the Parakanã's expression *awai'yma* as "without conscience," but it literally means "not (being a) person."[31] When the dreamer surrenders his perspective he becomes other, and thus a danger to his kin. The same is true of killers. In the past, when returning from a warfare expedition, the warriors had to abandon their bow and enter into seclusion. Their folks, particularly the women, would remember them that they are kin, not others: "Do not have anger toward us," they would say. All measures were taken to avoid a complete alteration of the killers' point of view.

However, to be a killer or a shaman in Amazonia unavoidably implies the cumulating of more than one perspective, and a certain capacity of alternating between them or employing both at the same time. Not all perspectives are equal. Because agency is variously distributed among the entities of the cosmos, and the capacity for predation is a hallmark of powerful agency, the shaman, as the warrior, is commonly associated with predators like the jaguar. To become a puissant shaman one must entertain a special relationship with ferocious beings, eaters of raw meat and blood. This relationship implies a sharing of perspectives. The shaman's ambivalence stems from his serving, in person, as a point of articulation between his perspective and that of his ferocious familiar spirits.

The most obvious manifestation of this fact is the shaman-jaguar metamorphosis, where the former actually become the latter, as Wilbert clearly shows for the Campa complex: "Campa jaguar shamans can adopt a jaguar form upon embarking on their far-flung journey in search of food. Human food does not nourish them when they are in jaguar form. Rather, were-jaguars of this kind eat people, which appear to them as peccary. They travel long distances so as to avoid eating their friends and kin. Especially during the months of March through June were-jaguars are on the prowl of children or in shamanic terms young 'peccary,' and again, as jaguars, shamans are unable to distinguish their own human children from others. Thus, when in the form of jaguars, shamans *are* jaguars: they see like them and they think like them" (1987:194). In the same vein, Vilaça writes about the Wari' shaman: "The negative facet of shamanic agency concerns his capacity to turn into an enemy at any moment, attacking his own people, and possibly causing death. Such action is unintentional, almost a 'technical failure': the shaman's vision becomes deficient and he starts to see his kin as enemies or animal prey. The effect is as if his different bodies merge in such a way that he, as Wari', adopts the animal's point of view" (1999:250).

The alteration of perspective, the intimate rapport with dangerous spirits, the capacity of magically killing people, the cannibal connotation of the initiation and the healing practice, and the going-jaguar—all these facts contribute to making the Amazonian shaman a redoubtable figure.

Conclusion

Amazonian shamanism is not a loving animism, as its middle-class urban vulgate want us to believe. It is better understood as a predatory animism: subjectivity is attributed to human and nonhuman entities, with whom some people are capable of interacting verbally and establishing relationships of adoption or alliance, which permit them to act upon the world in order to cure, to fertilize, and to kill. As I suggest elsewhere (Fausto 1999a), however, the capacity of familiarizing other subjectivities, of having them as allies, depends on predation in warfare and hunting.

Whereas neoshamanism is turned on the remodeling of individual subjectivities, indigenous shamanism is concerned with producing new persons and social relationships from the stock of human and nonhuman subjectivities existing in the cosmos. The question is, then, how can one acquire a surplus of intentionality and agency, and avoid being deployed of his or her own? If there is no ontological difference between predator and prey, how can one maintain oneself in the position of predator and not of prey? Amerindian warfare and shamanism seem to revolve around this question.

Understandably enough, the predatory act is the lost fact in modern, urban, middle-class shamanism, which purged the phenomenon from all its ambiguous attributes. It is thus no wonder why the jaguar, although a recurrent figure, is depicted as an endangered species and not as a dangerous predator. Neoshamanism subjects others' thoughts to Western thinking and moral standards: there must be good and bad, both a light and a dark side, and a clear-cut frontier in order to demarcate a basic contrast of ethic. There is no such dichotomy in South American shamanism, which thrives on ambivalence.

One of the difficulties of the sixteenth-century missionaries in translating Christian texts to indigenous languages was to find a suitable equivalent for God, because there was no such thing as an indigenous supreme divinity to be translated into a unique (although trine) God. Further, to make things worse, once the missionaries had chosen one among various possibilities, they had to rid him of his ambiguous attributes. If God were a jaguar, their task would have been much easier.

What does it mean not to base a cosmology on a clear-cut opposition between good and bad? What kind of society does so? These are questions that have haunted Western thinking since the sixteenth century. Nevertheless, the answers have always been a mere repetition of the very dichotomy that causes the questioning. Choose your side: the noble or the fierce savage? Hobbes himself actually preferred the latter, whereas Rousseau would have favored the former. Nowadays some people make a living by selling one or the other image, while others just comfort their hearts in defending one of them. The choice is less motivated by facts than by the approach one has to one's own society. Again, no novelty here. The "state of nature" had the same function for sixteenth- and seventeenth-century philosophers: it was a way to distinguish between the original and the artificial in human nature so as to judge European society at the time.

In any case we must recognize one fact: the very culture that bases its ethics in a universal distinction between good and bad has developed (among many other things) an insurmountable capacity for violence and destruction. Indigenous cultures that prospered in ambivalence, on the contrary, were not so successful. A famous Jesuit missionary once said, maybe in a burst of despair, that the best form of preaching for people like the Tupinambá was with the sword and the spear. He was only partially right. The Europeans conquered South America with the word and the sword, a mixture that proved to be much more efficient than the fine blend of blood and tobacco that characterizes Amazonian shamanism.

Notes

I wrote this article during my stay in France as visiting researcher at the Laboratoire d'Anthropologie Sociale (CNRS/Collège de France). I would like to thank Philippe Descola for the invitation to France, and the Coordenadoria de Aperfeiçoamento de Pessoal do Ensino Superior (CAPES) for providing the means for my sojourn. My thanks also go to Aparecida Vilaça for her comments on a first version of this text, and above all to the Parakanã among whom I collected the data presented here. My fieldwork was carried out in 1988–1989, 1992–1993, 1995, and 1999, and was supported by Financiadora de Estudos e Projetos, Associação Nacional de Pós-Graduação em Ciências Sociais, the Ford Foundation, Universidade Federal do Rio de Janeiro, and the Wenner-Gren Foundation for Anthropological Research.

1 I took the liberty of extracting the passages cited in this paragraph from the sites "Shamanism: Working with Animals" (*www.animalspirits.com*), "Amazon Spirit Quest" (*www.biopark.org*), and from Dr. Thomas Pinkson's page, maintained by the 7th Direction (*www.7thdirection.com*).

2 The Jesuits oscillated between considering the shamans' powers a mere imposture or an effective demoniacal force. Father Dobrizhoffer, for instance, seems to prefer the first alternative, whereas Ruiz de Montoya was inclined to accept the second. The former quotes a dialogue he had with the Abipones about the metamorphosis into jaguars: "'You daily kill tigers in the plain,' I said, 'without dread, why then should you weakly fear a false imaginary tiger in the town?' 'You Fathers don't understand these matters,' they reply, with a smile. 'We never fear, but kill tigers in the plain, because we see them. Artificial tigers we do fear, because they can neither be seen nor killed by us'" (1970 [1784]: vol. 2, 77–78).

3 Recounting his encounter with a Guarani group yet unconquered, Dobrizhoffer writes: "His [the cacique's] son, a handsome boy of ten years old, had all his face painted with small black stars. 'You think', said I, 'to adorn your face with these stars, but you have disfigured it most wretchedly. Come, behold yourself in this mirror.' Having looked at his face a little while, he hastened to some water to wash it, and he, who with his naked limbs, had just before come to me a perfect Pyracmon, when he had wiped off the soot, seemed transformed into a Daphnis" (1970 [1784]: vol. 1, 78). On the church's attitudes toward the masquerade in the Middle Ages, see Schmitt 2001.

4 Viveiros de Castro suggests that Cunhambebe's statement may be understood as "a jaguar-becoming, where 'jaguar' is a quality of the *act*, not of the *subject*. . . . Even if the object of becoming is imaginary, the becoming is real, and the ferocious alterity is a quality of the verb, not its predicate" (1992:271). On Staden's account, see Forsyth 1985 and Whitehead 2000.

5 I have analyzed the historical transformations of Guarani shamanism in order to show that there has been an almost complete dissociation between the shaman and the jaguar, and the replacement of predation by the concept of "love" (*mborayhu*). I have called this process "dejaguarification" (Fausto 2001b). There are interesting parallels between the Guarani case and other examples of historical transformation of shaman-

istic systems in Amazonia. I am thinking especially of the Yanesha (Santos Granero 1991), and the upper Río Negro peoples (Hugh-Jones 1994; Reichel-Dolmatoff 1975; Wright 1992).

6   When talking about shamans and dreamers, I employ the masculine pronouns. Among the Parakanã, as in most Amazonian societies, the great majority of dreamers are men and the activity is supposedly restricted to them. This does not mean that there are no women who dream, but that the activity is genderized as male, even when the dreamer is a woman.

7   The word *opetymo* seems to result from the combination of the noun *petym* ("tobacco") and the verb *'o* ("to eat").

8   There is a specific term to speak of the concrete forms in which the *karowara* may present themselves in the patient's body. This term is *topiwara* and comprehends monkey teeth, some species of beetles, stingray stings, and sharp-pointed bones; in sum, every tiny, pointed object when animated by a shaman. Among other Tupi/Guarani-speaking people, *topiwara* are the shaman's auxiliary spirits, the majority of which are animal spirits.

9   *Jawataranga* can be analyzed as *jawa(ra)-tarang-a* (jaguar—to wear out—nominalizer). Other Amazonian peoples seem to draw the same association between the giant otter and the jaguar. Among the Yágua of Peru, for instance, the former is named "aquatic jaguar" (Chaumeil and Chaumeil 1992:27).

10 Once the Parakanã told me that just after contact some killers vomited whenever they took Western medication, and this vomiting made them lose their *pajé* (shamanic power). They supposed that there was an incompatibility between the drugs and the stench of blood in their mouths, and they believed to have discovered an efficient neutralizer for it.

11 *Akwawa* is a general category for all entities in their condition as a person, who are not a member of ego's group. In other words, all "real" enemies and all dreamt interlocutors.

12 In the first sense, one may say: "The white man is distributing his stuff" (*omajarang aka Toria oma'ejiroa*). In the second sense, one may say: "I going to hunt and kill the game" (*aata weha ijokao ma'ejiroa*).

13 Let me briefly note that an important connection here that I cannot develop in this essay is the idea that homicide is linked to a long life and the curing of diseases. The Parakanã say, for instance, that one kills an enemy "for his illness" (*ojemonawa-pé oja*). On this theme, see Fausto 2001a:308–14.

14 For a thorough exploration of this dream, see Fausto 2001a:358–62, 2001c.

15 A man who has slain a jaguar may bring its corpse to the village and dance with it in order to favor the dreaming about a jaguar.

16 In this case, the Parakanã do not say that it is the dreamer in "his real skin" (*ipireté*) that enters into the beast, because the skin here is the jaguar fur. When I asked Iatora about who effectively dressed it, he said: "I, indeed" (*ije été*).

17 I am drawing here on Strathern's notion of partible persons (1988:178–79) without conceptualizing, however, all relations as gift exchange.

18 See Fausto 1999a, where I argue that the ritual killing in the *opetymo* is connected to real killings. See also Fausto 1999b, where I develop the idea that a central feature of Amazonian warfare is the producing of many effects from a single death.

19 Two *opetymo* were realized after a warfare expedition: one just after the warrior's return, the other to mark the end of the posthomicide taboos. In this occasion, the killer announced his intention to dance and make his victim's hair fall as a reference to the corruption of the corpse.
20 Once a man said to me that women do not suffer from the swelling of the spleen because they do not shoot people (which is not entirely true in what concerns western Parakanã history). A woman contended, however, that the proximity to a killer may occasionally contaminate them with the victim's blood.
21 These trees are regionally known in Portuguese as *carapanaúba* and *quina*. The Parakanã call them, respectively, *marawa* and *inajarona*.
22 Whereas the latter is a diurnal rite of individually executed songs, focused on tobacco smoking and the killing of male enemies, the former is a nocturnal festival of collectively danced instrumental music, associated with eating honey and with sexual relationships between lovers.
23 To be precise, the Parakanã do not exactly associate blood contamination with predatory disposition. This state is connected instead to another part of the victim: the *kawahiwa*. This term is composed of the word for "fat" (*kawa*) and the suffix *ahiwa*, which occurs in key shamanic terms like "dream" (*ipoahiwa*), "song for curing" (*karahiwa*), and "oneiric prey" (*temiahiwa*). As I understand it, *ahiwa* is a modifier that indicates, at the same time, fierceness, danger, immateriality, and fertility (see Fausto 2001a:316–17).
24 *Tauari* (*Couratari* sp.) is a *Lecythidaceae*, whose inner bark is commonly used in Amazonia as a cigar wrapper. The Parakanã call it *petyma'ywa*, that is, "cigar or tobacco tree."
25 I point to this analogy when I analyzed the symbolism that makes initiation (and warfare rites) a kind of ritualized male menarche and a mode of male procreation (see Fausto 1999a:947; 952, 2001a:456–68).
26 "Naturally" is here the correct term, if we take it for not depending on intersubjective relation. Preadolescents may take infusions to retard the menarche but not to spur it. Menstruation just happens to them. What depends on intersubjective relation is the development of the breasts. The Parakanã say that boys "make breast" (*mokom*) on girls by having sexual relations with them.
27 For the expression "ontological predation," see Albert 1985, and Viveiros de Castro 1993:192. For a description of the phenomenon, see, among many others, Fausto 2001a, Viveiros de Castro 1996a; Vilaça 1992; Lima 1995; Sterpin 1993; Journet 1995.
28 For the Yanomami, see Albert 1985:341–81 and Lizot 1996; for the Wari', see Vilaça (1992:107–13); for the Matis, see Erikson 1986:194–97; for the Araweté, see Viveiros de Castro 1992:240; for the Juruna, see Lima 1995:203; for the Nivacle of the Chaco, see Sterpin 1993:43; for the Kayapó, see Vidal 1977:156–57, and Verswijver 1992:194–201; for the Timbira, see Carneiro da Cunha 1978:103–5, and DaMatta 1976:85–87.
29 The literature is full of examples in which the killer's digesting of the victim's blood replicates the familiarization of the victim's spirit. The Wari' provides the most clear instance. After the homicide the victim's blood-soul penetrates the killer's body and makes him fat, a fact that is compared to a female pregnancy. During the seclusion the blood is digested and transformed into semen, which will inseminate the women. Homicide leads thus to the constitution of two rapports of filiation: an actual one (the

killer fertilizes the women with the exblood, now sperm), and a spiritual one (the killer is conceived as the "father" of the victim's spirit) (see Conklin 1989:239-41; Vilaça 1996:120-23).

30 For some Amazonian peoples cooking is not enough, and a shaman must treat the food before it is safe for consumption. The "shamanizing" of food corresponds to its desubjectifying. On this theme, see Viveiros de Castro 1996b:119;139. For examples, see Arhem 1993:111; Hugh-Jones 1996:127-28; Crocker 1985:152; Vilaça 1992:66-68; and Kaplan 1975:39.

31 The expression is formed by the word *awa* ("person") plus the negative suffix *y'yma*. Whenever speaking of a dead person, it is suffixed to his or her name, meaning "the late so-and-so."

References

Albert, Bruce. 1985. "Temps du sang, temps des cendres: Représentation de la maladie, système rituel et espace politique chez les Yanomami du sud-est (Amazonie brésilienne)." Ph.D. diss., Université de Paris-X (Nanterre).

Andrade, Lucia M. M. de. 1992. "O corpo e os cosmos: Relações de gênero e o sobrenatural entre os Asurini do Tocantins." Ph.D. diss., Universidade de São Paulo.

Arhem, Kaj. 1993. "Ecosofia Makuna." In *La selva humanizada: Ecología alternativa en el trópico húmedo colombiano*, ed. F. Correa. 109-26. Bogotá: Instituto Colombiano de Antropología / Fondo FEN Colombia / Fondo Editorial CEREC.

Carneiro da Cunha, M. Manuela. 1978. *Os mortos e os outros: Uma análise do sistema funerário e da noção de pessoa entre os Indios Krahó*. São Paulo: Hucitec.

Chaumeil, Bonnie, and Jean-Pierre Chaumeil. 1992. "L'oncle et le neveu: La parenté du vivant chez les Yagua (amazonie péruvienne)." *Journal de la Société des Américanistes* 78: 25-37.

Conklin, Beth. 1989. "Images of Health, Illness, and Death among the Wari' (Pakaas-Novos) of Rondonia, Brazil." Ph.D. diss., University of California, San Francisco.

Crocker, Jon Chris. 1985. *Vital Souls: Bororo Cosmology, Natural Symbolism, and Shamanism*. Tucson: University of Arizona Press.

DaMatta, Roberto. 1976. *Um mundo dividido: A estrutura social dos Apinayé*. Petrópolis: Vozes.

Descola, Philippe. 1993. *Les lances du crépuscule: Relation Jivaros, haute amazonie*. Paris: Plon.

Dobrizhoffer, Martin. 1970 [1784]. *An Account of the Abipones, an Equestrian People of Paraguay*. New York: Johnson Reprint Corporation.

Erikson, Philippe. 1986. "Alterité, tatouage et anthropophagie chez les Pano: La Belliqueuse quête de soi." *Journal de la Société des Américanistes* 62: 185-210.

Fausto, Carlos. 1999a. "Of Enemies and Pets: Warfare and Shamanism in Amazonia." *American Ethnologist* 26 (4): 933-56.

——. 1999b. "Da inimizade: Forma e simbolismo da guerra indígena." In *A outra margem do ocidente*, São Paulo: Companhia das Letras.

——. 2001a. *Inimigos fiéis: História, guerra e xamanismo na Amazônia*. São Paulo: Edusp.

——. 2001b. "Si dieu était jaguar: Cannibalisme et christianisme chez les Guarani (XVI-XX siècle)." Paper presented at the École Pratiques des Hautes Études, Paris.

———. 2001c. "La conversion des ennemis: Un rêve amazonien." Paper presented at the École Pratiques des Hautes Études, Paris.
Forsyth, Donald W. 1985. "Three Cheers for Hans Staden: The Case for Brazilian Cannibalism." *Ethnohistory* 32: 17–36.
Furst, Peter T. 1968. "The Olmec Were-Jaguar Motif in the Light of Ethnographic Reality." In *Dumbarton Oaks Conference on the Olmec*, ed. E. Benson. 143–74. Washington, D.C.: Dumbarton Oaks Research Library and Collection.
Gallois, Dominique T. 1988. "O movimento na cosmologia Waiãpi: Criação, expansão e transformação do mundo." Ph.D. diss., Universidade de São Paulo.
Hugh-Jones, Stephen. 1994. "Shamans, Prophets, Priests, and Pastors." In *Shamanism, History, and the State*, ed. N. Thomas and C. Humphrey. 32–75. Ann Arbor: University of Michigan Press.
———. 1996. "Bonnes raisons ou mauvaise conscience? De l'ambivalence de certains amazoniens envers la consommation de viande." *Terrains* 26: 123–48.
Journet, Nicolas. 1995. *La paix des jardins: Structures sociales des indiens curripaco du haut Rio Negro (Colombie)*. Paris: Musée de L'homme.
Kaplan, Joanna. 1975. *The Piaroa: A People of the Orinoco Basin*. Oxford: Clarendon Press.
Lévi-Strauss, Claude. 1964. *Le cru et le cuit. Mythologiques I*. Paris: Plon.
———. 1966. *Du miel aux cendres. Mythologiques II*. Paris: Plon.
Lima, Tânia Stolze. 1995. *A parte do cauim: Etnografia juruna*. Rio de Janeiro: Museu Nacional/UFRJ.
Lizot, Jacques. 1996. "Sang et statut des homicides Chez les Yanomami centraux (Venezuela)." *Systèmes de Pensée en Afrique Noire* 14: 105–26.
Métraux, Alfred. 1946. "Myths of the Toba and Pilagá Indians of the Gran Chaco." *Memoirs of the American Folklore Society* 40: .
Müller, Regina. 1990. *Os Asuriní do Xingu: História e Arte*. Campinas: Editora da UNICAMP.
Reichel-Dolmatoff, G. 1975. *The Shaman and the Jaguar*. Philadelphia: Temple University Press.
Rivière, Peter. 1994. "WYSINWYG in Amazonia." *JASO* 25: 255–62.
Santos-Granero, Fernando. 1991. *The Power of Love: The Moral Use of Knowledge amongst the Amuesha of Central Peru*. London: Athlone Press.
Schmitt, Jean-Claude. 2001. "Les masques, le diable, les morts dans l'occident médiéval." In *Le Corps, les rites, les rêves, le temps: Essais d'Anthropologie Médiéval*. Paris: Gallimard.
Staden, Hans. 1928 [1557]. *Hans Staden: The True History of His Captivity*. Trans. and ed. by M. Letts. London: George Routledge and Sons.
Sterpin, Adriana. 1993. "La Chasse aux scalps chez les Nivacle du Gran Chaco." *Journal de La Société des Américanistes* 79: 33–66.
Strathern, Marilyn. 1988. *The Gender of the Gift: Problems with Women and Problems with Society in Melanesia*. Berkeley: University of California Press.
Verswijver, Gustaaf. 1992. *The Club-Fighters of the Amazon: Warfare among the Kayapo*. Working paper of the faculty of letters, University of Ghent, 179. Ghent: University of Ghent.
Vidal, Lux. 1977. *Morte e vida de uma sociedade indígena brasileira*. São Paulo: Hucitec/Edusp.
Vilaça, Aparecida. 1992. *Comendo como gente: Formas do canibalismo Wari'*. Rio de Janeiro: Editora da UFRJ.

———. 1996. *Quem somos nós: Questões da alteridade no encontro dos Wari' com os brancos*. Ph.D. diss., Rio de Janeiro: Museu Nacional/UFRJ.

———. 1999. "Devenir autre: Chamanisme et contact interethnique en amazonie brésilienne." *Journal de la Société des Américanistes* 85: 239–60.

Viveiros de Castro, Eduardo. 1992. *From the Enemy's Point of View: Humanity and Divinity in an Amazonian Society*. Chicago: University of Chicago Press.

———. 1993. "Alguns aspectos da afinidade no dravidianato amazônico." In *Amazônia: Etnologia e história indígena*, ed. E. Viveiros de Castro and M. Carneiro da Cunha. 150–210. São Paulo: NHII-USP/FAPESP.

———. 1996a. "Le meurtrier et son double chez les Araweté (Brésil): Un exemple de fusion rituelle." *Systèmes de Pensée en Afrique Noire* 14: 77–104.

———. 1996b. "Os pronomes cosmológicos e o perspectivismo ameríndio." *Mana: Estudos de Antropologia Social* 2 (2): 115–44.

Wagley, Charles. 1976. "Xamanismo tapirape." In *Leituras de etnologia brasileira*, ed. E. Schaden. 236–67. São Paulo: Companhia Editora Nacional.

Whitehead, Neil. 2000. "Hans Staden and the Cultural Politics of Cannibalism." HAHR, 80: 721–52.

Wilbert, Johannes. 1987. *Tobacco and Shamanism in South America*. New Haven: Yale University Press.

Wright, Robin. 1992. "Guardians of the Cosmos: Baniwa Shamans and Prophets." *History of Religion* 32 (1): 32–58.

The Wars Within: Xinguano Witchcraft and Balance of Power

Michael Heckenberger

> Sometime later [after the first white men came], when there were [again] many children, Kálusi [Karl von den Steinen] arrived . . . in the time that the white men had become "good." . . . But, afterward, the deaths began. The witchcraft diseases [kuríhe] arrived. We became few. In the time the white men came [again]; they brought [back] the witchcraft diseases, the old ones, the witches. The witchcraft arrows flew. Many died. — Kuikuru elder, quoted by B. Franchetto

In the upper Xingu River region of southern Amazonia, matters of life and death and of "good" and "evil" are intimately tied to conceptions of witchcraft. It is, the Xinguanos firmly believe, the root cause of most misfortune and illness. Mishaps can occur by accident, and nonhuman spirits and "monsters" can cause sickness and death. The witch—the assault sorcerer or "dark shaman"—stands out most clearly, however, as the embodiment of evil in the world. Although human in form, witches lack empathy for other humans and act for purely personal motives: rivalry, spite, jealousy, vengeance, and the like. Spirits can also show indifference to human suffering and purposely do harm, but they exist outside of human society. They can be good or bad, and, while dangerous, they are not considered inherently evil—if you make the appropriate observances but otherwise don't mess with them they generally do little harm. Witches, on the other hand, exist within society as humans, yet they also work against human society and need little or no provocation to persecute their victims.

We might therefore view witchcraft as the antithesis of society, its dark side or alter ego. By its antisociality, however, witchcraft is a root metaphor for sociality; it implicitly defines what is socially appropriate, good, beautiful, disciplined, moral, and ultimately what is human, through witchcraft's inappropriate, bad, uncontrolled, immoral, inhuman-ness. Witches are precisely what humans ought not to be: individualistic, self-serving, and opportunistic, parasites that victimize and kill innocent people who are often powerless to resist. Dark shamans control or channel a destructive evil force, a raw coercive power that undermines the most basic moral values—sharing, humility, charity, etc.; the many over the one—and threaten human life. Not surprisingly, witchcraft is met with an equally deadly response, a similarly destructive power: execution. This coercive power, this institutional violence, is viewed as legitimate, even socially sanctioned, and is administered through ritualized trials, ordeals, and social dramas. Counter-witchcraft is thus both a juro-political instrument administered by chiefs and prominent men, and an ethno-medical technique applied by shaman and counterwitches to rid society of spiritual parasites and pathogens.

Witchcraft is a central concern of Xinguanos, and in the upper Xingu as elsewhere in the region it has been widely noted by ethnographers. Actual instances of presumed witchcraft, counterwitchcraft, or accusations and executions, however, are rare, and ethnographic cases involve isolated cases or solicited descriptions of past instances. Furthermore, in contrast to native Amazonian perspectives, which often place great emphasis on dark shamans and their ways, witchcraft has received relatively little attention in regional ethnology. Like the related issues of politics, ritual, and ideology, in general witchcraft has been overshadowed by anthropological inquiry into domestic economics and human ecology, mythology, and kinship, in part due to the long-held assumption that power was absent or subdued among Amazonian peoples (Clastres 1987; Lévi-Strauss 1943; Steward 1949). For Amazonia there are no classic ethnographies or broad comparative studies of the topic—such as exist for Europe, Africa, Melanesia, and North America—from which to frame regional comparisons.

Nevertheless, the upper Xingu is one of the better-known places of Amazonian witchcraft. In fact, case studies from the upper Xingu have provided definitive examples of how witchcraft functions as a mechanism of social control (Dole 1966); how it operates within the context of chiefly rivalry and politics (Ireland 1996); and how witchcraft and power relations, within the triad of chief, shaman, and witch, fluctuate according to differing historical contexts, particularly regarding disease (Heckenberger 2000b). Researchers have noted witchcraft throughout the twentieth century, and virtually all the ethnographies from the 1950s forward recognize it as a central feature of Xinguano peoples. They describe it in the form and manner I witnessed in the 1990s (see, e.g., Basso 1973; Carneiro 1977; Dole 1962, 1966; Gregor 1977), and my experiences agree with most of what they say.

Witchcraft was a critical element of my ethnographic experience. Seven people died during my first stay with the Kuikuru (Carib-speaking Xinguano), five of whom were firmly believed to be the victims of witchcraft. The experience was for me very personal, emotional, and immediate because several victims were members of my adoptive family, the family of the primary chief, and people for whom I care a great deal.[1] Although each person died of a different illness with different symptoms, the deaths were seen as linked, particularly those most closely related to the chief. It was in the eyes of the Kuikuru an epidemic of witchcraft, and the aim, in the eyes of many, was to upset the balance of power in the village and more broadly. Indeed, a war was brewing just beneath the surface, within society, and emotions and stress ran high.

Witchcraft was not part of my research "design": I did not go looking for it or ask questions and seek answers about it. But, unavoidably, it became a central aspect of my research: it found me. Witchcraft must be understood historically, it is not a constant institution but rather varies in direct proportion to the frequency of illness, misfortune, and death experienced in a region. I was fully cognizant of the fact that much of the history of witchcraft over the past five centuries was tied to "the great dying," the sobering reality that from the sixteenth century onward many people died in epidemics.[2] What I realized only later was that, as today, the vast majority of these deaths were attributed to witchcraft, in one way or another. I wasn't prepared for the centrality of witchcraft in understanding Xinguano history.

Three things in particular about witchcraft stood out in my mind. First is the intensity of the experience. It is about illness, death, and loss, and because these issues are not viewed as natural but typically the actions of other members of the community it also revolved around jealousy, fear, and hate. In other words, witchcraft is extremely emotional, particularly for the people most immediately affected by it and for everyone in the midst of it. Second is the intensity of political climate: the atmosphere was charged and the divisions between people and interest groups were accentuated. Third, in the midst of such an agitated or turbulent social climate, is the efficacy of singular events and people. There is much more to witchcraft than social role playing or working out structural rules; it is, as we might expect of something so central to life and death, defined by contingency, negotiation, and strategy.

Xinguanos and Others

Xinguano (upper Xingu) society refers to a population of closely related communities that inhabit the topographic basin formed by headwaters of the Xingu River as they descend from the northern flanks of the central Brazilian plateau into the Amazon basin. The Xinguanos are settled agriculturalists and fisherpeople, who live in large, more or less permanent villages, internally ranked according to birthright and political power and integrated into a broader political body, Xinguano society. The regional society is pluriethnic and composed of diverse communities (twelve in 2003), speaking five distinctive languages: two Tupian languages (Kamayura and Aueti), two Arawak languages (Yawalapiti and Mehinacu/Waura), and four dialects of one Carib language (Kuikuru, Kalapalo, Matipu, and Nafuqua). They all differ somewhat from one another, in part related to their divergent histories in the region, but all generally share the same cultural values and traditions, and all form a moral community and define themselves as a people. They are "human," what the Kuikuru call *kuge*,[3] and other peoples, whether indigenous or not, are considered a little less human: prone to violence, unpredictable, and wild (*nikogo*)—like witches.

Xinguanos are not typical of broader Amazonian cultural patterns, at least not those traditionally viewed as typical of all or most of the region by anthropologists working there: that is, as small, egalitarian, politically autonomous, and impermanent "tropical forest tribes." Xinguano peoples are also notable for their unique way of accommodating cultural pluralism within a peaceful, if not always harmonious, way of life. Virtually surrounded by groups that valorize aggressive masculinity and bellicosity, Xinguano actively avoid open hostility and abhor violence and murder. Ritualized "warfare" occurs between Xinguano communities, specifically in the context of the intertribal spear-throwing competitions between two villages, and, more generally, the wrestling matches that occur between villages, especially the chiefly funeral ceremony.[4] Open hostilities or warfare between communities is virtually unknown, although armed conflicts between Xinguanos and other indigenous groups have occurred multiple times in the past, even though seldom at the instigation of the Xinguanos.[5]

Violence, aggression, and blood are epistemologically linked: blood causes aggressive or violent tendencies, it makes people violent and people are stigmatized, dangerous, for having human blood "on their hands." This belief is rooted in creation myths, for the Kuikuro did not accept the bowl of blood offered them by the creator. This distinguishes them from their neighbors, traditionally warlike groups of Tupian and Gê-speaking peoples, and from white people (who did accept the blood offering), and it permeates their lives, most obviously in their food restrictions on game (Heckenberger 2001). This belief forms the ontological foundation of otherness for the Xinguanos: it is what makes them "good," "peaceful," and "beautiful," and what makes others much less so—"wild Indians," white people, and witches— those against whom war must occasionally be waged.

There is one major exception to Xinguano taboos against bloodshed—witches, as with other dangerous and life-threatening animals, like jaguars, anacondas, poisonous snakes (there are food taboos for these creatures but they are killed routinely). Killing witches is not only accepted in some situations, but is sanctioned by chiefly decree and at least partial public opinion. Overt aggression seldom occurs outside of the witchcraft complex, the immoral and covert actions of witches and the overt and legitimate (although dangerous and stigmatized nonetheless) actions of counterwitches, diviners, chiefs, and executioners, bent on rooting out and eliminating the hidden evil lurking in the midst of human society. Their response is commonly decisive, whether through ritual or warfare, and retaliation against enemies is equally decisive, with the single-minded purpose to destroy the enemy, whether within or without.

Triangle of Power: Witches, Chiefs, and Shamans

Witchcraft, following convention, describes the aggressive and immoral use of supernatural techniques (Walker 1989:3). In the anthropological literature, witchcraft is commonly addressed from either a sociological and psychological perspective: the former focused on the functions of witchcraft and the actions it entails, the latter on beliefs and the effects they have on individuals. But, as Lawrence notes, "sorcery and healing must be placed in the total cosmic framework that people conceive to exist: not only in the human socio-political structure and not only in the religious system but simultaneously in both" (1987:21). On the one hand, witchcraft is in the realm of institutional violence, along with feuding and warfare, but, on the other hand, it lies squarely in the domain of the supernatural, like shamanism.

In an overview on sorcery and witchcraft in Melanesia, Stephen (1987) helps frame certain issues relevant to Amazonia, as Africa had once before helped define problems in Melanesia. Indeed, Amazonia shares much in common with Melanesia—and elsewhere, for that matter (i.e., "witchcraft" in "precapitalist" societies and the idiosyncracies of the region or its cases will shed light on very general issues). As Stephen notes, witches and sorcerers (shamans)[6] both channel spiritual power, although "their mediation of that power is in opposite directions. . . . The sorcerer accepts responsibility for life and death and thus gains influence; the witch is forced to take blame for misfortune and death and thus faces social ruin" (251). The sorcerer, Stephen suggests, is defined by cosmic responsibility, controlled/active use of cosmic power, support of the moral order, and is socially rewarded. Shamanism is an instrument of the powerful. The witch, in contrast, is defined by cosmic blame: the uncontrolled/passive use of power for destructive ends and against the social and moral order. It is a position held by the weak, the antisocial, and the punished.

Stephen further notes that in societies "with marked structural inequalities—as between junior and senior, wife-givers and wife-takers—sorcery within the community may (although not necessarily) be deemed appropriate to maintain the relationship of dominance or privilege. Where the only important structural differentiation is between insiders and outsiders, then sorcery will be deemed proper only against the enemy or its use may be eschewed altogether" (273). This also rings true for Amazonia, although we might frame the question differently, as focused inward versus outward, based not merely on what is seen as proper but what is deemed possible. It is a war within society over power, between rivals but not openly enemies.

Witchcraft is about power, it is, like power in general, about the ability of some individuals to coerce or control others due to their special status or role. Witchcraft occurs primarily in the context of rivalry and threats between individuals of certain social statuses; that is, it occurs against certain individuals by certain individuals. Thus there is a close relationship between witchcraft and the chieftaincy, as there is between witchcraft and shamanism. But this invisible power is a double-edged blade, a weapon of the weak, because its boundless threat humbles even the most powerful. And the powerful, because they have the power to indict others of it, mete out the only form of violent punishment known to the Xinguanos; counter-witch ordeals and execution.

Power is diffusely distributed in Xinguano communities, but we can distinguish two primary sources of it through the interpenetrating dimensions by which individuals acquire influence and control others. The first is secular and involves the personal efficacy and success of individuals, in trade, industry, and family, for instance, and is achieved without significant interaction with or control over supernatural forces. The second source directly involves the supernatural as well as some special abilities to "channel" the generally unseen forces of nature and the cosmos: that is, "invisible" power. All adult men and women have some capacity to control "spirits," most notably in the numerous rituals that involve forest and aquatic spirits, but some individuals have significantly greater means to control cosmic power. For example, chiefs control ancestral power, shamans control the spiritual power of nature, and witches (dark shamans), like curing shamans (those who do not enter trance to commune with spirits) control several forms of practical magic.

In Amazonia, there has been a common tendency to conflate diverse social roles under the generic term shaman, which has come to refer to any religious specialist or healer; that is, men and occasionally women who have some special, typically achieved, control over supernatural forces. The Kuikuru have shamans who can go into trance and shamans who cannot, herbalists who also heal the sick, and the unknown or suspected witches and known counterwitches. Unlike some places, where shamans primarily act as intermediaries or conduits of spiritual forces that generally affect human conditions, Xinguano shamans largely deal with illness, both *kwifi oto* (create or exacerbate it) and *fiati* (diagnose and, hopefully, remedy it). When they cannot remedy it and the patient dies, they can only implicate the source of the illness through trance, and it then falls to the family or the chief to mete out justice. Powerful shamans, those who can induce trance, may divine the source of an ailment or misfortune, a witch or spirit, but the job of dealing with this spirit is largely up to others. Shamans do not, generally, do battle with evil spirits but rather merely look for them. Once found, the spirit or witch must be dealt with through ritual.

Good shamans, intermediaries between the world of body and spirit, can channel spiritual forces to diagnose misfortune and treat illness. Dark shamans, masters of witchcraft, stand in opposition to them, creating and guiding illness and misfortune, also in the liminal realm between humans and evil spirits. Xinguano witchcraft and shamanism are about health and illness and the bodies of people, but not all bodies are equal. Thus, another social role and institution almost invariably comes into play, that of chiefdom.

In some social contexts witchcraft colors all social relations, through fear, anger, and powerlessness (Basso 1984), but witchcraft and shamanism are also costly business—that is, it is expensive to support the ritual actions used to counter witchcraft and not everyone has the means to do it. Witchcraft executions are not only personal affairs of revenge between the aggrieved and their presumed assailants, but also juro-political instruments of social control and moral judgment. Ideally, an execution should be carried out with the authorization of the primary village chief, even though chiefs publicly denounce both witchcraft and witch executions and commonly criticize others for indulging their authority to liberally—unjustly—kill witches (Gregor 1977; Ireland 1986).

The term chief (or headman) is no less problematic. Xinguanos have chiefs (*anetï*),[7] men and women who rise to unusual prominence owing in large part to hereditary privilege. They also have "great" men and women, individuals who rise to public prominence due to their notable political actions: they act "like a chief" in public events. Further, they sometimes become de facto chiefs, and their power rivals that of the "great" chiefs, the *anetï hekugu*. Then there are a variety of men and women, who due to their heritage (*anetï ñsoño*, or secondary chiefs) or their achievements—for example, as bow-masters, wrestlers, singers, dancers, story tellers, or craftspersons—are considered "great," but generally they do not aspire to political leadership.[8]

Each person is constructed by a complex interplay between heredity, the achievements and motivations of the individual, and, for lack of a better word, serendipity. Chiefs are born to power: a chief is a person born of an *anetï* line, although they can become anything they wish, or are coerced into becoming. Chiefs can be shamans, they can be also good musicians, craftsmen, and so forth, or, as is commonly the case, good at many things (*loki*). The reverse is not true: although diverse factors cumulatively define individuals, if a person is not born of the right bloodline or of the right substance, *anetï*, they will never become a chief, although chiefly rank is not isomorphic with prominence or political power (Heckenberger 2001). Further, an established or "sitting" chief is not generally thought to be a witch. In fact, owing to their public prominence, chiefs and their families are the preferred targets of witchcraft: chiefs and witches are traditional enemies. In this context it is important to note that although it is uncommon for chiefs to be witches, witches are often their accomplices or henchmen.

Like chiefs, witches are not born but made. Indeed, we might say that chiefs are born to power (legitimate power) and witches to evil (illegitimate or immoral power). Like chiefs, witches are taught by their fathers through an arduous process, one that involves a long apprenticeship that changes the body and mind of the initiate. Such changes include procedures like replacing the eye fluid in order to see better at night, attaching poisonous ants to the fingertips to harden them against poisons lethal to the untrained hand, and spending time in a covered pit beneath a bonfire to prepare for the inevitable antiwitchcraft, the *kune* (see Carneiro 1977 and Gregor 1977 for more description). Thus, like chiefs, not everyone can become a witch, it is highly secretive and typically passed down from father to son. Not all sons of witches become witches, however, and only rarely does accusation implicate directly fathers or sons (I was also told that women become witches).

Unlike chiefs and witches, shamans do not inherit special substance, special knowledge, or corporeal discipline from their parents, grandparents, or older ancestors. Individuals may well aspire to become shamans, although they typically decide to become one after receiving a vision while gravely ill. Shamans generally are not seen as inheriting their shamanic qualities, although the predisposition does run strong in some families and varies within the region. With the Kamayura, for instance, chiefly authority and shamanism are closely linked. In fact, shamanism is something of a village specialty among the Kamayura, and the most powerful shamans are the reigning chiefly family. During my time in Amazonia the Aueti chief was a specialist in counterwitchcraft, which, as was pointed out to me, is something of a village specialty. Each villager is said to know something about witchcraft, because the counterwitch, the primary chief in this case, uses some of the same techniques (making charms) and substances (often considered poisonous to others) that the witch uses, and some counterwitches, I was told, may even be reformed witches. There are eight shamans among the Kuikuru, only two of whom can divine or go into trance, at least independently from the others (occasionally groups of shamans will perform a "soul-recovery"), but neither of these two are primary chiefs.

Chieftaincy is about power. Although it is not only about power, the dominant idiom is hierarchy, the type of hierarchy that creates pervasive structural inequalities and is considered characteristic of transitional societies—between "egalitarian" society and the state is the chiefdom. Witchcraft is likewise about power, and is intimately tied to the strategies and negotiations of people. Dole (1973, 1966), suggests that the "occasional killing of a supposed sorcerer is a process of social selection through which antisocial individuals are eliminated. Witchcraft is a social ill, and there can be no doubt that society will try to purge itself of these 'marginal' people, and it seems likely that 'marginal' people are often implicated." Dole (1966) and Carneiro (1977) both describe such instances, in the former case through an example of a powerful shaman successfully implicating a witch, and, in the latter, how an accusation was deterred due to the threat of retaliation. Ireland (1996) forcefully argues, through precise genealogical histories spanning over a century, that there is much more to witchcraft executions than this: it is not only about struggles between the powerful and the weak but about power more generally, including between the powerful. Witchcraft conforms to certain planes of social structure—in other words it commonly involves specific social roles, notably chiefly rivals. Thus, while perhaps there is a correlation between "marginal men" and suspected witches, as Dole suggests, some rather prominent individuals are also "suspected," on occasion.

Witchcraft and Disease

"The great irony about Kuikuru witchcraft," Carneiro notes, is that although "it probably does not exist" in terms of Western explanations of illness, "nothing is more firmly rooted in the mind of a Kuikuru than the notion that most of his afflictions are directly due to sorcery, and that a number of persons he comes into contact with every day are witches" (1977:222). Illness and death are always seen as the result of malevolent forces, witches, evil spirits, and monsters: *etseke*. In the upper Xingu, actual instances of witchcraft are rare and are generally known through accusations and countermeasures, as elsewhere in the Americas (Walker 1989:3). It is not something carried out in public, but instead is a series of actions done, to great extent, in secret. It is a very sensitive and emotional topic, one that people do not talk about freely or spontaneously. Accusations, divinations, and executions are likewise private and dangerous affairs.

There are various medical techniques, esoteric knowledge, and specialists to treat illness, many of which are put to work, often repeatedly, when someone is not well. Regardless of diagnosis and treatment, however, all agree that the root of illness, what causes it, is spiritual not biological in nature. Cures are naturally spiritual, first and foremost, although practitioners—shaman, herbalists, and, today, health monitors (indigenous "nurses")—treat both the symptoms and the cause. Thus, while many Kuikuru who have been exposed to Western medical practitioners and ideas for over half a century have a good notion of the epidemiological theory of disease transmission, they believe that witchcraft lies at the heart of most illness and death. Why one person gets sick and recovers while others die, or why one person gets ill, or their house gets struck by lightning, or they get bitten by a snake, and others don't, is because they were targeted by some evil force, usually witchcraft.

There are many spirits that can also do harm; in my household alone, I saw various types. Among the more dramatic were three attempted soul recoveries, all on the same small boy (discussed below) and in each case from forest and water spirits (see Basso 1973; Carneiro 1977). The spirit of the *ihagaku* (jawari)[9] was thought to have caused an illness in the chief's mother who was already weakened by long-term illness, and appropriate ceremonies and basic shamanistic treatment were conducted. At one point I was thought to have been attacked by Ahaça, the spirit called "father of the forest," after having spent the day in an archaeological site far from the village and deep in the forest (I was diagnosed and treated for malaria). In another case an elderly woman from a neighboring house, long thought bewitched, was apparently killed by Tuangi (Mavutsini), the creator for seeing his magical shell necklaces stashed in the forest (or so she told a kinswoman in a dream after her death). These attacks can lead to death, but death usually is attributed not to a failed offering but a misdiagnosis.

The more common source of human suffering is witches, both flying witches and other changelings, who take on other forms to travel great distances and steal into neighboring villages.[10] Some are so powerful that they can raise an evil wind that destroys whole villages, others can bring pestilence or predation to crops, or draw mosquitos or lightning to villages or individual houses. In one case a witch brought a jaguar to the door of one Kuikuru family to lie in wait for its unsuspecting victim, in this case a young boy who was killed by it. Although some witches are believed to be able to breathe illness onto people, witchcraft generally involves the use of diverse "charms" (Gregor 1977), and assault sorcerers or witches are "masters of charms"—what the Kuikuru call *kurífe oto*. The Kuikuru recognize two primary techniques, both involving tiny fragments (*exuviae*) of the intended victim: the witch secrets away the charm, which leads to prolonged sickness and death, or, more commonly, they shoot it into the victim with a tiny arrow and the victim then soon dies.[11]

Witchcraft is cited in Xinguano narratives as a general force that seems to come in waves. According to the Kuikuru, the "old ones"—the old evil—had returned in the time of Karl von den Steinen (*Kalusi*): witches have always been there to threaten society, but were of varying strengths and number. I was told of witches that could conjure an "evil wind" that infected whole villages, who had, in fact, laid waste to several villages in the early- to mid-twentieth-century epidemics. The destruction of whole villages is also remembered by the Waurá for this time (Ireland 1988). These narratives no doubt refer to epidemics in the area, but, as Ireland suggests, traditional "theories of disease cannot account for an epidemic of communicable disease, unless it is viewed as the result of an epidemic of witchcraft" (1988:170).

Disease and witchcraft are linked and, therefore, witchcraft and countermeasures are directly correlated with the frequency of illness and death. In the past, in recent centuries, there have been several episodes of catastrophic depopulation due to epidemic diseases, each eventually running its course and leaving the survivors more biologically and culturally "adjusted" to the reality of epidemics, at least temporarily, but also taking staggering tolls on regional populations. The first wave of direct contact was in the mid-1700s, when *bandeirantes* seeking fame and fortune in the remote hinterlands of colonial hegemony, as often as not reaped in human souls, "descended" and "domesticated" Indians as converts and slaves, and with them also came disease. Catastrophic diseases apparently struck even earlier based on the decreased village size and abandonment of large tracts of land. Epidemics of "witchcraft diseases" occurred when the white man (Steinen) returned.

Witchcraft is very real in the eyes of the Kuikuru and, in fact, there are physical clues (markings, charms, visions in dreams) referring to its existence.[12] As is commonly the case, however, it is the beliefs that people have about the abilities and actions of others, rather than direct observation or knowledge of the dark ways, that guides the actions people take to avoid attacks or to counter them (see Middleton and Winter 1963:4). The fact is that any death can be attributed to witchcraft and any person, or virtually any person (chiefs are seldom seen to be witches), can be a witch. Witches, like other individuals, are socially constructed through suspicion, innuendo, accusation, and, notably, ritual techniques that attempt to root out the guilty: witch trials and hunts typically involve indictments and often have a verdict. Witchcraft is thus not only about the number of deaths but also certain deaths or types of deaths, particularly those of chiefs.

The Witch-Hunt

It was the height of the rainy season when I first arrived in the Kuikuru village in January 1993. Village life was relaxed, as this was a relatively slow time owing to the heavy rains. The mood was also upbeat because there was much to be happy about: leadership was strong; crops were plentiful; the village population, some 330 persons, was the largest it had been since the 1800s; their anthropologist had come to town with a new motor boat, gifts, and novelties; and the end of the rains, the time of harvest and festival, was coming. Things were good.

The prosperity of the Kuikuru village and the community's satisfaction with its situation was in part a reflection of strong village leadership, in particular the primary village chief—the *hugogó òto*. This was manifest in public opinion, support of the chief's projects and aspirations, and, ultimately, the request by the community at large to construct a *tajïfe* (chief's house). The *tajïfe* is one of two structures in the village that are built by the community but are "owned" by the chief and comprise his symbolic estate. A beautiful village is embodied in the chief as the "owner" or "custodian" (*oto*) not only of the *tajïfe* and *kuakutu* (men's house), but of the village center itself—the *hugogo*, just as the chief is objectified in the beautiful village, the constructions, the monuments, that the community builds in the name of and places in guardianship of the *hugogó òto*,[13] who, so objectified, represents the center, the ancestors, the community.

Lurking just at the edge of this prosperity was misfortune, in this case the malicious actions of witches. Death is a part of life, and Xinguanos are no stranger to it. Witchcraft, at least the threat of it, is therefore omnipresent, but it is not really a common part of daily life. Fears, suspicions, and rumors about someone not feeling well, about minor illnesses, or about things that happened in the past are common, but things that herbal remedies or basic shamanic healing "cure" are passed over quickly. People often get seriously ill and die, but many people recover and many deaths go by with only little debate and no redressive action. Only grave illness, serious misfortune, and death typically result in "witch scares," and usually when such problems occur in numbers. And, further, only some deaths demand full-blown witch-hunts, and these do not happen every day.

A death in the family. I was away from the village when the deaths began in late March 1993. I had gone to Brasília and Río de Janeiro for a couple of weeks to collect further supplies and report back to the outside world that all was well. When I returned, however, things were not well, particularly for my new Kuikuru family, that of the chief, the *hugogó òto*. His eldest son and heir had died several days before I returned. This death and three more in close succession, including the toddler sons of the *hugogó òto* and another chiefly (*anetï*) couple, colored many aspects of village life for the next nine months. In fact, the formal mourning period only ended some thirteen months later, in August 1994, at the completion of the *kuarup*, the chiefly funeral ritual that is the keystone of Xinguano ritual life.

Little could have prepared me for the changes that had transpired in the village in those brief few weeks, and nothing would be the same afterward. At 11 P.M. when I arrived back in the village it was dark, much like the first time I had strolled into the Kuikuru village. But now a difference could be sensed immediately. The men's house in the center of the village had been reduced to a skeleton, with only a few stubby posts and a pile of rubble vaguely discernable. And something else was amiss, something more deeply evocative: soon after I had entered the imposing central plaza (a quarter kilometer in diameter), I could hear a low wailing emanating from the houses that lay across the plaza—where I lived—opposite the port road from which I had entered the village.

The chief's son—heir apparent to the line of ancestral power that long ago had passed through his great-grandfather, his grandmother, and then to his father—had died the most horrible death, in the Kuikuru eyes: it was just at the time when he was preparing his public debut from more than a year of household seclusion (a rite of passage that all Kuikuru pass through, but that is particularly long and important for chiefly individuals). The death of the chief's son only confirmed what he had long felt: his rivals were responsible for the death and illness of his family members, including both his mother's long-term illness (she had been essentially confined to her hammock the whole year I was there) and his own personal ailments, which he had been treated for repeatedly, both in and out of the village. A couple of days after I returned, a relative of the chief arrived from a neighboring village to pay his respects. During his brief visit he implicated a man in a third village as the witch. This man—a "known" witch—remained the primary suspect throughout the four-month witch-hunt that began upon the son's death and afterward. The chief was certain throughout the investigation that the witch did not act alone but was supported by political rivals, yet he was never fully certain, or certain for long, who precisely they were.

A strong suspicion of guilt is sometimes enough to prompt a kinsman to avenge himself on a suspected witch, but this is a wholly personal act and is not viewed as legitimate by society. To justify an execution there are trials that should be performed, namely the *kuné* counterwitchcraft ritual that, if conducted properly, will reveal the witch (see Carneiro 1977). The trial involves the help of a shaman and a counterwitch and is usually carried out only by prominent families because it is extremely expensive. Furthermore, the execution must be authorized by the village chief. In the present case, because the bereaved was the village chief there was therefore no justifiable way to seek vengeance except through the meticulous operation of the *kuné*.

Trip to the Karajá. On April 4, three days after arriving back in the village, I left again to accompany the chief and two of his young brothers on an expedition to visit an elderly Karajá man, who lived some five hundred miles away on the Araguaia River. The night before, the chief had explained to me that, after his son's death, the family had begun preparations for the *kuné*. In preparing the body for burial, they had removed several parts (head hair, the fleshy tip of the right index finger, and a small bit from the thumb palm of the left hand) to be incorporated into the *kuné* charm. These pieces, *exuviae*, were all carefully guarded in a coffee can in the small house where I now lived. For security, the chief set armed guards at both doors of the house, as well as sentinels at each of the three major road entrances to the village: the witch could take on one of many forms (e.g., a jaguar, a deer, a dog, an airplane) and come into the village in the dark of night to steal the *exuviae*, which were intended for charms meant not only to identify but to kill them.

At mid-day we set out for the village of the Karajá, traveling upriver to the first stop at the border post of the Parque Indígena do Xingu. We arrived at the post as dusk fell, which was profoundly unsettling to my companions because in the small, open motorboat we were especially vulnerable to attack by the witches in one or another of their night guises. This trepidation continued during our overland trip to the Brazilian town of Canarana, but as we put distance between us and the post it began to subside.

The old Karajá shaman was in São Felix when we arrived, but the chief and his brothers went with him to the village of Santa Isabel the next day. I was not present as the shaman tied the hair of the deceased son into four small "dolls" in human form to be incorporated by a Xinguano specialist into a counterwitchcraft charm. Indeed, I did not see the dolls until the day, a week or so later, that a specialist in counterwitchcraft (considered a kind of "good witch," but a witch nonetheless) incorporated them into the finished charms. I did, however, help prepare the payment of several kilos of glass beads and other valuables.

Death of the second son. On our return to the Kuikuru village on April 13 more dire news awaited us: two more Kuikuru were gravely ill—the youngest toddler son of the Kuikuru chief and a pregnant woman. Although things were already astir and witchcraft was on the tip of many tongues, the issue of witchcraft and the identity of the witch became more intense with additional illnesses, particularly after a young Kuikuru girl reported that she had been visited by the suspected witch. The witch had, reportedly, secretly visited the Kuikuru village one night and, among other things, asked the young girl about the whereabouts of Afukaka and several villagers. He also hinted that he had indeed killed the chief's son. I learned then that this witch had once lived in the Kuikuru village and was considered responsible for the death of several other Kuikuru. He was forced to flee when the brother of one of the victims had attempted to kill him.

The ill feelings about the death of the chief's eldest son were exacerbated by the increasingly grave illness of the youngest son. Further tension, over the proper treatment of the toddler, emerged between a FUNAI nurse, who had arrived in the village while we were away, and the Kuikuru shamans, of which there were eight in 1993. Soon after I arrived in the village, the nurse sought me out to convince me, so that I might convince the chief, that his son was mortally ill from meningitis, she thought, and that he needed to be taken to Brasília as soon as possible for treatment. On the other side, several shamans explained to me that this would be a serious mistake because the child's soul had been "stolen" by a spirit, and to remove him from the village, to further separate him from his disembodied soul, meant certain death. Although the chief acknowledged the sincere concern and reasoning of the nurse, he agreed with the assessment of the shamans, and he allowed them to attempt a soul recovery (see Basso 1973; Carneiro 1977).

The soul recovery required a collective effort of multiple shamans, smoking together in a circle sequestered in the house of the patient, thus joining their forces with the principal shaman in a trance. First they attempted, to no avail, to recover the soul from the stump of a large tree behind the house where they thought a forest spirit had sequestered it. They then attempted, without success, to recover it from the nearby lake, and then again from the tree trunks that lay, like fallen giants, in front of the house (the remnants of the permanently canceled project to build a chief's house). Shamanistic diagnosis is not an exact science, and various things were tried, but more and more the chief became open to the idea of radical measures: taking the patient to the city. We set off to meet a plane coming from Brasília, via the FUNAI Posto Leonardo, where, after further efforts by a Kamayura shaman in the Yawalapiti village adjacent to the post, the younger son died before the plane arrived.

On returning to the village, the body of the deceased child was prepared, washed, painted, and adorned. Like his older brother, hair was collected from the body as were the flesh of the right index fingertip and left palm. The body was interred in a deep (two meter) single pit and a small pot was placed over the head. The fingertip was placed on a heated griddle in the village center. The heat caused the tip to jump, signifying the finger of the deceased victim pointing to his assailants. The appropriate body parts were gathered and guarded overnight with those of the older brother. Early the next day, we were off to the Aueti village, some four or five hours away by foot and motorboat, to prepare the next step of the *kuné*.

Trip to the Aueti. We walked for about an hour from the Curisevo River port to the Aueti village, and we spent much of the time talking—the chief, his younger brothers, and I—about the histories of the area, the relations between the villages, and the plants and animals we encountered along the way. But I could feel a tension building as we neared our destination. Our talk became less jovial, more serious, and then simply died out as we approached the village. The memories of the events that brought us here closed in upon us, just as the closed space of the forest opened into the fields and parklands encircling the village. We were here on serious business, here to traffic with witches, good witches in this case, but witches nonetheless: holders of a deep, ancient knowledge that is the root of most human suffering.

Unlike most Xinguanos, who often travel to visit relatives in other villages, major village chiefs generally do not informally visit other villages. Their presence is a public affair, the occasion of unusual formality and ceremony, and is typically a harbinger of major happenings or special, usually ritual, events. Relations between the Aueti and the Kuikuru are especially tense. Not only do the two speak entirely different languages but few close ties of kinship link the two villages.

We were met in the village with the usual friendly reception that Xinguanos extended to any visitor, the same hospitality that had made my transition into the Kuikuru village so smooth. The youngest brother and I, less encumbered with the formality of high office and renown, made the rounds that afternoon; the chief and his next younger brother did not venture out but stayed in the chief's house, where formal visitors are received. We ate fish and *beijú* in the chief's house and the chiefs talked among themselves, and queried me about the white man, my work, and other things. Much of it was about the surge of witchcraft and the deaths in the Kuikuru village.

Early the next morning, the task at hand took on a concrete form. The Kuikuru and Aueti chiefs discussed the payment: two shell necklaces and three shell belts. After payment was made, we went to a clearing in the forest close behind the chief's house, where the Aueti chief, the counterwitch, prepared the charms to be brought back to the Kuikuru village to place in the *kuné* pot.

The kuné. The *kuné*, well described by Carneiro (1977), is a form of counterwitchcraft, a pot in which the charms of counterwitchcraft are boiled. However, the *kuné* is more than an inanimate object—it is spiritlike and it must be fed and cared for, it is the capture and control of raw spiritual force. To conduct the *kuné*, the chief partitioned off a third of his house with sheets of black plastic. The hearth was set up in the house of the chief's "uncle" and stepfather-in-law, where he and his family had set up residence. The *kuné* was begun two days after we arrived back at the village on April 21. During the first week of the *kuné*, evidence was mounting that the witch was indeed the man implicated earlier.

The chief contracted one of the two shamans (of eight) who could successfully enter into trance through inhalation of large doses of tobacco smoke. Even though the shaman was a close relative of the chief (their fathers being first parallel cousins), the shaman was subtly implicated at various stages of the witch-hunt, either as an accomplice or an actual witch. He had been, in fact, indicted for witchcraft some decades before, which resulted in his move along with his kinsfolk to the Yawalapiti village in the mid-1970s. In several conversations, the chief told me that he questioned the shaman's truthfulness or motives; nonetheless, throughout the *kuné* ritual the shaman came to the house in which I lived every few nights to counter the actions of the witch who, in an effort of self-defense, was trying to spoil the *kuné* pot by placing charms meant to corrupt it.

The shaman would come to the house and go into trance by inhaling large quantities of tobacco smoke, during which time he could consult with diverse spirits regarding the actions of the witch, the location of the *kurífe* planted in and around the village to destroy the *kuné*. One elder chief from another village plainly described what I also suspected; he said, "you do know that it is that old shaman that is helping your friend [tending the chief's counterwitchcraft device] who is planting the charms" (see also Gregor 1977). This shaman produced various small charms consisting of small pieces of twine or other discarded knickknack—the *exuviae*—wrapped in beeswax around a small twig (the Kalapalo use larger ones, he once told me). Various people described "sightings" of things that demonstrated witchery: the witch screaming at night and plunging into the river to escape the intense burning sympathetically produced through the counterwitchcraft; a set of jaguar footprints over the deceased's grave, a sure sign that the witch, in the guise of a jaguar, had visited the village.

The *kuné* lasted nearly four months. During much of this time, the shaman cared for it nearly every other night, and the chief and his family labored through the strenuous tasks of providing water and fuel for it. But in the end it did not kill the witch. Several failed execution attempts were made, but the chief tired of the whole business, himself valuing human life so much that even the shadow of a doubt was unacceptable. The indicted man was neither a threat nor a rival to the chief. The man was indeed marginal, having been repeatedly accused of witchcraft and forced to flee village after village, but was no longer a member of the Kuikuru village. The primary suspect throughout the witch-hunt was a man from a neighboring village who had lived in the Kuikuru village about ten years before, seeking refuge from the Kalapalo village of Aiha due to an earlier accusation. He fled Aiha to the Magiapei (Nafuqua) village, but returned to Aiha when his situation in the Nafuqua village deteriorated, once again as a result of witchcraft accusations. (This supports Basso's (1973) observation that one accusation leads to another; that is that witches have a life history).

A threat more insidious than witches, because there is virtually no way to retaliate, comes from the witches' accomplices: people who contract witches to avenge some perceived threat or slight from their political rivals. In the present case, the chief was certain that, in the case of both of his sons, multiple people conspired in the attacks on his family, including the chief felt, his grandfather (his namesake), his mother, his two sons from his first wife, and younger son of his second wife.

Five years after the *egitse* (*kuarup*) funeral ceremony was held in 1994, the *ihagaku* (*jawari*) was held (in 1999) to mark the end of the long *kuarup* cycle and the end to the formal mourning. However, regarding the veneration of the dead, there are constant reminders for the living. Still today, the principal bridge—a massive construction of tree-trunk footings sunken deeply into the wet ground, large (one to two feet wide) logs with flat tops or, commonly, hand-hewn boards from large trees—is "owned" by the son. Many complain of the difficulties of arriving at the Kuikuru village; when I arrived in fact, at the height of the rainy season, we waded through high water ranging in depth from thigh to chest level. Still, I look back at it fondly and sadly. It was not just any death.

Conclusion

During my stay in the Kuikuru village I spent many hours in my hammock thinking about witchcraft. In fact, it was hard not to because, given the recent deaths, scarcely a day went by when I wouldn't hear some mention of witchcraft. The problem I often thought about was visibility, the inability to visualize things at different scales of analysis and, thus, the common pitfall of retrodicting present conditions into the past or, worse still, assuming that invisibility meant irrelevance. No matter how central or important the institution of witchcraft is in the present, how can we be certain that it was so in the past; in other words, how do we extend our observations about the ethnographic present into the past? Or, more precisely, how do we compare different types of things, different types of "bodies," at different spatio-temporal scales?

We are on firm ethnological ground to suggest that witchcraft has very ancient roots, perhaps leading back, in one form or another, to the earliest groups who entered the Americas in late Pleistocene times. At the minimum it is a central feature of many Amazonian peoples, particularly Arawak and culturally related groups (e.g., Bakairi, Karajá) in southern Amazonia. In one form or another witchcraft relates to a medical theory—shamanism and so forth—from elsewhere, a thousand years ago or before. The roots of witchcraft run deep and to speak of the ultimate causes in the past of something like witchcraft, something for which there are few historical clues as to its existence, let alone its nature, one must suspend history. There is little point, therefore, in searching for the "ultimate" or "root" cause of the witchcraft complex itself, its existence, what overarching function it served, or what "caused it" at its moment of origin. Like most things, the absolute origins of an institution—the origin of the related ideas and practices—are hard to fix very precisely.

We can, however, consider proximate (historical) causes and their immediate effects, gauged in terms of real people, communities, institutions, families. Surely there have been significant changes in the institution of witchcraft but we can at least be fairly sure that it, in some form or another (something like *kwifi oto*), existed in the past, and that shamans and chiefs battled with witches (we can more clearly retrodict contemporary chiefs, at least, into the past due to the continuity of their "place," the spatial metaphor of their person, the plaza; see Heckenberger 2001). What is constant is that human agents negotiate between the past (tradition), the present historical situation, and the future they have in mind for themselves. The problem is twofold: first, there is the frequency and nature of illness and death, and, second, there is the nature of the social and political relations in relation to it. What differs is the historical contexts through which the institution, changing and reinterpreted but showing substantial consistency through time, actually passed through over time, the actual social relations and actions that are tied to it and that reproduced the meanings through action.

The Xinguano case demonstrates once again the efficacy of the unseen— the cultural, social, and political forces that lie behind the more visible material conditions of subsistence technology and demography. It is not possible to fully address the question of historical efficacy here (see, e.g., Foucault 1980; Sahlins 1981), the effects of things seen and unseen, the "reality" and social agency of things, whether human or not. What is clear, however, is the efficacy of witchcraft to move people to action. It is something seemingly so esoteric as to be overlooked altogether in many considerations of political power and economy, cultural evolution, and human ecology, as well as mythology and kinship, because these notions are antimythic (forgotten) and antisocial.

Xinguano witchcraft, which by and large is only visible in the fairly narrow time frame of the present or recent past, provides several important insights into Xinguano history. First, it demonstrates that history is far more complicated, structurally, at all levels, than is commonly portrayed: its situation is complex. Witchcraft also demonstrates, in particular, the importance of political factors, power, ideology, and ritual in structuring people's lives, and, therefore, that narrow views of cultural structures or changes in them that ignore the importance of culture in favor of ecology, behavior, or adaptive fitness will surely fall wide of the mark in understanding cultural diversity and change in Amazonia. Witchcraft also suggests that broad characterizations of, for instance, shamans, chiefs, and witches, particularly as generalized types, ignore the marked variability within and between Amazonian societies: that is, simply put, there are innumerable interests involved that resolve into diverse and flexible social roles, and that actors mold cultural, social, and ecological "structures" to their wills, actively.

However, the structures that mold people, that constrain subjects as they are constructed in the context of diverse power relations, operate at diverse social scales; that is, of the persons. The person, in other words, is fractal and resolves into different "bodies" at different scales: among which we might recognize, for conceptual if not analytical purposes, a distinction between a historical person (the "cultural body"), a social person (the "body politic"), and an individual in the world of social and historical relations (the "mindful body") (see Scheper-Hughes 1994; Wagner 1991). Analytically, these correlate, crudely, with quantifiable social entities (communities, families, individuals), and although each of them is commonly visible they operate, or have lives, at different spatio-temporal scales. That is, our models of the nature or origin of witchcraft or its influence on other things, sociological or psychological, political or religious, structural or contingent, are scale dependent. They operate over the long-term of historical periods, the demographic curves of epidemic depopulation recovery over generations; the middle-term of operating systems and the actual institutions or schema that underlie them—shamanism, chieftaincy, or witchcraft; and the short-term of actual acts that generate these longer histories and larger bodies.

My interest is Xinguano history, particularly its history on a large scale, the "big" picture of major patterns over generations, centuries, and millennia. Little was known about this history in 1992 when I went to the field, but from an anthropological perspective this history began late, after about 1885 when reports from the ethnological expedition led by Karl von den Steinen first brought news of the area and its people to the attention of the Western world. The year I spent with the Kuikuru is to some hardly an event, but it is significant in the view of decades or generations; further, we can narrow the "event horizon" to more discrete moments in time that, likewise, had a tremendous influence on the flow of things.

Notes

1   I stayed with the Kuikuru from January to December 1993; the deaths occurred between March 26 and December 25, 1993. Witchcraft was an issue that came up, in one way or another, in each of my subsequent visits to the Kuikuru village in August 1994, November 1995, October 1996, July 1999, and August 2000, as well as during the several months between 1991 and 1997 when I traveled with Xinguano leaders in Brazil. The National Science Foundation (1992–1994), Social Science Research Council (1992–1994), William T. Hillman Foundation (1995, 1999), and the University of Florida (2000) are all gratefully acknowledged for grants that supported my research in the upper Xingu.
2   Heckenberger 2000a. Archaeological evidence that corroborates the long-term presence of Old World epidemic diseases in the upper Xingu, documenting a massive reduction in village and regional population after approximately 1550–1650, only became available through this research (Heckenberger 1996, 2000b).
3   Unless noted, I use Kuikuru terms throughout, although the same terms exist in other languages as well.
4   These rituals, known as the *jawarí* and *kuarup*, following the Kamayura terms (*ihagaka* and *egitse* by Kuikuru) are well described in Agostinho 1974 and Basso 1973, among others.
5   The best-known example is the 1930s assassination of the Yawalapiti chief and abduction of multiple women by the Aueti, and the subsequent retaliation raid by Yawalapiti and allies (Coelho 2000). According to some, the Yawalapiti chief was killed in this attack because he was a suspected witch. But, this was not the view held by the Yawalapiti, who saw the attack as open warfare and murder.
6   There is no distinction made here between a sorcerer and a witch (see also Carneiro 1977). It might be noted, however, that what Melanesianists commonly refer to as sorcerer is more or less synonymous with what Amazonianists call shaman; and thus witches are dark shamans.
7   *Anetï* is the word for any member of the chiefly "class" born of a chiefly ranking mother or father, but it is also used to refer to anyone who, de facto, operates like a chief.
8   Basso describes these bow-masters as specialized warriors, although my own experiences lead me to conclude that this status is more generalized, referring to men whose acumen with the bow makes them particularly good hunters and fishermen, or useful in those times when armed conflict arises. Note that some individuals show markedly different feelings about aggressive conflict or "bravado" within the confines of the general nature of Xinguano soft-spokenness.
9   Here Kuikuru words are used with Kamayura (Tupi-Guarani) words, as generic terms, in parentheses.

10 These are commonly jaguars or other animals, but on occasion a "one-eyed" airplane.
11 See Carneiro 1977 for a discussion of the many details of the witchcraft complex, including apprenticeship, techniques, and countermeasures (see also Basso 1973 and Gregor 1977 for general discussions).
12 This is not always the case because I observed among the Kalapalo, for instance, that the *eté òto* occupied, or "owned" the chief's house; and among the Kuikuru and Yawalapiti, at least, the *hugogó òto* owns the center, the men's house, and the chief's house.
13 Carneiro 1977 provides an excellent summary of the divination ritual based on interviews he conducted in 1975 (although he never witnesses a *kuné* ritual).

References

Agostinho de Silva, Pedro. 1974. *Kwarup: Mito e Ritual no Alto Xingu.* Sao Paulo: Editoria da USP.

Basso, Ellen B. 1973. *The Kalapalo Indians of Central Brazil.* New York: Holt, Rinehart and Winston.

———. 1984. "A Husband for His Daughter, a Wife for Her Son: Strategies for Selecting a Set of In-Laws among the Kalapalo." In *Marriage Practices in Lowland South America*, ed. K. M. Kensinger. 33–44. Urbana: University of Illinois Press.

———. 1995. *The Last Cannibals: A South American Oral History.* Tucson: University of Arizona Press.

Carneiro, Robert. 1977. "Recent Observations on Shamanism and Witchcraft among the Kuikuru Indians of Central Brazil." *Annals of the New York Academy of Sciences* 293: 215–28.

Carrasco, D. 1989. "Preface." In *Witchcraft and Sorcery of the American Native Peoples*, ed. D. E. Walker Jr. ix–xi. Moscow: University of Idaho Press.

Clastres, Pierre. *Society Against the State.* Trans. Robert Hurley. New York: Zone Books.

Dole, Gertrude E. 1964. *Endocannibalism among the Amahuaca Indians.* New York: New York Academy of Sciences.

———. 1966. "Anarchy without Chaos: Alternatives to Political Authority among the Kuikuru." In *Political Anthropology*, ed. M. J. Swartz, V. W. Turner, and A. Tuden. 73–78. Chicago: Aldine.

———. 1973. "Shamanism and Political Control among the Kuikuru." In *Peoples and Cultures of Native South America*, ed. D. R. Gross. 294–307. New York: Doubleday.

———. 1993. "Homogeneidade e diversidade no alto Xingu vistas a partir dos Cuicuros." In *Karl von den Steinen: Um seculo de antropologia no Xingu*, ed. V. P. Coelho. 375–403. São Paulo: Editora da Universidade de São Paulo.

Foucault, Michel. 1980. *Power/Knowledge: Selected Interviews and Other Writings, 1972–1977.* Ed. C. Gordon. New York: Pantheon.

Franchetto, B. 1993. "A Celebração da história nos discursos cerimonias Kuikuru. In *Amazonia: Etnologia e historia indigena*, ed. E. B. Viveiros de Castro and M. M. Carneiro da Cunha. 95–116. Campinas: Editora da Unicamp.

Gregor, Thomas. 1977. *Mehinacu: The Drama of Daily Life in a Brazilian Indian Village.* Chicago: University of Chicago Press.

Heckenberger, Michael. 1996. "War and Peace in the Shadow of Empire: Sociopolitical Change in the Upper Xingu of Southeastern Amazonia, A.D. 1400–2000." Ph.D. diss., University of Pittsburgh.

———. 2000a. "Estrutura, história e transformação: A cultura xinguana na longue durée." In *Povos indígenas do alto Xingu: Cultura e história*, ed. B. Franchetto and M. J. Heckenberger. Rio de Janeiro: Editora da Universidade Federal do Rio de Janeiro.

———. 2000b. "Epidemias, indios bravos, e brancos: Contato cultural e etnogenese no alto Xingu." In *Povos indígenas do alto Xingu: Cultura e história*, ed. B. Franchetto and M. J. Heckenberger. Rio de Janeiro: Editora da Universidade Federal do Rio de Janeiro.

———. 2001. "Xinguano Hierarchy and Political Economy: The Symbolic Foundations of the Native Amazonian State." Manuscript.

Hugh-Jones, Stephen. 1995. "Shamans, Prophets, Priests, and Pastors." In *Shamanism, History, and the State*, ed. N. Thomas and C. Humphrey. 332–75. Ann Arbor: University of Michigan Press.

Ireland, Emily. 1986. "Our Chiefs Do Not Spill Their Anger: Secrecy and Covert Leadership in Witchcraft Executions." Paper presented at the 85th annual meeting of the American Anthropological Association, Philadelphia.

———. 1988. "Cerebral Savage: The Whiteman as Symbol of Cleverness and Savagery in Waura Myth." In *Rethinking History and Myth: Indigenous South America Perspectives on the Past*, ed. J. Hill. 157–77. Urbana: University of Illinois Press.

———. 1996. "Chefia e dinâmicas políticas entre os Waura." Paper presented at the 20th annual meeting of the Associação Brasileira de Antropologia, Salvador.

Lawrence, P. 1987. "De Rerum Natura: The Garia View of Sorcery." In *Sorcerer and Witch in Melanesia*, ed. M. Stephen. 17–40. New Brunswick: Rutgers University Press.

Middleton, J., and E. Winters. 1963. *Witchcraft and Sorcery in East Africa*. London: Routledge and Kegan Paul.

Sahlins, Marshall. 1981. *Historical Metaphors and Mythical Realities*. Ann Arbor: University of Michigan Press.

Scheper-Hughes, Nancy. 1994. "Embodied Knowledge: Thinking with the Body in Critical Medical Anthropology." In *Assessing Cultural Anthropology*, ed. R. Borofsky, 229–39. New York: McGraw-Hill.

Stephen, M. 1987. "Contrasting Images of Power." In *Sorcerer and Witch in Melanesia*, ed. M. Stephen. 249–304. New Brunswick: Rutgers University Press.

Steward, Julian. 1949. *Handbook of South American Indians, Vol. III: The Tropical Forest Tribes*. Washington, DC: Smithsonian Institute.

Wagner, Roy. 1991. "The Fractal Person." In *Big Men and Great Men: Personifications of Power in Melanesia*, ed. Maurice Godelier and Marilyn Strathern. 159–73. Cambridge: Cambridge University Press.

Walker, D. E. 1989. "Introduction." In *Witchcraft and Sorcery of the American Native Peoples*, ed. D. E. Walker Jr. 1–10. Moscow: University of Idaho Press.

Siblings and Sorcerers: The Paradox of Kinship among the Kulina

Donald Pollock

In this essay I explore shamanic and nonshamanic forms of sorcery, and I locate the demarcation between them along the divide that separates public/political arenas from private/domestic contexts. I suggest that the demarcation represents one facet of the Kulina cultural paradox of "siblingship," the paradox that all members of an endogamous village are close kin ("siblings" in the Kulina metaphor) and yet many are also potential marriage partners (Pollock 1985b:2000). Shamanic sorcery is a form of discourse about the public performance of siblingship, while nonshamanic sorcery engages the zone of sexuality and affinality. Moreover, the social disruptions of contact with Brazilians over the past sixty or seventy years and the reconfigurations that have resulted in the matrix of Kulina social life have shaped and nuanced these forms of sorcery and their semiotic potential for discursive commentary on social life.

The Kulina are an Aruan-speaking group living in western Brazil, where some 2,000 group members live in villages scattered throughout the Purus/Jurua region of the Brazilian states of Acre and Amazonas.[1] The Kulina are closely related to the Deni (Koop 1980).[2] My research was conducted among the Kulina of the upper Purus River, in particular among the community that lived in the village called Maronaua in the late 1970s and 1980s, many of whom now live in the village called Sobral at the site of the abandoned rubber-tapping camp locally known as the Seringal Sobral. Maronaua was a relatively large village of roughly 130 people when I first arrived in 1981. Some 30 or so former residents had recently moved to Sobral but returned often for visits and still regarded themselves as members of a single local group that had, perhaps temporarily, fissioned over a political dispute.

Shamanic Sorcery

The ability to perform shamanic sorcery derives from the incorporation of a substance called *dori* into the bodies of young men undergoing shamanic training. Senior shamans place dori from their own bodies into the bodies of initiates. Ideologically, all young men undergo this training as a part of socialization into adulthood, and consequently all Kulina men possess this corporeal potential for commission of sorcery. In other words, the ritual context of shamanic training is also the rite of passage into adulthood for all young men.

Dori is a complex substance that condenses multiple semantic realms. I have described the concept at some length elsewhere (Pollock 1992; 1994a; 1996), and thus will give a somewhat abbreviated perspective here. Dori is the substance that permeates and largely defines the bodies of men. It creates maleness and the properties of maleness; adult male gender in humans (and possibly in animals) is attributed to possession of dori (Pollock 1985a; 1992). Dori is related to semen; when adolescent boys undergo shamanic training and acquire dori, they must not engage in sexual relations or their dori will be lost along with the newly forming semen, the corporeal mark of their adult male identity. Dori is described as a dangerous, caustic substance that would be poisonous to its owner/possessor if not acquired in the carefully controlled setting of ritual training; this poisonous property makes it the shaman's weapon.

Dori gives shamans the ability to heal, but it also renders adult men capable of inflicting harm, even killing, human enemies and game animals. As a sorcerer, a shaman extracts a portion of the dori from his body and mystically hurls it into the body of his victim. There it grows until it kills the victim. Kulina sorcerers may opt merely to harm an enemy, and in such a case shamans can extract the dori from the body of the victim before death results.

The qualities of male gender with which dori invests adult men are found in their most basic, raw form in the jaguar, the *dzumahe*.[3] The jaguar is regarded as a solitary, dangerous hunter, a carnivore who hunts at night when the spirit forms of animals and shamans are about in the forest. These qualities are often most socially notable in their absence. A brief mention of a case I have described elsewhere illustrates this point. A young adult man I call Awano lived at Maronaua at the time of my first research in that village. He spent a great deal of time tapping rubber, which is a Brazilian, or *karia*, rather than Kulina economic activity, although Kulina sometimes tap small quantities of rubber to buy Brazilian commodities. In spending his time in this way it was felt he was neglecting his proper duties as a husband and son-in-law, in particular through his failure to be a productive hunter. Early one morning Awano was subjected to a ritual intended to "give him the ability to kill." Awano's skin was burned on his upper arm and the poisonous secretions of a large frog were rubbed into the burn. The frog poison caused him to convulse, vomit, and temporarily pass out. While such intentional poisonings are widely known in indigenous Amazonia, and have even been explained as a form of (unintentional) therapy for intestinal parasites, the Kulina explicitly described this poisoning as a kind of injection of dori intended to jolt Awano back into adult malehood, especially as a hunter. Indeed, burning the upper arm as a site for the application of the frog poison explicitly mimics the Brazilian/Western practice of injecting medications into the muscles of the upper arm: Awano received, in effect, a medicinal dose of dori in a particularly potent form.

Dori, then, is present in a number of forms, and is in other animals and even in a few plants. Dori, as the quintessence or exaggerated form of male gender, is normally balanced by the "tame" or socializing qualities of female substances such as breast milk, which balances male semen in the formation of a child, and the fermented manioc beverage called *koidza*[4] that women prepare to "tame" and resocialize hunters returning from the forest. Male animals possess dori, and thus are prohibited as food for parents of an infant who is nursing; the dori of male animal meat interferes with the taming or "completing" effects of mother's milk.

Sorcery Illness

Dori is also the generic term for sorcery-induced illness, the illness caused when a sorcerer hurls or injects a portion of his dori in the body of a victim. As an illness, dori is treated in the context of a curing ritual called *tokorime*. The *tokorime* ritual is held only in the dry season, and normally at night, although especially difficult cases of dori illness may lead to the ritual being extended into the daytime. In the *tokorime* curing ritual, shamans become transformed into the *adzaba* spirits, and invoke the spirit forms of animals to assist in curing. Shamans, typically two or more in alternation, enter the village from the nearby forest and sing with the women of the village, who form a large semicircular ring around the sick patient. The shamans snort tobacco snuff and enter into a trance, in which they become transformed into the *adzaba* spirits who suck out the dori on the afflicted area of the patient. In curable cases of dori, the process is repeated for several hours, and the patient is pronounced healed.

Dori illness is understood to be the result of a sorcery attack, and when the patient is cured in the *tokorime* ritual, the sorcerer is typically identified as a senior shaman in another village. Doho, the headman of the village called Santo Amaro, several days downriver from Maronaua and Sobral, was commonly identified as the sorcerer-cause of episodes of dori in the upriver villages. In these cases, accusations of sorcery against shamans such as Doho in other villages certainly direct public sentiment outward, preserving the ideological harmony of kin living together within the village. The act of affirming the conviction that village consociates would never harm each other through sorcery is arguably more important than identifying or punishing the sorcerer. For example, on the several occasions during my research when Doho visited Maronaua, he was happily greeted as a favorite cousin and in-law, and when I pointed out that he had caused numerous cases of dori in the village, people responded with a kind of dismissive reply that Doho would never seriously harm anyone; indeed, in the diplomatic context of intervillage ritual it seemed bad form even to mention these earlier accusations.

When a patient dies of dori, the entire nature of the incident changes; the Kulina assume that the sorcerer is present in the village, and it becomes critical to identify and kill the sorcerer. Not surprisingly, men identified as sorcerer-killers are socially marginal or lacking in political resources and support within the village. In the most dramatic case that I witnessed, a prominent elderly man died after two frantic days of nonstop curing rituals. The sorcerer implicated in his death was a visitor from a village on the Envira River—an old friend who had the misfortune to arrive in Maronaua just as his friend and host, a double irony, took ill with a respiratory infection. In the end, the accused sorcerer was clubbed to death and his body was thrown in a stream.

The denial of a proper burial is prescribed for sorcerers killed in revenge for their fatal dori attacks. With a normal burial, the spirit, *kurime*, of the deceased travels down to the underworld village of peccary spirits, where the human spirit is eaten and transformed into a white-lipped peccary, the *hidzama*. Shamans call these peccaries up into the forest where they can be hunted and eaten. The process is a cyclical one in which spirit substance is continuously reincarnated as human then peccary, each a kind of food for the other (Pollock 1993a). Sorcerers, however, are denied this reincarnation; for several days their spirits wander the village where they were killed, but ultimately they are eaten by a jaguar and are not reincarnated as either peccary or a human. Jaguars, incidentally, gain a measure of their malign nature from eating the spirits of sorcerers.

Sorcery accusations, or the threat of such accusations, have long been regarded as a form of social control, a view that is perhaps not so much wrong as incomplete (see, e.g. Douglas 1970; Geschiere 1997: 215–23). Among the Kulina the possibility of being accused of sorcery is without doubt a concern for men whose behavior places them at various social and cultural margins, though it did not, in my experience, coerce them into conforming to more acceptable social norms. At Maronana, and later at Sobral, for example, a man I call Bodo was often spoken of as a possible sorcerer, and with each case of dori in the village his name was mentioned until it became clear that the patient would recover, whereupon suspicion was redirected to a man in another village. Bodo clearly feared the consequences of a patient's death, however, and he periodically left the village to travel to his mother's village of Santo Amaro when complaints about his behavior became too loud or frequent. Bodo was regarded as lazy; he rarely hunted and too often chose the easy option of fishing. He lived with his father-in-law despite having three children, a point at which he should have built his own house. And thus it was not simply his wife who complained of too much fish and not enough meat; his father-in-law should have been able to rely on Bodo to hunt for the household, but couldn't. When things got too uncomfortable for Bodo he retreated to Santo Amaro, and I have heard that his returns to Maronaua and later to Sobral were also flights from possible sorcery accusations at Santo Amaro.

The cultural logic and techniques of shamanic sorcery are straightforward, but the social conditions of sorcery are complex. Indeed, I have suggested that, the Kulina use sorcery as a displaced discourse on other social issues; a brief discussion of sorcery-caused illness will make this clear.

Dori, in the form of an illness caused by a shaman-sorcerer, is said to resemble a stone in the body that grows unless it is extracted. The symptoms of dori illness are vague and may include almost any discomfort, pain, or unease that an individual reports. However, not all pains or discomforts are diagnosed as dori; rather, a diagnosis of dori is highly contextual. Virtually all nonfatal cases of dori are diagnosed only following interhousehold conflicts. That is, aches, pains, and other discomforts are generally ignored or appropriated to a nonmystical illness category, but outbreaks of violence between households are invariably followed by diagnoses of dori and *tokorime* curing rituals (Pollock 1996). Diagnosis of dori and shamanic curing do not even require sickness to precipitate the process. In the case of the elderly man mentioned earlier, his death and the revenge killing of his sorcerer-murderer were followed by serial shamanic treatment of virtually every resident of the village. Moreover, in general after the successful cure of dori illness, a second ritual is held in which all village members dance for hours at night in a large circle in the center of the village, singing songs that have themes of order and beauty in the world. I refer to dori illness and its treatment as a displaced discourse because the Kulina believe that dori is caused by harmful sorcery attack and do not explicitly connect the illness and the precipitating episodes or context of interhousehold violence, yet my data show that this relationship between interhousehold violence and dori illness is constant and predictable.

It is clear, then, that dori illness, ideologically the result of sorcery attacks, is at another level a response to disrupted interhousehold relations: that is, public failures of conviviality, according to Overing and Passes (2000). It takes the form of projecting blame outward to shaman-sorcerers in other villages, and affirms the social value of harmony and cooperation—again, conviviality is an appropriate term—that underlies relations among village members. Even in the case of fatal sorcery attacks, the sorcerer is identified among those who have no kin ties to village members, or whose claims to kinship have been compromised by their chronically antisocial behavior. In each case sorcery is declared to be something that the close kin comprising the village—a community of siblings, actual and metaphorical—would never commit against one another.

Sorcery is thus articulated with siblingship as something of its opposite. Siblingship is one metaphor for village membership: "we are all siblings," as people say to underscore the relations of cooperation and support, peacefulness and mutuality, that characterize sibling relations. Sorcery is the metaphorical opposite: antisocial, dangerous, secret, and potentially fatal. Sorcery accusations directed out of the community implicitly assert the expectations of conviviality of community membership: "our siblings" would never harm us; harmful sorcerers are found in other villages.

Those dangerous sorcerers are, ideologically, affines. Despite a preference for village endogamy and cross-cousin marriage, Maronaua and Sobral, the sites of the *kurubu madiha* group of Kulina,[5] regard the members of the Santo Amaro village, the *pitsi madiha*, as potential and in many cases actual affines, and each forms the primary locus of attack sorcery against the other. For example, Bodo, mentioned after, was a *pitsi madiha* who married into the community at Maronaua (young men in Maronaua occasionally travel to Santo Amaro looking for eligible young women for marriage).

Sorcery's articulation with siblingship thus reveals a complex dimension to this issue, one that I describe as the paradox of siblingship for Kulina. Specifically and briefly, villages composed ideologically of siblings are also ideologically endogamous: some of these siblings must be converted into potential affines for marriage. The paradox lies in the fact that many village members are simultaneously siblings and affines, and the relations expected of affines, from sexual access to sorcery attacks, are prohibited among siblings (Pollock 2001). The Kulina are not unique in this regard; some of the social consequences of this kind of paradox were explored a number of years ago by Ellen Basso among the Kalapalo (1970, 1975) and by Joanna Overing among the Piaroa (Overing-Kaplan 1972, 1973). I will not explore here the broad range of the interesting consequences of this paradox or dilemma for the Kulina (see Pollock 1985, 2001), but I will pursue briefly the implications of the paradox for violence and sorcery.

Interhousehold violence is not common in Kulina villages, but violent acts can be very aggressive and village members become extremely distressed when, for example, a woman attacks her husband's lover with a machete or a burning log, or men threaten each other with shotguns or knives. Violent disputes between individuals are often resolved, however, and harmony is typically restored after a *tokorime* curing ritual and its subsequent ritual of social reconciliation. A more serious and complex case is worth a brief examination to illustrate the more subtle forms that violence can take. When I first arrived in Maronaua in the dry season of 1981 I found that *tokorime* rituals were being conducted every night in the village. Over the next several weeks I learned that the village had become divided the week before my arrival over a dispute between the senior headman, Rimana, and his younger brother, Waki.

The details of the dispute are complicated and more ideologically than physically violent. Rimana led a faction that looked to the Brazilian National Indian Foundation (FUNAI) for future support of the village. Rimana had received vague promises of an airstrip, health care, and even electrical generators. And, just as important, FUNAI would support Rimana's political position. His brother Waki, however, had allied himself to the Catholic missionary organization, the Conselho Indigenista Missionário (CIMI). A Brazilian family had been placed in the village by CIMI, and this family, although technically missionaries, had adopted the CIMI position of looking after indigenous rights rather than pursuing any overtly evangelical goals. A large quantity of medications had already been supplied to the village by CIMI, which had also built a schoolhouse where the missionaries hoped to start literacy training. Waki, the younger brother and a weaker political figure, was supported by the CIMI missionaries, who found him a more pliable ally than Rimana.

The resources designated by FUNAI to the region were overtaxed, and it is unlikely that the organization could ever have provided the material benefits that Rimana sought. Rather, I believe that FUNAI's implicit goal was to encourage Rimana to expell the CIMI missionaries, who were regarded as troublesome and illegal intruders in this indigenous area. Some time not long before my arrival, the missionary family returned to Maronaua from a trip to Brasilia, and their return precipitated a series of angry disputes between Rimana and Waki over their presence. Rimana insisted that the missionaries leave the village, while Waki, recognizing that the missionaries were an extremely valuable source of support for his own political aspirations, refused to allow them to be expelled. Rimana then announced that he would take his own supporters to the abandoned rubber-tapping camp down-river, the Seringal Sobral. Unfortunately for Rimana's plans, many of his political supporters and allies were reluctant to move; Maronaua had good hunting, established gardens, and substantial houses. To many, even to rebuild houses, which the Kulina adapted in a variation of the local Brazilian caboclo style, was more effort than the dispute seemed to justify. After all, people told me, FUNAI was merely a promise but the CIMI missionaries were already in the village, acting daily to help people. This Rimana took only a small group of about thirty people to Sobral, about one week before I arrived.

As this brief and somewhat simplified account suggests, my arrival in Maronaua more or less coincided with a particularly serious political conflict, one that was, moreover, between two brothers. While not physically violent, the dispute disrupted or threatened the conviviality of village relations and the obligatory harmony of siblings—in this case a pair of especially powerful siblings—and the social tensions that it provoked were immediately translated into a virtual epidemic of dori illness. Indeed, by the time I arrived in the village I found *tokorime* curing rituals being performed all night, every night, for numerous patients. Significantly, the sorcery attacks' ideological projection of blame outward onto sorcerers in the Santo Amaro village was so marked that even Rimana returned to Maronaua to assist in the *tokorime* curing rituals (a participation that doubtless was also a form of self-immunizing from accusations of sorcery). I suspect that, over their history, Kulina villages have periodically divided along similar social lines and in comparable disputes, and the resulting communities ultimately come to regard each other as distinct *madiha* groups that are also the loci of sorcery attacks.

Affines and Enemies

Dori is not the only form of illness that can be caused by the intentional use of mystical forces; the Kulina describe another illness, one caused by the (mis)use of the hallucinogenic drug ayahuasca. While at one level dori sorcery might be understood as a discourse of siblingship and conviviality, the complex of beliefs surrounding ayahuasca illness draws on concerns about affinity and the social tensions of sexuality. Together, both reveal facets of the paradox of kinship and affinity in a Kulina village.

While Kulina do not use ayahuasca in shamanic practice, they do take it regularly during the dry season in nighttime rituals. Ayahuasca *(Banisteriopsis caapi)* allows its users to communicate with spirits in the sky. Its use is not associated with curing but rather is connected with visions of the future and of the mythic past. Notably, both Kulina men and women take ayahuasca; the Kulina regard it as an introduced drug they acquired from the local Panoan-speaking peoples, and they call it by the same Panoan term, *rami*, that is used by the Kaxinaua and the Sharanaua along the upper Purus.

The focus of my original research among the Kulina of Maronaua was traditional ethnomedicine (Pollock 1994a, 1996), and in abstract discussions of illness Kulina occasionally mentioned a rather mysterious condition called *ramikka dzamakuma*, "ayahuasca fever" or "ayahuasca sickness." *Ramikka dzamakuma* is caused when a man wishing to seduce a woman prepares an infusion of ayahuasca by boiling the vine, and then smears her hammock and clothes with the liquid. The drug acts initially as an aphrodisiac, and produces the desired amorous effects. However, within a few days the woman falls ill and may die unless she is treated by a special variety of shaman called a *wiwimade* (literally "storyteller"), who is skilled in the specialized use of ayahuasca. The serious threat posed by this illness lies in the fact that only the local Panoan Indians are *wiwimade* shamans, and they are usually happy to let Kulina suffering from illness die.

Ramikka dzamakuma is somewhat mysterious inasmuch as it appears to be largely mythical or hypothetical; no one suffered from this illness during my research and no one could point to a case that was unambiguously *ramikka dzamakuma*. I interpreted the illness as having a kind of virtual or potential character, a logical entailment of Kulina notions of illness and personhood but rarely if ever a reality in practice. Like beliefs about aphrodisiacs in other cultures, *ramikka dzamakuma* is also a fantasy about sexuality and sexual access, and from this perspective it offers some insights into Kulina notions of affinity and sexuality as opposed to siblingship and conviviality.

The description of the preparation and use of ayahuasca as an aphrodisiac is suggestive; it mirrors a complex of beliefs and practices surrounding illness and its treatment, and it is in this sense that "ayahuasca fever" is immanent in Kulina notions of illness and personhood. The ayahuasca prepared for "normal" consumption in vision-inducing rituals is mixed with a variety of other plants to produce the desired hallucinogenic effects, and the mix is taken by drinking. However, to produce the aphrodisiac the vine is boiled alone and is applied to the hammock and clothes where it will be absorbed into the skin. When powerful substances, especially powerful-smelling substances, penetrate the skin they produce transformations in the person, and *ramikka dzamakuma* works a fundamental transformation on the person who takes it in this inappropriate way. While milder-smelling substances can be used to enhance one's attractiveness, strong-smelling substances produce more profound effects: tobacco snuff transforms shamans into spirits; good-smelling substances are rubbed on a corpse to help transform the dead into a peccary spirit. Ayahuasca used as an aphrodisiac drug transforms the victim, but at the price of poisoning her.

The paradox of *ramikka dzamakuma*—that the potion that is used to attract and seduce a lover will ultimately kill her—condenses and expresses the more general Kulina view of affines and potential affines. These are relationships surrounded by behavioral taboos and prescriptions, expectations and rules. While the metaphor of siblingship extends to all community members a free and easy conviviality and the linked identities of shared substance, sexuality and marriage demarcate that a community of "siblings" be divided into two groups: kin and affines—that is, those with whom sex is forbidden and those who are potential or actual sexual and marriage partners. It is the affinal side of the social universe to which an attitude of shame is extended, to which obligations of hunting and gardening are owed, and to which sexual access is available. At a marriage ritual, affines lash one another with thick whips made of tapir hide attached to a handle. To court or seduce a sexual partner is a metaphorical act of aggression, and just as sorcery attacks are typically attributed to members of affinally related communities, so too is the mystical illness of *ramikka dzamakuma* caused by the aggressive act of seduction between potential affines.

Siblings and Sorcerers

I have relied here on the highly apposite concept of "conviviality" proposed by Overing and Passes and their colleagues to capture the sense of cooperation and easy, if obligatory, hospitality that surrounds life in the Kulina villages where I have worked, inasmuch as it appears to describe life in so many indigenous Amazonian communities (Overing and Passes 2000:14). Conviviality is not merely a cultural prescription (as Overing and Passes note it may even be incompatible with prescriptions and formal rules for social life), it is also a shared psychological style of experiencing one's "self," and although my interest in this essay has been focused on developing a cultural account of Kulina sorcery, it is tempting to introduce a psychological perspective as well. As Stephen has commented in her study of Mekeo magic, humans in social life seem to display a *desire* for a well-defined, bounded self (1995:320), even when in cultural terms local conceptions of personhood present the "unbounded" person so familiar in lowland South American research. In a Kulina community, where the permeability of personhood is stressed and a fluid, open self is valued, desire for a bounded self must be repressed. Moreover, the "openness" of personhood, the cultural assumption of overlapping identities and shared substance among community members, leaves the self vulnerable to attack or penetration by sorcerers; the very openness that is both the prerequisite and consequence of conviviality is also the vulnerable point at which sorcery penetrates. It is not surprising, perhaps, that the Kulina image of sorcery's malign weapon is an intrusive, penetrating mystical substance that draws on the same logic of shared substance that unites members of a community.

If Stephen is correct, and if such a psychological style also entails that the desire for a bounded sense of self be repressed in order to achieve the openness of social life, we may understand how assaults on that self trigger such violent responses. Among the Kulina, fatal sorcery attacks require the killing of the sorcerer by dramatically violent means, by bludgeoning, in the cases I have witnessed, and reportedly in other cases by arrows, shotgun blasts, and axe blows. Affinity and sexual access, which demarcate the self through behavioral prescriptions and social obligations, are threats to the permeability of the self that is always at risk in siblingship; *ramikka dzamakuma*, the dual face of seduction and murder, captures the violence of this threat to the experience of one's self in a Kulina community.

In a Kulina village one's metaphorical siblings represent the universe of conviviality, and vice versa, but affinity and sexuality represent the major threat to the harmony of siblingship; the preference for village endogamy continually entails that some of these "siblings" be converted into affines or potential affines and the openness of the self that one experiences in relations with one's siblings is continually threatened by the intrusion of relations based on more-explicit rules of conduct, structure, and calculation of reciprocity. Attack sorcery by shamans, and the metaphorical violence of the seducer, represent, in effect, too little regard for the conviviality of siblingship on the one hand, and too much desire for the sexual access of affinity on the other. They frame the essential tension of Kulina social life, the paradox of siblingship and affinity and of sorcerers and seducers.

Notes

1 I use an orthography for the Kulina language that is based on the International Phonetic Alphabet, but I should acknowledge that to do so is partly a political act. The Summer Institute of Linguistics (SIL), a fundamentalist Protestant missionary organization, developed an orthography for the Kulina language that it has used in its ethnographic publications, educational materials, and Bible translations in Peru (e.g., Adams 1962, 1963). The SIL orthography is based on the Spanish values of letters (e.g., where I write *madiha* the SIL writes *madija*), and thus I find it less useful than my own, especially when roughly 90 percent of Kulina live in Brazil. Unfortunately, literate *madiha* in both Peru and Brazil are also writing *madija*. So it goes.
2 I suspect from the Deni ethnography that they are in fact a Kulina group that has become regarded as separate and to some degree distinct. Their language appears to be at least a closely related dialect of Kulina. Even their name, *deni*, is the Kulina pluralizing suffix used with the name of each Kulina local group; the Kulina at Maronaua are the Kurubu *madihadeni*, for example: the *kurubu* fish people.
3 In the upper Purus dialect of the Kulina language the /o/ often becomes /u/ and the terminal /i/ becomes /e/. In the SIL orthography the term dzumahe is dsomaji.
4 Claire Lorraine (2000) has noted that among the Kulina of Amazonas the term *koidza* refers to a ritual in which large quantities of the drink are consumed. Among the Ku-

lina of the upper Purus, the term *koidza* refers to the drink itself, and the Brazilian term *mariri* has been adopted for the ritual. See also Adams (1962:184) where she defines *cohuidsa* as *la bebida fermentada*, while Kanaú and Monserrat (1984:12) define *coidsa* as *festa tradicional do povo kulina* for the Kulina of the Igarapé do Anjo of the upper Río Envira.

5 Kulina villages are more or less coterminus with named, localized subgroups that typically are named after animals: the *kurubu* is a local fish and the *pitsi* is a species of monkey.

References

Adams, P. 1962. "Textos Kulina." *Folklore Americano* 10: 93–222.
———. 1963. "Some Notes on the Material Culture of the Kulina Indians." *Antropologica* 1 (2): 27–44.
———. 1976. "Ceramica Kulina." *Peru Indigena* 10 (24–25): 82–87.
Árhem, Kaj. 1981. *Makuna Social Organization*. Uppsala: University of Uppsala.
Basso, Ellen. 1970. "Xingu Carib Kinship Terminology and Marriage: Another View." *Southwestern Journal of Anthropology* 26: 402–16.
———. 1975. "Kalapalo Affinity: Its Cultural and Social Contexts." *American Ethnologist* 2 (2): 207–28.
Conklin, Beth A. 1996. "Reflections on Amazonian Anthropologies of the Body." *Medical Anthropology Quarterly* 10 (3): 373–75.
Douglas, Mary, ed. 1970. *Witchcraft Confessions and Accusations*. London: Tavistock.
Geschiere, Peter. 1997. *The Modernity of Witchcraft: Politics and the Occult in Postcolonial Africa*. Charlottesville: University of Virginia Press.
Goldman, Irving. 1963. *The Cubeo*. Urbana: University of Illinois Press.
Gow, Peter. 1997. "O parentesco como consciência humana: O case dos Piro." *Mana* 3 (2): 39–65.
———. 2000. "Helpless: The Affective Preconditions of Piro Social Life." In *The Anthropology of Love and Anger*, ed. J. Overing and A. Passes. 46–63. London: Routledge.
Kanaú [Abel O. Silva], and Ruth M. F. Monserrat. 1984. *Dicionário Kulina-Português, Português-Kulina*. São Paulo: Centro Ecumênico de Documentação e Informação.
Koop, Gordon, and Sherwood Ligenfelter. 1980. The Deni of Western Brazil. Dallas: Summer Institute of Linguistics. Museum of Anthropology Publication 7.
Langdon, E. Jean. 1996. *Xamanismo no Brasil: Novas Perspectivas*. Florianópolis: Editora da UFSC.
Langdon, E. Jean, and Gerhard Baer, eds. 1992. *Portals of Power: Shamanism in South America*. Albuquerque: University of New Mexico Press.
Lorrain, Claire. 2000. "Cosmic Reproduction, Economics, and Politics among the Kulina of Southwest Amazonia." *Journal of the Royal Anthropological Institute* 6 (2): 293–310.
McCallum, Cecilia. 1996. "The Body that Knows: From Cashinahua Epistemology to a Medical Anthropology of Lowland South America." *Medical Anthropology Quarterly* 10 (3): 347–72.
Overing Kaplan, Joanna. 1972. "Cognation, Endogamy, and Teknonymy: The Piaroa Example." *Southwestern Journal of Anthropology* 28: 282–97.
———. 1973. "Endogamy and the Marriage Alliance: A Note on Continuity in Kindred-Based Groups." *Man* 8 (4): 555–70.

———. 1975. *The Piaroa*. Oxford: Oxford University Press.
Overing, Joanna, and Alan Passes, eds. 2000. *The Anthropology of Love and Anger: The Aesthetics of Conviviality in Native Amazonia*. London: Routledge.
Pollock, Donald. 1985a. "Food and Sexual Identity among the Culina." *Food and Foodways* 1: 25–42.
———. 1985b. "Looking for a Sister: Culina Siblingship and Affinity." In *The Sibling Relationship in Lowland South America*, ed. Kenneth Kesinger. 8–15. Bennington: Bennington College.
———. 1992. "Culina Shamanism: Gender, Power, and Knowledge." In *Portals of Power: Shamanism in South America*, ed. E. Jean Langdon and Gerhard Baer. 25–40. Albuquerque: University of New Mexico Press.
———. 1993a. "Death and Afterdeath among the Kulina." In "Death, Mourning and the Afterlife in Lowland South America," ed. Beth Ann Conklin, a special issue of *Latin American Anthropology Review* 5 (2): 61–64.
———. 1993b. "Conversion and 'Community' in Amazonia." In *Conversion to Christianity: Historical and Anthropological Perspectives on a Great Transformation*, ed. Robert Hefner. 165–97. Berkeley: University of California Press.
———. 1994a. "Etnomedicina Kulina." In *Saúde e Povos Indígenas*, ed. Ricardo V. Santos and Carlos Coimbra. 143–60. Rio de Janeiro: Fundação Oswald Cruz.
———. 1994b. "The Culina." In *The Encyclopedia of World Cultures: South America*. 146–49. New Haven: Human Relations Area Files.
———. 1995. "Masks and the Semiotics of Identity." *Journal of the Royal Anthropological Institute* 1 (3): 581–97.
———. 1996. "Personhood and Illness Among the Kulina." *Medical Anthropology Quarterly* 10 (3): 319–41.
———. 1998. "Food and Gender among the Kulina." In *Food and Gender: Identity and Power*, ed. Carole Counihan and Steven Kaplan, 11–28. New York: Gordon and Breach.
———. 2001. "Partible Paternity and Multiple Maternity Among the Kulina." In *Cultures of Multiple Fathers: Patrible Paternity in Lowland South America*, ed. Stephen Beckerman and Paul Valentine. 42–61. Gainesville: University of Florida Press.
Rüf, Isabelle. 1972. "Le 'dutsee tui' chez les indens Kulina du Perou." *Bulletin de la Société Suisse de Americanistes* 36: 73–80.
Shapiro, Judith. 1974. "Alliance or Descent: Some Amazonian Contrasts." *Man* 9 (2): 305–6.
Siskind, Janet. 1973. *To Hunt in the Morning*. New York: Oxford University Press.
Stephen, Michele. 1995. *A'aisa's Gifts: A Study of Magic and the Self*. Berkeley: University of California Press.
Townsend, Patricia, and P. Adams. 1978. "Estructura y conflicto en el matrimonio de los indios Kulina de la amazonia peruana." In *Communidades y Culturas Peruanas*, 139–60. Lima: Summer Institute of Linguistics.

*Being Alone amid Others:
Sorcery and Morality among
the Arara, Carib, Brazil*

Márnio Teixeira-Pinto

Tchibie is now a mute and feeble old woman. Almost totally debilitated, she walks with great difficulty and barely manages to leave the hills where she has been living for a long time. For decades, she and her family had to remain hidden because a FUNAI team was trying all means to contact them.[1] After wandering around for years, Tchibie and her family finally found a place to hide from the white man, but now they have been discovered. Because there is no way for them to live isolated anymore, they agreed to move from their hilltop shelters to a new place where the FUNAI personnel assured them they would be physically better and safer. After descending the hills for awhile on her own, Tchibie eventually needed help, and for a couple of hours she had to be carried on the backs of one of the FUNAI employees. She is the oldest person of her family, whose history is a rich amalgam of tragedy, survival strategies, and a striking disclosure of many aspects of Arara social existence. The debilitation of her health is like a sorrowful sign of her family's desolate and miserable social existence, which began when they were forced into isolation as a result of sorcery accusations.

Soon after Tchibie became a widow for the second time, she was taken in marriage by her eldest son. This was not the first incestuous match in the family, for her own husband had previously married their own daughter. The context for this history of incestuous relations began many years ago, when Tchibie and her first husband were banished from living with the rest of the Arara people. At that time they had two boys and a girl. Later, her first husband died leaving her with six children. She then married another man, apparently a non-Indian—nobody knows (or says) who he was or even how they met. She had one other daughter with him and one more son before

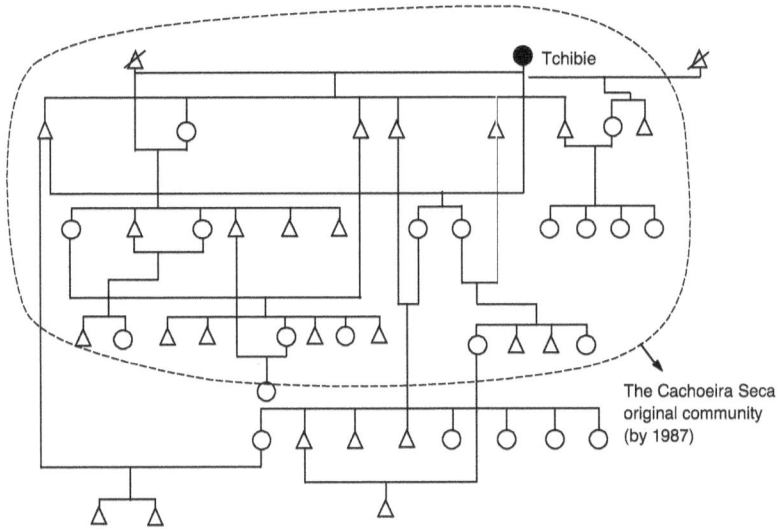

Figure 1. The Arara subgroup of Cachoeira Seca.

he also died. Then she became the first wife of her oldest son, and had two more daughters.

More than twenty years have passed since the beginning of this gloomy history. Now the FUNAI team has finally contacted Tchibie's family hidden on the top of the hills near the left bank of the upper Iriri River. The whole group amounts to a single extended family of almost thirty people, most of whom are offspring of incestuous unions (see figure 1).[2] They were finally settled near a small creek called Cachoeira Seca, alongside one of FUNAI's indigenous posts. There they built an extemporaneous village, with many small huts resembling temporary hunting shelters. The absence of the traditional way of organizing a village, in which a house represents a social unit acting as a cohesive group, expresses the absence (even the abandonment) of the traditional rules that govern interpersonal interactions. Many efforts have been made to get them to live closer to other Arara subgroups around the Laranjal Indigenous Post, located a few hours' travel time down the Iriri River[3] in order to help them reorganize their social life. They are now known as "the Arara of the Cachoeira Seca."[4]

Isolation and Incest: Sorcery and the Discipline of Shamanism

In this essay I analyze the connections between banishment, sorcery, shamanism, morality, and certain foundations of social life among the Arara.

Through a description of aspects of Arara cosmology—their notions of personhood, formal partnerships, and reciprocity—I will show how expulsion is an exemplary sentence to be applied to those who decide to break the moral rules connected to the use of certain technical skills. Subordinating technical abilities to the moral rules of generosity and unselfishness is an overall procedure typical of the Arara. From ordinary handicrafts to specialized shamanic practices, every skilled activity of the Arara is to be controlled by a firm precept of vigorously avoiding the suspicion of greed or stinginess. This is most evident in regard to shamanic knowledge and exercise.

Most conditions of Arara social life, as symbolically conceived by them, are so dependent on certain shamanic activities that the practice of shamanism becomes threatening for the community and risky for practitioners. Using shamanic skills for promoting collective well-being is one of the stronger moral imperatives attached to individual skills. It seeks to avoid the use of shamanism to practice sorcery, which amounts to a selfish appropriation of shamanic powers. As an inappropriate use of shamanic skills, Arara sorcery is a violation of the very foundations of sociality. Banishment, which means isolation, is the destiny of those who are suspected of sorcery and therefore accused of egoism and selfishness. This is what happened to Tchibie and her first husband. Their history is amazingly simple, and their adaptive response astonishingly awkward. Their destiny was a byproduct of Arara sanctions against those who are suspected of sorcery, found guilty and finally condemned to leave their communities. Furthermore, because they were living in an area subject to massive and violent nonindigenous invasions since the 1970s, they also had to hide from contact with intruders.[5]

Political autonomy and economic independence are at the foundation of Arara traditional social organization (Teixeira-Pinto 1993b, 1995a). The existence of small subgroups, of about thirty to forty people living dispersed over a wide area, has always been the pattern of Arara social life, and is still in practice today. The largest Arara settlement, the Laranjal village, includes many different and autonomous subgroups, each having their own gardens, hunting paths, and even a particular schedule to bathe in the river or visit the FUNAI facilities in search of health care or industrial tools and goods. Yet, a tight network of interaction and collaboration among the different subgroups underlies the independence of each subgroup. The difference between formal independence and real isolation, which led Tchibie and her family to continuous incestuous matches, points to the opposition between living according to an established "social contract" that sustains Arara society as an enduring and consensual moral community, and living in complete abandonment of it.

Sorcery and the Moral Bounds of Shamanism

I argue here that through the analysis of the conditions of sorcery we can perceive significant aspects of Arara sociality, which paradoxically are revealed in its disruption. The accusations and consequences of sorcery can reveal the limits of what we may call an Arara "social contract" based on the nature of the moral conceptions that inform and create most of their practices, whether collective or individual. A contrast between being alone, selfish, and violent and being generous, reciprocal, mutual, and integrated within a network of cooperation and interdependence is presented as the two major limits of the native moral spectrum of possible human ways of acting. In this essay I will review the argument that the potential use of shamanic powers to produce damage to others is at the core of Arara definitions of sorcery, even though this is already a cliché, a commonplace, and even a trite statement about sorcery. But the Arara include a further aspect to this issue that I find absorbing: because all Arara adult men must be initiated into and are at least partial practitioners of shamanic tasks, all of them potentially and permanently can be suspected of being sorcerers. Possessing some shamanic abilities is part of what is expected of a male person. Moreover, most of Arara social life is thought of as being produced and reproduced by shamanism. Thus sorcery appears as a typical instance of a common yet essential skill that can turn into a dangerous practice that threatens the very possibility of collective life. This characteristic of sorcery reveals the fragility of the foundations of Arara social life, and in this sense sorcery is not only a moral deviance of correct shamanic actions but also, and mainly, a defiance of society as a whole and a conceptual challenge for the Arara understanding of the moral aspects of sociality.

Part of what is considered as something only a shaman can accomplish in the world is the production of ideal metaphysical conditions that make social activities logically and symbolically possible.[6] Another part is the control over several regular cooperative tasks such as gardening, and the organization of rituals (not to mention daily healing and physical care) that are accomplished through shamanic intercession. As important as shamanism is for general aspects of social life, it is also a permanent source of danger and threat. This fragility of life's status is an essential aspect of the Arara way of understanding human relationships, and it is at the foundation of the moral gist of sociality.

The moral constraints and closeness of formal ties of friendship and cooperation between individuals are what control the potential use of shamanic powers for malevolent purposes. Evoking many other Arara institutions, shamanism also has the status of being something that has to be used as a "gift" (that is, something that exists under the exclusive condition that it will be given to someone else [see Lefort 1967]). In no morally acceptable way can a shaman act on his own behalf. Hence, along with its harmful utilization, shamanism for any self-benefit stands as one of the main causes of sorcery accusations. Yet the threads that connect the use of shamanic arts and crafts with attitudes toward others are extremely fragile and constantly subject to rupture. Denying the decisive quality of Arara shamanic powers (that it has to be used only in someone else's favor) means ignoring the main properties and values needed to sustain collective life. In this sense, sorcery is an instance of an anticollective action, a supreme sign of egoism, and an exaltation of the individual over the collective, and should be recognized as such through the banishment of contumacious suspects. At the heart of Arara social life there is this manifest contradiction: the same conditions that make conviviality possible are precisely what can also put it at risk. Sorcery is the practice that reveals this contradiction most clearly.

My arguments have obvious inspiration in other authors, ethnographies, and analyses. However, in the interest of simplicity and brevity I will not offer comparisons or detailed citations.[7] A much lengthier work on Arara and Amerindian moralities is a long-term project that I have just begun to undertake.

The Form and Meaning of Autonomy and Dispersion, Difference and Constraint

The Arara were the last Carib-speaking people to accept permanent contact with Brazilian national society. There were, however, many indigenous groups historically called Arara in the Xingu and Iriri river basins who had similar histories of being affected by indigenous and nonindigenous groups induced by the occupation of Amazonia throughout the century. More recently, the construction of the Trans-Amazonian Highway, along with the growth of the many towns that developed from colonization projects along the new road, have been the source of the main impact on the traditional indigenous population.[8]

Historical information about the Arara points to a pattern of territorial dispersion between the Tapajós and Tocantins rivers (see Nimuendaju 1932; Tocantins 1877; Von den Steinen 1894). Linguistically, the Arara belong to the same dialectic family as the Apiacá of the Tocantins (extinct), the Yaruma (extinct), and the Txicão-Ikpeng (living in the Xingu Indigenous Park). All of these are peoples whose spatial dispersion in the area between the Tocantins and Tapajós rivers covered the valley of the middle Xingu and Iriri rivers where the Arara were recently found (see Menget 1977: ch. 2). The Arara occupy a marginal geographical position when compared with the larger demographic concentrations of the Carib-speaking peoples of the Guyanas and the tributaries of the upper Xingu River (cf. Basso 1977). For a long time they shared the same area with several Tupian-speaking peoples (Shipaya, Curuaya, Mundurucu, Juruna), and the Gê-speaking Kayapó. Such extreme historical influences are important for understanding Arara singularities among other Carib-speaking peoples.

Much of the reality of the Arara way of life is a subtle adaptation of traditional patterns. Instead of the traditional dispersed local groups, now many different residential units emerge as the smallest sociopolitical units. Nevertheless, local groups have retained their main status of independence and autonomy, all despite living mostly within a single village. Their main settlement, around the Laranjal Indigenous Post, is in fact a conglomerate of distinct social units, each with a slightly different history of relationships with each other. If it weren't for its peculiar history of isolation and incest, the Cachoeira Seca-Iriri subgroup could simply be seen as another typical Arara social unit. However, the independence and autonomy of each subgroup go along with the network of multiple connections between them. Due to its peculiar history, the Cachoeira Seca-Iriri group has no connections of any kind with the others, a sign of its imposed seclusion.

A residential unit is built on a combination of two distinct norms: uxorilocality and a certain degree of personal autonomy. Uxorilocality is required for a first marriage, but prestige, personal affinities, solidarity, and cooperative agreements can influence any residential arrangement (Teixeira-Pinto 1995a). If affinal ties are important aspects for setting up a residential group, another condition is that a household should behave as a real cooperative unit: coresident adult men should always be helpful and reciprocal with each other in the tasks the group must collectively perform (hunting during the dry season, preparing the communal garden during the rainy season, etc.). Each household is centered on an elderly headman, and ideally, living with him are his unmarried sons and daughters, and eventually his sons-in-law. Yet since the Arara tend to be polygynous, uxorilocality becomes a very relative and unstable principle.

There are many matrimonial strategies to prevent the difficulties created by uxorilocality vis-à-vis a man's multiple marriages. In bypassing the paradox of uxorilocality in the context of polygyny, affinal ties replicate: a man marries two sisters or a woman and her sister's daughter. A marriage with a very young girl can likewise be arranged, thus avoiding uxorilocality. At the most, the best matrimonial strategies are those that can add wives without appending in-laws.

Unlike the postmarital unit to which a man belongs, the natal group receives the signs of consanguinity and its related circumstances. Those who are born within the same residential group are defined as mutually *iebï*, people who partake of the same physical "substances" (Teixeira-Pinto

1993b). This community of substance realizes practices of gifting, sharing, and cooperating in an extremely generalized fashion. But when a man gets married, he leaves behind him his natal family and consanguineal kin, and begins to live with his father-in-law and his affinal kin in the new household. While there, a man becomes a member of a hunting team, which is much more than an economic activity: belonging to a household implies the establishment of a large set of formal ties of solidarity, cooperation, and moral commitments between those associated through shared residence. By and large, the shift from the natal group and consanguineal domain to the new affinal household arena corresponds to the passage from an informal ground of conviviality to a strict field of formal interactions.

The relationships of a man with his natal group, however, never cease. Occasional meetings and planned rituals, usually held during the dry season, reconnect a man with his natal relatives. These gatherings invariably begin with a large collective hunt that one household offers to another. The hunters are to act as guests visiting another local group's settlement. Nowadays where living arrangements are basically within a single village, hosts and guests share the same arena, but observe traditional roles: a household team leaves the village for a prolonged stay in the forest where they must kill as much game as they can, while the other household remains in the village preparing large amounts of *piktu*,[9] which must be offered in exchange for the meat. All of this activity forms an exchange cycle of meat for drink, which will be sustained until the end of the dry season: a residential group initially hunts to offer the game to another which will reciprocate with the *piktu*. Afterward they both change roles.

The demographic and the postmarital residential patterns, along with the exchange cycle between households, imply a very clear dynamic whose formal structure, sociological mechanisms, and associated moral aspects can be seen by observing both households, natal and postmarital, to determine the nature of the connections that are established between the individuals. The mutual individual associations with natal kin and with the new coresidents are a very significant characteristic of Arara social life. The complex logical, symbolic, and psychological connections between individuals are a significant feature for defining the nature of personal bonds that entail social involvement and the moral commitments among them.

A household, while not being a named entity with a clear jural status, does act as a corporate group, although it does not constitute in itself a "house" in the analytical sense (see Lévi-Strauss 1981, 1986; Carsten and Hugh-Jones 1995). Households do have political independence and economic autonomy enough to secure their freedom in relation to the strategies for interacting with other households. The matrimonial alliances that anchor their existence are always defined by the headman's wider political motives. It is important to agglutinate a group of individuals because a large and efficient hunting team provides prestige to the headman in the network of interaction that involves the several households.

Further, the dry-season hunting routine also has its structuring function within the household team. All men of the same household must hunt together during the entire season. They arrange themselves into a team with an internal organization that decides on the length of stay in the forest as well as the preferential places to build the temporary hunting camps. Although they do not act as a single unit in carrying out their hunting objectives but rather divide themselves into many formal partnerships, Arara men are always expected to act in pairs.

There are two different types of formal partnerships. The first, which occurs on a regular basis, is called *ibirinda* and is associated with the collective hunt throughout the dry season: wandering around with a fellow in the forest suffices to establish a formal link of *ibirinda* between two men.[10] The second, called *uoktangat*, occurs during conflicts and hostilities against traditional enemies: a joint act of killing an enemy produces a sort of deep identification between the partners.[11] Between the two formal partnerships the only sociological difference is that an *ibirinda* association always is initiated between people who live within the same household, while the war partnership, *uoktangat*, connects people from two distinct groups. Both partnerships are permanent and last even in a situation where the initial condition for their existence has already come to an end. Each time a collective expedition is realized, former pairs of *ibirinda* can join or new ones can be formed. Because the collective hunt is the primary male activity during the dry season, the *ibirinda* partnerships are constantly created, renewed, or remade. Likewise, even though there were neither traditional combats nor enemies to be killed in the customary way, there were still five pairs of *uoktangat* living in the village of Laranjal in 1994.

Within a household the nature of the ties that unite men are not homogeneous: there are parents and sons, uncles and nephews, grandfathers and grandchildren, siblings, brothers-in-law, sons-in-law, and fathers-in-law. Yet the formation of hunting partnerships must obey certain exclusive criteria: the unit of parent and son, or two siblings, or grandfather and grandchild cannot act together. The basic relations that settle partnerships are real affinal ties (a son-in-law with his father-in-law, two brothers-in-law together, etc.). Besides the affines, an unmarried maternal uncle and his nephew (keeping in mind that the Arara are basically uxorilocal) are also recognized as virtual and privileged partners for hunting. The reason that prior relations among hunters excludes them from formal partnerships is that the compulsory solidarity that comes from consanguinity would make the ethical imperative completely useless. That is, it is because they are built on relations of real affinity (and on the mother's brother–sister's son links) that the *ibirinda* or *uoktangat* partnerships, emerging from hunting or raiding, are distinguished from pure kinship and consanguinity.

Between these "partners" extremely formalized ways of cooperation and solidarity take place. Actually, the extreme formality of typical Arara ways of behaving draws the attention of anyone who visits them for long or even for very short periods of time. In fact, in both the most ordinary activities (gardening, hunting, harvesting) to ceremonial practices (drinking manioc beer, playing flutes, dancing) and the more extraordinary and highly ritualized procedures associated with their famous "bellicose passion" (raids, killing, dissection of an enemy's corpse; see Teixeira-Pinto 1997) the Arara constantly operate in pairs. Indeed, "to act in pairs" appears to be a pervasive metaphor for a general Arara ideal for social ties. To act in pairs means that each person establishes connections with another to accomplish what they are supposed to do. However, to act in pairs doesn't imply any sort of immutable connection between two specific individuals that once established would prevent them from being connected to another partner. Rather, it only means a model of relation that can connect n persons in sets of two.

Because the Arara are much more inductive and seductive than coercive, a call for cooperation (*mate ibirindamitpït uro*) is a spark for Arara sociality. Nevertheless, even when not formalized through that explicit request, the simple act of asking someone to do something is a very effective way to be connected with somebody else and to become involved in a situation in which they must meet expectations to render aid. There are two main sets of cooperative activities, one that is structured by very formal and predictable rules, and another that is built around more informal and unpredictable practices. The first is connected with dry-season collective hunting and the war expeditions and killing of enemies in the past, while the second is associated with year-round ordinary hunting and the daily consumption of manioc beer.

Even though it is quite possible to go alone for occasional hunting, Arara hunters prefer to invite someone else to accompany them. There are different expertises in hunting techniques and variations in skill, in addition to the fact that two hunters can kill and carry more game than can one. But none of these facts alone are responsible for their preference for going hunting with a partner. There is no good in being alone because it can trigger a general feeling of sadness, gloominess, and melancholy. In the Arara glossary for personal affective states, there are at least three emotional qualities associated with loneliness: *tïmorangne, tïpongne,* and *ipo'pra*, the translation of which obviously presents many problems. Their contextual roots can help us to understand the differences. *Tipongne* is connected to the sensation of feeling "unhappy," while *ipo'pra* is a sort of nostalgia or yearning for, or missing, someone. *Timorangne* is a more generic and diffuse feeling of "distress" without a definite causation but always associated with the wider condition of being in the world. The all-embracing category the Arara use to describe this terrestrial existence is *otamnoptanã*, the noun derived from the verb *otamnoptobot* that denotes the "loss" of anything.[12] Relatively widespread throughout Amazonia, the idea of an initial catastrophe giving form to the actual world has not just a descriptive value for the Arara but also serves as the main foundation for their morality. For them, geomorphology immediately brings to mind the cosmological history of privation and the subjective conditions of living in the terrestrial domain. For this reason, the connections between individuals are not only a necessary adaptation but a temporary solution for an isolated individual's hardships.

In this sense the symbolic and psychological links between two formal partners are much more important than any sociology could anticipate. By being *ibirinda* or *uoktangat* two formal partners always have many reciprocal obligations. Besides collaboration in practical activities, to assist each other in any sort of disablement, especially when one is returning from the forest, is among their main duties. Because of this, being partially skilled in the shamanic arts for curing a partner comprises part of the attributes expected of any adult man.

Even in relation to practical activities, two formal partners are connected in a deeper way. Among the *ibirinda* for instance, the one who kills game must give it to the other partner to carry the whole time. When arriving at their destination, the one who killed the animal chooses the way that the meat should be prepared by the partner who carried it from the forest, or even by a former *ibirinda*. During a hunt it is extremely rare that just one partner has success in killing. So together they do in a joint way something that each one of them could be doing independently: killing, carrying, preparing, etc. A greater ethical imperative seems to transform the apparently simple possibility that something fully achievable individually may in fact be accomplished in an independent way: an imperative of complementarity and an ethic of solidarity and cooperation solidly joins those who are involved in a common task.

In brief, the general picture of what goes on among the *ibirinda* is as follows: a slain animal is carried by the partner of the one who killed it; if both are successful, each one will carry the game of the other. As they arrive in the village, they lay the game on the ground and address the partner, saying "that's your game." If both carry game, both will do the same, formally returning the game to whom it belongs. But they don't even touch the game they kill; instead they almost immediately choose someone else (a former *ibirinda* partner) and ask him to cut up the flesh. After the game is cut into pieces, the hunter (or hunters) asks someone else (the third actor on the stage besides the hunter himself, yet always a former partner) to cook the game. When cooked, the hunter finally asks his father-in-law or the oldest man present to help him, after which the hunter and all the others feel free to do the same. What is going on here? Game, even one animal, can generate a network of sharing and the circulation of food (or goods). Hunting (which presupposes a hunter!) is appropriated in a very collective way, creating, using, and reinforcing the social ties between the hunters. If there is individual achievement, it is incorporated into community life. Between a hunter and his game, deep links of interindividual connections are established.

But this is not the only formal partnership, neither is it the only illustration that formal ethics of solidarity, cooperation, and complementarity play a very important role. In the case of the distribution of manioc beer, *piktu*, almost the same thing happens. *Piktu* is made mainly by women by masticating, and then later fermentation. In the daily drinking gatherings, every man shows up with large bowls full of drink. Each offers generous portions to another (an old man and formal partners are among the chosen) always holding the pot (a calabash) with his own hand. But after a little while he gives his whole bowl full of *piktu* to the same person who drank first, who will take care of the distribution from then on. Because every man shows up with a bowl the characters may change, but the "script" and the overall model will remain: each one will distribute the *piktu* that was produced and presented by another. Thus, the collective appropriation of manioc beer is another reaffirmation of the very nature of Arara social connections among individuals. Everything must always be done in relation to others. Henceforth, despite being sociologically divided into many different social units and enjoying a reasonable degree of personal autonomy, the Arara end up being linked to a network of multiple connections that crosscut the multiple fields of sociality.

The great gatherings and rituals enacted during the dry season also have the objective of affirming and sustaining on a more permanent and regular basis the relations between autonomous and independent social groups and, concurrently, the formal engagements between nominally free individuals. It is in this context that trust and suspicion mediate individual adhesion to the Arara "social contract," and that the use of shamanic powers and its infringement that characterizes sorcery appear embedded in the moral dimension of Arara sociality.

The Shaman as Giver: Producing Well-Being

All Arara shamanic tasks are related to special ways of accessing occult powers. An infusion called *omiatchembïlï*, made from a vine I was not able to identify, has some (but not major) importance.[13] Certainly it is central to initiation into the shamanic arts, but afterward it can be left aside as its primary condition. Prepared through a gradual and constant cooking of the vine leaves and stem, the infusion is to be taken after long sessions of vomiting provoked by the exaggerated ingestion of warm water. After lying down in their hammocks in a temporary camp far from the village, every man must drink the infusion for hours and hours (even days). Weakened from expelling all previously consumed food and intoxicated by the infusion, the men probably are induced to have visions defined as the entrance into the supernatural world. This visual familiarity with metaphysical being is one of the meanings of initiation.

As stated, the infusion and the trance it purportedly induces are not absolute conditions for the shamanic practice. There is no public session of shamanism during which the consumption of any substance occupies an important place. Most of the shamanic activities are secret labors done in the forest. It is after the shaman's return from the forest and his relating of what he has done, seen, or discovered that the others note the shaman's deed. However, the social legitimacy of the shamans' words seems to come from the fact that they are supposed to have acquired the technical competence to identify and comprehend metaphysical beings, occult signs or omens, having already been initiated and having practiced the consumption of the infusion. Such metaphysical beings are said to act on this terrestrial level where most things are immediately visible to skilled eyes,[14] and in such a way they can be perceived even in unaltered states of consciousness. Thus trance is, technically speaking, not a sine qua non for gaining access to metaphysical realities.

At present, every man is not only entitled to be initiated but actually obliged to do so. For healing purposes all men must develop such technical abilities as only shamanism can provide. A "real person" must have the necessary skills for acting as healer for his kin and his formal partners (see below). Yet this generalized initiation (avoiding any gendered discussion) has many consequences for the social dimension of Arara shamanism. In general, an obvious consequence is the extreme proliferation of active shamans and the corresponding dispersion of shamanic capacities and dilution of competence to deal with metaphysical causalities and casualties.

Further, there is the dissipation of the frontiers between the cosmological levels of the visible and the invisible, the natural and the supernatural, the physical and the metaphysical. Because the existence of such limits is always a possible basis for the emergence of specialists in its crossing, the Arara assume a different cosmological configuration that seems to unravel even more the tenuous lines that would give the shaman's role any major specificity. It is in the traditional forms of healing and looking after the many problems that could affect the person that this dilution of shamanic powers manifests itself much more clearly.

Every adult man should know how to perform some healing procedures, in part to take care of his own wife (or wives) and children but also, or mainly, to comply with the social obligations toward formal partners. In general, any severe health impairment goes along with afflictions that affect the person. Only wounds with open skin infection or other clear, even if small, manifestations are defined as injuries that take place entirely on the body in its physical sense. Shamanic healing procedures apply by and large to diseases in which the person's afflictions have an important role, whether as cause or as foreseen consequence.

The Person: Afflictions, Control, and Healing

Despite their conceptual independence, the person and the body are intrinsically connected on the physical level.[15] If not all body illness compromises the person, any disablement of the person reflects on the body, and the body is also the means to gain access to the person's condition and its afflictions. It is through the concrete manipulation of body parts, components, and substances that a shaman can produce a cure. Also, the body components and substances are the elements through which sorcery can afflict the person.

The main body attribute is its capacity for movement: a body without life is simply "still matter" or an inactive "thing." An organism without movement is not a proper living thing. To be alive, as the Arara understand life and the living, is to have the capacity of *otchitotketpït*—moving, being animated, and being able to "go away" from one place to another. The idea of movement, which broadly is the capacity to shift through different places, goes along with the very notion of life. However, even though the end of bodily motion is a criteria for the identification of life, it is not the definitive sign of death. Death is also a process. It is common to say that "someone died a little" after a serious accident, a major fight, or a wound that produces abundant bleeding even for a little while. With the end of bodily motion one continues to "die" gradually, until everything consummates in full. Even during one's lifetime, a process of continuous mortification is entailed by the gradual loss of the person's vitality. Many processes play important roles in this continuous mortification during the lifetime: the immanent aging of the "hard parts" of the body, serious accidents impacting on the "soft" parts of the body, pathogenic factors associated with infections or other alterations produced in the person through body lesions or wounds, and even different sorts of direct predation by malign beings that dominate metaphysical settings.

The person's vitality is tied to the vital substances that circulate inside the body (see Teixeira-Pinto 1989). Identified by the radical /*kuru*/, the vital substances are the object of an incessant search as a condition for the maintenance and reproduction of life. Almost all body liquids and secretions are marked by the radical: blood (*imānkuru*), sperm (*ekuru*), saliva (*ilaptchikuru*), breast milk (*mongukuru*), urine (*tchikuru*). All of these are metabolic transformations of the substances /*kuru*/ acquired during life. There also are free kinds of /*kuru*/ substances, such as some tree secretions (*ieikuru*) or the bitter cassava juice liberated through pressing manioc tubers (*ekuru*). These free occurrences of /*kuru*/ substances are defined as the natural food of some metaphysical beings that wander about within the world, and they are considered extremely dangerous for the human being. The free occurrences of /*kuru*/ substances are also the subject of countless classes of taboos. Touching, seeing, or even talking about them in certain situations (the proximity of a hunt, for example) can produce the physical state of *uopra'* (see below). They must avoid touching blood (circulatory as well as menstrual) and any other tacky and viscous substance that recalls male sperm. Everything that seems to have /*kuru*/ in free form represents danger because it is the favorite nutrient of the harmful living beings that circulate in the world and the chief factor attracting their malefic actions.

Existing in all living beings, the /*kuru*/ substances circulate in the world in a very precise way: if animals have it, it is because they have gotten it from other animals or plants that have gotten it from the soil that, in turn, got the substances from the dead animals that lie directly on the earth. A precious source of vital substances is fermented drink, mainly those that are elaborated from root crops whose profitable parts grow inside the earth, the many species of potatoes and cassavas that the Arara cultivate. The earth is responsible for the overall processing and circulation of vital substances. Thus, the reason that the Arara do not put a dead body in the earth is that a dead body still keeps part of its vital liquids and thus would be reintroduced within the /*kuru*/ circuit. It is precisely to avoid the deceased's direct contact with the soil that they lay the corpse down on an elevated platform. A dead person buried on a platform above the ground represents the antithesis of the fermented drink made from vegetable roots grown inside the soil.

Elsewhere (Teixeira-Pinto 1997) I have shown that, while opposed to fermented drink, an Arara corpse lying on a platform is the logical counterpart of a sacrificed enemy, which is ritually transformed into a decorated skull, set on top of a tree trunk, and reduced to the symbolic (fertilizing) value of fermented beverage. During an impressive ceremonial, a large amount of beverage is left at the base of the trunk, just as it was brought by the ritual character represented by the decorated trunk. Also, the women drink large quantities of the brew while claiming they are "taking a child from the trunk," a clear reference to the reproductive meaning of both the beverage and the killing of an enemy.

The human acquisition of the /kuru/ substances comes mostly through consumption of the fermented drink: the roots that they use in its preparation absorb the substances that animals lose in the soil (see Teixeira-Pinto 1989). The different manners of consuming the *piktu* produce modifications in the person's status, their place within the social world, and the many formal relationships of cooperation and solidarity that the Arara cultivate. The joint consumption of fermented drink creates and informs the social and symbolic context that involves the person. On the other hand, the interruption of the process of acquisition is what defines death as a gradual and uninterrupted loss of the person's vitality.

The Arara fear hot things placed on or "inside" the bodies because they could burn and dry up organic substances. Further, there is no good in eating hot things because doing so could "dry up the inside." The risk is greater for those who more often practice shamanism. They should keep intact their vital substances that provide them with the conditions of access to the metaphysical powers (which have vital substances as their preferential food). Major burns or bleeding is damaging to a shaman's ability, for a dried man loses contact with other living beings in the world. Physical impairment, illness, and states of indisposition are also defined as alterations in the substances circulating inside the body. For these a shaman might prescribe or conduct therapies. It is through the same symptomatology that a shaman can identify evidence that something of sorcery is inside the body of a sick person.

Changes in a person's state must receive treatment based on alimentary taboos. The first, *uo'pra*, is an indisposition associated mostly with menstrual blood that is identified in cases of constant failure in hunting. Emanations from menstrual blood (*imandem*) of a careless woman who, during her period, prepares food or touches objects later manipulated by the men, can penetrate through the fingernails, go up through the fingers and arms, and reach the shoulder articulations. To avoid it, apart from the many restrictions imposed on women when menstruating, all the adult men must use an armlet (*mbïa*) around the biceps of the left arm (the one that holds the bow).

Not always does this armlet avoid the penetration of harmful emanations from menstrual blood into a man's body. Each failure or error in the hunt (the importance of which will depend on a subjective evaluation that takes into consideration a man's traditional performance in the hunt) entails the suspicion of an *uo'pra* state. Hunters can submit to rites to remove the bad luck and reestablish good hunting fortune. The *uo'pra* state is not embodied in the mistakes or accidents involving a man, although these empirically reveal the bad luck: it is the animals that feel the strange emanations of a man contaminated by menstrual blood and then run away from the hunter's sight or behave in a strange or atypical manner and thereby tangle up the shot. The animals can also feel the emanations that come with the arrows (or bullets or cartridges) manipulated by someone who could contaminate. But not every animal can fully perceive a state of *uo'pra*. At times it is the peccaries (or the tapirs, etc.) who foresee the magical infections, and they do so in such a way that for each individual animal species avoiding a hunter there exists a specific therapy or native medicine.

There are four classes of medicines used for problems related to the state of *uo'pra*, all of which act through the same general principle: pieces of an animal skin are rubbed on the hunter's arms and face. This action is supposed to work through odor (*inun*) transmission from the animal to an afflicted hunter: odors left on the hunter's body neutralize menstrual blood emanations as if through aromatic essences they approximate the hunter and game, predator and prey—the tie that had been removed by the effects of menstruation. Surprisingly, there are no medicines for problems in the deer hunt (*kariamï*): the only procedure to overcome eventual failures in hunting a deer is to play the *tïdïdï*, the flute made out of an enemy's skull.

Broadly speaking, everything that "gets into" or "gets out" of a human body can change the person's state. Emanations from menstrual blood, a child who is born (the fetus is made by the semen that goes out of the father's penis to the mother's uterus whence it will come out after the proper time), or any alterations imposed by living beings or malicious attitudes are only instances of the sorts of things a person's state can be subject to. Accordingly, every possible way of treatment and cure is also a process of introducing or removing something from a sick body.

There exists a mild form of sorcery (*tchano*) that is made of thorns put on a hammock or in a tree in the usual path of the victim, which then penetrates the skin and infects various vital organs. It can, however, be removed by simple massages and shamanic extractions. The many general infections produced by the hidden forces of the forest are also conceived either as direct penetrations (strange beings invading the victim's body) or as indirect contagion (a metaphysical being who sees those who are careless in the forest and then spits some sort of miasma that invades the victims). Death, or mortification, is seen as a loss, extraction, or deprivation of the person's vital substances.

The distinct ways of proceeding with shamanic anamnesis, treatment, and cure always take into consideration the way a person is constituted, and thus each involves slightly different processes of "getting into" and "getting out": food, drink, medicines, or pathogens are elements that can change a person's state. Yet we have already seen how the medicines act through transmission of odors to the skin of a patient. Therapy by extraction, one of the most evident procedures performed by shamans, is called *ikurukitpït*—a verb that also denotes the common action of cleaning, wiping, and washing. The shaman, without any trance or special preparation, massages, fastens, twists, wrings, and sometimes blows over the hurt or sore body parts. An anamnesis is performed mostly when there is no physical evidence of lesion or injuries because there is a risk of *tchano* or other extrasensitive source of infection and contamination. To differentiate between a simple illness (*abudup*) and a pathological state of diffuse etiology is something that only a skilled shaman is capable of doing. The shamanic therapy of massages and extractions, *ikurukitpït*, acts on objects and substances that are merged or conflated with those that normally give vitality to the person. The association between the substances that naturally compose a regular human physiology and those that penetrate through exogenous processes can lead to the aggravation of the morbid state and, eventually, start the process of mortification because the pathogenic agent can damage the circulation of the vital substances in the body and impair its capacity for movement.

Besides the aromatic therapies and those done through massages or extractions, there also are some treatments based on diet. Food taboos apply to two different changes in a person's state: when they are *uo'pra*, as in the situations described above, and when they are *amïlï*, just after the birth of a new child or when a wife is "too pregnant" as they say. Both *uo'pra* and *amïlï* are included in a more general pathological situation called *mangupe*, in which dissimilar etiologies can lead the person to bodily or mental instability, unexplained weakness, or undetermined *aboulias* (*akarak puinan*). These are types of indisposition in which there are no discernible wounds, lesions, or pains, and thus cannot properly be considered a disease (pain and "illnesses" are *abudup*). For these states of unexplained weakness there exists a remedial herb bath (*manguepti*) and food restrictions. The difference between the dietary restrictions for *uo'pra* and *amïlï* lies in the fact that the one who protects himself after the birth of a new child, apart from the quantity of food and the sort of meat he can consume, must also eat alone without any contact or physical proximity to others.

Apart from his healing function a shaman must also perform two other tasks, both dealing with metaphysical powers. First, a shaman's expertise provides the logical and symbolic conditions for success in hunting practices. Second, it is the shamans who are in charge of collective protection against the perils and risks of living. The first task is achieved through a very simple shamanic ritual that is performed at the beginning of a new period of the year when men hunt collectively (during the dry season), while the second task depends on the chances or even the need of encountering the powerful mythical jaguar (*okoro*).

The Hunt: Game for Assuring Collective Well-Being

Techniques of identification, search, attraction, and persecution of animals comprise the empirical side of any hunt. There are many complex techniques but virtually all are shared by all adult men. The transformation of these hunting techniques into a social effective reality is done only by means of their subordination to and control by a set of social imperatives of cooperation, solidarity, and generosity (mostly connected with the formal partnerships and the acquisition and sharing of meat and fermented beverages). On the other hand, all hunting activity is also placed under the symbolic model that defines meat as equivalent to fermented beverage. Every game animal obtained is to be exchanged for fermented drink. There is a clear complementarity between those who produce the brew in the village and those who kill animals in the forest, just as there is complementarity between game and fermented beverages. It is this logical association that embodies the deep foundations of the Arara social world. Furthermore, the transformation of animal flesh into meat to be appropriated by humans implies symbolic mechanisms essential for the understanding of the very nature of Arara sociability.

Nearly every animal species is under the metaphysical control of spiritual beings called *oto*, who act as the animal owners or wardens. It is only through a kind of agreement between humans and the *oto* that the former can hunt. This agreement has a twofold expression, the first of which is through the musical festivities that precede the hunters' return from their long expeditions, in which the Arara give notice to the *oto* that the humans have killed many animals (see Teixeira-Pinto 1997, chs. 1, 4); and the second is through animal domestication (*iamït*). What exactly then, is the importance of the *oto* for human existence?

Apart from the minor food taboos imposed on specific occasions, the Arara have a diet with only a few restrictions. Indeed, they do not abstain from anything: they eat toads, vultures, electric fish, and almost everything that crawls, walks, flies, or swims. Virtually omnivorous, the Arara exclude from their diet only creatures that, even though apparently animal in nature, surpass a "natural quality." Sloths, anteaters, owls, and otters (as well as other mustelids) tend to be avoided by the Arara because they are animals that are not under the protection and control of an *oto*. In effect, to have an *oto* as a metaphysical patron is an exclusive condition (although a paradoxical one) for an animal to be edible. The practical condition of being edible is to be "huntable," and thus to have a spiritual warden is the precondition for being subject to human predation.

The Arara end their big collective hunt by the end of the dry season, when it is time to resume agricultural work. With the rains coming, the collective hunting activities begin to cease, and the drinking, the parties, and the gatherings in general also decrease. Gardening seems almost to be an asocial or even antisocial activity; Arara sociability is most generally associated with hunting and drinking. Indeed, everything happens as if the abundance of meat and fermented drink were the exclusive elements that could make Arara social life possible. But the interlude that comes with the rains and agriculture lasts just until the next dry season. Before a new dry season comes it is necessary to prepare for it as a new suitable time for hunting.

While the other men are still busy with the gardening work a solitary shaman takes a walk into the forest, where he goes to execute an oral rite. Pounding on the forest floor, shaking the foliage, and beating the trees, the shaman repeats many times:

> tamït'pra uro
> iamït'pra tangie
> ibirinda pïn!
>
> I do not have pets anymore
> I do not have any pet at all
> Give me another pet!

These words are a nonliteral translation of the formula used by a shaman: the word *iamït* designates both pets and foster children. The shaman talks to a specific *oto*, requesting the young of a particular species so that it can be raised by humans. The *oto* are said to keep such animals inside a big box, and when it is opened mature and young animals are liberated together, and humans can find the young in the forest.

The Arara have special houses for pets. The relation between *iamït*, breastfeeding, and alimentary interdiction is significant, because a pet must be fed as immature humans are: with women's breast milk. Breast milk is *mongukuru*—something full of the vital substance that composes, forms, and sustains the organic processes that partially constitute the person. Feeding the pets with human milk means they become consubstantial with humans, and this is the main reason why the Arara prohibit the killing and eating of pets.

On the other hand, if those who raise pets as *iamït* cannot kill and eat that particular animal, those who demand young animals from an *oto* shall for a certain period stop hunting for the species under the control of that specific *oto*. However, there is nothing to limit the action of all other men who, roaming in the forest, can meet the animals conceptually liberated by their *oto*: in other words, a shaman asks for pets, and then the hunters come through and kill the other animals that were also liberated. Thus, a man can kill animals only with the proviso that someone else (a shaman or any adult man) refrains from doing so through the interdictions that come with the *iamït* magical formula. This is in actuality a very tricky strategy, which helps us to identify another aspect of the *iamït* institution. If the one who asks for pets is forbidden to hunt that animal species, would it necessarily mean that he can't eat that species? Nobody says they cannot eat it if somebody else kills them!

What is the symbolic nature of the meat that Arara eat? Appropriately, it lies in the conception that meat is something that exists under the sole condition of being given in exchange for fermented drink. Thus the conceptual nature of meat nullifies the agreement celebrated between humans and metaphysical powers through the *iamït* formula. The interdictions on hunting and the restrictions on eating imposed on someone (or a few hunters) are the real conditions for hunting and eating by many. The *iamït* shamanic formula for obtaining pets, as a symbolic condition that makes hunting and the acquisition of meat possible, emerges as a sort of deliberate human perfidy. Even though acting as a trickster is a common characteristic among Amerindian shamans, here the Arara seem to have added a little extra.

The very foundations of human relationships—that is, the symbolic attributes of meat being equivalent to fermented drink—involve betrayal, fraud, and perfidy regarding the supernatural beings that provide the means for its achievement. Human existence and sociability depend on a kind of treachery. The effectiveness of the *iamït* magical formula lies in its circumlocution, which restricts the *iamït* from killing but at the same time deceives and deludes the animal's metaphysical warden, thus redoubling the probability of success in hunting by other men. The most interesting thing here is that such trickery is the initial circumstance of the real possibility of social life, because it depends on the exchange system of fermented beverage extracted from root crops for the meat of animals hunted under the metaphysical conditions of the *iamït* formula.

Every year at the end of the Amazonian rainy season, a shaman goes to the forest to perform another *iamït* ritual, which is done explicitly to prepare the animals' spiritual warden for the great slaughter of the oncoming dry season when the men resume collective hunts. A single shaman in the forest is thus symbolically capable of setting forth again the general framework that supports full life in society: the betrayal of the cosmological powers whose existence entitles the animals to be hunted, exchanged, and eaten.

This is done as a condition for community well-being, the very existence of human sociality. It could be stated that a single shaman going to perform the *iamït* ritual in the forest is acting in the strict sense of the other's collective living. It happens to have almost the same meaning as other typical shamanic tasks: the encounters with the mythical jaguar.

The Jaguar: Perils and the Shamanic Anticult

A shaman encounters an *okoro* without anybody seeing or knowing. Unlike many other Arara traditional activities, it is not possible to go to one of these encounters with a jaguar accompanied by anyone else. An encounter with *okoro* is defined as a solitary and unwitnessed task. What is learned during initiations is that, while in an alleged altered state of consciousness caused by the direct consumption of the *omiatsembïlï* infusion, or after its regular use over a long period, one can see, observe, and identify many metaphysical beings, of which the jaguar in the context of shamanism is certainly one. Both the direct consumption of the infusion and the trance state itself do not seem to be absolutely necessary to the shamanic practice, however. It is said that many *okoro* who are well-trained in shamanic techniques and in other magical practices could achieve without ingestion of any substances a mental state in which they can contact supernatural beings. It is also said that a persistent practice of encountering metaphysical powers, together with self-control, can enable a shaman to recognize without too much effort signs of a supernatural being's presence and activities unperceived by normal eyes.

What the shaman does when he encounters an *okoro* is called *ikurukitpït*, the same concept used to designate shamanic therapeutic massages and extractions. The term also designates the act of "cleaning" or removing any filth or impurity from some object or body. For healing practices the meaning seems quite evident: the penetration of strange objects or substances into human bodies causes a corporal imbalance, which can be recovered by shamanic massages and "extractions." In the healing setting, *ikurukitpït* actually suggests a "cleaning" of impurities that contaminate and harm a sick body. In encounters with the jaguars, however, the same term that is used for a very specific activity leads to some interpretive problems. A literal association would lead us to suppose that the proximity of *okoro*—the immediate cause of which is to promote the shaman's encounter with the jaguar—should be also considered as a kind of "malfunction" (like an illness or any indisposition) to be dealt with and controlled by the exercise of *ikurukitpït*. Yet illnesses and any unascertained organic indispositions (*abudup*, *mangupe*, etc.—the most common sicknesses that normally require shamanic treatments) have very precise etiologies and prescriptive therapeutics: they are "penetration effects" caused by invisible agents and eliminated by shamanic massages and extractions. It is said that okoro approaches humans because they are "angry" (*ikurin*), and it would be to appease the jaguar that the shaman goes to an *ikurukitpït* session. If there is nothing extraordinary about an aggressive jaguar, why should a shaman go to an *ikurukitpït okoro*, as if he were about to perform a sort of shamanic healing? The answer to this lies in the jaguar's twofold nature: they can be either the hateful divinity Akuanduba or a deceased Arara relative. The Arara define death as a process of liberation of the person's components. Through the multiple beings into which a corpse is transformed, most of them harmful to the living, any death reveals a quantum of violence and aggressiveness that are embedded in the temporary junctions that forge a live human body. A corpse transformed into a feline is just an emblem of the overall condition of living in this world.[16]

However, aggressiveness, violence, and predation, which are what a jaguar epitomizes as the natural precondition of the world, must not be allowed to exist among living relatives: everything in Arara social life is explicitly thought and done to avoid and remove the hazards of untempered behaviors that can prolong misfortunes among the living. An Arara myth recounts how, after an almost perfect life in the sky, the Arara were condemned to live a very afflictive life on earth (which is nothing but the leftovers of the mythical sky's ground), and unrestrained and uncontrolled behavior would lead them to a tremendous open clash, equal to that which destroyed the original cosmological architecture. Akuanduba, the most powerful supernatural being in the Arara pantheon, inflicts punishment on them in many ways, such as sending noxious beings to harm people, transforming corpses into jaguars to scare those who are still living, and masquerading himself as a black jaguar, the largest and most terrifying predator.

None but a very powerful shaman can approach a black jaguar. On a more regular basis the shaman's aim is to seek out those jaguars that are the reappearance of deceased relatives in a new bodily form. Wapurï, one of the most prestigious shamans at the time of my fieldwork, once told me he would go to meet a jaguar just to stimulate its memory that the people alive in the village are still its "relatives" and thus should not be prey of its voracity. And so a shaman goes searching for those jaguars that in life are related to the living Arara. Here the act of *ikurukitpït* seems to recall its earlier meaning as a technique to return a body to its regular state.

The deceased bodies, through the transformations they are submitted to and the new living forms they assume, return to adhere to previous aggressive and violent ways of behaving. Therefore the *ikurukitpït* action, when seeking to recover the original relations between a jaguar and the ones that are still alive, would have as its meaning the removal of much of the aggression, violence, and virtual predation that dead people have while under the jaguar skin. These are ways of acting which must be banned from the community as a whole. Thus a shaman directs himself to controlling the dangers of hostility, aggression, violence, and predation that accompany a dead person garbed in a fine jaguar skin. Its very presence among the living proclaims that hostility, anger, and belligerence are intrinsic qualities of this world, and it demands immediate shamanic action. What is interesting here is that *ikurukitpït* as a shamanic action toward the jaguar as a dead person's specter does not apply to any of the many other "spirits" that a deceased body releases after the end of the body's movements: *tcharupãngmã, ikaualãngmã*, and *editen*. It is only the *okoro* that is subjected to the extreme loss of memory that entails the deep forgetfulness of the former affiliation with the living people. Being solitary and, above all, a predator, a jaguar is the paramount embodiment of what should not constitute the rules, values, and ways of behaving among living people.

Death is also a revelation of the nature of the Arara person. The multiple beings into which the corpse's parts are transformed are the embodiment of the essential parts of the person during the transitory life of the physical body, and most of these beings emerge into a nonsocial way of living. It is precisely around the body (its fabrication, reproduction, and maintenance through the consuming of food and drink that are the objects of human exchanges) that social ties among the living are built. Thus the fragmentation of the body after death, the postmortem destinies of the bodies, point to a solitary existence due to the loss of the qualities that characterize social life.

In the Arara imagination, solitude always goes along with aggressiveness, violence, and the chance for predation. The loss of ties of solidarity implies solitary beings. The revealing of the violent constituents of the person is connected to the loss of ties among the living (kinship, affinity, partnerships, and social links in general). In this sense the expected results of the shamanic action, when he evokes the former relations between the dead and the living, is to recover the ties of solidarity. The shaman therefore acts in the name of solidarity ties that must be in force among relatives and thus avoids the aggressive and violent nature intrinsic to the person's constitution, despite the fact that death constantly reveals its own aggressive nature. Although part of being alive can always be revealed by the nature of being dead, a shaman is expected to act in the name of the living and reflect the values and rules for being alive.

By renewing the connections that once joined the jaguar and the living, the shaman expresses the precaution that the living must maintain against hostility, aggression, and violence among humans. Everything here suggests a kind of "inverted ritual of passage," because reconverting a potential predator into a relative is like bringing a modified being back to its previous state. Hence the action of *ikurukitpït okoro* aims at regaining a peaceful and gentle relative from a wild and predatory jaguar through the shaman's symbolic agency on the metaphysical scene. It is then quite clear that shamanic encounters with jaguars have nothing to do with any kind of worship or cult, but rather very much the contrary. And it is also an inversion of the shamanic formula addressed to the *oto*. As I describe above, the *iamït* oration is designed to establish links between humans and animals so that animals can become, through a trickster strategy, objects of human predation that, once hunted and reduced to the mere status of meat, accompany fermented drink as the nourishment for human bodies and social solidarity. On the other hand, when approaching the jaguars, a shaman intends to avoid its predatory passion and set apart any belligerence, hostility, or violent behavior precisely by reconstructing the links between the dead and the living.

The control over virtual violence through its conceptual subordination to the solidarity that must define all relationships among the Arara is what is symbolically engraved on the shamanic actions toward the *okoro*. Thus a shaman's periodic encounters with the jaguars symbolize the opposition between life and death in such a way that the degree of the dissimilarity between being still alive (*enge*) and being already dead (*irumbot*) becomes valuable for the moral aspects of human living. But it is not the simple opposition between life and death that plays an important role here. The simple fact of being alive (*engouete*) does not produce any good for the moral grounds of human existence. It is the set of associations between death, aggression, and loneliness, on the one hand, and life, sociality, and the moral commitments to a peaceful and generous way of life, on the other, that fulfills the meaning of existence. However, solitude, and therefore aggression, predation, and death are the natural attributes of living in the world after the original catastrophe. And they are the cosmologically imposed conditions from which human sociality must escape. By aiming to avoid the solitude that can lead anyone to selfish and aggressive behavior, the Arara have built up a strong network of multiple formal individual connections.

Conclusion: Sorcery's Outrage

As the very shamanism that is its source, Arara sorcery does not involve any obscure techniques, hidden skills, or mysterious science, nor is any specific initiation into it needed. It works in exactly the same way as the shamanic arts; or, rather, it works in exactly the reverse way from shamanism, though taking advantage of the same corpus of knowledge about the functioning of the world and its connections with states of the person and the body. It is on the person's and the individual's bodies that sorcery makes itself evident. Sorcery acts by forcing magical "penetrations" into a body, thus jeopardizing the normal physiology of the corporeal "substances" that compose a body and sustain the more subjective aspects of the person.

Sorcery can be produced through a healing procedure, through magical formulas addressed to metaphysical powers asking for help to harm someone the next time he is found wandering in the forest, or through any other means normally available to shamans. It is always manifest as sudden changes, considered inscrutable or beyond ordinary understanding, in bodily functions and/or the person's affective states. It is just like the predation process imposed by malicious cosmological beings or by shamanic procedures that, instead of extracting harmful agents out of sick bodies, introduce pathogens inside them. Because of it, sorcery is a kind of inversion of the expected role of a shaman. There is only one way to differentiate between the two possible causes of ailments (a foreseeable attack by cosmological beings and an outrageous attack by a deviant shaman, which can be any adult man), and that is to think back to try to determine whether in recent history someone would have any reason to be upset and wish to cause any harm.

The motivations a shaman can have to act in such a way are defined as *otchinme*, a concept comparable to jealousy, selfishness, or acting in "self-benefit"—that is, not acting toward the benefit of others. Previous quarrels, disputes, serious disagreements, or even political aspirations are among the reasons one can use to make an accusation of sorcery against someone. At first everything appears just as a suspicion without an actual suspect. Being a victim of sorcery is the first complaint; then, after being announced in a public meeting on the village patio, normally during a gathering for drinking manioc beer, the complaint can evolve to a formal accusation, depending on the acceptance of the assertions. This is the kernel of the whole process: convincing others of the seriousness of the facts and symptoms described and the probability of being produced by sorcery. If in the previous days the person who is claiming to be a victim of sorcery has actually been involved in a conflict situation with another person, the chances of being victimized by sorcery increase. This is the main reason why every man ought to avoid becoming involved in serious disputes, quarrels, or any situation that can develop into a suspicious or a straightforward accusation of sorcery. Being thought of as generous, kind, and cooperative slightly increases the chances of not being accused, and bad behavior, even on occasion, can lead to inclusion on a list of suspects of those considered capable of acting as a sorcerer. There is no clear evidence of identifying the source of sorcery as always being from the outside. On the contrary, given the sociological and moral dimensions of shamanic powers, the tendency is to look to the inside of the local group or to a nearby household to try to discover the guilty one. It is quite clear, then, that the only possible limit for not being included on a list of suspects of sorcery lies in the moral aspects of interindividual social bonds.

The technical possibility of using the same shamanic competence to cause damage instead of well-being puts the whole society on a dead-end route. Because the only chance of existing in this world includes being dependent on shamanism, it is existence itself that appears to be fragile and unstable. There is no way of understanding human sociality without understanding the risk of being subject to sorcery, as there is no other way of determining any cosmological support for human sociality. What sorcery does is exactly reconnect human existence with the undesirable cosmological conditions of living on this terrestrial level. And this is the greatest risk that human sociality is subject to. This is the conceptual challenge that sorcery presents: human sociality depends on the inversion of the cosmological determinants, which in turn depends on shamanic powers to create the conditions for living outside the violent cycle of predation that characterizes the whole world, which are the same powers that can reintroduce the harmful cosmological forces into human social existence. Yet, while human sociality depends on a collective agreement, its rupture depends only on an individual decision: a shaman who decides to break the moral imperative to use his skills only for the benefit of others. Because this is what everyone should avoid by all means, there is a virtually universal agreement about the punishment to be applied: that is, banishment, an imposed isolation that is the admission of individual autonomy (to be fully experienced now) and, paradoxically, also the reaffirmation of the very nature of human sociality. As understood by the Arara, there is a striking fragility within social life, for it depends on the strength of the moral commitments between individuals. Otherwise, the only other choice would be living alone.

Tchibie was in the first generation of a family condemned to live on its own, with the only chance of reproducing itself through incestuous unions. For many years, Tchibie and her family lived a secluded life, which was not interrupted by any native involvement but rather by FUNAI's intervention. It was the massive nonindigenous intrusion into the Arara's traditional territory that led FUNAI to contact them. Most likely, from the Arara point of view, they would have remained cloistered within their own misfortune of isolation and incest. Nevertheless, their incestuous history was simply evidence that isolation and solitude are probable destinies for those who have decided to abstain from, or are suspected of having broken, the "social contract" and moral understanding about what it means to live together, as if they were able to live alone even amidst many others.

Notes

I am deeply grateful to Robin Wright for his gifted revision, which transformed my sometimes obscure writings into a more intelligible English. This essay is dedicated to Miriam Hartung, who helped me make sense of my own solitude. I am grateful for her lovely presence and affectionate support.

1 FUNAI is the abbreviated name of the Fundação Nacional do Índio, the official Brazilian agency for indigenous affairs.
2 Almost unique in the kinship and Amazonian literature, the recurring incestuous unions among the Arara, mainly among the Cachoeira Seca subgroup, is the subject of a forthcoming essay. Here, despite the evident interest of the case, they appear only as an example—one taken from real life—of what can happen to those who break the moral rules linked to the powers of the shaman. For a general analysis of Arara kinship and marriage practices, which include polygyny, intergenerational unions, and, in particular circumstances, the formal possibility of incest in the form of a marriage with a half-sister, see Teixeira-Pinto 1995a and 1997.
3 The Arara have two contiguous yet officially distinct territories: the first, which is quite small but completely legalized, is reserved for the Arara of the Laranjal; the second, which is larger but recently interdicted and under different sorts of economic and political pressures, is reserved for the Arara of Cachoeira Seca-Iriri. In general, the chances for the physical and social reproduction of the Arara as a whole depend both on the conservation of the two areas and on the rejoining of the broken ties between the two segments of the population.
4 The official name of the reservation where the Indians were settled is Cachoeira Seca-Iriri.
5 Between 1970 and 1980, the nonindigenous population in the region increased by more than 200 percent due to Brazilian government policies for the occupation of Amazonia.
6 See chapter 1 of Teixeira-Pinto 1997 for a discussion of the connections between shamanism and the conditions for activities such as hunting and gardening.
7 My views on several aspects of Arara shamanism and sociality is clearly influenced by some of Overing's inspiring analysis on both topics (1985, 1990, 1993, 1999) as well as works by Perrin (1995), Hamayon (1982), and Langdon (1992 and 1996). Regarding the subject of "morality," many insights were gained from reading the collection edited by Howell (1997).
8 See Teixeira-Pinto 2001 for a more in-depth presentation of the Arara's recent history in relation to contact with Brazilian national society.
9 A fermented beverage made of masticated manioc flour and warm water.
10 Modified by the possessive *ï*, ibirinda literally means "my other."
11 *Uoktangat* is obscure even to the Arara; they told me that it is "just a noun."
12 See below for a short description of Arara cosmology. See also chapter 2 in Teixeira-Pinto 1997 for a more detailed description and analysis.
13 The largest concentrations of the vine are in the northern areas of the Arara traditional territory, but after the construction of the Trans-Amazonian Highway the Arara were restricted to the southern part of their area, where there are only a few places they can find the vine. However, I am quite sure that the limited importance of the infusion has no connection with the territorial constraint.

14 The history of the formation of the present Arara cosmos defines this terrestrial level as the domain to which flows everything that remained after a primordial catastrophe. The primordial cosmos was shattered after a fight between two people related through the category *ipari* (matrilateral cross-cousins or, in general, an affine). The land on this terrestrial level is said to be what was left of the primeval cosmological floor, which broke up and fell from the sky after the combat. That floor was also the edge of the domain where every benign being used to live. Beyond the frontiers of that level there were only different kinds of malicious beasts with atrocious behavior living in a permanent cruel quarrel—in short, a horrifying existence. With the cosmological breakup, the coexistence of all types of living being began to be an imposed necessity. As a result of all of this, even extraordinary and evil creatures can now appear on the terrestrial plane. In order to distinguish in the fauna what is ordinary and beneficial from what is extraordinary and vicious, one needs to develop expertise through the shamanic experiences.

15 The relation between the body and the person is rather complex. In brief, the Arara notion of person is like a synthetic principle that temporally unifies the multiplicity of body parts. After death, the body is separated (through the intercession of Akuanduba under the jaguar skin) into many different parts, from which just a few retain the more subjective aspects that define the person—its cognitive abilities, feelings, memories, wishes, and yearnings. This person status is analogous to the cosmological attributes associated with the terrestrial level, where the human body received its actual morphological constitution. The tense conceptual composition between unity and multiplicity is what is expressed in both the person and the terrestrial domain (see Teixeira-Pinto 1993a and 1997).

16 In other works I have presented a full description of the metaphysical transformation of deceased persons and the consequences of this transformation for Arara social life (see Teixeira-Pinto 1993a and 1997, ch. 2).

References

Basso, Ellen. 1977. *Carib-Speaking Indians*. Tucson: University of Arizona Press.

Carrithers, M., S. Collins, and S. Lukes. 1985. *The Category of the Person*. Cambridge: Cambridge University Press.

Carsten, J., and S. Hugh-Jones. 1995. *About the House: Lévi-Strauss and Beyond*. Cambridge: Cambridge University Press.

Hamayon, Robert. 1982. "Des Chamanes au Chamanisme." *L'Ethnographie: Voyages Chamaniques Deux* 78 (87/88).

Howell, Signe. 1997. *The Ethnography of Moralities*. London: Routledge.

Langdon, E. Jean M. 1992. "Dau: Shamanic Power in Siona Religion and Medicine." In *Portals of Power: South American Shamanism*, ed. E. J. M. Langdon and G. Baer. Albuquerque: University of New Mexico Press.

———. 1996. "Introdução: Xamanismo—velhas e novas perspectivas." In *Xamanismo no Brasil: Novas perspectivas*, ed. E. J. M. Langdon. Florianópolis: Editora da UFSC.

Lefort, Claude. 1967. "A Troca e a luta dos homens." In *O método estruturalista*. Rio de Janeiro: Zahar Editores.

Lévi-Strauss, Claude. 1981. *A via das máscaras*. Lisboa: Editorial Presença/Martins Fontes.

———. 1986. *Minhas palavras*. São Paulo: Brasiliense.

Menget, Patrick. 1977. *Au nom des autres: Classification des relations sociales chez les Txicão du haut-xingu*. Paris: EHESS.

Nimuendaju, Curt. 1932. "Idiomas indígenas do Brasil." *Revista del Instituto Etnológico de Tucumán. Universidad de Tucumán*, 543–618.

Overing, Joanna. 1985. "There Is No End of Evil: The Guilty Innocents and their Fallible God." In *The Anthropology of Evil*, ed. D. Parkin. Oxford: Basil Blackwell.

———. 1990. "The Shaman as a Maker of Worlds: Nelson Goodman in the Amazon." *Man* 25 (4): 602–19.

———. 1993. "Death and the Loss of Civilized Predation among the Piaroa of the Orenoco Basin." *L'Homme* 126–28: 191–212.

———. 1999. "Elogio do Cotidiano: A confiança e a arte da vida social em uma comunidade amazônica." *Mana* 5 (1): 81–108.

Perrin, Michel. 1995. *Le Chamanisme*. Paris: PUF.

Teixeira-Pinto, Márnio. 1989. *Os Arara: Tempo, espaço e relações sociais em um povo karibe*. Rio de Janeiro: PPGAS/Museu Nacional.

———. 1993a. "Corpo, morte e sociedade: Um ensaio sobre a forma e a razão de se Ésquartejar um Inimigo." *Revista Brasileira de Ciências Sociais* 21 (February): 52–67.

———. 1993b. "Relações de substância e classificação social: Alguns aspectos da organização social Arara." *Anuário Antropológico* 90: 169–204.

———. 1995a. "Entre esposas e filhos: Poliginia e padrões de aliança entre os Arara." In *Antropologia do parentesco: Estudos ameríndios*, ed. E. Viveiros de Castro. Rio de Janeiro: Editoria da UFRJ.

———. 1995b. "Histórias de origem e relações ambíguas: Notas comparativas sobre um simulacro da questão étnica no Brasil." *Brasil em perspectiva: O debate dos cientistas sociais*, ed. M. A. Gonçalves. N.p. Rio de Janeiro: Relume/Dumará.

———. 1997. *IEIPARI: Sacrifício e vida social entre os índios Arara*. São Paulo/Curitiba: HUCITEC, ANPOCS/Editora UFPR.

———. 2001. "História e cosmologia de um contato: A atração dos Arara." In *Pacificando o branco*, ed. B. Albert and A. Ramos. 405–30. São Paulo: UNESP.

Tocantins, Antônio M. G. 1877. "Estudos sobre a Tribu Mundurucu." *Revista do Instituto Histórico e Geográfico* 40: n.p.

Von Den Steinen, Karl. 1894. Na gema do Brasil. *Gazeta de Notícias*, 203–267.

*Sorcery and Shamanism in
Cashinahua Discourse and Praxis,
Purus River, Brazil*

Elsje Lagrou

Sorcerers, healers, and shamans, with their manifold methods and different characteristics and attributed powers among the Pano-speaking peoples,[1] are classified by the Cashinahua of the Purus River into two distinct groups: the *dauya*, "the one with medicine" who kills and heals through the use of medicinal plants; and the *mukaya*, "the one with bitterness" who heals and eventually kills with the help of spirits (*yuxin*) through a bitter substance (*muka*) that is a materialization of *yuxin* power. While the first specialist is initiated in his art by men, the second depends on the *yuxin* themselves to confirm his power. Despite this apparently clear distinction, it is my intention here to demonstrate that this terminological dualism conceals a conceptual continuum of overlapping practices and specialists that follows the logic of Cashinahua dualistic thought in general.

The Cashinahua sociological and cosmological thought system is characterized by a dynamic dualism in which alterity is produced from sameness and sameness from alterity, where each element of an opposed pair (moiety *dua*/moiety *inu*, Boa-water/Inka-fire) partakes of its opposite, and form lies in the bounded and relatively stable intermixing of complementary opposites (bone/skin, body/spirit, male/female, kin/affine, etc.). In such a world, body, identity, and the problem of alterity are not issues of category or classification but rather are relational and philosophical issues.

It has been shown in the literature on Pano-speaking peoples that whereas some peoples have a myriad of intermarrying groups, the Cashinahua stress their moiety system. The many spirits, deities, and mythical characters, some of which are held in common by different Pano-speaking groups, are organized by the Cashinahua into a cluster of dualities, in which the master of water beings is the boa/anaconda and is semantically linked to the moon, while the master of the sky, called Inka, has thunder and lightning and the jaguar and the harpy eagle as his representatives and is semantically associated with the sun. This cosmological dualism, based on the complementary qualities of the perishable and the imperishable, is used in moiety symbolism and in ritual language. This dualism, however, involves a dynamic and complex relation between terms that insistently questions a substantialist definition of identity and difference. Through recurring inversions of role and position in the naming system and ritual, and through constant definitional paradoxes in discourse, the question of sameness and otherness becomes salient as the central theme around which Cashinahua ontology revolves. Cashinahua discourse on the activities of dark shamans, and on the possibility that any human being could turn into one, is consistent with this view. If the Tupi-speaking Kagwahiv say that everyone who dreams has a bit of a shaman (Kracke 1987), the Cashinahua would say that everybody who has some knowledge has a bit of a dark shaman.

The puzzling concept of *nawa*, stranger, as opposed to *huni*, human being, is paradigmatic to Cashinahua (and in general Panoan) ambiguity in relation to a fixed definition of boundaries between self and other, and will suffice to illustrate my point about Cashinahua dualism. *Nawa* can be used as a term to denote "real" otherness: strangers and potential enemies, like the white colonizers or mythical *inkas* (cannibal gods). When such people or game animals are invoked or named in ritual songs, they are always called *nawa*. But *nawa* is also used in the ethnological literature to refer to a broad range of different Pano-speaking peoples (the Nawa of the Yuruá-Purus region, including the Cashinahua, Yaminahua, and others), or as part of an ethnonym attributed to and by Panoan neighbors, in which case it comes to mean "people," as in such forms as *cashi* (vampire bat) *-nawa* (people) or *yami* (stone axe) *-nawa* (people). *Nawa* can also be used in terms denoting one of the moieties or name-giving sections inside one's own community.

This shows that a single concept can occupy all the different positions of a scale going from the pole of complete otherness and enmity to the pole that includes the collective notion of self, denoting membership in one of the subdivisions that define the interior of one's own community. This does not mean, however, that the term *nawa* loses its intrinsic relational character while *huni* occupies the pole of identification. No matter how close it comes to the concept of self, *nawa* will always mean someone other than oneself. This is the reason why no one will ever refer to himself or herself as *nawa*, nor will the word *nawa* be used to refer to a person who one wants to feel close to. In this sense *nawa* remains the other, although an other that can easily be transformed into the same, by switching points of view. *Nawa* and *huni*, enemies and kin are opposites, but enemies can become kin, and kin can become *nawa*. The Cashinahua universe is a universe in constant transformation where different beings and complementary roles occupy contiguous positions.

Thus even if among Panologists the Cashinahua have been famous for their dualistic thought, I will demonstrate that the Cashinahua place more emphasis on continuity than on mutual exclusiveness. The same holds true for the pair of specialists in Cashinahua discourse on the practice of dark shamanism. Both the "owner of medicine" (*dauya*) and the "one with the bitter substance" (*mukaya*) have their dark side, being healers as well as sorcerers.[2] In between these two poles there is a continuum of other specialists who also deal with the subject of healing or killing by means of the use of substances or manipulating energies or beings called *yuxin*. Thus the opposition established between the two kinds of shamans conceals a broad spectrum of different specialties, giving us the strong impression that the figures of the *dauya* and the *mukaya* play the role of logical limits of two different kinds of methodologies for dealing with well-being and misfortune that are to a certain degree more coexistent than mutually exclusive in everyday practice and discourse.

When analyzed in this way, Cashinahua practices related to illness and health resemble much more those of other Panoan groups such as the Katukina (Lima 2000) and Yawanahua (Pérez 1999). One striking difference with these groups, however, is the fact that among the Cashinahua healing practices are more diluted into an overriding concern with well-being and growth and less crystallized into fixed roles and specializations.[3] Thus what seems to be part of a standard initiation for every knowledgeable adult male among the Cashinahua is seen to give rise to a spectrum of specialized healers among the Yawanahua and, to a lesser extent, the Katukina. In this way, whereas *xinaya* for the Cashinahua means no more than a "knowledgeable man (or woman)" whose knowledge includes a wide variety of healing plants and ritual songs, for the Yawanahua *xinaya* indicates a special kind of song healer, openly recognized as such by his community.

All scholars who have studied the Cashinahua, myself included, have been puzzled by their lack of stress on the shamans among themselves relative to the great deal of emphasis they place on shamanism in their cosmology, in which the agency of other beings, plants and animals included, can be used by humans to affect the well-being of other humans without the use of physical violence. This is the reason for the heuristic use of comparative sources in this paper. Not only is it healthy, for theoretical reasons, to transcend the rigid, and to a certain point artificial, ethnic boundaries imposed by ethnologists on their subjects of study, but in this case comparative data are extremely relevant because they reveal both the surprising homogeneity of a regional indigenous thought system with respect to dark shamanism and the particular position that the Cashinahua occupy in this field.

Thus, among the Cashinahua the invisibility of knowledge related to sources of health and illness-producing substances and songs is not accidental, and it is my aim here to analyze the reasons for this concealment —not of practices but of roles and publicly recognized power. Therefore, whereas among the Culina, the close neighbors and traditional enemies of the Cashinahua, almost all males are shamans or sorcerers, according to what they, the Cashinahua, and Culina scholars (Pollock 1992) say, the Cashinahua affirm that they have lost all of their powerful specialists—sorcerers and shamans alike. This state of affairs, however, is not seen as a weakness but rather as the result of a conscious control of knowledge and power that has not been lost, because it is out there even though safely concealed from excessive exposure and use.

Nevertheless, the *dauya*, and the *mukaya* continue to occupy an important place in Cashinahua discourse, and I describe below the way they function in discourse as logically distinct and necessarily complementary. It should be noted, however, that the nonexclusive character of attributes related to the *mukaya* or the *dauya* is consistent with Cashinahua dualism, where identity always entails a participation in the identity of one's opposite (Lagrou 1998). This is also consistent with the Cashinahua worldview in which the distinction made between matter and soul does not correspond to the classical mind/matter dualism of Western thought traditions. Thus, because plants are imbued with as well as vehicles of spirit matter and energy (*yuxin*), it is not possible to sustain the classical explanation that plant medicines treat illnesses with a "natural" cause while shamanism treats illnesses due to "supernatural" causes (Kensinger 1995:211, 215). Ambiguity here is not used to conceal a lack of clarity but rather to reveal an underlying complexity of thought and action. If I have known *mukaya* and *dauya* poison users only through discourse and never in practice, the real persons I have known were all somewhere in between, with several male and female adults knowing a good deal about plant medicines and poisons as well as about *yuxin* beings, their fertile and lethal omnipresence, and ways of dealing with them. In this essay, I intend to present the everyday practices of the "knowledgeable" adults whom I observed in the field, along with the discourse about "real" dark shamans, who are almost always placed at a safe distance in space and time.

Dauya, *A Category of Accusation*

Dau indicates medicine as well as poison, and it is in the sense of "poison user" that the sorcerer gains existence in Cashinahua discourse as a category of accusation, ready to emerge in periods of conflict and village fission. While today, as in the past according to earlier documents (Capistrano de Abreu 1941 [1914];[4] see also Kensinger 1995 on the fifties), the source of danger from the inside seems to reside much more in the possible use of sorcery in the form of poison by kin, the source of danger from the outside has been attributed to the use of shamanism by close neighbors, especially the Kulina or, occasionally, the Yaminahua, a closely related Pano-speaking group.

Panoan peoples vary in the emphasis they place on the presence or recent disappearance of sorcery, and they embrace a great variety of techniques ranging from songs and poison put in contact with bodily substances of the victim to the more classical Amazonian shamanic darts that are sent to kill people at a distance. Manuel Sampaio, the young Cashinahua leader of a recently founded village called Nova Aliança, put the question in the following terms:

> When people knew the use of poison and shamanising, kinsmen killed kinsmen. When people started to die from the white man's illnesses, we lost a great amount of people. We decided that we needed to grow, if not we would disappear. We had already diminished very much. Now our villages are growing. Many new children have been born and the Nation [*nação*] of the Cashinahua has become big again. In this new village, which is celebrating its third birthday today, eighteen children have been born and only two have died. This is so because our village is a happy village. Nobody should ever kill kinsmen again. Today the Culina still kill their own people with *duri*. They also kill our people with *duri*. Our old people still know the poison which can kill but nobody knows how to take away *duri*.

In similar terms, during E. Coffaci Lima's fieldwork she encountered several Panoan Katukina who stated emphatically that for them sorcery was a thing of the past. She also states however, that there were a few episodes in her stay where her suspicions were aroused. One of Lima's interlocutors stated, "When I was a child, of the size of this boy [pointing to a boy of twelve years old], people were dying all the time of *rao*" (2000:151). Note that the term *rao*, the Katukina equivalent of the term *dau*, which among the Cashinahua clearly refers to substances of plant or animal origin, can also refer to a bewitching oration (153–54). Thus, the Katukina took the decision to eradicate what was seen to be a permanent inclination toward instant vengeance through sorcery (*rao*) each time someone had been insulted. The explicit motivation for this collective declaration of intentions was to let the population grow and to permit kin people to cohabit in the same village.

The same decision was taken by the Yawanahua (Pérez 1999:151), where pepper and tobacco powder have fallen in disuse because of their explicit associations with sorcery. Pérez mentions a community meeting organized by the old and new village heads where a collective agreement was made not to use sorcery anymore. Among the Yawanahua the use of poison as well as killing songs are known, and people say both were used with frequency in internal conflicts. Among their neighbors, the Katukina, the Yawanahua are held responsible for several deaths that have occurred (Lima 2000:153, 155).

Among the Marubo, on the other hand, sorcery is still held to be responsible for the majority of sudden and unexplained deaths: "Some informants affirm that sorcery is very much used today, since 'all illness has this cause.' . . . They say that in the old days "wrong songs" were only used by very angry people, but now people are angry all the time with each other, there are fights between different big houses, they want to kill each other . . . For this reason, they affirm, this rapid depopulation is occurring, with even the smallest children dying" (Montagner Melatti 1985:170). Among the Marubo, along with the Shipibo and Yaminahua, poison is much less frequently used than sorcery songs.

If the Katukina accuse the Yawanahua of sorcery through songs, the Yawanahua hold the Cashinahua responsible for the death of Antonio Luis, a famous warrior who obtained many wives through raiding against his Pano enemies and in this way became the founding father of the actual Yawanahua community. The method of killing used by the Cashinahua sorcerer was to add poison to the tobacco snuff of the great leader and shaman (Pérez 1999:16).

When Kensinger first arrived as a missionary among the Peruvian Cashinahua in the 1950s, it was the medicine man, *huni dauya*, whom he feared as potential "agent of the devil" and not the *mukaya*, the shaman (1995:225-27).[5] Actually, Kensinger never knew a practicing *mukaya*, even if some Cashinahua would say today that in those days they still existed. If they existed, the Cashinahua systematically denied it at the time, or only would admit that some used to have *muka* but lost it (Kensinger 1995:218).

Still, with regard to the "witch doctor" whom Kensinger finally befriended after the latter healed his infected foot with herbal medicine and with whom he ended up collaborating in the field of healthcare, we read the following: "I was expected to treat the "symptoms" while he addressed his treatment to the "cause(s)," particularly where his diagnosis included supernatural agencies" (1995:227).

This statement is particularly important for my argument, although it goes against the idea that the *dauya* would treat natural causes of illness and the *mukaya* the supernatural causes (Kensinger 1995:214). Pérez (1999) equally has called attention to the necessity of including healing with plant medicines in the field of shamanism, but he still defends the opposition between illnesses with mechanical causes that are to be healed through plant medicine, and illnesses caused by the intentional agency of *yuxin* beings, or sorcerers, to be healed through healing songs.

Many examples I collected (Lagrou 1991, 1998) of illnesses treated with herbal medicine involve the treatment of those caused by spirit beings of the forest world: when a baby cries at night it is understood that a *yuxin* is attempting to abduct its soul, and thus herbs are burned to frighten the spirits away; when an adult has been caught by *yuxin* the treatment is herbal baths and medicine squeezed in the eyes (to treat the eye soul); if the *yuxin* of game animals come, not to steal the wandering soul but to transform the body of their victim into one of them, once again humans use plants to combat them.

Let me illustrate my point with a case study I followed in my fieldwork. Six months before my arrival, six-year-old Philomena started to suffer from what seemed to me to be epileptic attacks. The first hypothesis, given to me by her parents, was that *kuxuka*, the dolphin, had transformed into a handsome man and attempted to abduct her when she was alone by the river. She then fell in the water and almost drowned, but was saved by her father. That night she had her first fit. Eye drops, baths, and smoking, all of which were deployed to ward off *kuxuka*, did not help her recover, and having observed several of the girl's fits, Augusto Pinheiro, the herbal doctor (*dauya*), decided that the problem was the "peccary child." Antonio Pinheiro, a middle-aged man who was learning the art of healing with Augusto (his adoptive father and brother-in-law), described to me the phenomenology of the peccary child as follows: "The peccary child bites its tongue and pushes us violently away, striking out randomly. Aah!, aai!, it screams, foaming at the mouth and trembling. She caught this illness because her parents ate peccary while her mother was pregnant or maybe when she was nursing."

Augusto prepared a mixture of ten plants, each of which had the name of a part of the peccary's body (peccary hair, skin, testicles, ears, etc.) and told the parents to wash their child with it at night and in the morning. The problem eased and after several weeks the parents left the herbal doctor's house and returned to their village. A month later, however, the problem started again. Two possibilities were proposed: either the illness was not provoked by the peccary but by some other animal causing similar grimaces and spasms, or the parents were not observing the prescriptions of sexual continence and fasting. Augusto was convinced that the parents had not kept the food and sex taboos during pregnancy or nursing, but he was equally sure that they were not able to observe the taboos correctly during this time. Only when he was sure that they were keeping their fast would he be able to cure the illness and exclude the other, more dangerous possibility of it being due to a capybara child. As Antonio stated, "The capybara child's teeth chatter, *xenx xenx*, they bite. Without medicine you die"

(Amen bakeirã hawen xeta xenx xenx amiski hawen mestekinã dauuma mawamiski).

The naming of the illness, such as peccary child, capybara child, etc., as well as the diagnosis through observation of the bodily movements of the child who is unconscious and possessed by the illness-causing agent, suggest strong evidence for exploring an interpretation of illness as a dangerous and uncontrolled process of becoming other and nonhuman. The body mimics its invader in such a way that its human existence is placed in danger. The *yuxin* could be taken away by the peccary to cause the body to die, or it is also possible that the whole person might disappear, as seems to have happened to several youngsters in the villages of Peru who, I was told, got lost in the forest where they transformed into wild animals and never were seen again. Sad or angry people, unsatisfied with their relationships with close kin or spouses, are said to be prone to hear *yuxin* callings at night, and then disappear as they "sleep walk" into the forest.

This example clearly shows that herbal doctors (*dauya*) and their counterparts, poison owners (*dauya*), do deal with the world of *yuxin* and not just with "natural" or "mechanical" causes, whatever these might be thought to mean for the Cashinahua. Matter is the vehicle of *yuxin*. Animals with a strong *yuxin* are not only killed but consumed raw with the intent to communicate with the *yuxin* of their owner (as is the case of the ritual killing of the boa and the *oropendola* bird I describe later on). Plant substances—from ayahuasca, tobacco, and *dade* to the manifold plant extracts squeezed in the eyes—are used to alter perception; to see the world differently (a recurrent theme in Pano mythology). And it is the same idea of increased power through materialization that can be held responsible for the success of shamans who can visualize the pathogenic agents they extract from the bodies of their patients (Lévi-Strauss 1974:205–26).

The idea that poison is materialized *yuxin* is also manifest in the precautions taken by the sorcerer, not only after killing when he is saturated with the blood of his victim,[6] but at the very moment of touching the poison. He who does not observe the diet and talk properly to the poison at the time of touching it will die. Only he who knows how to talk to the poisonous plant will escape. Sometimes merely passing by a poisonous plant can be lethal. According to Antonio: "The poison to kill is red. When you pass it, you say, 'I know you already,' and you keep going. You look at it from a distance. If you say, 'I never saw this medicine'; you die. Or if you touch it without knowing, you will really get ill. There is a plant medicine used by the *dauya* in order not to die when he touches poisonous leaves."

Like the vine and leaves of ayahuasca[7]—said to be the transformed body parts of the first man who learned to drink the brew with the snake people—it is claimed that poisonous plants are the transformed body of the first sorcerer, an old woman named Yuxankudu. And that is the reason, explain the Cashinahua, why they "have *yuxin*" (a quality to be distinguished from "to be *yuxin*").

The myth of origin of poisonous plants was told to me by Antonio in the following way:

> Yuxankudu (the old grey woman) was the first one who knew how to use poison. She used to kill when she was desirous of human flesh; children, men, and women alike she killed. One day Yuxankudu was sitting in a corner, counting pieces of charcoal. For each piece of charcoal she pronounced the name of her victim and the reason for his or her death. A little girl, her granddaughter, was listening. The old woman mentioned that she had gone to the riverbank to get clay for her pottery. She leaned forward so much that her thing, *xebi* (vagina), became visible. Her son-in-law saw it and took her with force. Then he fled away, but she turned in time to see his back. She cried. At a small river she got poison with a conch, cooked it, and kept it with her. When she arrived home, she mixed the poison into the food of her son-in-law. He got a high fever and diarrhea, and then he died. Thus went the story of the old woman. The girl went home and told the widow's wife what the old woman had done. His kin decided to kill her. The old woman heard them and fled. Tawaxeni-buxka, a blind man, got up from his hammock and told the victim's father where the old one had hidden. They went after her but she kept running away. It was time to organize *nixpupima* (a rite of passage for girls and boys) in her village. Thus the people went to her hiding place and told her, "Grandmother, there will be the party of your grandchild, come and baptize your namesake." And the old one went. One brother came jumping with a corncob stuck in his buttocks and she laughed. Then another brother appeared and hit her with a club. She died. They burned her in the fire and from her blood grew poison. In the beginning everybody knew, but they forgot and now people know the leaves but don't know how to touch it without dying."

Another myth, collected by Capistrano de Abreu (1941 [1914]:194–95), associates the origin of poisonous plants with a great deluge, which meant the beginning of a new existence. The sky fell to earth because the inhabitants of the sky cut down too many trees. Everybody on earth died, only Macari and Maticiani survived, each clinging to a high tree. They married and had two children, Muru and Batan, the ancestors of the Cashinahua. Until that time illness did not exist. But poisonous leaves fell down to earth, rain soaked them, they putrefied and the wind stirred them up, dissipating illness where it passed.

What can be learned from this story is that the Cashinahua associate the origin of illness with the existence of poisonous plants, much more so than they associate it with the power of human thoughts, songs, and words. It is this source that sorcerers are said to tap when they want to kill. The poison can affect its victims in various ways. The consumption of poisoned food causes violent vomiting, dizziness, high fever, and almost immediate death. Sometimes the dark shaman attacks his victims directly, scratching their foreheads with the long nail of his right thumb. He hides his poison under the nail of the thumb of his right hand as well as inside his bamboo earrings, which are capped with wax or resin.

But poison can also act without direct contact with the victim's body. Thus a poisoned arrow flying over the victim's head or a poisonous leaf burned over a fire are believed to cause death. The smoke, carried by the wind, can cause deadly dysentery and fever, killing whole villages. People take considerable care to dispose of and bury excrement, hiding it from eyes with potentially evil intent. Otherwise a *dauya* might find it, mix it with poison and cook it in a banana leaf over a fire. If this happens, a person will first feel a terrible headache around midnight, and will then be afflicted by a deadly diarrhea and start vomiting uncontrollably.

The young Budu, Capistrano's informant (1941 [1914]:150–54), had known a *dauya* that had been killed because he was accused of putting poison in the excrement of the son of Budu's namesake. Also, the sudden death of his own mother had been attributed to an old *dauya*. As in the previous case, revenge had been taken on the supposed sorcerer. The old man lived in the same house as Budu's mother and she died shortly after an incident in which she had been laughing with her kin and the old man felt offended, thinking they were laughing at him because he was thin. He became very angry. When Budu's mother went to the river to take a bath, he followed her and put poison in her skirt. On her way back she started to feel the pain, and she died the same night. Because he was considered to be the only *dauya*, "man with medicine," in the longhouse, the old man was killed and burned.

Antonio reported to me in detail the same procedure of hiding poison in the woman's skirt. At night the woman first feels a headache, then starts vomiting and risks death the same night. When a sorcerer has recently killed someone, Antonio explained, he dyes his hands black with *genipapo* and the whites of his eyes become red (he is "full of," or contaminated by, the blood of his victim). The *dauya* is, in Antonio's words, a furious person with no sense of humor: "If you make fun of his bald head, because *dauya* are always bald, if you think it's funny, he puts poison on you. If you are stingy [*yauxi*] with him, he puts poison on you. If you refused to have sex with him, he puts poison on you. If you were stingy with me [he gives here a mischievous smile] I could poison you. If you scolded me, I could poison you, if I were a *dauya*. A *dauya* never eats meat and does not smell any perfume. When he kills someone he spends a month without talking to anybody. He cannot touch a woman. I do not want to know about *dau*, I do not want to die."

From the following description we can see that we are dealing with a phenomenology typical of sorcery accusations. The description of the character of the sorcerer is a personification of antisocial behavior and power abuse, a kind of man who would never be tolerated in a village. Among the Krahó, who are Timbira-speakers of the state of Maranhão, the figure of the sorcerer serves the same role of antithesis of social behavior, contrasting with the generosity of the village head. His sorcery is the crystallization of social retention and lack of reciprocity, and serves therefore as a metaphor for death itself (Carneiro da Cunha 1978:12–17). On the other hand, among the Cashinahua, not all deaths imply revenge and the search for someone to be accused. Sorcery accusations appear only as an explanation for sudden, unexplained deaths of healthy and strong people. When Budu's mother died, her *yuda baka* (body soul) appeared to her kin people and revealed the identity of her murderer (Capistrano 1941 [1914]:143).

Only once did I hear about suspicions that an old man might be preparing himself to put his knowledge of poisonous plants into practice. This happened not in the context of a sudden and unexplained death calling for revenge but rather in the context of a village fission, in a tense and conflictive atmosphere. During an ayahuasca session, the village head's son had a vision in which the father of the leader of the separatists wanted to poison him. This vision worried the boy's close kinsmen seriously, but once the secessionists left and left the village in peace, the fear and animosity calmed down again. This episode is another illustration of the fact that, for the Cashinahua, it is the *dauya* and not the *mukaya* who more clearly represents the figure of the dark shaman, ready to emerge in accusations during episodes of conflict.

In the village of Fronteira, an incident between government representatives and the mourning widow and brothers of a young healthy woman who was about to give birth but died suddenly could be understood in the same terms of sorcery suspicions arising in situations of sudden loss and tense social relations. The pregnant woman had a headache and was subsequently medicated by her brother-in-law, who had access to the village pharmacy in the absence of the nurse. He gave her a whole tablet of painkillers and an injection of unidentified content, and she died immediately of what seemed to be a brain hemorrhage. When her husband arrived home the same day and was informed of the tragedy, all the men involved in the accident got drunk to cope with the situation.

At that moment a delegation of two government representatives from FUNAI who were working with indigenous peoples arrived at the village. The drunken widow, his brother, and his brothers-in-law approached the two men, asking them for explanations of the following paradox: why had the doctor and nurses of a vaccination campaign a month before decided only to vaccinate pregnant women? Was it a campaign to exterminate the Indians? Was the woman who had died that day the first of a series of victims to come? How did they explain this coincidence, which seemed to be the confirmation of a rumor that had been circulating on the Purus River ever since the doctor and nurses had visited all the villages, vaccinating only pregnant women? The government representatives had no answer to the villagers' angry questions, and they had to spend the night hiding in the government-owned radio house in the village to protect themselves from the mourners who threatened revenge. Only the next day, when everyone was sober again and the anger had subsided somewhat were the government officials able to leave their hiding place and begin negotiating with the mourning community.

This incident follows the same logic of traditional sorcery accusations: the nurses had applied their *dau* in the powerful form of injections (which penetrate the skin as magical darts) on healthy people and, worse, on pregnant women. People were suspicious and now the suspicions had been confirmed: the injections were starting to show their lethal effect. At this moment, as though to confirm the interpretation, the government representatives arrived and were threatened by the mourners. The event also shows another important aspect of Cashinahua experiences with illness after contact: the cause of illness may come from the outside much more frequently than from the inside.

Mukaya: *At the Top of an Iceberg*

As mentioned above, dark shamans or sorcerers—people who cause harm to their own kin—appear more often in Cashinahua discourse in the form of *dauya* "poison users" than in that of specialists who talk to other beings, *yuxin*, loosely translated as spirits. Thus for the Cashinahua the more one can materialize harmful energy, the more effective it becomes. The *dauya* acts or is supposed to act at the limit between the visible and invisible use of violence, at the limit between the use of material and immaterial means of inflicting harm. The *mukaya* goes one step further on the path of dominating and visualizing invisible power. And we will see that other techniques, in which material substances are used to invoke invisible powers, can be placed somewhere in between the domains of the *dauya* and the *mukaya*, and are used and known by the majority of adult men and women.

Whereas among the Culina, shamanism expresses the quintessence of masculinity—with the accumulation of *duri*, the shamanic substance, the result of a successful concentration and domestication of youthful male desire (Pollock 1992:25–40)—among the Cashinahua hunting and shamanism, at least in its restricted *mukaya* version, are dealt with as logical opposites (Kensinger 1974, 1995; Deshayes 1992). The first sign of a man's calling to become a *mukaya* is his failure to kill animals, not because they escape him but because they talk to him. Thus what characterizes the *mukaya* among the Cashinahua is his extraordinary capacity of communication with other beings, a technique that can easily be used to cause harm to other human beings because it is the *yuxin* who control and cause illness and death.

Not only for men is the call of *muka* (the bitter shamanic substance) considered to be counterproductive in terms of gender performance, but it is also dangerous to women because women with *muka* are said to become compulsive wanderers.[8] During pregnancy, the interference of *yuxin* produces deformations in the child's body, which is why exceptional births, like babies with six fingers or a closed ear, are called *yuxin bake* (spirit's children) (Lagrou 1998:47, 69–74).

This incompatibility of dominant male and female roles with the requirements and restraints put on a *mukaya* may be one of the more important reasons for its low popularity among Cashinahua men and women, while among the Culina almost every adult male is said to have some *duri*. Thus, among the Cashinahua there are many testimonies of men and women being called by the *yuxin*, yet almost none of these callings is answered in a positive way. When someone has been caught by the *yuxin*—a process described in terms of a violent assault and combat resulting in the victim's fainting ("dying"), followed by the planting by the yuxin of *muka* in his or her heart—the victim will look for the *mukaya*'s alter ego, the *dauya* (medicine man), who will prescribe or treat him or her with herbal baths or, in extreme cases, make them eat rotten fish or meat in order to keep the *yuxin* away.

It is important to point out once again the method used by the Cashinahua to defend themselves against incursions of the *yuxin*. The *yuxin* represent nonhuman beings; they are characterized by their alterity with respect to what most strongly defines human identity. Humans have their agency, perception, and cognition (in the form of manifold souls) embedded in a fixed and solid body that has been molded by close kin living together. This thinking body has strong emotional roots embedded in memories of caring. *Yuxin* beings, to the contrary, are wandering beings with no roots and no fixed form; they belong to a realm mostly invisible to human beings, and although they are not immaterial their relation with matter is one of fluidity and transformation, not one of solidity. For the Cashinahua the most effective way to keep away these floating beings and images of change and alterity is to make them invisible, sealing off the body with smoke, painting, protective baths, and food—that which most clearly defines the constitution of a living human body.

I only know of one woman, Delsa, who acknowledged that she was a follower of the path of a shaman. She did not claim to have *muka* and was therefore called a *yuxian* (someone who lives with *yuxin*) instead of a *mukaya*, but her prayers had the power to heal thanks to her spiritual snake husband, Yube Xeni. Delsa, the first of two wives of the leader of the village Fronteira, became a *yuxian* following a frightening experience in one of the most dangerous places of otherness known to the Cashinahua: the hospital. The story she told me goes as follows. While pregnant with her last child, she was in town accompanying her husband. When she was about to deliver, the doctors wanted to operate on her in order to sterilize her. They were acting in accordance with the wishes of her husband. Delsa, however, refused vehemently. She said that if she herself no longer wanted to bear children, she could use her own methods to achieve this. In Cashinahua society it is women and not men who control fertility.

Thus, with the threat of control being taken from her while in the hospital and about to deliver, Delsa "went crazy." She screamed and punched, not allowing the doctors to get away with sterilization. During her fit, Delsa also had visions. It seems that the hospital, the place where people go to die, has a large quantity of *yuxin* wandering around. After a certain period of time, later back in the village, she learned to gain control over her visions.

Delsa started first of all to receive the visits and teachings of her deceased father, who had also been a *yuxian* (shaman), and later on she "married" Yube Xeni (the snake *yuxin*). From that moment Yube Xeni came to make love to her at night, and because of her new *yuxin* husband Delsa said she no longer had sex with her human husband. One of the signs of her alliance with the world of *yuxin* was her deformed mouth—people say the *yuxin* are eating her mouth away—while another sign is her successful healing of fever in small children.

Although Delsa is a *yuxian* and not a *mukaya*, she does share some of the *mukaya*'s characteristics: for example, both are chosen by *yuxin* and their conviviality implies both sexual abstinence and sexual alliance with *yuxin* beings.[9] Delsa's initiation started at the moment she was at the end of her period of fertility and thus would not interfere with gender-specific sensibilities and the production of human beings. Her initiation through visions and dreams with a deceased kinsperson, in this case her father who had also been a shaman (*yuxian*) and who decided to transmit his power to her, as well as her sexual union with the powerful snake Yube Xeni, shaman par excellence, shows obvious similarities with the initiation of other Panoan song healers and shamans, especially among the Katukina (Lima 2000:134-43). However, no materialization of spiritual power had been involved in Delsa's case and no mention was made of her powers to produce illness.

The *mukaya*, on the other hand, belong to a category of shamans, famous in Amerindian ethnographic literature, characterized by their ability to materialize the spiritual power harnessed inside the shaman's body, which may cause harm or kill victims from a distance. The imagery involved resembles that of warrior's shooting invisible arrows or darts to equally invisible enemies. The healing powers of this kind of shaman invariably involve the power of making visible harmful objects that have been extracted by sucking them out of the victim's body. Anthropologists and their Panoan interlocutors alike tend to attribute the quality of shaman (translated as *pajé*) to only this kind of practitioner.

It is difficult to know who was responsible for making this phenomenology a kind of paradigm of shamanism, whether it was the anthropologist looking for the 'real' shaman or an indigenous tendency to establish a hierarchy of powers dealing with the invisible. The fact is that some Panoan groups affirm never to have had such shamans (*pajés*)—such as the Yawanahua (Pérez 1999:110), Yaminahua (Townsley 1988; Calavia 1995), Sharanahua (Siskind 1973:43), and Cashibo (Frank 1994; Pérez 1999:114), while others affirm that they do or did, such as the Marubo (Montagner Melatti 1985:401), Shipibo (Illius 1992), Katukina (Lima 2000:128-29), and Cashinahua.

It is interesting to note that the Panoan groups given above that claim never to have had shamans capable of extracting and sending bewitching substances are exactly the groups where another version of shamanism, manifest in the use of bewitching and healing songs, is very much alive (Pérez 1999:114). Still, among the Marubo and Katukina, who do or did have their version of the *mukaya*—which they called *romeya* ("the one with tobacco," a tobacco materialized in the same way as *muka*, a bitter and magical substance in the body)—song healers and sorcerers nevertheless do play a very important role. While Lima (2000:128) calls attention to the reproduction of a dualism of shamans among the Katukina who value their (deceased) *romeya* (real shaman) over their song healers (*rezador*, *shoitiya*, or *koshoitiya*) because the latter do not have the power to heal sorcery, Pérez (1999:110-14) stresses the fact that the Yawanahua never used this kind of dualism. All shamans are said to be capable of gradually accumulating different kinds of powers, those of plant healers (*niipuya*) along with those of the *xinaya* (song healers), and, at the top of the ladder, the *yuvehu* (plural of the important entity *yuve*) or *tsimuya*, the one with bitterness, who is characterized by his power to incorporate spirits. The Yawanahua do, however, distinguish clearly between illnesses healed with plant medicine and others healed through magical songs, in a much more radical way, it should be said, than do the Cashinahua themselves.

Further reflection on other interesting similarities and differences between Panoan groups is beyond the scope of this essay, but some provisory conclusions can be drawn nevertheless. One fact that stands out regarding the variety in Panoan sorcery and healing methods is that the *dauya* among the Cashinahua might be seen to be to the *mukaya* what specialists in healing and bewitching songs are to the *mukaya's* equivalent in other Panoan groups. In other words, if almost everywhere the supposedly "real" shaman, the one Panoans share with their neighbors, tends to disappear, those specialists most strongly feared as sorcerers remain: among the Katukina, Yaminahua, and Yawanahua they act through bewitching songs, while among the Cashinahua they act through poison.

If the power of sorcery found shelter in other techniques that seem always to have coexisted with the technique of sending darts, what then would have been lost with the absence of a *mukaya*, labeled as the only "real" shaman? One strong attribute of the *mukaya* was his capacity to call and communicate with *yuxin* spirit beings at free will. It is, therefore, the privilege of communication with the spirit world that has been lost with the figure of the *mukaya*. In another work (Lagrou 1998) I have shown how this communication and the perception of *yuxin* is diffused throughout everyday life. If we use the capacity of this kind of communication as a criterion to define the shaman, we would be once again in the position to affirm with the Kagwahiv that almost "everyone . . . has a bit of a shaman" (Kracke, 1987).

Almost all of the techniques that have recently been described for the Katukina (Lima 2000) and especially for the Yawanahua (1999) as characterizing different trajectories and initiation methods to become song healers (in Portuguese, *rezadores*) whose songs have both the power to kill and to heal, I have registered as isolated techniques used by adult men and women in private or collective rituals with the intention to enter into contact with *yuxin* beings and their powers (Lagrou 1991, 1998).

Thus there are the different rituals involving the killing of a boa (*yube xeni*) and the consumption of different parts of its body by men and by women, separately, to obtain luck in men's hunting expeditions, or to enhance a woman's intelligence in the learning of designs or to obtain fertility or control it (Lagrou 1991, 1996). The same ritual, however, can also be realized with the intention to bewitch someone by means of the *yuxin* of the boa. All old men, I was told, know how to kill by speaking to the *yuxin* of the boa, because they ate its heart. In this way they have become like *yube* himself, and their words have power. A list of the names of men who performed the ritual, accompanied by a long period of fasting and abstinence, would follow this speech with the *yuxin*. Interestingly enough, these ritual performances would not give rise, among the Cashinahua, to special roles and statuses; this was, my interlocutors would say, something all old people knew and had done several times in their life. Although their blowing and songs were considered to be powerful and extremely dangerous, these men were not called healers (Lagrou 1998). It is interesting to note that among the Katukina this same encounter with the boa or anaconda, without killing or consuming it, implies the beginning of an initiation process in the arts both of song healing and of shamanism. The encounter produces dizziness in the hunter and can be completed with the transference of *rome* (a shamanic substance of which the anaconda is the owner) (Lima 2000:132–38).

Another Cashinahua private ritual that is practiced in the woods is part of a sequence of initiation rituals of which, preferentially, every adult should have taken part at least once in his or her life. I refer here to the ritual consumption of different parts (leaves, stem, root) of a plant called *dade*. I never witnessed such a ritual, however, and its content is surrounded by mystery. *Dade* is administered to small children to strengthen them and enhance their concentration. Women take the plant to get pregnant or, conversely, as a temporary contraconceptive (Lagrou 1998:72). In the case of contraception, the ritual is performed before menstruation. The consumption of *dade* is followed by some months of strict dieting, and its effect and consequences are said to be equivalent to those of the ritual killing and consumption of the boa. The acquisition of the capacity of communication with *yuxin* is one of the possible consequences of the encounter with *dade*. Thus it is the use of a substance, a practice in which the *dauya* is specialized, that will give extraordinary power to a person's words, a practice traditionally ascribed to the *mukaya*.

In one of my conversations with Cashinahua villagers, we discussed the danger and power of twins, whose words were said to have the power to kill because of their status as spirit children (*yuxin bake*, *yubebu*) conceived through intercourse with the spirit of the boa. To emphasize their strength, twins were compared to *dade*: "When one [of the twins] dies, you cannot tell the other, otherwise the other also dies. He is like *yube xeni* [boa]. He has the power of *kuxuka* [the dolphin]. He is like *dade*." This same *dade* is said by the Yawanahua to be a hallucinogen used in the initiation of song healers and shamans (Pérez 1999:18).

Finally, there is the ritual use of ayahuasca, which is another example of how much the world of plants is imbued with *yuxin* agency and how much this agency is prone to materialize in plants. It is this relation between energy and substance that approaches the two kinds of specialists—

one working with substances and the other with words—in such a way that they can only in theory be considered to be mutually exclusive.

Song healers among the Shipibo, Marubo, Yawanahua, and Katukina all make use of ayahuasca in their healing rituals. In some cases, such as the Shipibo, Katukina, and Marubo, the patient is present at the healing sessions, while in others the patient is absent, such as among the Yawanahua where prayers are sung over a cup of manioc beer that will be offered to the patient who is asleep at home in his hammock (Pérez 1999:115). During these healing rituals, however, the healer does not use the drink alone.

In contrast with many other reports on the ritual intake of ayahuasca, the Cashinahua do not restrain from meat or fish at dinner before taking the brew. They say that if the owner of the ingested animal appears in a vision, something that is considered almost inevitable, they will deal with him through song. It seems almost as though they eat the animal to see its *yuxin* in a vision. Ayahuasca can be taken by all adult men and adolescents, and in some cases by women. I witnessed only one woman taking the brew; she was from another village and was accompanied by her husband. Elderly people tend not to take ayahuasca, alleging they are already too tired and that their eye soul (*bedu yuxin*) has already learned how to dream.[10]

Ayahuasca is taken with the intent to get information about distant places and their beings, the hiding places of game, the real intentions of opponents in conflicts, the motives of visitors, future events, and illness-causing agents. It is also an event where sorcery can be used, and thus the Cashinahua of the villages where I worked (Cana Recreio, Moema, Nova Aliança) were wary of taking part in the ayahuasca ritual of their more distant kin and neighbors in the village of Fronteira, who were famous for putting sorcery in the brew through their strong thoughts and songs. Two or three specialists of the vine were considered to be especially dangerous in this sense, and, in the eyes of their relatives living in villages nearby, they could be dark shamans.

As with all other methods of dealing with the world of *yuxin*, the ritual intake of ayahuasca has two sides—it can either heal or inflict illness, depending on how it is used. Although I did not witness any healing session with ayahuasca, one session was described to me by Antonio Pinheiro in the following terms: "When the vine brew is prepared, the patient is called to come close. You ignite the lamp. You tie up his hammock, and then you tie up yours. You sit very close to him. Then you drink the vine and when you are drunk, you sing, sing, sing, and sing until you find his illness. If they put poison, they will discover it. If they put something else, illness, you discover it. Then you tell him on the spot, if he will be all right, you tell him, 'you will be all right, friend,' or whoever, right? Or father, brother, uncle, of any kind, you tell him: 'you will be all right.' If he will die, you tell him also, 'ah, I think you will not escape. There is no way.' In this case the people cry. You would feel sorry, wouldn't you?"

Induced by my questions, Antonio explained that if the cause were *muka* it would have to be sucked out, but only if it had not yet spread out, because in that case the victim would invariably die. A close look at this description of a healing session with ayahuasca shows us that, more than about healing itself, Antonio is speaking about the use of this ritual to help the healer to discover the cause. Kensinger (1995:211) mentions this same possibility for a *mukaya* to use *nixi pae* (ayahuasca) to acquire more information, a new song, or the indication of another plant.

Other Cashinahua, however, were emphatic in stressing that what defines a *mukaya* is exactly his ability to discover the truth about illness or future events by means of his direct intercourse and communication with *yuxin*, without having to resort to the help of ayahuasca or any other substance. It should be noted, though, that if all of these instruments and means to induce trance states do not identify the *mukaya's* practices and capacities (because his power resides in not needing any psychotropic substance) they will have an important role in the process of initiation and preparation (Kensinger, 1995:211). Other methods used by someone wanting to become a *mukaya* include very intensive dreaming and solitary walks in the forest with the intention of being caught by *yuxin*. During the seizure the *yuxin* will plant their substance in the shaman's body.

Regarding the use of substances by the *mukaya* to enter a trance state, an exception should be made for tobacco snuff (*dume*). *Romeya*, the equivalent of the Cashinahua term *dumeya* ("the one with tobacco"), indicates among the Marubo and Katukina a specialist with attributes very similar to those of the *mukaya*: he can call spirits at will, and he has a magic substance in his body that he can materialize in the form of shamanic objects and then send to victims in the form of invisible darts. He can also suck out the same kind of objects from the bodies of his patients. The name of the bitter substance that has been introduced into his body by the spirits (*yuxin* or *yové*) is *rome*: tobacco. The link is intrinsic. The Cashinahua also have a myth about a very powerful shaman with the strength to conquer all the powerful monsters inhabiting the paths that separate the houses of his kin. This shaman, whose name is Dume Kuin Teneni (*tene*, real tobacco, a *dumeya*), has a body smell so bitter that each time he takes a bath the fish die as if by poison.

Tobacco snuff is not, however, a privilege held for shamans. Common men can use tobacco snuff to help concentrate on hunting, or they can use it in combination with ayahuasca in order to clear their vision. Yet, when prepared in a special way, tobacco is the quintessential healing substance.

According to Antonio: "Pure tobacco, we use to heal illness. It is a mixture of, in our language, ashes of *xiun*, *yapa*, and *biunx*. The white man calls them *murici*, *manixi*, and *yandé*. These really strong ashes are mixed with the tobacco powder. If you have illness in your body, any kind of illness, and pain in your bones, you sniff tobacco powder, get drunk, and you can cure. You pass your spittle on the person and spread it out over his body."

Tobacco helps the *mukaya* to enter a trance state and take off in search of the lost soul of an ailing child. As Antonio further states:

> When a child is ill, it cries all the time. It cries. The one that is calling is her soul. Her mother calls, *Huwe!* [Come!] The child is sleeping. It is her soul that is crying from far away. When it arrives, the child wakes up immediately. Thus the *mukaya* sniffs the tobacco powder to get drunk, to be able to find her, right? He goes to the forest, to try to find her soul in the cemetery, or else, just in the forest. Sometimes he stays for hours in the forest trying to find her. He returns from the forest with *achiote* from the souls, *genipa* from the souls, smoked meat from the souls, beads from the souls. He also brings with him a parrot's young, *bawa bake*, an orange-winged parrot's young, *txede bake*, and a parakeet, *pitsu*. Sometimes also a monkey's young. He brings them at the spot, together with the child's soul and accompanied by many souls. The *mukaya* playing flute and the souls, *yuxin*, all decorated as in the *katxanawa* ritual. Then the *mukaya* does the following: At this point Antonio passes his hands under his armpits, rubs his hands, puts them together in the form of a horn and blows in the supposed patient's fist. Afterward he blows on its heart, on the front and on the back. Finally he blows on the feet and on the knees. Then he continues with the *mukaya*'s words.... Always saying, '*heneai mi peai!*' [let go, you are all right]. He turns her face, the 'dead' child's face. Then she starts to move, her body is warming up, her heart is beating, she opens her eyes and says: 'I was sleeping.'

This detailed description of the recovery of a soul by a *mukaya* shows Antonio's profound familiarity with the scene, although the Cashinahua say they have not seen practicing *mukayas* since the 1950s. Antonio, himself a modest healer (*rezador*), confessed to me his desire to become a *mukaya*, but his second family was too young and his wife was against it. For a *mukaya* the prohibition to eat any kind of sweet food or meat is not limited to periods of initiation or practicing but rather holds for the time he wants to keep the *muka* in his body. As soon as the diet is violated, the *muka* disappears. Not only can a *mukaya* not eat meat, he is also not allowed by the *yuxin* to kill game. Yet another severe restriction, difficult to combine with everyday life, is the prohibition of sexual intercourse.

The Initiation of a mukaya

Sources agree on the fact that the *mukaya* gets his knowledge and power from the spirit beings and not from men. This was what Capistrano's young informant told him in the beginning of the century: "It was the *yuxin* who taught the *huni kuin* who got their *muka* from the *yuxin*" (1941 [1914]:161). Kensinger states: "The shaman learns his art from the spirit beings who give him his *muka*" and that "any person, male or female, with a propensity for dreaming may become a shaman" (1995:217). And Antonio affirms the statement with details: "A *mukaya* does not need to be *deku* (dexterous), nor *unan* (intelligent, learned), because it is the *yuxin* who acts. *Yuxin* heals through him. *Muka* is *yuxin* acting in his body. It is in this way that he learns with the spirits."

The same idea seems to hold for the Katukina (Lima 2000:143) and is accepted as a possibility among the Shipibo-Conibo and Marubo,[11] who all share the kind of shaman most closely related to the *mukaya* of the Cashinahua. Other Panoans (Lima 2000) and especially the Yawanahua (Pérez 1999) would not conceive of this possibility of initiation without human masters. It is important, however, to recall at this point that the kind of specialist discussed here is absent among those groups that stress the initiation of healers over their election by the *yuxin* themselves.[12] It should be noted, however, among the Yaminahua of the Purus River (Townsley 1993) as well as the Yawanahua that healing and sorcery songs are composed of mythic themes. To be a healer among the Yawanahua means therefore to possess a solid knowledge of this mythical universe, a knowledge only obtained through initiation by another *xinaya* (the one with knowledge).

At this point it is necessary to invoke the existence of a third important figure among Cashinahua specialists. This figure, who is called the *txana ibu* ("the song leader"; also translated as owner of the *oropendola* birds) is said to *xinan haidaki*—that is, "to know a lot" (note the similarity of this term with that for "healer" among the Yawanahua; *xinaya*). The importance of the presence of a song leader for the well-being of a village cannot be stressed enough (see Lagrou 1998; see also Kensinger 1995, McCallum, 1989). The song leader is responsible for the performance of prophylactic songs at all important public rituals and private rites of passage; for example, at the end of the seclusion of a newborn child, where in that case the song leader sings for protection while passing the *genipa* paint onto the child.

I call attention to the importance of the song leader because he seems to me to be the missing link to understanding the apparent contradictions between the existing data on Cashinahua shamanism and the new information that has recently become available for other Panoan groups, thus constituting a continuum of shamanistic practices where previously much less was known. Although no explicit healing powers are attributed to the *txana ibu*'s function, it nonetheless comes very close to the healing specialists described by Pérez, Lima, and Montagner Melatti for other Panoan groups. *Txana ibu* undergoes a long period of training under the guidance of a master song leader. His songs are necessary to invoke the benevolence of all *yuxin* beings that underlie the abundance, fertility, and well-being of everyday life. His songs also intend to make the *yuxin* beings happy (*benimai pakadin*), and his help is invoked when unpretentious prayers or blowing is required. I use the word unpretentious because I never saw any of these "knowledgeable men" claim recognition for a successful healing. The only help requested was for him to pass some of his strength and knowledge onto a weak person through massage with his own sweat. The *txana ibu* is a kind of instructed adult who has experienced several initiation rituals associated among other Panoan groups with shamanic power: the ritual killing and consumption of a boa, of *dade*, of ayahuasca and tobacco snuff, and of pepper (in this case from the beak of an *oropendola* bird, in order to obtain an infallible memory as part of his consecration as new song leader).

This is not to say that the song leader of the Cashinahua is equivalent to the healers/shamans of the Yaminahua, Yawanahua, Katukina, and others. Much to the contrary, the differences are as important as any similarities — first because the *txana ibu* are not considered to be healers and, second, because their power does not seem to have a dark side. The *txana ibu* does not claim knowledge of bewitching songs. Yet if his ritual songs are performed wrongly, the results for the community can be disastrous. Also there is the specialization of the *txana ibu* that is systematically combined with that of *dauya*, the specialist in plant medicine. And it is because in the case of illness the *txana ibu*'s prayers and silent songs are always accompanied by herbal medicine that this side of his activity in the field of healing has been left in a shadow. Knowledgeable Cashinahua men are not famous for their power of healing and killing through song—only the prophylactic and propitiating purpose of their praxis is stressed—but they are famous for their knowledge of poison. This is why, in my view, the dark side of shamanism among the Cashinahua is to be found in the use of poison, a practice for which the transmission of knowledge by a master is indispensable. Thus a specialization between Panoan groups seems to exist, where some stress their knowledge of the power of songs and words while others are famous for their control over the power of lethal substances.

Let us return here to the different forms of initiation of a *mukaya*. In situations of emotional vulnerability, an individual can be caught by the *yuxin*. This is one way of obtaining the shamanic substance *muka*. Accidents of this kind are not exceptional, and several of them were told to me. In all cases, however, kin people intervened with herbal baths and plant medicine squeezed in the eyes to interrupt the victim's acquaintance with the world of *yuxin* and to make them stop dreaming (Lagrou 1991:32–44). But a person can also actively look for an encounter and alliance with *yuxin* beings. Such an individual will become listless, wander alone in the forest, and come back without game. A young Cashinahua, Osair Siã, described an initiation by *yuxin* to me in the following terms: "A shaman [*pajé*] can give life and take it away. To become a shaman, you go alone into the forest and decorate your body with bark and palm leaves. You lie down on a crossroads with arms and legs spread out. First come the nightly butterflies, called *husu*, covering your whole body. Than come the *yuxin* eating the *husu* until they touch your head. You embrace them with all your force. The *yuxin* become transformed into a *murmuru* palm tree, full of thorns. If you are strong enough and do not let go, the palm tree will transform into a snake that coils itself around your body. You hold on; it transforms into a jaguar. You go on holding it in your grip and thus it goes until you are holding nothing. You succeeded in the test and go on to explain to the *yuxin* you want to receive *muka*. The *yuxin* will give it to you."

Antonio described to me the transference of the *muka* substance itself: "Then, they say that when he 'dies,' the soul puts, he plants, *sempa*, you know. We call it *sempa* [resin] in our language." I then asked him, "What kind of a mixture is *sempa*?" He replied, "It is a mixture of *sempa* and *muka*. He is going to plant *muka* in his heart. When he plants *muka* and *sempa* and *tamakana*, they say that when it is big, when it is growing, it starts to whistle. The soul [*yuxin*] in his heart whistles, whistles until it is grown up and big. People say: 'this man does not want to eat meat any more,' because he has *sempa*, the meat will turn into *sempa*."

A very similar account, with the addition of more-precise details, can be extracted from the eyewitness story from the early 1900s of Capistrano's young informant: "When the *yuxin* gave *muka*, they went to get *dau*; they made a *paçoca*, like a pill, of *dau*; they made a little ball, put it in his whole body, a small ball of *dau* in his body; in his body to become a *mukaya*" (1941 [1914]:161).[13] We learn from this text that the material used by the *yuxin* to materialize their power in the initiate's body is called *dau*, plant medicine. Thus we can conclude that the one who has medicine incorporated in his own body, the bitter medicine of the *yuxin*, *muka*, does not need to use medicine any more. He is medicine and poison himself.

Capistrano's informant also claimed to have seen the *muka* of a shaman, called Yawabiti, he had known as a child: "When he [the *mukaya* Yawabiti] showed them his *muka*, I saw it. The *muka* were a small ball of poison (*dau*), a small piece of a knife, he showed them a small wood splinter, he showed a bead; I saw everything." And he concludes: "Nobody would have the courage to scold Yawabiti, the *mukaya*. If they would scold him, he would throw *muka* on them and they would die if Yawabiti threw *muka* on them" (163). The richness of detail here leaves no doubt that the *mukaya* was once a shaman of flesh and blood. Yet when accusations of sorcery appear, also with respect to the past, as in the rich documentation gathered by Capistrano, the target is systematically a *dauya* and not a *mukaya*.

We can organize the different causes of illness in Cashinahua etiology following the words of Capistrano's informant Budu: "A Cashinahua can die from illness or from poison" (140). Illness can be due to all kinds of causes: the revenge of *yuxin* in the case of transgressions of food taboos or when people invade a *yuxin's* territory; attacks by the souls of the dead who throw *muka* on their victims or kidnap their soul; long-lasting illnesses that don't kill but cannot be healed either, causing a clearly localized pain in the stomach, heart, or chest, attributed to an attack with *duri* by the Culina (this kind of illness needs to be healed by foreign shamans); and, finally, illnesses, such as headache and intestinal parasites, considered to have been originated at the beginning of time.[14] Illnesses accompanied by strong diarrhea and vomiting that cause a sudden and unexplained death, on the other hand, are not real illnesses but rather have a sorcerer as their cause. These are illnesses for which there has never been a cure, the Cashinahua say, not even when there still were *mukayas* around. This kind of death has only one answer: the sorcerer is killed and burned. People still fear the older generation for their knowledge of poisonous plants, but no records following those written down by Capistrano have registered the accusation and execution of a sorcerer during this last century.

Conclusion

I hope to have shown here how Cashinahua discourse and practice related to the dark side of shamanism partakes of a thought system characterized by a dynamic dualism where identity depends on the inclusion and incorporation of alterity and where self partakes of the identity of other. This thought system does not separate soul from matter or energy from substance. When harm is inflicted on human beings, the possibility of the agency of a dark shaman is invoked. Panoan literature shows two methods of inflicting harm from a distance. The first is one that depends on the use of words and songs; it is a method intended to make *yuxin* beings act in accordance with the wishes of the bewitching agent, and is manifest to the Cashinahua in the figure of the *mukaya*. The second method, embodied in the figure of the *dauya*, depends on the use of substances that can or cannot be put into direct contact with the victim's body. Whereas other Panoan groups have been shown to specialize in the first cluster of techniques, the

Cashinahua clearly consider themselves to be more efficacious in the latter. People who don't claim a specialist's role, on the other hand, do use a rich variety of techniques to deal with *yuxin* beings with the intent to cause prophylactic or lethal effects on their own lives or that of other human beings, showing through daily practice that everyone "has a bit of a shaman" and that matter is as much imbued with *yuxin* agency as the words and songs of shamans.

Notes

1 See especially Pérez 1999 on the Yawanahua, and Montagner Melatti 1985 on the Marubo.
2 It should be noted that the difference in question is not one between healer and sorcerer, as seems to be the case among Peru's Arawak-speaking Matsingenka who distinguish terminologically between the healing shaman (*seripi'gari*) and the sorcerer (*matsika'nari*) (Baer 1992:87). The Panoan Shipibo of the same region, on the other hand, clearly state that it is of the nature of the shamanic healing act itself that "to remove *nihue* [the illness causing agent] from a sick body" means "to cast it on another living being who doesn't possess enough *xinan* [knowledge, power] to repulse it. Thus, in curing one, he is always bewitching another" (Illius 1992:75-76). This situation results from the fact that the shaman cannot destroy the substance. Also among the Arawak-speaking Kulina, traditional neighbors of the Cashinahua in Brazil, shaman's and sorcerer's roles are linked. "The shaman's role in illness is not limited to the treatment of the *dori* [illness-causing agent]. He also identifies the enemy shaman who is presumed to have caused the illness, normally (with nonfatal illnesses) a shaman from another village" (Pollock 1992:32). Shamans and sorcerers are not distinguished terminologically: both are *dzupinahe*. Their antisocial aspect is translated as *bruxo* (witch) and *feitiçaria* (sorcery) (Pollock 1992:39).
3 This characteristic approximates the Cashinahua to other Panoan relatives, like the Matis (Erikson 1996). Erikson called attention to the fact that among Panoans the role of the shaman is a temporary and delicate matter and is much less stressed and institutionalized than among many other Amazonian groups (Erikson 1986: 196, 205), although the data of Townsley (1988, 1993) for the Peruvian Yaminahua of the Purus River; Illius (1992) on the Shipibo-Conibo; and Montagner Melatti (1985) for the Marubo do not seem to confirm this hypothesis. Among the Matis (Erikson 1996 and n.d.) no specialists in the use of "bitter substance" have survived the trauma of contact with Western society. The class of bitter substances includes ayahuasca, tobacco snuff, toad poison, and the shamanic bitter substance *muka*. The author argues that after contact, and after the loss of most people in the older generation, nobody felt strong enough to handle these dangerous substances. Therefore, the Matis seemed to have specialists only in the domain of sweet (*bata*) substances. The Matis argued that they were all "children," having lost their old ones, "those who know." But this situation is seen as transitory by the Matis themselves who seem to have reintroduced the ethnically important but "bitter" and dangerous practice of tattooing, as well as the use of toad poison. This happened after Erikson's last visit in 1982.
4 Capistrano de Abreu is a well-known Brazilian historian of the late nineteenth and

early twentieth century, who is famous for establishing the basis of a new approach to the history of Brazil. Alongside his brilliant career as historian, Capistrano devoted many years to the study of the language and mythology of the Bacairi of Mato Grosso and the Cashinahua of Acre. Capistrano worked with two Cashinahua informants at his house in Río de Janeiro, where he compiled what was until recently the most complete collection of myths transcribed in vernacular language, with interlinear transcription and literal translation.

5 Kensinger befriended the headman because he cured him, but he became the "witch doctor's" rival: "I suspect that my distrust of him was greater than his distrust of me; after all, I thought he was the devil's agent" (1995:225). He adds, "My missionary colleague objected that accepting treatment from the witch doctor would be to dabble with the Devil's medicine" (227).

6 To be impregnated with the blood of one's victim is a very widespread idea among Amazonian people (see Albert 1985, for the Yanomami; Viveiros de Castro 1986, for the Tupi), and it has also been noted for the Panoans by Erikson (1986).

7 Ayahuasca is a strong hallucinogenic brew widely used in the region. The basic ingredient of ayahuasca is the *Banisteriopsis caapi* vine. Different groups in the region use a variety of plants to enhance the effects of the vine, but most frequently used is a leaf from the *Psychotria viridis* tree, which is considered to be responsible for the vivid visions produced by the brew. This leaf is the only addition to the vine used by the Cashinahua. For a description of its chemical composition and ritual setting, see Der Manderosian et al. 1970:7–14.

8 According to Antonio: "M. P. almost learned it. We would not let her because she is a woman. When someone has *muka*, she wanders around everywhere. She was walking around like crazy with the spirits. We took hold of her and put the plant *yuxin nemani* in her eyes. If she would see spirits again, we would bath her with *tuduan*. And if she would continue, we would give her rotten fish."

9 This "mystical marriage," however, is not as clear for the *mukaya* as it is for some other Panoan groups, as among the Katukina (Lima 2000:138), the Marubo (Montagner Melatti 1985:409–10), and the Shipibo-Conibo (Saladin d'Anglure and Morin, 1998:60). Yet it should be seen as no accident that the myth of origin of the use of ayahuasca among the Cashinahua, said to be experienced by every novice introduced to the experience of the hallucinogenic brew, is about exactly the same theme of mystical marriage with the snake woman—a member of the snake people who own the brew. Ayahuasca is one of the substances used on a regular basis by almost all Panoan novices in the arts of shamanism, although in some groups, as among the Cashinahua, its use is not restricted to apprentices of shamanism.

10 Where the Peruvian Cashinahua tend to distinguish between a dream soul (*nama yuxin*) and the eye soul (*bedu yuxin*) (Kensinger 1995; Deshayes 2000), the Cashinahua from the Purus River on the Brazilian side of the border consider eye and dream soul to be one and the same (Lagrou 1991, 1998; McCallum 1989).

11 Árevalo Valera 1986:152; Montagner Melatti 1985:416; also Lima 2000:143.

12 Yaminawa (Townsley 1988; Calávia Saez 1995); Sharanawa (Siskind 1973a), also Lima 2000; and Yawanawa (Pérez 1999).

13 The transcription in Cahinahua has been adapted to actual linguistic standards and the interlineal translation in Portuguese. The English translation is mine.

14 Deshayes (2000:30–31) calls this last kind of illnesses "memory illnesses" because its

origin is situated in mythic times. Thus the origin of headache could be found in the myth of the jaguar mother-in-law who used to eat her grandchildren. Her son kills her and burns her body; a piece of burning wood touches his forehead and causes the first headache. The myth of origin of intestinal parasites, an example I collected, explains that intestinal parasites came about as a result of the sexual intercourse of a woman with a giant earthworm. Furthermore, when the woman's new husband, the jaguar, was cleaning and thus healing her, she did not wait until the end of the ritual, and therefore people will always have intestinal parasites.

References

Albert, Bruce. 1985. "Temps du sang, temps des cendres: Représentation de la maladie, système rituel et espace politique chez les Yanomami du sud-est (Amazonie brésilienne)." Ph.D. diss., University of Paris-X (Nanterre).

Arévalo Valera, G. 1986. "El ayahuasca y el curandero Shipibo-Conibo del Ucayali (Perú)." *América Indígena* 46 (1): 147–61.

Baer, G. 1992. "The One Intoxicated by Tobacco: Matsigenka Shamanism." In *Portals of Power: Shamanism in South America*, ed. E. J. Langdon and G. Baer. 79–100. Albuquerque: University of New Mexico Press.

Calavia, O. 1995. "O nome e o tempo dos Yaminawa." Ph.D. diss., University of São Paulo.

Capistrano de Abreu, J. 1941 [1914]. *Rã-txa hu-ni-kui~: A língua dos Caxinauás do Rio Ibuaçú. Grammática, textos e vocabulário Caxinauás*. Rio de Janeiro: Edição da Sociedade Capistrano de Abreu, Livraria Briguiet.

Carneiro da Cunha, Manela. 1978. *Os mortos e os outros*. São Paulo: Hucitec.

Der Manderosian, A., et al. 1970. "The Use and Hallucinatory Principles of a Psycho-Active Beverage of the Cashinahua Tribe." *Drug Dependence* 5: 7–14.

Deshayes, P. 1992. "Paroles chassées: Chamanisme et chefferie chez les Kashinawa." *Journal de la Société des Américanistes* 78 (2): 95–106.

———. 2000. *Les mots, les images et leurs maladies chez les indiens huni kuin de l'Amazonie*. Paris: Loris Talmart.

Erikson, Philippe. 1986. "Altérité, tatouage et anthropophagie chez les Pano: La belliquese quête du soi." *Journal de la Société des Américanistes* 72: 185–210.

———. 1996. *La griffe des Aïeux. Marquage du corps et démarquages ethniques chez les Matis d'amazonie*. Paris: Peeters.

Frank, Ernst. H. 1994. "Los Uni." In *Guía etnográfica de la alta amazonía*, ed. F. Santos and F. Barclay. 103–237. Quito: Flacso/IFEA.

Illius, B. 1992. "The concept of Nihue among the Shipibo-Conibo of Eastern Peru." In *Portals of Power: Shamanism in South America*, ed. E. J. Langdon and G. Baer. 63–77. Albuguerque: University of New Mexico Press.

Kensinger, Ken. 1974. "Cashinahua Medicine and Medicine Men." In *Native South Americans: Ethnology of the Least Known Continent*, ed. P. Lyon. 283–88. Boston, Little, Brown.

———. 1995. *How Real People Ought to Live: The Cashinahua of Eastern Peru*. Prospect Heights, Ill.: Waveland Press.

Kracke, Wald. 1987. "Everyone Who Dreams Has a Bit of a Shaman: Cultural and Personal Meanings of Dreams. Evidence from the Amazon." *Psychiatric Journal Ottawa* 12 (2): 65–77.

Lagrou, Elsje. 1991. "Uma etnografia da cultura Kaxinawá: Entre a Cobra e o Inca." Master's thesis, Federal University of Santa Catarina.

———. 1996. "Xamanismo e representação entre os Kaxinawá." In *Xamanismo no Brasil: Novas perspectivas*, ed. E. J. Langdon. 197–231. Florianópolis: Editora UFSC.

———. 1998. "Cashinahua Cosmovision: A Perspectival Approach to Identity and Alterity." Ph.D. diss., University of St. Andrews.

Lévi-Strauss, Claude. 1974 [1958]. *Anthropologie Structurale*. Paris: Plon.

Lima, E. Coffaci. 2000. "Com os olhos da serpente: Homens, animais e espíritos nas concepções katukina sobre a natureza." Ph.D. diss., University of São Paulo.

McCallum, Cecilia. 1989. "Gender, Personhood and Social Organization amongst the Cashinahua of Western Amazonia." Ph.D. diss., London School of Economics.

Montagner Melatti, D. 1985. "O mundo dos espiritos: Estudo etnográfico dos Ritos de Cura Marubo." Ph.D. diss., Universidade de Brasília.

Pérez, L. P. Gil. 1999. *Pelos caminhos de Yuve: Conhecimento, cura e poder no xamanismo yawanawa*. Master's thesis, UFSC.

Pollock, Donald. 1992. "Culina Shamanism: Gender, Power, and Knowledge." In *Portals of Power: Shamanism in South America*, ed. E. J. Langdon and G. Baer. 25–40. Albuquerque: University of New Mexico Press.

Saladin d'Anglure, B., and F. Morin. 1998. "Mariage mystique et pouvoir chamanique chez les Shipibo d'amazonie péruvienne et les Inuit du Nunavut canadien." *Anthropologie et Sociétés* 22 (2): 49–74.

Siskind, Janet. 1973a. *To Hunt in the Morning*. Oxford: Oxford University Press.

———. 1973b. "Visions and Cures among the Sharanahua." In *Hallucinogens and Shamanism*, ed. M. Harner. New York: Oxford University Press.

Townsley, G. 1988. "Ideas of Order and Patterns of Change in Yaminahua Society." Ph.D. diss., Cambridge University.

———. 1993. "Songs Paths: The Ways and Means of Shamanic Knowledge." *L'Homme* 33 (2–4): 449–68.

Viveiros de Castro, Eduardo B. 1986. "Escatologia pessoal e poder entre os Araweté." *Religião e Sociedade* 13 (3): 2–26.

The Enemy Within: Child Sorcery, Revolution, and the Evils of Modernization in Eastern Peru

Fernando Santos-Granero

Accusations of child sorcery, and the punishment and execution of child sorcerers, was common practice among four of the six Arawak-speaking peoples living in the Selva Central region of eastern Peru, including the Asháninka, Ashéninka, Nomatsiguenga, and Yanesha (see map).[1] Until very recently, however, the consensus opinion was that Peruvian Arawaks had abandoned these practices around the 1970s as a result of the mass conversion to Evangelism, Adventism and Catholicism, the rapid expansion of formal education and health services, and greater integration into a market economy. Confirming evidence of this opinion came from the fact that no actual cases of child witchcraft were reported in the literature after 1970.[2] It thus came as a surprise when, in the mid-1990s, several anthropologists and other professionals working with Peruvian Arawak communities involved in an armed struggle against the communist organization Shining Path and the Túpac Amaru Revolutionary Movement (MRTA) began to report that accusations of child witchcraft had resurfaced.[3]

Most of this information was passed on by word of mouth among specialists working with these Arawak groups. It was (and still is) believed that if child witchcraft became public it would only reinforce existing prejudices about the "savagery" of Amazonian indigenous peoples. Similarly, the first (and until now the only) written references on the reemergence of this phenomenon were succinct and very cautiously worded (see Fabián Arias 1994:297, 1995:165; Fabián Arias and Espinosa de Rivero 1997:62). Even serious international organizations working directly with or assessing the situation of the Asháninka in past years, such as UNICEF-Peru, Médecins sans Frontières, and the United Nations Commission on Human Rights,

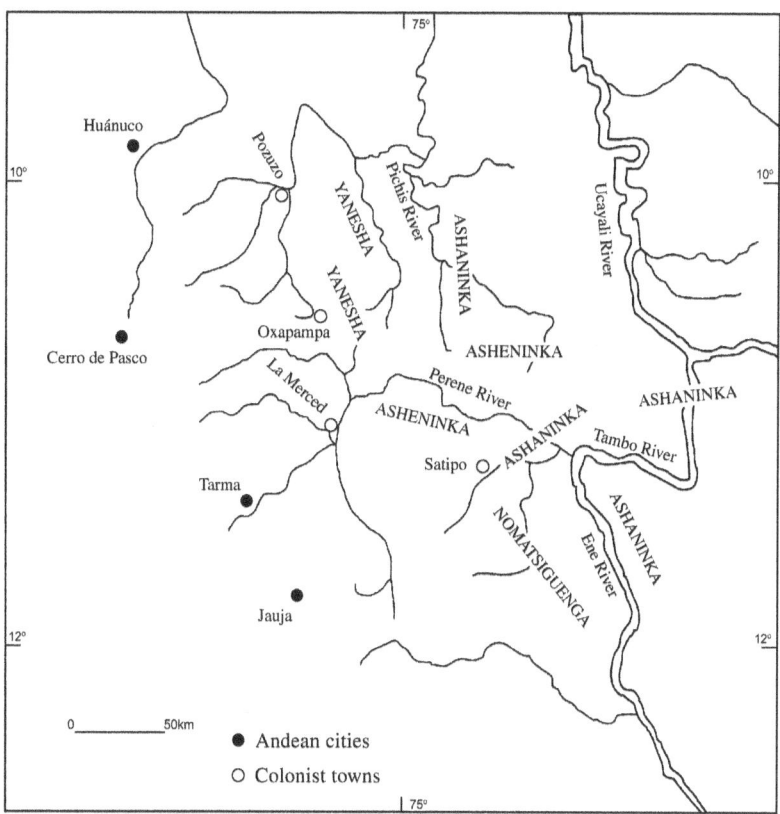

Map 1. The Arawak-speaking peoples of eastern Peru. (Map compiled by author)

do not mention this practice in their public documents. Given their close knowledge of the region, it is difficult to believe that they have been unaware of this phenomenon.

Doubtless, this conspiracy of silence is well intentioned. It aims at averting bad publicity that could prevent Peruvian Arawaks from securing their civil rights in a context in which they have experienced the full impact of terrorist and counterterrorist violence for more than a decade. It is thus with great trepidation that I have decided to write this essay, and I do so with the conviction that it would be worse if this topic were to be exploited by sensationalist journalists. In an insightful essay on the creation of new cultural "traditions" by the Tukano of the Vaupés River basin, Jean Jackson asked the sensitive and very pressing question: "Is there a way to talk about making culture without making enemies?" (1989:127). The challenge for me, as well as for all of the contributors to this volume, is to find ways of talking about cultural practices that are odious to Western sensitivity without

The Enemy Within   273

either making enemies out of those who practice them or providing their enemies with arguments to deny them their rights.

In a previous essay I inquired into the possible origins of the belief in child sorcery among Peruvian Arawaks (Santos-Granero 2002). I argued there that the historical sources lacked all evidence suggesting that Peruvian Arawaks believed in child witchcraft in contact times or during the colonial era. And I proposed that this belief originated in the attempt by Peruvian Arawaks to appropriate mimetically the mystical powers that missionaries attributed to St. Christopher and the Christ child in preventing plagues and epidemics. In this essay, I explore the sociological rather than the ontological aspects of the practice of child sorcery.

Native Beliefs and Rationale

The first reference to Peruvian Arawak child sorcery appeared in 1880 in a report by Franciscan missionary Bernardino González on his sojourn among the Yanesha. In the report he asserts that natives believe that illnesses and deaths are the result of witchcraft, and that they even attribute these afflictions to their own children and closest relatives (see Izaguirre 1922-29: vol. 10, 400). A decade later in 1893, Father Gabriel Sala (1975:438-39) expanded on these beliefs, offering a detailed description of the plight of Yanesha child witches. Later, French diplomat and traveler Olivier Ordinaire, in an account of his 1885 trip from Peru to France through the Amazon, stated that the Asháninka and Ashéninka believe that child sorcerers are responsible for many diseases. Franciscan missionary Tomás Hernández reported similar beliefs in 1896 among the Nomatsiguenga of the Pangoa Valley. Whereas early accounts provide a more or less detailed depiction of the external or visible aspects of the practices surrounding child sorcery, they say very little about the rationale behind them. How do children become sorcerers? Why and how do they bewitch people? Why is it necessary to torture them? Why do accused children accept their fate without resistance? Why, instead of defending them, do their relatives join in the ritual torture and execution? And why are child witches killed and their bodies disposed of in such cruel ways? To answer these questions I shall resort to the scant and fragmentary literature on the subject, complementing it with my own field data on the Yanesha.

The Asháninka and Ashéninka believe that child sorcerers (*matsi, máci,* or *machi*) are initiated in the art of witchcraft during their sleep (Weiss 1975:292). In their dreams, they are visited by any of a number of demonic teachers (*kamári máci*) who are under the orders of Korioshpiri, the "father" or "ruler" of all demons. These demonic teachers, which include birds (cuckoos, nocturnal swallows), insects (grasshoppers, crickets), and the souls of other live or dead human sorcerers, appear to the sleeping child under human guise (Tessmann 1999:51; Weiss 1975:292). The evil spirits of the dead (*shiretzi*) are also reported as possible teachers of witchcraft (Rojas Zolezzi 1994:239). The visiting demons place animal or fish bones, palm-leaf slivers, or other small objects in the child's palm, and then knock them off so that they will get buried in the ground. Once buried, these objects cause somebody to fall ill. Demonic teachers urge the child to bewitch someone, likening victims to edible forest animals. They also give them human flesh to eat so that they develop a taste for it. After repeated visitations from demonic teachers, the targeted children begin to dream that they themselves bury these pathogenic objects. With the passage of time, they lose their human nature and become demonic witches.

The Nomatsiguenga also believe that children may learn witchcraft from a number of demonic teachers, particularly various kinds of birds (Shaver and Dodd 1990:103). Among the Yanesha, it is believed that a child becomes a sorcerer (*amaseñet*) when another adult or child sorcerer rubs her or him with a special plant (Smith 1977:103), or when children paint each other with the juice of the flower of the *ranquëch* tree (species not identified). These substances penetrate into the child's heart, endowing him or her with evil powers. If a shaman does not treat the affected children by sucking these substances out of their bodies, they will inevitably lose their humanity and become demonic sorcerers. I was told that children could also become sorcerers if *aseñac*, the curved-billed hummingbird, flies over them. This bird is considered to be an assistant of Yosoper, the chthonic ruler and master of all demonic beings, and thus it plays an important role in the dissemination of evil (Santos-Granero 1991: 113–14). In addition, both the Yanesha and Asháninka believe that children can learn sorcery directly from active children sorcerers.

What persons are most likely to become, or be accused of having become, *matsi* or *amaseñet*? Among the Palcazu and Pichis Asháninka, the accused were adult women or girls and only very rarely a boy (Ordinaire 1988:93; Elick 1970:212). Other sources claim that both girls and boys could be accused of being sorcerers, although more often than not the accused were little girls (Pérez Marcio 1953:166; Brown and Fernández 1991:152). This is also true for the Pajonal Ashéninka (Rett Bragg, personal communication). In general, sources on the Asháninka and Ashéninka coincide in that the accused was "the most defenseless member of the community, usually a girl child, especially if it is an orphan or captive taken in a raid" (Weiss 1975:292; see also Palomino Arana et al. 1936:513; Uriarte 1982:211). Orphan children accused of sorcery were generally fatherless rather than motherless (Navarro 1924: 24). Among adults, the most vulnerable to accusations of sorcery were women who did not have husbands to defend them (Navarro 1924:24; Torre López 1966:64; Weiss 1975:292).

Among the Yanesha, the accused were mostly "orphans, widows and destitutes" (Batlle 1905:248). One early source states that shamans generally blamed someone "weak and powerless, some poor orphan, who has nobody to defend him or look after him" (Navarro 1967:395). Sources on the Yanesha are not consistent as to gender preferences among children accused of sorcery: some suggest that boys and girls were equally accused (Sala 1975 [1893]:438); others that men, women, and children could be accused, but that more often than not the accused was a girl child (Smith 1977:103–4; Bullón Paucar 1976:152). I was told that both girls and boys could be accused, and the same was reported for the Nomatsiguenga (Shaver and Dodd 1990:103).

Bad-tempered, sulky children were primary targets for accusations of sorcery. Children who were disobedient or disrespectful of adults were also suspected of witchcraft. The same happened, however, with children who stood out because of their pleasantness or sagaciousness (Sala, 1975 [1893]:438). In all these cases the common theme is that these children do not behave as children are expected to do. Although the marked tendency is for children devoid of kinship relations (orphans, war captives) to be accused, one of the most astonishing aspects of Peruvian Arawak child sorcery is that quite often the accused children are close relatives of their victims and even members of their extended households, including biological and classificatory children, siblings and spouses (see Stahl 1932:36; Torre López 1966:64; Weiss 1975:294; Shaver and Dodd 1990:103).

Child witches may, for a certain time, be unconscious of their evil powers, and thus act as such unknowingly. However, most sources suggest that once children induced to learn sorcery become conscious of their powers, they use them purposefully. This is especially true when they become older. It is important to note in this regard that adult women and men accused of sorcery "are understood to have been witches since childhood who somehow escaped detection" (Weiss 1975:292). In other words, although they are adults they fall within the category of child sorcerers. It is also important to keep in mind that child sorcerers—whether actual children or adults—are considered to be different from "professional" sorcerers who have become so during their training as shamans.[4]

Child sorcerers who are still unconscious of their evil powers give vent to them when they become angry with someone. Once conscious of their powers, they can put them to work by reflecting angrily on their victim. For both the Asháninka and the Yanesha, anger, especially when expressed openly and violently toward a relative, is a dangerous feeling; it not only disturbs the balance of power but it also leads to witchcraft (Elick 1970:213; Smith 1977:104; Santos-Granero 1991:101). When child witches are angry at someone, they instruct their demonic helpers to gather bodily secretions (mucus, hair, fingernails), scraps of leftover food (animal and fish bones, manioc fibers, chewed coca leaves), or other objects that have been in close contact with the victim (*chonta*-wood splinters, palm-leaf slivers, thorns, and more recently plastic bags, fishing lines, nails, bottlecaps, broken glass, or small pieces of metal), and bury them in the floor of the victim's house. Child sorcerers may also visit the house of their victims to rob a scrap of food refuse from them or search clandestinely among the garbage surrounding the house to gather a bit of leftover food (Tessmann 1999:51).

The Asháninka and Ashéninka insist that the objects excavated by accused children "are not simply discarded refuse, but rather are found tied or wrapped in a leaf, or otherwise showing evidence of being especially prepared" (Weiss 1975:293). Child witches ritually manipulate and bury these objects. Through notions of "contagious magic" (Frazer 1996:13) the buried objects are thought to enter into the body of the victims and make them ill. Also, the soul of child sorcerers can visit the victim while he or she is asleep and thrust the prepared charm into the victim's body (Tessmann 1999:51). These actions may be accompanied by singing and other ritual operations. Child sorcerers can also direct their "death wish" to cause a poisonous snake to strike the victim (Tessmann 1999: 51; Elick 1970:213).

When someone falls ill, the patient's relatives resort to a friendly shaman (*seripiari*, or *sheripiari* among the Asháninka in general; *pa'llerr* among the Yanesha) to cure him or her. Shamans use a variety of techniques to cure patients, including blowing tobacco smoke over the victims' bodies and sucking from their bodies the pathogenic objects that a variety of nonhuman agents (ants, termites, wasps, stone or salt spirits, demons, and erring shadows) might have introduced into them. If this therapy does not work it indicates that the illness is the product of human witchcraft, so shamans strive to identify the person responsible for sending the evil charm. They do this through divination, consultation with their mystical helpers in dreams and astral voyages, or interpretation of their patients' dreams (Elick 1970:214; Weiss 1975:293; Santos-Granero 1991:103–21). If the child witch belongs to the victim's household, they grab her or him immediately; if not, the victim's kinsmen or warriors designated by the acting shaman assail the household of the person identified as a witch and bring her or him to the patient's house (Elick 1970:214; Stahl 1932:35).

Once the child witch has been detained he or she is subjected to harsh punishments. Such punishments have two objectives: first, to force child sorcerers to reveal where they have hidden the evil charms that have made the patient ill, and, second, to make them cry, because it is believed that by crying they will forget the evil arts they have learned (Weiss 1975:293; Rojas Zolezzi 1994:240). To achieve this hot peppers may be rubbed into their eyes, or they may be hung upside down over a smoking fire or tied on a smoking rack (Sala 1975 [1983]: 438; Eichenberger 1966:122; Shaver and Dodd 1990:103). Accused children are also confined to an attic above a smoking fire in order to make them cry, thus preventing their demonic teachers from finding and helping them. In addition, accused children are starved because they are believed to feed mystically on human flesh (Weiss 1975:293). From time to time the confined children are forced to search for the pathogenic objects they have purportedly buried, digging them out with a stick. While they do this they are beaten with sticks or vines, whipped with stinging nettles, or submerged in water until they almost drown (Torre Lopez 1966:64; Weiss 1975:293; Shaver and Dodd 1990:103). Peruvian Arawaks believe that child sorcerers "are invincible in the face of death, and ... that tortures cannot kill them" (Shaver and Dodd 1990:103). It is precisely because child sorcerers are considered to be no longer human, in fact, that they are tortured in ways that would otherwise be regarded as extremely cruel.

Accused children generally submit without resistance to the demands of their accusers, a fact that has puzzled missionaries and scholars alike. This submission seems to be linked to the widespread belief that child sorcerers may, at least for a while, not be conscious of the powers they possess. In such cases, children accused of being sorcerers do not protest their innocence, for they feel "that the accusation itself constitutes proof that [they] must be what they say" (Elick 1970:214). In fact, neither the intentionality or lack of intentionality of alleged child sorcerers is important; both accusers and accused believe that child sorcerers are under the control of maleficent forces (Torre López 1966:64–65). If accused children do not offer resistance, as is often the case, it is because after repeated accusations they come to believe (and to dream) that they are sorcerers.

The life histories I collected of Yanesha men accused of being sorcerers when they were children indicate that, generally, accused children had already been singled out as potential sorcerers and had a record of minor accusations. Indeed, Yanesha shamans (*pa'llerr*) and priestly leaders (*cornesha'*) held periodic cleansing rituals for children who showed signs (such as hot temper, gloominess, disobedience, and disrespect) of having been introduced into the arts of witchcraft. These rituals included confinement, ingestion of tobacco concentrate and other herbal concoctions to induce vomiting, special diets based on cold, boiled, and saltless foods, vigils, sexual abstinence, and cleansing of the evil substances that turned them into witches.

Equally puzzling is the fact that parents of accused children rarely try to defend them; they can even turn against them with unusual fury. I would argue that this is in part associated with the ideology of kinship. Bewitching someone from another lineage or extended household is a very grave misdemeanor that puts at risk the delicate balance of solidarities that hold together the different households composing a given settlement. But bewitching someone from one's own extended household, let alone one's own parents, is an even graver offense. If the transgressors dared to breach the norm of solidarity among close kin it means that they are, doubtless, under demonic control (Torre López 1966:64). Parents whose children are accused of bewitching someone from another extended family might try to defend him or her, but if the social pressure is too strong and they persist, they risk being killed themselves (Pérez Marcio 1953:168). In contrast, parents whose children are accused of bewitching them or a close relative often reacted violently against the accused.

If the victim improves, the accused child is beaten, ritually cleansed, and released. If the victim dies, the child witch is invariably condemned to death (Stahl 1932:36). The type of execution depends on the wishes of the victims, their relatives, and the acting shamans. Child sorcerers can be bludgeoned (Sala 1975 [1893]:439), garroted (Ordinaire 1988 [1885]:93; Stahl 1932:36), drowned (Pérez Marcio 1953:168), stoned (Bullón Paucar 1976:70), shot with arrows, or burned alive (Navarro 1967:395; Izaguirre 1922–29: vol. 12, 114). They can also be buried head first and face down into an armadillo hole (Weiss 1975: 293), left in the forest tied to a tree to be devoured by jaguars, or covered with honey and tied up naked to a tree close to an anthill (Pérez Marcio 1953:168). The corpses of dead children witches are generally burned and/or disposed of by throwing them into a river.

These extremely cruel and otherwise unusual forms of execution and body disposal are intended, first, to prevent the demonic teachers of the dead children sorcerers to revive them, and, second, to prevent the "shadow soul" of the dead child witch from staying in the area and teaching the art of witchcraft to other children. If the bodies of executed child witches were simply to be thrown into the bush, their mystical helpers could breathe life into them again (Weiss 1975:435). Their souls would join those of their demonic teachers, becoming one of them and eventually teaching other children the art of sorcery (Weiss 1975:293, 437). To destroy children witches in body and soul, the Asháninka not only burned and disposed of their bodies, but also destroyed and burned all their belongings (Uriarte 1982 [1938]:212).

Sources describe the execution of child sorcerers as carried out in the midst of a grand nocturnal celebration—in which large amounts of manioc beer is consumed—that is organized by the relatives of the deceased and the shaman who had treated him or her (Izaguirre 1922–29: vol. 12, 114; Navarro 1967:395; Palomino Arana et al. 1936:513). The objectives of these celebrations are not clear, and the only source that discusses the subject asserts that they celebrate "the death of the innocent [child accused of sorcery], and that of the person who died" (Uriarte 1982:211). In other words, they seem simultaneously to have the traits of a funerary ritual in honor of the deceased and of a cleansing ritual on behalf of the community.

Child witches blamed for the death of a person were not always killed. As a result of increased missionary influence and state presence, beginning in the 1920s some Peruvian Arawaks began to hand over accused child sorcerers to white and Mestizo colonists or to traders in exchange for manufactured goods, such as cloth, pots, machetes, and shotguns (Weiss 1975:293; Brown and Fernández 1991:152). Although this custom saved many lives, it also led to an active trade in children who were treated by their owners as servants and slaves (Palomino Arana et al. 1936:513). To save accused children sorcerers from being executed or sold as slaves, Catholic and Adventist missionaries also became involved in this trade (Gridilla 1942:67; Pérez Marcio 1953:175).

Situating Child Sorcery

Most information on Peruvian Arawak child sorcery is generic; very few actual cases of child sorcery are reported in the literature and those few are quite sketchy. A review of these cases is indispensable, however, to situate this practice in social time and space. I present here three of the most detailed and reliable cases reported in the literature, together with a discussion on the historical circumstances in which each took place. As we shall see, most of these cases took place in contexts of external pressure, violence, epidemics, social disruption, and collective movements of resistance or evasion, often with messianic overtones.

Case 1: María Josefa León, Nomatsiguenga girl of Pangoa, 1896.

In 1896, Domingo, the brother of Churihuanti, chief of the Nomatsiguenga settlement of Pangoa, died of severe stomach pains. The local shaman was called in to identify the witch that was responsible for his death. He blamed María Josefa, a fatherless nine-year-old girl, and condemned her to be shot with arrows or burned alive. After passing this sentence, the relatives of the dead man organized a ritual drinking celebration. At night, while they were celebrating, María Josefa managed to untie herself and escape. She took refuge in the house of a Chinese man who had settled in the colony that had grown around the neighboring Franciscan mission. Alerted of María Josefa's escape, Churihuanti and his followers pursued her. However, the Chinese colonist took the girl to the missionaries, who, in turn, turned her over to colony authorities. Three times Churihuanti, his relatives, and followers went to the colony to demand that the girl be returned to them or that the missionaries kill her. But each time their demands were rejected. This generated great resentment among the local natives. (Reported by Franciscan missionary Bernardino Izaguirre [1922–29: vol. 12, 114–40])

Two years before these events took place the Franciscans had founded a mission and colony close to the Nomatsiguenga settlement of Pangoa (Izaguirre 1922–29: vol. 12, 111–50). By then the Nomatsiguenga knew that, coming from the west, the white men (*viracochas*) had occupied most of the Chanchamayo and Chorobamba valleys, displacing the Ashéninka and Yanesha from their lands; destroying the native ironworks that had functioned since the Spanish were expelled from the region in 1742; taking over the salt mines of the famous Cerro de la Sal; and even removing the remains of Juan Santos Atahuallpa, the charismatic leader of the 1742 uprising, from his tomb and shrine in the uplands of Metraro. They also knew that, from the east, white rubber extractors and their native allies were carrying out raids against the Ashéninka, Asháninka, and Yanesha to procure women and children in order to transform them into sexual slaves, domestic servants, and peons. Nonetheless, the craving for iron tools, firearms, and the mystical powers that had allowed the whites to create, or usurp all the fine things the natives possessed led Churihuanti, the settlement chief, to welcome the missionaries and the fifty Andean families that came with them to cultivate coca, sugar cane, and tropical fruits.

Peace between natives and foreigners lasted a short time. In 1895, the missionaries reprimanded Churihuanti and his people for killing and robbing an Irish miner who had entered the area with the aim of looking for gold. This engendered much resentment among Churihuanti's supporters, who from then onward began to harass the colonists by entering into their houses without invitation, stealing their possessions, and eating their food. The sudden death of Churihuanti's brother in early 1896 took place in this context of deep antagonism. The missionaries' decision to protect María Josefa, the alleged witch, from Churihuanti made matters even worse.

By then, the loyalties of the Nomatsiguenga were divided. The majority supported the aggrieved Churihuanti and his relatives; but a few families sided with the Franciscans. In subsequent weeks tensions mounted, and new conflicts arose between the local Nomatsiguenga and the foreign colonists. Some conflicts ended in killings. Churihuanti attempted to persuade the Nomatsiguenga families loyal to the missionaries to join him, but to no avail. As a result, Churihuanti threatened to kill them and their alien friends. After gathering a party of two hundred warriors from the Perené,

Ubiriqui, Yurinaki, and upper Tambo river valleys, Churihuanti attacked the missionaries and settlers, who together with a group of loyal Nomatsiguenga families had taken refuge in the mission house. The local shaman extended his mystical protection over the confederates, assuring them that the bullets of the foreigners would not injure them; they only had to blow in their direction to turn them into leaves. Although many indigenous warriors were killed in the confrontations that followed, the native alliance defeated the foreigners, forcing them to abandon the region. The fleeing missionaries took María Josefa with them.

The case of María Josefa was not isolated. Late-nineteenth-century sources are full of reports of children accused of being sorcerers. In 1893, Sala (1975 [1893]:439) suggested that epidemics and the killing of child witches were driving the Yanesha to extinction. Carranza (1894:31) noted that the practice of accusing children of causing disease through witchcraft was extensive among the Asháninka. And Izaguirre (1922–29: vol. 12, 146, 158) recounts several instances in which Franciscan missionaries rescued children accused of sorcery among the Asháninka and Ashéninka. Doubtless, then, the 1890s was a period when accusations of child sorcery were common.

Case 2: Conija, Ashéninka girl of Yurinaki, circa 1923.

Around 1923, Comabe, an Ashéninka man living in the settlement of Yurinaki on the confluence of the Yurinaki and Perené rivers, became ill. Comabe had converted to Adventism earlier that same year. When he fell sick, his nonconverted neighbors called Chollaco, the local shaman, to determine who had bewitched him. Chollaco went to Comabe's house and, after drinking manioc beer, chewing coca leaves, consuming tobacco concentrate, and invoking his spirit helpers, he accused Conija, Comabe's daughter, of being the guilty witch. Chollaco appointed the girl's older brother to punish her and force her to unbury the evil charms that had made her father ill. Conija was separated from the rest of the family and locked in the attic, where she was starved and subjected to smoke. From time to time she was forced to go down and dig up the dirt floor with a knife in search for the charms she had allegedly buried to bewitch her father. Throughout these searches she was constantly beaten and insulted. This went on for several days, but because her father increasingly got worse the shaman condemned her to death. By then Conija was extremely thin and weak. Her brother took her to the riverside, bludgeoned her, and threw her body into the river. Because Comabe still did not recover, the shaman repeated his detection ritual. This time he accused the sick man's wife. However, to avoid being tortured,

Comabe's wife hanged herself. Shortly after, during one of his visits to Yurinak, Adventist missionary Ferdinand Stahl cured Comabe, and the latter returned to the Adventist faith. (Reported by Adventist historian Alejandro Bullón Páucar [1976:96-97])

The 1920s was a period of great change and strain for the Yanesha and Ashéninka of the upper Perené River Valley. In 1891, Peru granted British holders of Peruvian bonds one million hectares in this area. By 1920, the British-owned Perené colony had planted 650 hectares of coffee along the left bank of the upper reaches of the Perené River, thus displacing many of the native families that lived there (Barclay 1989:112). Because local natives were considered to be unreliable, the colony depended until 1922 on immigrant Andean laborers (Barclay 1989:121). This situation began to change in 1922, when Adventist missionary Ferdinand Stahl obtained permission from the colony to establish a mission in Metraro.

Stahl was very successful in both attracting the Ashéninka to the mission and in persuading them to work for the colony (Barclay 1989:124). Part of his success was due to the fact that the messianic and apocalyptic elements of Adventist discourse coincided with similar "traditional" Peruvian Arawak beliefs. The site Stahl chose for his mission enhanced even more the messianic appeal of his discourse. Metraro was the place where Juan Santos Atahuallpa—the eighteenth-century messianic leader who, at the head of a multiethnic army, expelled the Spanish from the Selva Central region—established his headquarters. It was also the site where he was buried. His tomb, lodged in a large ceremonial building, had been the object of annual pilgrimages and celebrations until 1891, when his body was disinterred by Peruvian authorities and transferred to the highland town of Tarma (Santos Granero 1992:256).

By the time Stahl settled in Metraro, the Yanesha, Ashéninka, and Asháninka were experiencing strong external pressures. European and Andean colonists had displaced most of the native inhabitants from the valleys of Chanchamayo and Chorobamba and were now advancing downriver along the Perené Valley. Further havoc had been caused four years earlier in 1918 during the pandemics of influenza that swept the world. All these events were taken as signs of the impending end of the world, and Stahl's apocalyptic preaching could have only confirmed this perception. Soon, the Ashéninka identified the missionary as Pawa, the solar divinity, who had come to save them (Bullón Paucar 1976:74). The news that Pawa had arrived spread rapidly throughout the region, frequently preceding Stahl himself.

Stahl's presence and growing success generated conflicts with nonconverted local groups. Sarate, the chief of a large Ashéninka settlement close to the headquarters of the Perené colony and a man renowned for his bravery, became a sworn enemy of Stahl, using his influence to hinder the latter's evangelical efforts (Stahl 1932:53; Bullón Paucar 1976:72–74, 141–47). People in several other settlements were also firmly opposed to his presence (Bullón Paucar 1976:83–85, 139). In fact, by curing Conija's father and persuading him and other settlement members to return to the Adventist faith, Stahl and the converted families gained the enmity of Chollaco, the local shaman, and of his supporters (Bullón Paucar 1976:99–103, 180–81) (see fig. 1).

Despite this opposition, by 1928 Stahl's fame and prophecies regarding Christ's second coming and the imminence of the Last Judgment had extended far beyond the area in which he preached, generating a mass religious transformative movement that, according to Bodley, "promised the total destruction of the White man and the return of a messiah (1970:111). All along the Perené and Tambo rivers, as well as in parts of Pangoa and the Gran Pajonal, the Ashéninka and Asháninka concentrated in large settlements modeled after the mission at Metraro. They stopped using liquor and tobacco and believed that Christ's coming would end in a cataclysmic event during which the earth would be burned and the unbelievers would die—a notion that must have intensified the conflict between converts and nonconverts (Bodley 1970:111).

All these notions led to an increase in the accusations of child witchcraft, as becomes evident from reports by Adventist missionaries and historians (Stahl n.d., 1932; Herndon 1963:127–28). Franciscan missionaries operating in the region during this period also noted this phenomenon (Navarro 1967:391, 394–95; Gridilla 1942:67). In fact, accusations of child sorcery reached such a point at this time that, in 1922, the Catholic Church founded the mission of Puerto Ocopa in the lower Perené River region, with the specific purpose of "rescuing children and youngsters condemned to this sacrifice" (Torre López 1966:83; Ortiz 1978:208–8). By 1927, all thirty-five children in the charge of the Franciscan nuns of Puerto Ocopa were orphans who had been bought from their accusers (Gridilla 1942:67).

> Case 3: Oijani, Asháninka girl of the Perené River, circa 1939.
>
> Around 1939 a man died in an Asháninka settlement close to the Adventist mission of Sutziki on the Perené River. The local shaman identified Oijani, a seven-year-old girl, as the guilty witch. She was described as a beautiful girl whose large, black eyes have a deep gaze that captivates—a sure sign, according to native parameters, that she was a witch. The shaman determined that Oijani should be executed the next day and her body burned. Her father accepted the shaman's verdict. Her mother did not but pretended she did, for she had decided to escape with her daughter to the neighbor-

Figure 1. A photo of Chollaco, an Ashéninka shaman of the settlement of Yurinaki, 1920s. Chollaco was a sworn enemy of the Adventist missionary Ferdinand A. Stahl. He accused a young girl, Conija, of bewitching her father, Comabe, who had converted to Adventism shortly before falling ill. Eventually Chollaco also became Adventist. (Bullón Paucar 1976)

ing Adventist mission of Sutziki. She did not tell her plans to her husband because she was not sure that he would agree with her. That night, Oijani and her mother escaped in a canoe toward Sutziki, seven hours distant downriver by canoe. Shortly after, someone realized that they had escaped and alerted the kinsmen of the dead man. Led by the shaman, a party of forty men composed of the victim's relatives and other members of the settlement went after them. The pursuers overtook the two women when they were landing in the mission; they chased them but were intercepted by converted mission Indians. This allowed the mother to reach the mission house, where she entrusted Oijani to the care of the mission director (see fig. 2). The pursuers threatened the director with convoking a general Indian uprising and setting the mission on fire, but he did not give in, arguing that the child was now his. After two days of threats and negotiations, the pursuers left the mission promising they would come back to fetch Oijani, but they never did. (Reported by Adventist teacher Manuel F. Pérez Marcio [1953:168-75])

Oijani's plight took place during one of the worse periods of Peruvian Arawak history; a period characterized by recurrent epidemics and the deaths of thousands of people. It all started in 1928, the year when Adventist missionary Ferdinand Stahl left the region (Bodley 1970:112). In previous years Stahl's teachings had disseminated by word of mouth throughout the Selva Central, generating a vast transformative movement that was beyond his control. Central to this movement was the spontaneous relocation in large settlements structured like the Adventist mission of Metraro. The most important among these was Las Cascadas, located on the upper Perené River (Bodley 1970:112). The high population density of these settlements favored the spread of measles epidemics and other illnesses (Bodley 1970:115), and in 1928 hundreds of people died along the Perené Valley and adjacent areas —often, entire families were wiped out. Fearful of epidemics and disappointed because "the anticipated transformation failed to occur" (Bodley 1970:114), followers of the movement deserted the messianic settlements.

Beginning in 1929, a new group of Adventist pastors founded three new missions along the Perené River, the largest of which was Sutziki, with the purpose of regrouping families that had been attracted to the 1928 messianic movement (Pérez Marcio 1953:116; Barclay 1989:125). The prosperity of these missions, however, was short-lived. In 1933 the region was again struck by an epidemic of measles that in Sutziki killed 120 out of the 300 inhabitants (Barclay 1989:126). The missionary of Sutziki reported that the Ashéninka and Asháninka believed that the epidemic had been brought by the white men to wipe out the Indians (Barclay 1989:127). A medical doc-

Figure 2. A photo of Oijani, an Asháninka girl of the Perené River, and the Adventist missionary who saved her, circa 1939. After being accused of having bewitched a man, Oijani was saved from execution by her mother, who took her to the neighboring Adventist mission of Sutziki. (Pérez Marcio 1953)

tor working in the area at the time reported that the epidemic killed many adults, and that following indigenous practices this resulted in an explosive increase in accusations of child sorcery (Pinto, cited in Ortiz 1978:197). Many accused children, he asserts, sought refuge in the mission of Sutziki.

The Ashéninka and Asháninka reacted in the face of the epidemic by mounting a violent nativist movement against the British settlers of the Perené colony, the Adventist missionaries, and the indigenous converts (Barclay 1989:127). Those in the Perené Valley simply stopped working for the British colony, and the missionary of Sutziki was forced to flee. The Ashéninka attacked the mission, killing many converts (Barclay 1989:127). They also threatened to attack the air base of San Ramón, built in 1928, presumably because they believed that the white men had brought the disease by plane. The killing of child witches spread like fire throughout the region. The missionary of Sutziki reported: "As a consequence of the epidemic, groups of savages kill the sick and the unprotected infants they find along the river banks" (Barclay 1989:127).

In 1937 new outbreaks of malaria affected the Chanchamayo Valley and the upper Perené region, resulting in extremely high mortality: 2,281 died in 1937 and 2,382 in 1938 (Ortiz 1969: vol. 1, 543). Many of the deceased were native people. In December of that same year a massive earthquake was felt throughout the entire region, causing many deaths and injuring many people (Ortiz 1967: vol. 1, 450). This catastrophe was followed by a new epidemic of measles in 1939 (Ortiz 1978: 196). The accusation of Oijani took place in this context. There is little information on the 1939 epidemic, but we know that accusations of child sorcery increased as on previous occasions. Not surprisingly, the Adventist mission of Sutziki and the Catholic mission of Puerto Ocopa became, in the early 1940s, a refuge for numerous accused children, who became known as *los salvados de la muerte*, or "those saved from death" (see fig. 3) (Pérez Marcio 1953: 175).

Child Sorcery at Present

The subject of present-day Peruvian Arawak child sorcery has been shrouded in silence, but a few cases have been reported by professionals working with Peruvian Arawak communities and some have appeared into the national press. I have chosen the following three cases because they depict very different situations. All took place among the Asháninka of the Tambo River area, but it must be noted that the rise in accusations of child witchcraft has also been reported among the Yanesha of the Palcazu basin, the Asháninka of the Pichis and Satipo valleys, and the Ashéninka of the Gran Pajonal uplands.[5]

Figure 3. *Los salvados de la muerte*, Peruvian Arawak children accused of being sorcerers, pose with Adventist missionaries in the 1940s. Children accused of being sorcerers sometimes sought refuge in Adventist missions; on other occasions Adventist missionaries saved them from execution by exchanging them for metal goods. (Pérez Marcio 1953)

Case 4: José and Isaías, Asháninka boys of P. [placename withheld], 1994.

In 1994 two "recovered" (*recuperados*) Asháninka boys who lived in P., a refuge community along the Tambo River valley, were accused of being sorcerers. They and their parents were under the control of Shining Path for eight years, then were rescued by the Asháninka self-defense forces and resettled in P. When they arrived in the community they took lodging with some relatives, but soon afterwards they quarreled with their hosts who accused their guests' children of being witches. As a result, the family moved out and started living on its own. By then the word had spread that they were all *terrucos* ("terrorists"). One day, José, the eldest son who was twelve years old, and his eight-year-old brother, Isaías, were found in the central plaza of the community singing Shining Path revolutionary songs while drawing with a stick in the dirt the communist sickle-and-hammer emblem. They were doing this in the midst of a group of local children. The two boys were reported to the president of the community and the lieutenant governor. Because they had been accused of sorcery in the past, and because their activities resembled the ritual operations of children sorcerers, who bury their evil charms in the dirt with a stick or draw magic symbols on the ground with sticks, the authorities accused them of bringing "bad habits" into the community—namely, teaching sorcery and "dirty politics" to the local children. The authorities handed over the boys to the local *ronda* (Self-defense Committee), and the *ronderos* beat the children and their parents. After doing so, they expelled the family from the community. (Compiled from reports in Fabián Arias 1995:165; Fabián Arias and Espinosa de Rivero 1997:40; and Beatriz Fabián Arias, personal communication)

Case 5: Silverio Paredes Imposhito, Asháninka boy of M. [place-name withheld], 2000.

In October 15, 2000, Silverio Paredes Imposhito, a twelve-year-old Asháninka boy of the native community of M., on the Tambo River, was found guilty of stealing 300 soles (approximately US$100) belonging to the community's health center. Silverio, his mother, his maternal grandfather, and his four younger siblings—each from a different father—had arrived in M. some years earlier, escaping from the violence that had afflicted their community. The boy was very bright and always said that he wanted to go to high school once he finished elementary school. Since his arrival, however, there had been several petty thefts. In three cases, the fatherless Silverio had been singled out as the thief and punished accordingly. Because of his recurrent misdeeds, people began to regard him as a possible child sorcerer. In October 14, when it was found out that the community's money was missing, the local authorities demanded in a public assembly that whoever had stolen the money should return it. Next day 200 soles appeared in the health center. The authorities suspected Silverio, who, they found out, had given 12 soles to a little boy, telling him that a third party had given him the money to deliver it to the little boy's mother. At dawn on October 16 the chief of the community, the lieutenant governor, and the health officer, together with the president and several members of the local Self-defense Committee, captured Silverio. He was pressed to confess. Because he refused, they tied him to a tree where there was a nest of *tangarana* stinging ants. Fifteen minutes later, Silverio confessed his crime, saying that he had robbed the money so as to be able to go to high school. The authorities untied him and took him to his home, where he said he had hidden the remaining missing money. But after searching in vain, Silverio passed out and never regained consciousness. He died next morning, on October 17. (Compiled from accounts in *El Comercio*, November 3–4, 2000; Expediente 2000; and oral sources)

Case 6: Simón, Asháninka man of S. [placename withheld], 2001.

In 2001, Valerio, the chief of the community of S. on the Ene River, fell ill. He immediately suspected that the sorcerer responsible for his illness was his neighbor, Simón, with whom he had recently quarreled over land issues. The inhabitants of S. had asked the government to recognize their settlement as a "native community" and to provide them with communal land titles. Simón, who was a "displaced" (*desplazado*) man from a community along the Tambo River valley, opposed this move. He declared publicly that he did not want to "live in community," thus prompting suspicions that he sympathized with Shining Path, which had taken a similar political stance against the government-sponsored juridical figure of *comunidades nativas*. In order to determine who had bewitched him, Valerio sought the services of the local shaman. The latter confirmed his suspicions. He told him that Simón had made him ill by hiding an evil charm in a tree hole. The chief's relatives then abducted Simón. They believed that the Ministry of Agriculture, which was reluctant to grant land titles to the community, had persuaded Simón to bewitch the chief. They beat him and then submerged him in the river repeatedly to make him confess that this was the case. Because Simón did not confess, some proposed that they should kill him. However, to avoid reprisals from the police they decided instead to expel him from the community. (Reported by Santiago Concoricón, Asháninka mayor of the Río Tambo district, personal communication)

These three cases took place in the context of extreme violence created by several forces: the insurgent activities of Shining Path and the Túpac Amaru Revolutionary Movement, (MRTA), the counterinsurgent actions of police and military forces, and the illegal activities of powerful gangs of drug traffickers. Below, I offer an abridged account of the situation in the Ene and Tambo river valleys, where the cases given above took place. It should be noted, however, that similar conditions have held during the past fifteen years in other areas inhabited by Peruvian Arawaks.

The Communist Party of Peru, most commonly known as Shining Path, began its military activities in 1980 in the highland department of Ayacucho. When in 1982 the police and, later on the army, began to put pressure on the insurgents in the Andes, they took refuge in the Asháninka territory along the Apurimac and Ene river valleys. At first they used the region as a temporary refuge area. Later on, they decided to settle more permanently and transform the region into a "liberated zone" where they could train recruits and provision themselves, and from where they could attack strategic targets in the rest of the country. They found support among the Andean colonists who in 1979 had begun to settle in these valleys, displacing the local Asháninka population from their lands.

In 1983 Colombian drug dealers also entered the area and began recruiting Andean colonists and local Asháninka to cultivate coca. To put an end to the opposition by the Franciscan missionary of Cutivireni, drug traffickers burned down the mission, including its church, in 1984 (Gagnon 1993:81). Shining Path took advantage of this situation and positioned itself as an intermediary between traffickers and local producers. This strategy succeeded. By 1985, Shining Path had struck an alliance with local drug dealers to secure permanent funding and arms (Hvalkof 1994:24). That same year, both groups consolidated their hold over the area and closed navigation along the Ene River. To increase their control, the insurgents forbade the local Asháninka to travel to the nearby valley of Satipo to work in the coffee plantations; they also forbade them to cultivate cash crops, such as coffee and fruit, and forced them to concentrate in the production of food staples. This created much resentment in some Asháninka communities, which saw their few sources of cash income disappear. In 1986, Shining Path began to expand its activities to the Asháninka settlements located along the Tambo River.

The modus operandi of Shining Path in the Ene/Tambo area was based on five steps: incursions to sack missions and projects promoted by nongovernmental organizations or rich merchants; indoctrination of the native population through community meetings; recruitment through persuasion or force of young men and children to train them ideologically and militarily in "popular schools"; creation of dispersed military camps composed of native militia and support personnel under orders of Shining Path commanders; and establishment of "support bases" and "open popular committees" grouping people from several military camps and native communities (Espinosa de Rivero 1995:121).

At first, the revolutionary political discourse put forth by Shining Path attracted many Asháninka. By calling for the destruction of the exploitative "old order" and announcing the advent of a more-just "new order" in which the Asháninka were to become "millionaires," the discourse by Shining Path shared many elements with native messianic myths—particularly with that announcing the return of Itomi Pawá, the son of the solar divinity, to this earth to bring justice and welfare to the Asháninka (Rodríguez Vargas

1993:53). Members of Shining Path intentionally underlined these similarities and even adopted shamanistic practices reminiscent of previous nativist movements. Thus, for instance, native witnesses report that in Shining Path camps they were fed soup containing scraps of metal, and that they were told that this would make them impervious to the bullets of the army (Fabián Arias and Espinosa de Rivero 1997:34).

Shining Path encouraged the dissolution of native communities (under the pretext that they were a remainder of the "old state") and their replacement by support bases. By 1989, the movement had managed to create fifty-seven support bases, each composed of two hundred to three hundred people, organized in five open popular committees (Fabián Arias and Espinosa de Rivero 1997:33). Life in these bases was strictly structured and disciplined. Shining Path columns were divided into "leaders" (*mandos*) and "mass" (*masa*). The leaders, mostly individuals of Andean descent, made all decisions and determined what could or could not be done; the mass, composed mainly of natives, was supposed to carry out unquestioningly subsistence and military activities. Shining Path commissars distributed tasks, imposed schedules, organized meetings, and established vigilance turns. They ruled camp life under the model of "three self-criticisms and fourth execution." Those who manifested discontent, dared to dissent, or attempted to escape were punished; if they persisted, they were killed. As a result of war, malnutrition, epidemics, suppression of dissenters, and political purges, many native people died in Shining Path camps (Espinosa de Rivero 1994:16–17).

In 1989, the army began a large military offensive in Ayacucho against Shining Path. The insurgents retreated into the Ene and Tambo valleys. By then it had become apparent to Shining Path leaders that the Asháninka were not natural allies and had little revolutionary potential. Thus, they escalated the forced recruitment of Asháninka men, and increased suppression of those communities that were reluctant to cooperate. To crush all local opposition, Shining Path attacked the local Asháninka federations—the Organización Asháninka del Río Ene (OCARE) and the Central Asháninka del Río Tambo (CART)—which they had attempted, unsuccessfully, to infiltrate. In November 1989, they killed three leaders of OCARE, including its long-time president, Isaías Charete, and one of the victims was crucified.

By 1990, Shining Path had achieved control of the whole Apurimac-Ene-Tambo river axis. As a consequence, fifty-one out of the sixty-six native communities that existed in this area disappeared as such (Espinosa de Rivero 1994:4). By then, however, the movement's authoritarian ways had alienated the sympathies of most Asháninka. In July 1990, CART decided to organize its own self-defense forces. Shortly after, three of its leaders were kidnapped and killed by Shining Path, marking the beginning of a general

Tambo Asháninka uprising. In only two months the Asháninka managed to push the insurgents upriver, beyond the community of Poyeni, which then became the boundary between the upper Tambo River, controlled by Shining Path, and the lower Tambo, controlled by the Asháninka. The Tambo River communities agreed to contribute a fixed monthly quota of men to the garrison of Poyeni to keep watch over the border and raid Shining Path camps to liberate their brethren.

These actions were all carried out without intervention of the army. However, in taking advantage of the new situation the army established military bases from 1991 to 1994 in the communities of Puerto Prado, Otika and Poyeni (Tambo River), Cutivireni, Valle Esmeralda and Kiteni (Ene River), and Puerto Ocopa (Perené River). From 1991 onward, the Asháninka self-defense committees initiated a counteroffensive against Shining Path in coordination with the army. In three years, the Asháninka self-defense forces managed to liberate around four thousand of the ten thousand Asháninka that were thought to be under the direct control of Shining Path (Fabián Arias and Espinosa de Rivero 1997:31). By 1995, the "displaced," "recovered," or "repentant" (*arrepentidos*) Asháninka population increased to around eight thousand.

Most displaced Asháninka sought refuge in the seven garrisoned communities or in the Tambo River communities that managed to retain their freedom. These refuge communities became heavily populated super-communities known as *núcleos poblacionales*, or "population nuclei." Because many young and adult men had died in the armed struggle or were still under control of Shining Path, a large part of the population was made up of broken families: widows, single mothers, and children, often orphans under twelve, who together composed up to 80 percent of the population of refuge communities (Rodríguez Vargas 1993:100). High population densities generated conflicts over land and women, aggravating the depletion of local natural resources and malnutrition. Density has also favored the spread of contagious diseases (diarrhea, skin rashes, tuberculosis), as well as recurrent epidemics of cholera, measles, and dengue. The cholera epidemics of 1991–1992 killed dozens of people in refuge communities, thereby inducing entire families to flee deep into the forest.

Life in refuge communities is as highly regimented as in Shining Path camps, inspiring deep rejection among the displaced Asháninka who have managed to escape from Shining Path control. Other conflicts between local and refugee populations spring from the fact that refugees came mainly from remote interior communities, whereas local populations in refuge communities are among the most integrated. As a result, locals consider refugees as less "civilized" than themselves, whereas refugees dislike and reject the foreign "civilized" mores of the locals. But, above all, locals suspect that refugees may be acting as spies for the insurgents. Consequently, refugees are constantly watched over, constrained in movement, discriminated against, insulted, and harassed.

The situation of violence in the region has decreased in recent years. Although the Asháninka and the army have not been able to totally suppress Shining Path, the number of attacks has been reduced to a minimum. However, the impact that two decades of violence has had over the Asháninka population is still discernible in the deep divisions that scar Asháninka society.

The Enemy Within

Accusations of child sorcery intensify during periods of great social disruption caused by external pressures over native lands, resources, labor, and bodies, but also over native cultural representations, values, and practices. These are times of violence and turmoil. Native people are displaced by force from their lands; they see their families separated, their landscape transformed by alien economic practices, their ironworks, health centers, and development projects destroyed; their shrines, sacred places, and churches desecrated; and their trading networks interrupted. These are also times of rapid economic change witnessed by the adoption of new tools and technologies, the prohibition to carry out certain productive activities, or the impossibility of practicing normal subsistence tasks. Changes in the sexual division of labor also occur as a result of new market activities, the demands of a war economy, or the adoption of new social mores. And changes in religious beliefs, political ideologies, and worldviews follow thereafter.

Above all, social disruption brings times of massive deaths, with entire families and even whole settlements wiped out by epidemics of influenza, malaria, measles, dengue, and cholera. Times when the sick are abandoned by their relatives with a little food to eat or are killed by locals fearing contagion when they escape to other communities; and when swarms of agonizing people crawl to the river banks in search for water to quench their thirst or cool down their bodies burning with fever. Times also when native people die in military confrontations with foreigners, often under very uneven conditions: bows and arrows against rifles, shotguns against machine guns. Times, in fact, when the dead are so numerous that it becomes impossible for survivors to bury them, and they end up being eaten by carrion birds or buried hastily in mass graves.

As unspeakable and disruptive as these externally induced circumstances are, however, they do not account fully for the escalation of accusations of child sorcery. Following Brown (1991), I suggest that Peruvian

Arawak child sorcery, like Amerindian millenarian movements, cannot be considered to be a simple response to external conditions—namely, colonial or neocolonial domination. Instead, child sorcery is intimately linked to the deep internal social fractures that develop when different positions and strategies are taken with respect to the presence of foreign agents.

A quick review of the cases I outlined above shows that accusations of child witchcraft always proliferate in contexts of internal conflicts between those who support and those who oppose the new faiths, dogmas, political ideologies, and forms of knowledge introduced by foreign, mostly white, "modernizing" agents.[6] As different in aims, methods, and rationales as they are, the activities of Franciscan missionaries, Adventists pastors, Shining Path or MRTA commandos, and state officials all have the effect of polarizing native peoples into defenders and opponents of modernization and change. In fact, the written evidence suggests that reaction with respect to these agents of change has often been pendular, with an initial phase of receptiveness, hope, and acceptance followed by a phase of disappointment, hostility, and open rejection. This is clearly what happened to Churihuanti and his followers in the 1890s, to those who converted to Adventism in the 1920s, or to those who voluntarily joined Shining Path or the MRTA in the 1980s. In all these cases, the option to modernize and the hope for a better life promised by the new faiths, dogmas, orthodoxies, and forms of knowledge brought in by the foreigners was followed by "traditionalist" backlashes calling for the defense of the status quo.[7]

I put "traditionalist" in quotes because, in each occasion, the defended status quo is dangerously similar to the utopias promoted by foreigners in the immediately preceding period. Churihuanti and his allies were probably angered when Peruvian authorities removed Juan Santos Atahuallpa's remains from his Metraro shrine. But the eighteenth-century Juan Santos was himself a foreigner who advocated hybrid beliefs and cultural practices combining Christian, Andean, and Amazonian motifs. The Catholic Asháninka of the Ene River became furious when drug traffickers and Shining Path burned down the chapel of Cutivireni, crucifying one of their leaders and forbidding them to carry out salaried activities. But, in the past, their ancestors had burned down Franciscan mission posts and had resisted attempts at involving them in market activities. Similarly, the Adventist and Evangelical Asháninka of the Tambo, Perené, and Pichis rivers opposed Shining Path and the MRTA for their antireligious discourse, their attempts to dismember the native communities created in 1974, and their restrictions against growing cash crops. But their ancestors frequently opposed the Adventist and Evangelical missionaries and rejected the legal notion of native communities because it threatened the unity of their ethnic territory. In brief, elements that in each past era were conceived of as symbols of oppression and of threatening change become in subsequent eras symbols of identity, ethnic cohesion, political autonomy, and cultural pride.

Historical evidence shows that, confronted with new ideas and cultural practices, many Peruvian Arawaks embraced change in the belief that it would improve their lives. The cases discussed above also show that, frequently, the accused children belonged to families aligned with foreigners or manifested a personal inclination for all things foreign. María Josefa's family was probably one of the first to support the Franciscans. The fact that she had a Christian name and sought refuge among the foreigners suggests that at the time when she was accused she had already been baptized and was familiar with the foreigners. Conija's family had recently converted to Adventism. We are told, however, that the new faith was still not firmly implanted in Yurinaki, and that many—including Chollaco, the local shaman—opposed it. Finally, Oijani's mother seems to have been receptive to Adventist preaching; otherwise we cannot understand her decision to take her daughter to the mission of Sutziki in opposition to her husband's wishes and at the risk of her own life.

Contemporary instances of child sorcery accusations are no different. The two Tambo Asháninka boys were recovered children; children whose families had joined—we do not know whether voluntarily or forcefully—the Shining Path movement, and were still fond of guerrilla songs and symbols. Silverio was also a child displaced by violence; his constant thefts proved, in the eyes of community members, that he had been badly influenced by Shining Path. In addition, he manifested an excessive craving for Western formal education, a craving that led him to steal the 300 *soles* that led to his death. Finally, by refusing to incorporate himself into the community, the displaced Simón proved his neighbors right in suspecting that he was a supporter of Shining Path, with its adamant opposition to the legal construct of "native communities." By attempting to obtain individual titles for his lands, Simón was also seen to support the ministry of Agriculture. At the time, the Ministry advocated a modernizing neoliberal agenda that sought to impose private property as the main form of property in rural Peru.

Professionals working in refuge communities in the Tambo and Ene river valleys assert that children and adults accused of sorcery "were frequently refugees that had fled from Shining Path camps" (Fabián Arias and Espinosa de Rivero 1997:83). A leader of the Asháninka Emergency Commission told me that the Tambo and Ene Asháninka believe that most refugees became sorcerers while living in Shining Path camps deep in the forest, where the evil spirits of sorcery abound. Anthropologists, social workers, and other professionals working in the Pichis River valley have informed me that during the 1989 Asháninka uprising against the MRTA, people who supported the Asháninka Army took advantage of the situation by killing many women and children reputed to be sorcerers—most of whom were widows and their daughters who sympathized with, or supported, the MRTA.

In contrast with the past, it is not necessary at present to actually bewitch someone to be accused of being a sorcerer. Other types of evil doings, such as stealing communal funds, teaching "dirty politics" to local children, or supporting anticommunity political initiatives are considered to be equally grave offenses. The common denominator of all these acts is that they are antisocial; they threaten the integrity of the bodies of individual Arawak men and women or that of the body politic as a whole. Child sorcerers infringe on the mandate that solidarity must exist among close kin; they bring in epidemics, they subvert the children of the collectivity by transmitting alien ideas, and they deprive the community of its resources. But above all they contaminate the collectivity by resorting to, passing on, and letting loose a wide range of evil powers. It is because of this that child sorcerers are perceived as the "enemy within," the rotten apple that infects the crate. Accordingly, they must be cleansed; if this is impossible, or if it fails, they must be purged.[8]

In the past, only shamans—acting out their dark side—were entitled to identify child witches; at present they share this prerogative with other, more secular, authorities. Periods of intensification of accusations of child sorcery among Peruvian Arawaks resemble "witch-hunts" in the broad sense; that is, an intensive searching out and harassment of those who hold unpopular views. Witch-hunts take place in contexts of rapid social change, social disruption, and personal stress (Schoeneman 1996). In this context, accusations can be derived either from ideological conflicts affecting the society as a whole, or from interpersonal conflicts induced by social change. Witch-hunts are always aimed at maintaining the existing social order or power structure. They are led either by those who want to preserve the status quo and orthodoxy vis-à-vis threatening new ideologies and mores, or by those who, having imposed a new orthodoxy and status quo, want to eradicate all vestiges of the old, competing orthodoxy. The persecution of Christians accused of all kinds of crimes and misfortunes during Roman times exemplifies the former situation; the hounding out of pagans once the Roman emperors had become Christian, and Christianity became the state's religion, exemplifies the latter situation.

In either case, the objective is to cleanse and purify society from individuals or groups that are perceived as polluting it: either "others" as specific subgroups that differ culturally from mainstream society or as categories of people who belong to mainstream society but who have become "others" in the eyes of their own people by virtue of their acts or thoughts. German and Russian Jews, Spanish Moors, central European Gypsies, and American Japanese exemplify, in different times and places, the first type of situation; witches in sixteenth-century Europe, clerics during the Mexican Revolution, kulaks under Stalin, and communists in the United States in the 1950s exemplify the second type. These others are singled out as responsible for the social, cultural, economic, and political crises afflicting their societies, either because they champion new subversive ideas or because they cling to old values and beliefs. They are enemies within, not only because they are perceived as being essentially different—generally "less than human"—but, above all, because they embrace different ideas and ideologies. Let us remember that Hitler pursued Jews not only because he considered them to be the antithesis of the Aryan race but, more important, because they were supposed to be communists plotting the destruction of the German state.

Child sorcerers fall into the second, and worse, type of others: people like us who have become others in disguise, and who for this reason are all the more dangerous. The ritual execution, or expulsion, of child witches, and the ritual celebrations surrounding these acts, seek to purge society of undesirable subversives. On the one hand they are meant to destroy child sorcerers in body and soul, obliterating all trace of them from the face of the earth. On the other hand, they have the character of an expiatory sacrifice aimed at "controlling the evil" and "disarming the forces of chaos" let loose by them (Torre López 1966:83–84). In brief, the ritual executions of child sorcerers are what we could call "rituals of identity"; rituals aimed not only at eliminating the dangerous others and the evil powers that threaten society, but also at bridging the social fractures induced by social change and restoring a sense of uncontested self-identity.

Whereas witch-hunts in Cameroon (Geschiere 1997), South Africa (Comaroff and Comaroff 1999), and Zambia (Colson 2000) are about occult economies and the mystical struggle between the old and the young to obtain the magical powers that will ensure them a portion of the riches promised by globalization, modernity, and millennial capitalism, Peruvian Arawak child sorcery is still about fighting revolutionary utopias and the evils of modernization. By directing their accusations toward children and women belonging to families that had embraced change, or who themselves manifested an inordinate interest in the new ideologies and modes of behavior, Peruvian Arawak shamans and leaders sought to contain change. Thus, selective accusations of child witchcraft can be seen as forms of social control and defense of existing power relations; namely those linking village headmen and local shamans to their constituencies or clienteles.

This in no way means that I support an interpretation à la Gluckman (1955) or Douglas (1970), for whom witchcraft accusations act as conservative mechanisms ensuring the preservation and reproduction of the status quo. On the contrary, following Thomas Schoeneman, I suggest that witch-hunts are self-defeating. As witch hunters "work to expunge the menace and maintain the incumbent power structure, [they] change the culture and its internal relationships" (Schoeneman 1996). Among Peruvian Arawaks, accusations of child sorcery seem to be aimed at families or kindred groups that, because they have little power within their settlements, ally themselves to foreign agents of change in an effort to gain leverage against current holders of political power. By concentrating their accusations on those who have embraced change, witch hunters deepen existing social and ideological fractures. They induce pendular reactions, with phases of witch-hunt and rejection of change followed by phases of openness to change and rejection of traditional values and practices. It is through this social and ideological historical dynamic that Peruvian Arawak child sorcery constantly engenders social change. As a consequence of these pendular changes, the defended status quo of today is exceedingly similar to the utopias promoted by foreigners in the immediately preceding period: the accused of today become the accusers of tomorrow; whereas the innovators of today become the diehard conservatives of tomorrow.[9]

Notes

I would not have been able to write this essay without the support of many persons who trusted me by providing information on the very sensitive issue of child sorcery. I particularly wish to thank Beatriz Fabián Arias, the first person to report the reappearance of accusations of child sorcery among the Tambo Asháninka, who was very generous with her time and information; Lucy Trapnell, who shared with me her extensive knowledge of the Perené Ashéninka and Pichis Asháninka, and took time to answer my many questions on the subject; and the Asháninka leaders—Jude Jumanga, Miqueas Sanchoma, and Sebastián Martínez of the Asháninka Emergency Commission, and Santiago Contoricón, mayor of the district of Río Tambo—who were extremely candid, sharing with me their concern about the recent intensification of accusations of child sorcery. I would also like to thank Frederica Barclay, Oscar Espinosa de Rivero, Leslie Villapolo, Blanca Reyna Izaguirre, Evangelical missionary Rett Bragg, Father Teodorico Castillo and Mother Leonilda and Mother Viviana of the mission of Puerto Ocopa, and Judges Carlos Leiva and Pedro Gonzalez of Satipo for their invaluable help. Finally, I would like to thank Olga F. Linares, who, as always, improved my English.

1 For practical reasons, I will refer to these four Arawak groups as Peruvian Arawaks. The two Peruvian Arawak peoples of eastern Peru among whom child sorcery has not been reported are the Machiguenga of the upper Urubamba River and the upper Madre de Dios River, and the Yiné, or Piro, of the lower Urubamba River.

2 Whether this lack of information indicates that the belief in child sorcery was abandoned, had simply subsided, or was concealed from the eyes of outsiders is now open to question. Anthropologist Lucy Trapnell (personal communication) told me that many years after she did fieldwork in an Ashéninka community located in the upper

Perené River she found out that, at the time that she lived there (1976), two boys had been accused of being sorcerers and were constantly harassed by their accusers. Similarly, many years after she worked in an Asháninka community in the Pichis River valley she was told that while she was there (1979) a boy accused of sorcery had been executed. Also, anthropologists Soren Hvalkof and Hanne Veber (personal communication) affirm that the practice of killing child witches has persisted among the Ashéninka of the Gran Pajonal during the past decades.

3 I use the terms "child sorcery" and "child witchcraft" interchangeably, for I argue that Evans-Pritchard's (1980:227-28) distinction between "sorcerer" and "witch," based on his Azande material, does not apply here.

4 Men (but not women) can also become sorcerers during their training as shamans, when in dreams they are drawn toward evil by a variety of demonic agents (see Santos-Granero 1991:114). Peruvian Arawaks distinguish this type of sorcerer from those initiated as children by asserting that the former are "professional" sorcerers; that is, specialists to whom one may resort to inflict mystical harm on one's enemies in exchange for some kind of payment.

5 Lucy Trapnell (personal communication) told me that accusations of child sorcery have greatly increased in the 1990s in the Pichis River valley. In 1995, in a community located in this area, a five-year-old girl was accused of bewitching her mother; when her mother died, she was executed and buried with her, with the consent of her father. Evangelical missionary Rett Bragg (personal communication) informed me that the notion that grave illnesses are caused by child sorcerers—mostly young girls—is widespread among the Pajonal Ashéninka. In 1996, an Ashéninka girl was accused of being a witch and was punished by having her eyes rubbed with hot-pepper juices. Anthropologist Frederica Barclay (personal communication) told me that accusations of child witchcraft have reappeared among the Yanesha in the past decade. In 2000, leaders of the Federación de Comunidades Nativas Yanesha (FECONAYA) were asked to mediate in at least two cases of child witchcraft.

6 This is valid for periods of intensification of accusations of child sorcery. During intermediate periods, when accusations decrease, the nature of the conflicts that give rise to them seems to differ substantially. I suspect that the differences in the kinds of persons accused during periods of intensification or decline in accusations is also related to the dominant mode of identifying child witches: whether through divination rituals in charge of shamans or through patient's dreams. I plan to examine these issues in a future essay.

7 In fact, whenever the activities of foreign agents have threatened the status quo, Peruvian Arawaks have rapidly coalesced into large military confederations to drive them out, as manifested in the uprisings against the Franciscans (1896), the Adventists (1933), the MRTA (1989), and the Shining Path (1990) (see, for example, Renard-Casevitz 2002).

8 At present, cases like that of Silverio are rare. Children accused of sorcery are mostly given away, as if they were orphans, to local nonnative families or to nongovernmental organizations devoted to the protection of orphans and other children displaced by situations of violence (Fabián 1995:165). In other cases, child witches have been given away to Catholic and Adventist missionaries or to the authorities of nearby military bases, again as if they were orphans. Most of the accused children are removed from their communities by native authorities or traditional leaders who are more ac-

quainted and have more contacts with members of the national society. Some of these authorities charge a certain amount of money for each child they hand to individual families in the cities of Satipo, La Merced, Huancayo, and Lima. Parents of accused children offer little resistance to the removal of their children, but in some cases they have joined efforts to inquire about the fate of their child among the missionary organizations and military authorities to whom they were handed. Some of the alleged children witches have returned to their communities after a few years. In general, however, returnees have had problems reincorporating into their communities both because community members are suspicious of their activities and because during the time they were away they adopted foreign mores and values. More often than not returnees end up moving to other communities where it is not known that they had been accused of sorcery.

9 This is certainly the case with the Adventist Asháninka and Yanesha. Whereas in the 1920s and 1930s they were the main targets of accusations of child witchcraft, at present they support the elimination or expulsion of children suspected of having become sorcerers while under the influence of Shining Path and the MRTA. To justify their position they cite the Bible precept that states "do not allow a sorceress to live" (Exodus 22:18).

References

Amich, José. 1975 [1854]. *Historia de las misiones del convento de Santa Rosa de Ocopa.* Lima: Milla Batres.

Barclay, Frederica. 1989. *La colonia del Perené: Capital inglés y economía cafetalera en la configuración de la región de Chanchamayo.* Iquitos: Centro de Estudios Teológicos de la Amazonía.

Batlle, Antonio. 1905. "Memoria de la Prefectura Apostólica de San Francisco del Ucayali." In *Colección de leyes, decretos, resoluciones i otros documentos oficiales referentes al departamento de Loreto,* ed. C. Larrabure i Correa. Vol. 9: 245-48. Lima: Oficina Tipográfica de La Opinión Nacional.

Bodley, John H. 1970. "Campa Socio-Economic Adaptation." Ph.D. diss., University of Oregon.

———. 1972. A Transformative Movement among the Campa of Eastern Peru. *Anthropos* 67: 220-28.

Brown, Michael F. 1991. "Beyond Resistance: A Comparative Study of Utopian Renewal in Amazonia." *Ethnohistory* 38 (4): 388-413.

Brown, Michael F., and Eduardo Fernández. 1991. *War of Shadows: The Struggle for Utopia in the Peruvian Amazon.* Berkeley: University of California Press.

Bullón Paucar, Alejandro. 1976. *El nos amaba: La aventura misionera de Stahl entre los Campas.* Lima: Talleres Gráficos del Seminario Adventista Unión.

Carranza, Albino. 1894. "Geografía descriptiva y estadística industrial de Chanchamayo." *Boletín de la Sociedad Geográfica de Lima* 4 (1-3).

Colson, Elizabeth. 2000. "The Father as Witch." *Africa* 70 (3): 333-58.

Comaroff, Jean, and John L. Comaroff. 1999. "Occult Economies and the Violence of Abstraction: Notes from the South African Postcolony." *American Ethnologist* 26 (2): 279-303.

Douglas, Mary, ed. 1970. *Witchcraft Confessions and Accusations.* London: Tavistock.

Eichenberger, Ralph W. 1966. "Una filosofía de salud pública para las tribus indígenas amazónicas." *América Indígena* 26 (2): 119–41.

Elick, John W. 1970. "An Ethnography of the Pichis Valley Campa of Eastern Peru." Ph.D. diss., University of California, Los Angeles.

Espinosa de Rivero, Oscar. 1994. *La repetición de la violencia: Informe sobre la situación de los Asháninka de los Río Ene y Tambo — Selva Central*. Lima: Centro Amazónico de Antropología y Aplicación Práctica.

———. 1995. *Rondas campesinas y nativas en la amazonía peruana*. Lima: Centro Amazónico de Antropología y Aplicación Práctica.

Evans-Pritchard, E. E. 1980. *Witchcraft, Oracles, and Magic among the Azande*. Oxford: Clarendon Press.

Expediente. 2000. Expediente No. 00-472-150702 JXP/FL 70/Tomo IV. Inculpados: Manases Torres Chiampa y otros. Delito: Contra la vida, el cuerpo y la salud: homicidio culposo. Agraviado: Silverio Paredes Imposhito. Fiscalía Mixta Provincial de Satipo.

Fabián Arias, Beatriz. 1994. "La mujer asháninka en un contexto de violencia política." *Amazonía Peruana* 12 (24): 287–315.

———. 1995. "Cambios culturales en los Asháninka desplazados." *Amazonía Peruana* 13 (25): 159–76.

Fabián Arias, Beatriz, and Oscar Espinosa de Rivero. 1997. *Las cosas ya no son como antes: La mujer asháninka y los cambios socio-culturales producidos por la violencia política en la Selva Central*. Lima: Centro Amazónico de Antropología y Aplicación Práctica.

Frazer, James G. 1996. *The Golden Bough: A Study in Magic and Religion*. New York: Simon and Schuster.

Gagnon, Mariano, with William and Marilyn Hoffer. 1993. *Warriors in Eden*. New York: William Morrow.

Geschiere, Peter. 1997. *Witchcraft and Modernity: Politics and the Occult in Post-Colonial Africa*. Charlottesville: University of Virginia Press.

Gluckman, Max. 1955. *Custom and Conflict in Africa*. Oxford: Blackwell.

González, Bernardino. 1880. "Ojeada sobre la Montaña." In *Historia de las misiones franciscanas y narración de los progresos de la geografía en el oriente del Perú*, ed. B. Izaguirre. Vol. 10: 319–403. Lima: Talleres Tipográficos de la Penitenciaría.

Gridilla, Alberto. 1942 [1927]. "Los Campas." *Colección Descalzos* 4: 49–78.

Herndon, Booton. 1963. *The Seventh Day: The Story of the Seventh-Day Adventists*. New York: McGraw-Hill.

Hvalkof, Soren. 1994. "The Asháninka Disaster and Struggle." *Indigenous Affairs*/IWGIA 2: 20–32.

Izaguirre, Bernardino, ed. 1922–29. *Historia de la misiones franciscanas y narración de los progresos de la geografía en el oriente del Perú*. 14 vols. Lima: Talleres Tipográficos de la Penitenciaría.

Jackson, Jean. 1989. "Is There a Way to Talk about Making Culture without Making Enemies?" *Dialectical Anthropology* 14: 127–143.

Larrabure i Correa, Carlos, ed. 1905–8. *Colección de leyes, decretos, resoluciones i otros documentos oficiales referentes al Departamento de Loreto*. 18 vols. Lima: Oficina Tipográfica de La Opinión Nacional.

Navarro, Manuel. 1924. *La Tribu Campa*. Lima: Imprenta de Colegío de Huérfanos San Vincente.

———. 1967. "La tribu Amuesha." In *Oxapampa: Visión histórica y desarrollo de la Provincia de Oxapampa, en el Departamento de Pasco*, ed. Dionisio Ortiz. Vol. 2: 387–95. Lima: Imprenta Editorial San Antonio.

Ordinaire, Olivier. 1988 [1885]. "Del pacífico al atlántico y otros escritos: Monumenta amazónica, D1." Lima: Instituto Francés de Estudios Andinos/Centro de Estudios Teológicos de la Amazonía.

Ortiz, Dionisio, ed. 1967. *Oxapampa: Visión histórica y desarrollo de la Provincia de Oxapampa, en el Departamento de Pasco*. 2 vols. Lima: Imprenta Editorial San Antonio.

———. 1969. *Chanchamayo: Una región de la Selva del Perú*. 2 vols. Lima: Imprenta y Litografía "Salesiana."

———. 1978. *El perené: Reseña histórica de una importante región de la Selva Peruana*. Lima: Imprenta Editorial San Antonio.

Palomino Arana, César Rodriguez Helí, and Samuel Ramírez Castilla. 1936. Las hechicerías en las tres regiones del Perú. Letras. Organo de la facultad de filosofía, historia y letras, 5 (3): 506–14. Lima: Universidad Mayor de San Marcos.

Pérez Marcio, Manuel F. 1953. *Los hijos de la Selva*. Buenos Aires: Casa Editora Sudamericana.

Pinto, Manuel. 1978 [1940]. "La Colonía del Perené: Reseña Histórica de una Colonización de la Selva Pervana." In *Reseña Histórica de una Importante Región de la Selva Pervana*, ed. Dionisio Ortiz. 193–99. Lima: Imprenta Editorial San Antonio.

Renard-Casevitz, France-Marie. 2002. "Social Forms and Regressive History: From the Campa Cluster to the Mojos and from the Mojos to the Landscaping Terrace-Builders of the Bolivian Savanna." In *Comparative Arawakan Histories: Rethinking Language Family and Culture Area in Amazonia*, ed. J. Hill and F. Santos-Granero. 123–46. Urbana: University of Illinois Press.

Rodríguez Vargas, Marisol. 1993. "Desplazados. Selva Central: El caso Asháninka." Lima: Centro Amazónico de Antropología y Aplicación Práctica.

Rodríguez Vargas, Marisol, and Oscar Espinosa de Rivero. 1997. *Múltiples retornos a una misma tierra: La situación del pueblo Asháninka de los Ríos Tambo y Ene—Selva Central*. Lima: Centro Amazónico de Antropología y Aplicación Práctica.

Rojas Zolezzi, Enrique. 1994. *Los Asháninka: Un pueblo tras el bosque*. Lima: Pontificia Universidad Católica del Perú.

Sala, Gabriel. 1975 [1893]. "Tomo Tercero: Comprende el último decenio de 1882 a 1893." In *Historia de las misiones del convento de Santa Rosa de Ocopa*, ed. J. Amich. 437–43. Lima: Milla Batres.

Santos-Granero, Fernando. 1991. *The Power of Love: The Moral Use of Knowledge Amongst the Amuesha of Central Peru*. London: Athlone Press.

———. 1992. *Etnohistoria de la alta Amazonía, siglos XV-XVIII: Colección 500 años*. Quito: Abya-Yala.

———. 2002. "St. Christopher in the Amazon: Child Sorcery, Colonialism, and Violence among the Peruvian Arawak." *Ethnohistory* 49 (3): 507–43.

Schoeneman, Thomas J. 1975. "Witch Hunt as a Culture Change Phenomenon." Lewis and Clark College, www.lclark.edu/~schoen/culturetext.html.

Shaver, Harold, and Lois Dodd. 1990. *Los Nomatsiguenga de la Selva Central*. Lima: Ministerio de Educación / Instituto Lingüístico de Verano.

Smith, Richard C. 1977. "Deliverance from Chaos for a Song: Preliminary Discussion of Amuesha Music." Ph.D. diss., Cornell University.

Stahl, Ferdinand A. n.d. *In the Land of the Incas*. Mountain View, Calif.: Pacific Press Publishing Association.

———. 1932. *In the Amazon Jungles*. Mountain View, Calif.: Pacific Press Publishing Association.

Tessmann, Günter. 1999. *Los indígenas del Perú nororiental: Investigaciones fundamentales para un estudio sistemático de la cultura*. Quito: Abya-Yala.

Torre López, Fernando. 1966. "Fenomenología de la tribu anti o campa." *Folklore Americano* 14 (4): 5–104.

Uriarte, Buenaventura Luis de. 1982 [1938]. *La Montaña del Perú*. Lima: Gráfica 30.

Weiss, Gerald. 1975. "Campa Cosmology: The World of a Forest Tribe in South America." *Anthropological Papers* 52 (5): 217–588.

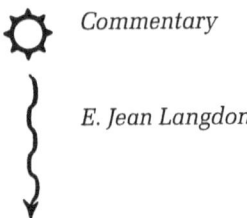

Commentary

E. Jean Langdon

Why another book devoted to sorcery, witchcraft, and shamanism? As classificatory paradigms in anthropology they have not proved to be particularly fruitful for comparative purposes. Acts of secret aggression in Amazonian cultures defy the labels of sorcery or witchcraft as defined by the African model, and the terms have been frequently used interchangeably, emptying their analytical value as universal categories. In a similar way, attempts to essentialize shamanism and shamans have not resulted in fruitful insights. On the contrary, such efforts have often led to simplifications and misconceptions about shamans and witches as social actors, without revealing the central ideologies and moral philosophies that underlie shamanism. Fortunately, the authors in this volume move away from a classificatory approach to these themes, directing them instead to the analysis of contemporary concerns in Amazonian ethnology, and in doing so they have been highly successful. They synthesize and underscore many of the new theoretical preoccupations and paradigms that have recently emerged, revealing the ambiguity and complexity of assault sorcery and shamanism as social, cultural, and political phenomena.[1] The particularities as well as common themes of Amazonian cosmologies are also revealed, and the essays contribute to the growing understanding of the organizing principles that distinguish their views of the universe and social praxis. The focus on assault sorcery as process rather than category has also yielded insight into the native notions of humanity, personhood, intention, and consciousness.

Just as there is a great variety of social actors (glossed as shamans, singers, healers, herbalists, etc.) performing rituals and administering substances for beneficial purposes in the Amazon, there is an equal complexity in the kinds of individuals who send harm to others and the methods they use, whatever their designation may be in native terminology. In cases where the shaman's position is ambiguous, such as the Kulina and Cashinahua, the aggressor may be the same person who heals. In other groups, such as those of the Río Negro area and the Warau of Venezuela, the classes of specialists are more elaborated and less ambiguous.[2] Those who cause harm are distinguished from beneficial shamans. Thus, categories of secret aggressors are culturally specific, and there are no distinguishing features, such as conscious intention, manner of acquisition of knowledge, nor methods employed, that cut across these cultures to permit the construction of a uniform definition of assault sorcery or their agents. The substances and techniques that kill—songs, spells, and invisible arrows, darts, or other projectiles—may be the same as those employed for beneficial aims. Río Negro poison-owners are classed as aggressors by their knowledge and use of poisons, but anyone who knows the proper spells can do harm. The Panoan people distinguish between categories of techniques but not between categories of shamans. The aggressor may be the other—representing a nonhuman, the enemy, another resident or ethnic group, or in-laws; or he or she may come from within the heart of the community itself, as among the Kulina, the Arawak of Peru, and the Arara. The accused may be brothers or sisters, healing shamans, deviants, or children. The case of the Arawakan children tortured into confessing misdeeds shows the outer limits of the phenomenon. They are distinguished from professional sorcerers and are marked by social marginality and the absence of extensive kinship ties.

We have been shown a dark side of the Amazonian universe and its inhabitants with harrowing images of darkness, predation, vengeance, and putrid stench. Although the particulars of this Amazonian cosmology differ from group to group, what is common is the notion of a universe propelled by the cyclic flow of vital energy that alternates between the processes of life and death, construction and destruction, health and illness, equilibrium and disequilibrium, and the production and reproduction of social life. The concept of energy is a key metaphor related to notions of the soul, power, desire and intention. Secret attacks bringing misfortune as well as preventative and restorative rituals are manifestations of the activation of this energy. Assault sorcery, like curing shamanism, is at the heart of Amazonian cosmology and society.

Discussions of South American cosmologies (e.g., Viveiros de Castro 1996) have emphasized that important plants, animals, special locations, and invisible beings are attributed the status of humans. These entities may differ corporeally from humans but, like them, they possess intentionality and "agency." Amazonian cosmology is about an "intentioned universe" (Viveiros de Castro 1996:126). Negative reciprocity represented through aggression, predation, hunting, and violence is essential to social processes, and illness and death are associated with images of asocial forms of behavior and eating, such as the practice of cannibalism or the consumption of blood, the jaguar's raw meat, or rotten and putrid food. Thus, Warau dark shamans, or Patamuna *kanaimàs*, perform the important function of using their negative powers to maintain the balance of the universe in a world where the netherworld-human relations depend on predation. The Parakanã do not differentiate ontologically between predator and prey, and it is important to maintain the position of predator and to avoid becoming the prey. George Mentore argues that the deadly and destructive forces associated with the shaman as spiritual hunter/warrior sustains the suppleness of Amazonian societies. The hunter/warrior qualities of the shaman are found also among the Arara.

This relation between shamanism, hunting, predation, and cannibalism is not necessarily as central to all the Amazonian cultures as it appears to be for the groups mentioned above. A good Cashinahua hunter cannot be a good shaman. However, one is struck by the shared images throughout these ethnographies associated with death and illness. Both are generally caused by aggressive activities and forces in the occult side of reality, whether they be instigated by humans or not. "Being eaten from the inside" is an extremely widespread image of illnesses that are attributed to invisible attacks. Putrid smells and other rotten qualities, particularly the stench of tobacco and blood, represent the decay of death as well as secret uncontrolled aggression.

Secret attacks are attributed to two kinds of figures, specialists (shamans, poison-owners, etc.) and deviant individuals who are marginalized by the social process. In both cases, the motives for aggression often depict human emotions associated with hate, vengeance, jealousy, envy, fear, compulsion, and desire. These negative qualities are projected onto both humans and nonhumans. To Carlos Fausto's quote "Amazonian shamanism is not a loving shamanism" we can add that humanity is not pictured as loving but rather as a group of beings full of contradictions and ambiguities that can be set in motion to bring misfortune to others. Donald Pollock's discussion of Kulina psychology is important because he interprets their vision of human desires as paradoxical, which avoids an essentialist negative or positive view of humanity.

This paradoxical or ambiguous nature of humans implies also a lack of a clear-cut definition of the essential characteristics of wrongdoers. The observation that the Parakanã do not distinguish between good and evil as essential qualities is true for most of Amazonian morality systems. Good and evil are relational and highly contextual, and what may be evil for one could be beneficial for the other. Native philosophy seems to imply that if death exists as a necessary evil for the cyclic universe, so also do negative human desires as the necessary opposite of human love, sociability, and collectivity. What constitutes a moral evaluation depends on one's involvement in the specific event (Read 1967).

Within specific contexts, accusations of assault sorcery are associated with antisocial behavior, deviance, marginality, and solitariness, but not necessarily with consciousness. Control of aggressive emotions is lost and the violent constituents of the person are released with the rupture of sociality. This rupture may occur in ongoing social life or in the rupture between life and death, when the dead forget their affiliations with the living and attack their own group. Waiwai moral philosophy counsels that everyone should guard against wrongly arousing his or her own destructive desires. The histories of Baniwa witchcraft accusations in this volume point out how the antisocial person is one who loses control over his thoughts and emotions. The Baniwa poison-owner is "no longer like a person," and his true body resembles that of a monkey. Echoing the theme of predation, uncontrolled violent emotions approximate the image of the jaguar, macaws, or other predators, and the distinction between human and animal becomes blurred.

Not only are sociability and solidarity collective processes that work to control individual motivations, they also are responsible for the exclusion of the accused. An understanding of the processes of exclusion can only be accomplished through all analysis of concrete events, such as that of Schultz (1976 [1960]), which details the marginalization and execution of a Krahó shaman.[3] The shaman's identity as an evil shaman was constructed through his excesses—his deviant behavior that set in motion the processes of social exclusion. The loss of kinship and social alliances were important factors leading to exclusion and execution. We see the same process in the examples of the Arawakan children and Tchibie, the old woman excluded from Arara society for years. They are socially constructed sources of evil and their identity is created through collective interaction and accusation.

The link between witchcraft accusations and social conflict has been researched by various ethnographers ever since Evans-Pritchard (1976 [1937]) pointed out that accusations indicate social conflicts. Indeed, "sociological" analysis has been successful for cross-cultural comparison. Several studies in this volume highlight the locus of social conflict: they shed light on ambiguities in gender and kinship relations as well as on public political conflicts. Pollock, along with Elsje Lagrou and Robin Wright, have characterized such accusations as social discourse, pointing beyond purely sociological considerations. They, as well as others in this book, have highlighted how the social processes of exclusion and the notions and activities surrounding invisible assaults constitute a moral reflection on the ambiguities of humanity, sociability, and cosmological forces.

The studies from the Xingu and the Amazon-Orinoco region describe the extensive political powers of the specialists in assault sorcery, particularly in the face of new contexts. Michael Heckenberg confirms Bastos's observation published in the mid-1980s that Xingu shamanism is more concerned with the realm of worldly political relations than with cosmological preoccupations.[4] New situations, including contact not only with other native groups but also with non-Indians and the political and economic processes of the state, have generated new uses of secret powers. Existing sorcery systems are the result of historical developments brought about by colonialism as well as internal forces. Salomon (1983) explored the transformation and operation of shamanic politics during the Spanish colonial rule in Colombia and Ecuador. Taussig's (1987) postmodern ethnography of the interplay of the imaginary and terror between colonialism and shamanic practices stimulated others to examine the role between the state and shamanism (see Thomas and Humphrey 1994). The articles by Robin Wright and Silvia Vidal and Neil Whitehead continue this interest. Shamanic powers have traditionally been important in the interethnic relations throughout the Amazon.[5] In the Río Negro, the messianic movements of the last century drew on shamanic powers and myth, joining Indians and non-Indians in search of redemption. Wright's history of accusations shows extensive shamanic networks that extend from the Río Negro to the Guahibo in the north and to the urban migrants and Mestizo population of São Gabriel da Cachoeira. New practices, such as Afro-Brazilian *macumba*, are incorporated into the arsenal of traditional techniques to defend or provoke harm. This exchange of sorcery techniques between ethnic groups resembles a similar phenomenon in the shamanic relations between the ethnic groups of contemporary Peru (Gow 1994).

In the Venezuelan context, sorcery practitioners who work to influence employment, loans, and political elections have important economic and political roles. In both Brazil and Venezuela there has been a rise in the number of Indian organizations negotiating for full citizenship and political power during the last twenty years. Conklin (2002) has recently argued that a generic shamanism emphasizing healing knowledge is playing a role in Indigenous politics in Brazil. The documentation here of assault sorcery provides a view of an important alternative route to empowerment in the larger society by showing how native traditions permeate what is generally perceived to be a modern democratic process, and there is a need for more studies of this nature.

The phenomenon of the child witches related by Fernando Santos-Granero is of a different nature, although it is also related to the discourse of accusations. Marginal children, not professional sorcerers, are accused of sending misfortune through intense emotions and are tortured until confession. The cruel treatment of suspected sorcerers is not new in the region. Califano and Idoyaga Molina (1983) have described how the Mashco, of the same linguistic group as those described by Santos-Granero, tortured and killed women accused of being witches. In the case of the children, such accusations and what can be seen as witch hysteria correspond to moments of crisis created by contact with the outside society. This correspondence was also perceived by Gray (1997), who states that the Arakmbut's contact with the greater society from the 1950s to the 1990s led to periods of increased conflict, epidemics, and crises that resulted in accusations directed toward women, followed by attempts at assassination.

In sum, the focus on secrecy and aggression has underscored the multiplicity of kinds of practitioners, techniques, and accusations that characterize the theme of shamanism in the Amazon. Its complexity and heterogeneity go far beyond the general notions that we hold about shamans, witches, and sorcerers and relativize the relation between good and evil. This book has contributed to the growing knowledge about Amazon cosmology and social relations by emphasizing its dark side. It supports the growing recognition that notions of nature and supernature as well as of good and evil are not perceived with the same duality as they are in European philosophy. It has also helped us gain a better view into the nature of power, which is present in various forms and degrees in the universe as well as in society. In the Amazon, power is linked to notions of emotions, person, intention, and consciousness as well as to the perceptions of the cyclic nature of the universe. Shaman specialists are able to access power to a greater extent than ordinary humans and have cultivated their knowledge for the intentional exercise of it. However, it is clear that they do not have a monopoly on secret assaults, and that this topic goes beyond that of shamanism. The secret aggressor, no matter how classified, points to the notion of person as constituted through social discourse and cultural and historical processes.

For some time it has been apparent that any cross-cultural definition of shamanism is difficult to establish, and as Vitbesky has argued, it is characterized by a "chameleon-like elusiveness" (1995:184). Besides confirming Vitbesky's observation, the essays in this volume also demonstrate this elusiveness to be true for cross-cultural definitions of witchcraft and sorcery. On the other hand, it does not support Parkin's (1991:2) suggestion that witchcraft and sorcery deserve no privileged place as analytical categories. The ethnographies here move beyond categories and focus on secret assaults as forms of symbolic, social, and political processes. The privileging of secret assaults contributes to the new themes and theories that have emerged since the 1970s. As discussed above, some of these ideas are specific to the growth of Amazonian ethnology. Others, however, pertain also to general paradigms circulating in anthropology as a whole since the 1980s: challenges to the nature/culture debate; notions of agency, personhood, and emotions; sociality and conviviality as constituent factors of social life; and the interplay of society, history, and power.[6]

Notes

1. The reference lists at the end of each chapter are an excellent source for the major themes and preoccupations currently in debate.
2. This does not eliminate ambiguity, as shown by the various essays on the region and also by Hugh-Jones's (1994) discussion of horizontal and vertical shamans.
3. Murphy 1974a and 1974b provide two case studies of the process of the destruction of the social person, although the situations therein do not lead to sorcery accusations.
4. Dole 1973 [1964] previously recognized the importance of the political role of the shaman among the Kuikuru of the Xingu.
5. In the mountain region of Colombia, existing pre-Colombian networks (see Langdon 1981) were extended to the non-Indian society after the conquest and today make up the complexity of actors and images portrayed in Taussig 1987.
6. See Ortner 1994 for a discussion of the evolution of these ideas since the 1960s.

References

Bastos, R. J. de Menezes. 1984-85. "O payemeramaraka Kamayura: Uma contribuição a etnografia do xamanismo do alto Xingu." *Revista de Antropologia* 27/28: 139-78.

Califano, Mario, and A. Idoyaga Molina. 1983. "Las brujas Mashco y Pilagá: Análisis comparativo de una estructura de dos grupos de América del Sur." *Revista Española de Antropologia Americana* 8: 155-71.

Colajaimi, A. 1982. "Praticas chamanicas y cambio social. La muerte de un hechicero achuar: hechos e interpretaciones." In *Relaciones interétnicas y adaptacion cultural entre shuar, achuar, aguaruna y canelos quechua*. Quito: Abya-Yala.

Conklin, Beth. 2002. "Shamans versus Pirates in the Amazonian Treasure Chest." *American Anthropologist* 104 (4): 1050-61.

Dole, Gertrude E. 1973 [1964]. "Shamanism and Political Control among the Kuikuru." In *Peoples and Cultures of Native South America*, ed. Daniel R. Gross. 294-307. New York: Doubleday.

Evans-Pritchard, Edward E. 1976 [1937]. *Witchcraft, Oracles, and Magic among the Azande*, abridged edition. Oxford: Clarendon Press.

Gow, P. 1994. "River People: Shamanism and History in Western Amazonia." In *Shamanism, History, and the State*, ed. N. Thomas and C. Humphrey. 90-114. Ann Arbor: University of Michigan Press.

Hugh-Jones, Stephen. 1994. "Shamans, Prophets, Priests, and Pastors." In *Shamanism, His-*

tory, and the State, ed. N. Thomas and C. Humphrey. 76–89. Ann Arbor: University of Michigan Press.

Gray, A. 1997. *The Last Shaman: Change in an Amazonian Community.* Providence: Berghahn Books.

Langdon, E. J. 1981. "Social Bases for Trading of Visions and Spiritual Knowledge in the Colombian and Ecuadorian Montaña." 101–16. In *Networks of the Past*, proceedings of the 12th annual conference of the Archaeological Association of the University of Calgary.

Murphy, Robert. 1974a [1961]. "Deviance and Social Control I: What Makes Waru Run?" In *Native South Americans: Ethnology of the Least Known Continent*, ed. P. J. Lyon. 195–202. Boston: Little, Brown.

Murphy, Robert. 1974b [1961]. "Deviance and Social Control II: Borai." In *Native South Americans: Ethnology of the Least Known Continent*, ed. P. J. Lyon. 202–7. Boston: Little, Brown.

Ortner, Sherry B. 1994. "Theory in Anthropology since the Sixties." In *Culture, Power, History: A Reader in Contemporary Social Theory*, ed. N. B. Dirks, G. Eley, and S. B. Ortner. 372–411. Princeton: Princeton University Press.

Parkin, David. 1985. "Introduction." In *The Anthropology of Evil*, ed. David Parkin. 1–25. Oxford: Basil Blackwell.

Read, K. E. 1967 [1955]. "Morality and the Concept of the Person among the Gahuku-Gama." In *Myth and Cosmos*, ed. John Middleton. 185–230. Austin: University of Texas Press.

Salomon, Frank. 1983. "Shamanism and Politics in Late-Colonial Ecuador." *American Ethnologist* 10 (3): 413–28.

Schultz, H. 1976 [1960]. "Condenação e execução de medico-feiticeiro entre os índios Kraho." In *Leituras de ethnologia brasileira*, ed. E. Schaden. 212–24. São Paulo: Companhia Editora Nacional.

Taussig, Michael. 1987. *Shamanism, Colonialism, and the Wild Man: A Study in Terror and Healing.* Chicago: University of Chicago Press.

Thomas, Nicholas, and Caroline Humphrey, eds. 1994. *Shamanism, History, and the State.* Ann Arbor: University of Michigan Press.

Vitbesky, Piers. 1995. "From Cosmology to Environmentalism: Shamanism as Local Knowledge in a Global Setting." In *Counterworks: Managing the Diversity of Knowledge*, ed. R. Fardon. 182–203. London: Routledge.

Viveiros de Castro, Eduardo B. 1996. "Images of Nature and Society in Amazonian Ethnology." *Annual Review of Anthropology* 25: 179–200.

*Afterword:
Substances, Powers, Cosmos, and History*

Andrew Strathern & Pamela J. Stewart

The fascinating and energetic set of writings presented in this volume, charting the essential ambiguity and fluidity inherent in the shamanic complexes of South America, raises comparative questions that go beyond the region while contributing powerfully to the regional theme of analysis itself. In reading these chapters we received an impression of overlapping and interweaving themes that define a regional texture of ethnographic information. At the same time we could discern parallels with analyses from New Guinea, whose volatile and dynamic societies, filled with interpersonal conflicts and loyalties, show close resemblances in general to the ethos of many societies in Amazonian South America. Much has been written about shamanic practices in South America: it is the classic case for such accounts. The chapters herein greatly deepen our understanding of these practices, in terms of the training and knowledge required for them, what stimulates and maintains them, and how they have mutated in contexts of change, such as Fernando Santos-Granero describes for eastern Peru and the Shining Path guerrilla movement. Above all, many (but not all, see Robin Wright on the Baniwa) of the chapters reveal the ambivalence of the world of the shaman, and the overlap between shamans and sorcerers expressed in the vision of light and dark shamans as discussed, for example, by Johannes Wilbert. These studies are historically grounded, showing how formations of ideas are profoundly shaped by historical experiences. Wilbert, although stressing the ideology of balance in the Warao vision of the cosmos, recognizes that the uneasy duality of Warao ideas has emerged from a history of disease, depredation, and internal gerontocratic exploitation by shamanic elders.

In our comments here, we select a number of themes that link these Amazonian portraits of rivalry, power, and disempowerment to comparable materials from New Guinea. Overall, it is very striking that through the chapters a pattern of rivalry, jealousy, and vengeance is found as one of the strong motivating forces for the activities of dark shamans as sorcerers or witches. A minor aspect of this central theme is that in comparing terminologies used in the chapters we find arising the old definitional question of the distinction between witchcraft and sorcery. When we examine indigenous terms for what Evans-Pritchard called "mystical attacks" we find a complex of significations that blend together or juxtapose elements relating to conscious agency, spirit action, the use of charms, the exercise of bodily powers, the imposition of terror, and the like. For this reason, no hard and fast distinctions between witchcraft and sorcery can be made. Readers of these studies have to realize, however, that what one author calls witchcraft another may label as sorcery (see Stewart and Strathern 2003). No matter what the specifics, the overall theme remains the same: the dark shaman or sorcerer concept is a recognition of the patterns of aggression between people that are fed by passions and generated out of the same complexes of social relationships in which positive affect is expressed.

It is perhaps for this reason that the pervasive ambivalence of the shaman's powers is exhibited, as among the Kulina described by Donald Pollock, for whom shamanic powers are gained through the actions of senior shamans placing *dori* power into the bodies of initiates. *Dori* is related to semen and is dangerous if not used in a controlled way, so that its holders can heal others but also use it to inflict harm. The idea that the body is the locus of power and that power is a kind of substance is one that fits well with many ideas from New Guinea. The Kulina concept of *dori* closely resembles male ideology among the Etoro of Papua New Guinea, as described by Raymond Kelly (1993), according to which the transmission of semen into the bodies of initiates both makes them grow and gives them knowledge. The workings of the ideas of the effects of the harmful use of *dori* is further comparable to notions formerly present among the Gebusi (who belong to the same region as the Etoro): interhousehold relations are disrupted by sickness, but blame is directed outward to sorcerers beyond the collective set of village siblings, and revenge is taken on the sorcerers, ideologically seen as affines. Among the Kulina, jaguars, in turn, are said to eat the sorcerer's spirit. (In the Gebusi case those who executed revenge killing on a sorcerer would eat the sorcerer's body, see Knauft 1985; Kelly 1993). The form that sorcery ideas take is that *dori* assumes the shape of a stone in the body that continues to grow unless it is extracted (comparable to the image of a tumor). Again, such a notion is closely paralleled by ideas from New Guinea, where healers are classically said to extract objects projected into people's bodies by sorcerers. In a related notion, the Melpa speakers of Mount Hagen had an idea that *kum* stones could jump up from a streambed where people drank water after eating pork and would then lodge in their throats, making them thereafter greedy for flesh and turning their minds to cannibalism. In turn, this Melpa idea of *kum* is similar to the concept of *karowara* among the Parakanã as discussed by Carlos Fausto, who states that *karowara* are "pathogenic objects, controlled by shamans, with no autonomous volition, only a compulsion to eat human flesh." In Melpa ideas, however, the *kum* can exist as wild entities, autonomous in themselves, that a ritual expert could capture, tame, and bend to his or her own will. A kind of symbiotic arrangement between "expert" and "pathogen" is thus envisaged in both Melpa and Parakanã cases, for in the latter, according to Fausto, "to acquire a curing power, a shaman must suck the *karowara* from a creature spoken of as the "master of the *karowara*."

Such parallels, with their concomitant differences in detail, do not seem to be the products of chance. They are, rather, a result of the overarching similarity of two basic ideas: first, that human life is set into a cosmos of interpenetrating powers that includes the environment and its wild creatures such as the jaguar; and, second, that power resides in the human body and its substances and is affected by the ingestion or expulsion of substances. Thus, for the Parakanã, blood and tobacco together encompass the shaman's powers. For New Guinea as a whole (i.e., West Papua/Irian Jaya and Papua New Guinea) we have argued these two points at length (Stewart and Strathern 2001). Both concepts amount to a basic form of ethnophilosophy that we can characterize as a humoral theory: substances and their powers constitute life and death within a cosmos in which balance is sought and fitfully attained. Within such a cosmos the practice of hunting, with its dangers, its shedding of blood, its demonstration of power, and its setting within the domain of the "wild," easily acquires a special symbolic significance. And also in such a cosmos sensory powers beyond that of sight can assume great import. In particular, hearing and smell, both vital for the process of hunting, enter into people's picture of the cosmos and its spirits.

In what we conventionally refer to as the "social" side, then, we have a narrative of the violent potentialities inherent in relationships; while on the "cultural" side there is the imagery of the body and its substances, set in a dynamic cosmic flow. This vision of the world is one that makes it particularly open to forces of change, which in turn can either offer opportunities to people or oppressively close off opportunities they once had. The overall process of change amounts to an exposure of self to outsiders, starting with affines in the community itself and ending with forces of the colonial or postcolonial state. The impact of Christianity stands out here, as it does also in New Guinea. A desire to incorporate others in order to gain advantage from them struggles with a fear of their powers and the experience of misfortune though interactions with them. A major point here is that in circumstances of change fears of sorcery/witchcraft may find heightened, rather than diminished, contexts of expression.

Silvia Vidal and Neil Whitehead bring out these points very clearly in their essay on Guyana and the Venezuelan Amazon. They indicate how "occult forces" are a part of "regional and national political processes," as Peter Geschiere (1997) has shown them to be in Cameroon politics in West Africa. They also delineate the processes, again familiar from Africa, whereby in unstable times messianic movements led by prophets were instrumental in reshaping political and ethnic groups. Shamanic and prophetic traditions converge in the image of Kuwai, a monstrous primordial being whose power is invoked in ritual cycles by shamans. These strong indigenous ideas, entering into millenarian movements, made their way into festivities for Catholic saints, and further into national politics, for example with the idea that the president of Venezuela had his personal shaman whose magic saved him from a bomb attack by leftist guerrillas. Interestingly, while the volatility and dangers of political life have become very marked in Papua New Guinea's Highlands regions, rumors there surround allegations that politicians raise their personal militias at times of elections, depending on guns not magic; while at local levels fears of witchcraft and sorcery can be intense, waxing and waning with the incidence of sickness, drought, and epidemics, and flourishing on the mills of rumor and gossip about the unseen realms of power that constantly shadow local contexts of life.

Vidal and Whitehead raise the comparative question of why and how "occult forms of ritual action become the accepted processes of the state" in some places and not in others. Perhaps in Papua New Guinea it is the relatively strong institutionalized presence of the various Christian churches and an ideology that the nation is a "Christian country" that make a difference there. But it should be noted that forms of Christianity and ideas of the occult feed off each other, as demonstrated by the Charismatics' slogan of waging "a war against Satan."

Among the Duna of Papua New Guinea, some individuals in 1999 attributed the putative rise in the activities of witches to the coming millennium, and the Seventh-Day Adventist compound attracted women who were at risk of being accused as witches in the nearby Baptist community. At local levels, then, witchcraft and Christianity are closely intermingled. Rumors and gossip spread fears widely, as Michael Heckenburger also notes for the Xinguano. The deaths of members of important families were more likely to provoke witch-hunts than deaths in general from sickness, so we find the usual correlation between witchcraft accusations and local politics. While these idioms, as we have said, are not marked at the national level, we do not suppose that this situation is necessarily stable, given the pervasive and fluid local context of ideas about occult powers.

One striking difference at the cosmic level seems to be the importance of the mythology of Kuwai, a fact that is remarked on in a number of essays herein. In Papua New Guinea there is no single overarching figure, other than that provided in Christian ideology by the singular representation of God. But it is equally striking to see how this apparent difference at the mythological level masks a similarity at the practical level.

In his work on the Baniwa Wright notes that the first ancestral death was supposedly caused by "poison," and that Kuwai "left all forms of poison in this world as vengeance for his own killing." Revenge, then, lies at the heart of all subsequent "mystical" killings. And in practice revenge remains a powerful element, as both motif and motive, in social life.[1] This fundamental emphasis is shared by Papua New Guinea societies. Kuwai's doings seem to percolate through a number of Amazonian contexts. Dominique Buchillet indicates for the Desana that Kuwai himself was a murderer who "'killed' young boys being initiated," and plants that grew where he died were said to be poisonous. George Mentore on the Waiwai writes that for these people "all death means murder," attributed to the work of dark shamans. Márnio Teixeira-Pinto on the Arara argues that treachery is seen as lying at the heart of sociability itself. And Elsje Lagrou, on the Cashinahua, notes that *dau* "means medicine as well as poison." What the permutations of these views of social life appear to indicate is the double-sidedness of life itself with its bright and dark sides: no conviviality without anger, no good company without violence (as Bruce Knauft [1985] put it for the Gebusi of Papua New Guinea);[2] no healing without killing, whether this is done by the same or different practitioners; no social act of aggression without its response in revenge; and no life without death—thus completing the cosmological cycle.

Perhaps revenge is too narrow a word for this cosmic principle, which Garry Trompf (1994) has called a "logic of retribution," around which contested and contesting narratives of legitimacy constantly play. This is what the dark shaman stands for, as Kuwai's myth tells us. And it is this that the shifting images of shamans, witches, sorcerers, healers, and ritual experts capture, whether in Amazonia or in New Guinea. The figures of terror and redemption blend into each other, conceptually and across the continents.

At the broadest level these studies capture the shifting dimensions and configurations of feelings from which the phenomenon of terror in general emerges, or can emerge, in human interactions. In the realm of terror, physical acts take place in a wider cosmic context of the imaginary. Death is interpreted as murder, a sidelong glance as an act of witchcraft, an ambiguous phrase as evidence of sorcery. Imagination, built on circulating suppositions and ways of locating meaning in the world, creates a heightened sense of fear associated with events and social processes. The ideas involved may not be clearly articulated but rather be part of what James Fernandez (1986) called the inchoate and Michael Taussig refers to as "implicit social knowledge" by contrast with "conscious ideology" (1987:366). As Taussig explains, submerged memories of the historical past and its continuing impact on the present are involved. He condenses this point into the phrase "history as sorcery." Among the Putumayo of Colombia, whom he studied, such ideas form around fears of the dead, especially the dead of precolonial times whose pulverized bones are thought of as arising and becoming an evil wind that blows to harm people, particularly those whose blood is weak. This vision of the ancient dead comes from the history of "the violent arrival and colonization by the Spanish" (372), in which many people were killed. As the pagan dead, the remembered figures may reasonably be seen as malevolent and vengeful. They occupy "the space of death" and "have been enfolded and iconicized into the bowels of the Christian cosmos as Antichrist figures." As a result, "the history of the conquest itself acquires the role of the sorcerer" (373). Shamans in turn invoke some of these images of the past, bending them to their own ambiguous activities as healers. The evil wind of the past blows into people's blood and it is the shaman's job to expel it with song. Taussig argues that the images of terror blend with the practices of healing, and his study shows how aspects of terror can be replicated and multiplied over time, along with the accumulated historical sensibilities and vulnerabilities of a particular people. When these processes are further dispersed across national borders in globalized contexts of communication we can see that the ambivalent figure of the shaman who uses senses of terror to offer practices of healing finds its counterparts on the stage of international politics.

Most significant here is the ultimate role of terror in shaping and reshaping identities. The global structure of politics has recently been reshaped in this way, with the decline of East-West confrontations and the rise of dispersed movements wielding violence as a political tool and operating in the thickets of "religious" fundamentalist rhetoric and ethnonationalist aspirations. Terror operates in these contexts as the ultimate weapon, forcing people out of an expansive sense of connections with others and contracting them into its own "space of death." In the face of such terror, the world has two contradictory, but related, appearances: one, as a globalized set of networks of power breaching all boundaries; the other, as a multitude of states trying to close these breaches. Contemporary politics has its own shamanic figures who move across this geographical landscape.

Notes

1. We discuss this idea further in Stewart and Strathern 2002. For an important study on the poetics and politics of death generally among the Patamuna people, see Whitehead 2002. Whitehead's detailed study raises many issues for comparative analysis, as he himself expresses in his conclusion.
2. On the Etoro people referred to earlier see Kelly 1993.

References

Fernandez, James W. 1986. *Persuasions and Performances: The Play of Tropes in Culture.* Bloomington: Indiana University Press.

Geschiere, P. 1997. *The Modernity of Witchcraft: Politics and the Occult in Post-Colonial Africa.* Charlottesville: University of Virginia Press.

Kelly, R. 1993. *Constructing Inequality: The Fabrication of a Hierarchy of Virtue among the Etoro.* Ann Arbor: University of Michigan Press.

Knauft, B. M. 1985. *Good Company and Violence: Sorcery and Social Action in a Lowland New Guinea Society.* Berkeley: University of California Press.

Stewart, P. J., and A. Strathern. 2001. *Humors and Substances: Ideas of the Body in New Guinea.* Westport, Conn.: Bergin and Garvey.

———. 2002. *Violence: Theory and Ethnography.* London: Continuum.

———. 2003. *Witchcraft, Sorcery, Rumors, and Gossip.* Cambridge: Cambridge University Press.

Taussig, Michael. 1987. *Shamanism, Colonialism, and the Wild Man: A Study in Terror and Healing.* Chicago: University of Chicago Press.

Trompf, G. W. 1994. *Payback: The Logic of Retribution in Melanesian Religions.* Cambridge: Cambridge University Press.

Whitehead, Neil L. 2002. *Dark Shamans: Kanaimà and the Poetics of Violent Death.* Durham: Duke University Press.

 *Contributors*

Dominique Buchillet is a researcher at the Institut de Recherche pour le Développement in Paris, France and has realized investigations on shamanism and medicine among indigenous Desana and Tariano peoples in Upper Río Negro region since 1980. She has published numerous articles on shamanism, indigenous concepts of health and illness, epidemics, and interethnic contact.

Carlos Fausto is an associate professor and the chair of the Graduate Program in Social Anthropology at the Federal University of Rio de Janeiro. His fieldwork in Amazonia has focused on the Parakanã, a Tupi-speaking people, and now among the Kuikuro, a Carib-speaking people. He is the author of *Os Índios antes do Brasil* (2000) and *Inimigos Fiéis: História, Guerra e Xamanismo na Amazônia* (2001), which won the Brazilian Association for Social Sciences prize for the best book of the year.

Michael J. Heckenberger is an assistant professor of Anthropology at the University of Florida, Gainesville. He specializes in historical archaeology focusing on the nature and development of late prehistoric social formations and the impact of Euro-American colonialism in Amazonia. He is currently involved in field research in the upper Xingu, southern Amazonia, the central Amazon and Acre in western Amazonia. He is the coauthor of *Os Povos do Alto Xingu: Cultura e Historia*.

Elsje Lagrou is a senior lecturer in the Graduate Program of Anthropology and Sociology at the Federal University of Rio de Janeiro. Her theoretical interests center on cosmology, ritual, shamanism, aesthetics, gender, and emotions among Amerindian people. Since 1989 she has been conducting field research among the Cashinahua in three villages located on the banks of the Purus River in the Brazilian rainforest near the frontier with Peru. She has published several articles in Brazil and abroad.

E. Jean Langdon is a full professor at the Universidade Federal de Santa Catarina, in Florianópolis, Brazil. Her research interests and publications center on shamanism, cosmology, narrative and the anthropology of health. Currently she is conducting research on the politics of Indian health in Brazil.

George Mentore is an associate professor of Anthropology at the University of Virginia where he teaches courses in Lowland South American societies, the Antilles, the politics of the body, the anthropology of emotion, and anthropological theory. He has worked for over twenty years with the Waiwai people of Guyana.

Silvia Margarita Vidal Ontivero did her Masters and Doctoral studies at the Instituto Venezolano de Investigaciones Científicas. She has been doing fieldwork among the Arawak-speaking groups of Venezuela, Brazil, and Colombia since 1973, focusing her research on the sociocultural, political, economic, religious, symbolic, and historical characteristics, as well as the past and present migratory patterns and sociopolitical formations and identities, oral traditions, and intercultural-bilingual education projects of the Arawakan peoples.

Donald Pollock is chair of the Department of Anthropology and co-director of the medical anthropology program at the State University of New York, Buffalo. In addition to his research among Kulina Indians in Brazil, he has been engaged in a project on the culture of tertiary care medicine in the United States, and is completing a study of the social history of physician autobiography.

Fernando Santos-Granero is a staff researcher at the Smithsonian Tropical Research Institute in Panama. He received his Ph.D. in Social Anthropology from the London School of Economics and Political Sciences. He was director of the Centro de Investigación Antropológica de la Amazonía Peruana (Iquitos) and research coordinator of the Area de Estudios Amazónicos de la Facultad Latinoamericana de Ciencias Sociales (Quito, Ecuador). He is the author of *The Power of Love: The Moral Use of Knowledge amongst the Amuesha of Central Peru* (1991) and *Etnohistoria de la alta amazonía, siglos XV–XVIII* (1992) and the coauthor of *Selva Central: History, Economy, and Land Use in Peruvian Amazonia* (1998) and *Tamed Frontiers: Economy, Society, and Civil Rights in Upper Amazonia* (2000). He is also the coeditor of the *Guía etnográfica de la alta amazonía* (1994, 1998) and *Comparative Arawakan Histories: Rethinking Language Family and Culture Area in Amazonia* (2002).

Andrew Strathern and Pamela J. Stewart are research collaborators and in the Anthropology department at the University of Pittsburgh, and are both research fellows in the department of Anthropology at the University of Durham, England. They have worked together as a research team in the Pacific, Europe (primarily Scotland and Ireland) and Asia (primarily Taiwan). They are the coauthors of *Minorities and Memories: Survivals and Extinctions in Scotland and Western Europe* (2001); *Remaking the World* (2002); *Gender, Song, and Sensibility* (2002); *Violence: Theory and Ethnography* (2002); and *Witchcraft, Sorcery, Rumors, and Gossip* (2003); and the coeditors of *Identity Work: Constructing Pacific Lives* (2000) and *Landscape, Memory and History* (2003). They are also coeditors of the *Journal of Ritual Studies* and are series editors for the Ethnographic Studies in Medical Anthropology Series with Carolina Academic Press.

Márino Teixeira-Pinto received his Ph.D. in Anthropology from Museu Nacional of the Federal University of Rio de Janeiro, Brazil. Some of his past positions include visiting scholar at the University of St. Andrews-Scotland; associate professor in the Federal University of Paraná, Brazil; and associate professor at the Graduate Program in Social Anthropology of the Federal University of Santa Catarina, Brazil. He is the author of numerous articles and essays. He has been carrying out ethnographic research among the Arara Indians since 1987.

Johannes Wilbert is professor emeritus of Anthropology and director emeritus of the Latin American Center at the University of California, Los Angeles. He has served as director of the Caribbean Institute of Anthropology and Sociology of the Sociedad and Fundación La Salle in Caracas, Venezuela. He specializes in South American ethnology with particular emphasis on native populations of the Orinoco Basin and has conducted repeated field studies among indigenous groups of that region, concentrating on the Warao of the Orinoco Delta. Wilbert is senior editor of the twenty-four volume, PEN literary award-winning series *Folk Literature of South American Indians* and the author of *Tobacco and Shamanism in South America* (1987); *Mystic Endowment: Religious Ethnography of the Warao Indians* (1993); and *Mindful of Famine: Religious Climatology of the Warao Indians* (1996).

Robin M. Wright is an associate professor of Anthropology at the Universidade Estadual de Campinas (São Paulo, Brazil) and director of the Centre for Research in Indigenous Ethnology. He has published widely in the areas of indigenous history, indigenist policy, and religion in Brazil, organizing a three-volume work on the conversion of indigenous peoples to Christianity in Brazil. He is the author of *Cosmos, Self, and History in Baniwa Religion* and *For Those Unborn* (1998). Since the 1980s, he has collaborated with numerous nongovernmental organizations working on behalf of indigenous rights, both in the United States and Brazil, as well as with indigenous organizations of the Northwest Amazon in the production of a volume on Baniwa myths.

Neil L. Whitehead is a professor of Anthropology at the University of Wisconsin, Madison and editor of the journal *Ethnohistory*. The author of numerous works on the native peoples of South America, his most recent publications include an edited volume, *Histories and Historicities in Amazonia*, and an ethnography of assault sorcery among the Patamuna, *Dark Shamans: Kanaimà and the Poetics of Violent Death*.

Index

Africa, 3, 8–9, 299
Akawaio, 53, 167
Alleluia. *See* Shamanism: alleluia
Amazonia, 9–10
Animals. *See* Birds; Insects; Mammals; Reptiles
Anthropology, 11, 109, 136–37, 183, 306
Arara, 215–43; cosmology, 242 n.14; incest, 215–16; personhood, 229, 237; sociality, 217–18, 220–25, 240
Arauan. *See* Deni; Kulina
Arawak-speaking peoples. *See* Asháninka; Ashéninka; Baniwa; Baré; Nomatsiguenga; Tariana; Terena; Warekena; Yanesha
Asháninka, 274; epidemics, 284, 286, 289–94. *See also* Shining Path
Ashéninka, 274, 282, 288
Assault sorcery, 113, 230, 239, 277; abandonment of, 248, 258–59; accusations of, 204–5, 311; and banishment, 117, 215, 217, 240, 309; and breath, 142–43, 145; and darts, 189, 258; and disease etiology, 112, 189; dori, 203–6; and effigies, 4, 29; and envy, 120; as evil spells, 89, 109, 114–15, 121, 124, 125–26, 143; and gender relations, 89, 117; hiuiathi, 4, 88–89, 104 n.11; interrogations and inquests into, 148, 192, 329; macumba, 91, 103; and missionaries, 208; motivations for, 89, 116–17, 119, 126, 150, 239, 276–77, 308; and personhood, 149, 211, 309; and political power, 120, 184, 310; and predation, 143, 236, 239; and secrecy, 119; and social conflict, 29, 121, 207, 309; through songs, 259; spirit attacks, 188, 256, 267; talen, 5, 63; and violence, 206; and warfare, 29, 147. *See also* Dark shamanism; Plants; Revenge; Warfare
Asurini do Tocantins, 160
Asurini do Xingu, 160
Aueti, 186–87, 194
Ayahuasca, 209, 251, 260–61, 269 nn.7, 9; and illness, 209–11. *See also* Plants; Shamanic substances
Azande, 3–4

Baniwa, 55, 83–108
Baré, 55, 57–59, 70
Beckeranta, 60, 78 n.6
Birds: hummingbirds, 275; macaws, 33, 34; oropendola, 265; swallow-tailed kites, 26. *See also* Hunting; Landscape; Plants; Shamanism; Spirit beings
Blood, 30, 33–39, 103 n.2, 163, 182; menstrual, 168, 229–30; stench, 161; sym-

bolism of, 158, 166–67, 168, 182. *See also* Shamanic substances: tobacco; Violence

Body, 12, 29, 42, 125, 139–40, 227–30, 242 n.15, 315; ailments, 114, 128 n.5, 231; dori, 203; /kuru/, 228–29; and soul, 94, 101, 115, 142. *See also* Assault sorcery; Dark shamanism

Bororo, 168

Burnham, Forbes, 52, 72–74

Cannibalism, 33, 41, 106 n.16, 147, 159. *See also* Jaguar transformation

Carib-speaking peoples. *See* Akawaio; Arara; Kuikuru; Patamuna; Trio; Waiwai

Cashinahua, 244–71; dualism of society and cosmology, 244–47; song-leaders, 264–65

Chiefs, 52, 56, 57, 184, 185–87, 190

Children, 144, 250–51, 260, 275–76

Child sorcery, 273–305; case histories of, 280–92, 301 nn.5, 8; and charms, 222; and dreams, 275; executions of, 279; as expiatory sacrifice, 299; and factionalism, 296; and kinship, 279; and missionaries, 274, 280, 283–84; and modernization (external change), 295–97, 299; and ritual purification, 279; as rituals of identity, 299; torture, 278; and trade, 280. *See also* Asháninka; Ashéninka; Diseases; Nomatsiguenga; Shining Path; Violence; Yanesha

Christianity, 62, 83–84, 94, 96, 101–3, 317. *See also* Missionaries

Clastres, Pierre, 133–35, 151 n.1, 152 n.7

Colonialism, 9, 46, 52–54, 57, 59, 62–64

Conviviality. *See* Social relations

Cosmologies, 21–23, 25, 84–85, 224, 227, 240, 307, 316. *See also* Rituals; Shamanism; Spirit beings

Counterwitchcraft/sorcery, 59, 115–16, 186–87; daunonarima, 4; use of exuviae, 115, 192; iupithátem, 90–91, 104 nn.12, 13, 105 nn.14, 15; omens, 97, 99; piya, 5; rituals, 90–91, 115, 191–92, 194–95, 277; spells, 129 n.16; witch-hunts and executions, 185, 190, 205, 300

Criollos, 58, 66

Cubeo, 90, 104 n.4

Dark shamanism, 3, 4, 46, 106 n.16, 139–40, 152 nn.8, 9, 180; and animal counterparts, 41, 106 n.16; dauya, 244, 246, 247, 253–55; and execution, 106 n.16, 179; in history, 56–59, 60–63, 93–98; hoarotu, 5, 6, 33–42, 47–48; kanaimà, 4, 6, 61–63, 72; and marginality, 309; Obeah, 52, 54, 71, 76; pitadores, 56; and poison-owners (manhene-iminali), 4, 87, 99; and political power, 65–66, 71, 77, 138–39, 141; and predation, 37–39, 42, 140–41, 143–45, 237, 308–9

Demons. *See* Spirit beings

Deni, 212 n.2

Desana, 109–31

Development, 64, 217, 219

Diseases, 46, 283, 286, 288, 294. *See also* Asháninka; Shamanism

Divinities: Akuanduba, 236; Hoebo, 33–39; Katsimanali, 55; Kuwai, 53, 55, 85–86, 89, 113, 128 n.6, 318; Makunaima, 6, 61–62; Miana, 33; Piai-ima, 6; supreme macaw, 34; Yosoper, 275

Dreams, 93, 104 nn.7, 10, 159–64, 170, 174 n.6; and child sorcerers, 274–75

Ethics: of conviviality, 12, 99, 148–49, 218–19, 224–25, 240; in research, 14–16, 273–74. *See also* Social relations

Evans-Pritchard, E. E., 3

Evil spells. *See* Assault sorcery

FUNAI (National Indian Foundation), 208–9, 215

Gender, 89, 169, 204, 256

Guahibo, 90, 105 nn.14, 15, 106 n.16

Guarani, 173 nn.3, 5

Guyana, 51, 71; House of Israel, 74–75; People's Temple, 75. *See also* Burnham, Forbes; Colonialism

History, 12, 181, 189, 197–98, 248, 268–69 n.4, 281

Index 325

Hunting, 147, 221–25, 230–34, 316. *See also* Magic; Shamanism

Incest. *See* Social relations
Insects: bees and wasps, 26, 115. *See also* Hunting; Landscape; Plants; Shamanism; Spirit beings

Jaguar transformation, 106 n.16, 158–59, 163, 167, 171, 203, 235–36; black jaguars, 106 n.16, 236; songs, 164–65; and warfare, 159

Kamayura, 186
Kanaimà. *See* Dark shamanism
Katukina, 246, 248, 258, 260
Kinship. *See* Social relations
Kuikuru, 182
Kulina, 202–14, 248
Kumua, 110–14, 117–18, 122; morality, 125; power disputes, 118; transmission of knowledge, 122–27, 129 n.14

Landscapes, 21, 241 n.14
Light shamanism. *See* Shamanism

Madness. *See* Counterwitchcraft/sorcery: iupithátem
Magic: charms, 56, 106 n.17, 188; formulas, 233–34
Maku, 116–17
Mammals: bats, 161; capybara, 161; jaguars, 158, 203, 236–37; otters, 161; peccary, 205. *See also* Hunting; Landscape; Plants; Shamanism; Spirit beings
Marubo, 249
Matis, 268 n.3
Melanesia, 183–84
Mesoamerica, 43
Missionaries, 61, 136, 158, 172, 208–9, 249; Catholics, 111–12, 173, 281, 284; New Tribes Mission, 101; Seventh Day Adventists, 283, 286
Modernization, 61, 64
Mutilation, 6, 61–62
Mythology, 118–22, 167–68. *See also* Cosmologies; Poisoning

New Guinea, 7–8, 314–17
Nomatsiguenga, 275, 280–82

Pano-speaking peoples. *See* Cashinahua; Katukina; Marubo; Matis; Yaminahua; Yawanahua
Parakanã, 157–78
Patamuna, 4–5
Perspectivism, 159–70
Peru, 283
Plants, 247, 250; dade, 260; sago, 25, 31. *See also* Poisoning
Poisoning, 67, 104 n.6, 113, 204, 251, 253–54; dau, 247, 255; manhene, 86–88, 104 n.4; mythology, 86, 252; poisonous plants, 251, 253; and prophets, 93, 95, 97–98. *See also* Dark shamanism; Shamanic substances
Power: and bodily substances, 8, 55, 255. *See also* Body
Prophetism, Messianism, and Millenarianism: Awacaipu, 60–61; false prophets, 60; in Guyana, 60; Kamiko (Camico), 37, 57, 92, 93–94, 100; in Northwest Amazon, 53, 57, 92, 99–101; among Peruvian Arawak, 283–84; Uétsu, 92, 94–98, 99–100, 106 n.18; and Venezuela, 53–54, 58. *See also* Shaminism

Reptiles, 26–27; alligators, 41; snakes, 120. *See also* Hunting; Landscape; Plants; Shamanism; Spirit beings
Revenge, 119, 205, 318
Rio Negro, 52, 58, 64, 67, 70, 110
Ritual, 70, 111, 160, 165, 166, 203–4, 225, 259–60; hierarchies of ritual knowledge, 24, 56; oho-lament, 146–47, 151 nn.12, 13, 14, 238, 264. *See also* Cosmologies; Shamanism; Spirit beings

Shamanic substances: caapi, 96; muka, 256, 266; niopo, 91, 96; omiatchambïlï, 226; pariká, 95, 99, 111; tobacco, 23, 31, 36–37, 158, 161, 166–67, 262–63
Shamanism, 1–3, 9, 10, 43–45, 55–56, 57–58, 63, 65–67, 84–87, 98, 104 n.5,

105 n.15, 111, 114, 125, 138, 140, 143, 150, 159, 162, 184–86, 203, 217–18, 226–27, 231, 235, 238 306; alleluia, 59; light, 25–30; mukaya, 244, 246, 256, 258, 262–65; neoshamanism, 157–58, 171–72; piya, 4–5; priest-, 22–25; weather, 30–32; yea, 111–12. *See also* Blood; Cannibalism; Cosmologies; Dark shamanism; Jaguar transformation; Kumua; Mammals: jaguars; Perspectivism; Prophetism, Messianism, and Millenarianism; Ritual; Shamanic substances; Spirit beings; State; Warfare

Shining Path (Sendero Luminoso), 272, 291–93

Social relations, 12, 121, 146, 149, 202, 206–7, 211–12, 218; in Arawakan societies of Venezuela, 56–57; of the Guyanas, 59, 88–89. *See also* Ethics

Sorcery. *See* Assault sorcery; Counterwitchcraft/sorcery; Dark shamanism

Soul. *See* Body: and soul

Spirit beings, 25, 28, 30, 31, 184, 188, 204–5, 232–33, 274–75; the ancients, 24; anhinga, 160; the dead, 96; Eenunai, 86–87; hebu, 5, 24; inyaime, 87; iupinai, 89; karowara, 160–61, 174 n.8; macaws, 34; yuxin, 244, 250–51, 257, 264, 266. *See also* Birds; Body: and soul; Insects; Mammals; Reptiles; Shamanism

Stahl, Jonathan, 283–84

State, 51–52, 63, 72, 135, 138, 150; Hobbesian, 76; shamanic, 58, 77

Tapirapé, 163
Tariana, 113, 124
Terena, 167
Toba-Pilagá, 167
Torture. *See* Body; Child sorcery; Mutilation

Trio, 153, n.15
Tukanoans. *See* Cubeo; Desana
Túpac Amaru Revolutionary Movement, 291
Tupian-speaking peoples. *See* Asurini; Aueti; Kamayura; Parakanã; Tapirapé; Tupinambá; Wayãpi
Tupinambá, 159

United States, 15

Vampires, 37
Venezuela, 52, 58, 63–64, 68–69
Vengeance. *See* Revenge
Violence, 134–35, 148–49, 151 n.3, 182, 208, 238, 281–82, 295, 319; and drug traffic, 292; killing, 132, 147, 161, 169. *See also* Body; Dark shaminism: kanaimà; Shining Path; Warfare

Waiwai, 135–56
Warao, 21–50
Warekena, 55
Warfare, 47, 159, 162, 170, 222
Wari', 171, 175 n.29
Wayãpi, 160
Western culture, 51, 133–34, 172; and subjectivity, 137. *See also* Colonialism; United States
Witchcraft, 87–88, 178–81, 185, 187–88, 196–98. *See also* Assault sorcery; Chiefs; Dark shamanism
Women, 89, 106 n.17, 166, 256–57, 276

Xinguanos, 179–201
Xingu River, 179, 219

Yaminahua, 248, 264
Yanesha, 274–75, 283
Yawanahua, 246, 249, 258–59, 264

Neil L. Whitehead is a professor of Anthropology at the University of Wisconsin, Madison.
Robin Wright is a professor of Anthropology at the State University of Campinas, Brazil.

Library of Congress Cataloging-in-Publication Data
In darkness and secrecy : the anthropology of assault sorcery and witchcraft in Amazonia / edited by Neil L. Whitehead and Robin Wright.
Includes bibliographical references and index.
ISBN 0-8223-3333-3 (cloth : alk. paper)
ISBN 0-8223-3345-7 (pbk. : alk. paper)
1. Witchcraft—Amazon River Region. 2. Magic—Amazon River Region. I. Whitehead, Neil L.
II. Wright, Robin.
BF1566.15 2004   133.4'3'09811—dc22   2003026535

www.ingramcontent.com/pod-product-compliance
Lightning Source LLC
Chambersburg PA
CBHW030521230426
43665CB00010B/713